S0-ARA-809

PRINCIPLES OF TRANSPORTATION ECONOMICS

The Addison-Wesley Series in Economics

Abel/Bernanke
Macroeconomics

Allen
Managerial Economics

Berndt
The Practice of Econometrics

Bierman/Fernandez
Game Theory with Economic Applications

Binger/Hoffman
Microeconomics with Calculus

Boyer
Principles of Transportation Economics

Branson
Macroeconomic Theory and Policy

Brown/Hogendorn
International Economics: Theory and Context

Browning/Zupan
Microeconomic Theory and Applications

Bruce
Public Finance and the American Economy

Burgess
The Economics of Regulation and Antitrust

Byrns/Stone
Economics

Canterbery
The Literate Economist: A Brief History
of Economics

Carlton/Perloff
Modern Industrial Organization

Caves/Frankel/Jones
World Trade and Payments: An Introduction

Cooter/Ulen
Law and Economics

Eaton/Mishkin
Reader to accompany The Economics of
Money, Banking, and Financial Markets

Ehrenberg/Smith
Modern Labor Economics

Ekelund/Tollison
Economics: Private Markets and Public Choice

Filer/Hamermesh/Rees
The Economics of Work and Pay

Fusfeld
The Age of the Economist

Ghiara
Learning Economics: A Workbook

Gibson
International Finance

Gordon
Macroeconomics

Gregory
Essentials of Economics

Gregory/Ruffin
Economics

Gregory/Stuart
Russian and Soviet Economic
Structure and Performance

Griffiths/Wall
Intermediate Microeconomics

Gros/Steinherr
Winds of Change: Economic Transition
in Central and Eastern Europe

Hartwick/Olewiler
The Economics of Natural Resource Use

Hogendorn
Economic Development

Hoy/Livernois/McKenna/Rees/Stengos
Mathematics for Economics

Hubbard
Money, the Financial System,
and the Economy

Hughes/Cain
American Economic History

Husted/Melvin
International Economics

Invisible Hand Software
Economics in Action

Jehle/Reny
Advanced Microeconomic Theory

Klein
Mathematical Methods for Economics

Krugman/Obstfeld
International Economics: Theory and Policy

Laidler
The Demand for Money: Theories,
Evidence, and Problems

Lesser/Dodds/Zerbe
Environmental Economics and Policy

Lipsey/Courant
Economics

McCarty
Dollars and Sense

Melvin
International Money and Finance

Miller
Economics Today

Miller/Benjamin/North
The Economics of Public Issues

Miller/Fishe
Microeconomics: Price Theory in Practice

Miller/VanHoose
Essentials of Money, Banking, and
Financial Markets

Mills/Hamilton
Urban Economics

Mishkin
The Economics of Money, Banking,
and Financial Markets

Parkin
Economics

Phelps
Health Economics

Riddell/Shackelford/Stamos
Economics: A Tool for Critically
Understanding Society

Ritter/Silber/Udell
Principles of Money, Banking, and
Financial Markets

Rohlf
Introduction to Economic Reasoning

Ruffin/Gregory
Principles of Economics

Salvatore
Microeconomics

Sargent
Rational Expectations and Inflation

Scherer
Industry Structure, Strategy, and
Public Policy

Schotter
Microeconomics

Sherman/Kolk
Business Cycles and Forecasting

Smith
Case Studies in Economic Development

Studenmund
Using Econometrics

Su
Economic Fluctuations and Forecasting

Tietenberg
Environmental and Natural
Resource Economics

Tietenberg
Environmental Economics and Policy

Todaro
Economic Development

Waldman/Jensen
Industrial Organization: Theory
and Practice

Zerbe/Dively/Lesser
Benefit-Cost Analysis

PRINCIPLES OF TRANSPORTATION ECONOMICS

KENNETH D. BOYER

Michigan State University

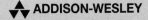 **ADDISON-WESLEY**

An imprint of Addison Wesley Longman, Inc.

Reading, Massachusetts • Menlo Park, California • New York • Harlow, England
Don Mills, Ontario • Sydney • Mexico City • Madrid • Amsterdam

Senior Editor, Economics	Denise Clinton
Senior Development Manager	Sylvia Mallory
Editorial Assistant	Rebecca Ferris
Managing Editor	Jim Rigney
Production Supervisor	Billie Porter
Senior Manufacturing Supervisor	Hugh Crawford
Cover Supervisor	Meredith Nightingale
Cover Designer	Richard Hannus
Cover Photo	Images © 1997 PhotoDisc, Inc.
Text Design, Composition, and Project Coordination	Elm Street Publishing Services, Inc.

Principles of Transportation Economics

Library of Congress Cataloging-in-Publication Data

Boyer, Kenneth Duncan.
    Principles of transportation economics / Kenneth D. Boyer.
      p. cm. -- (Addison-Wesley series in economics)
    Includes bibliographical references and index.
    ISBN 0-321-01103-1
    1. Transportation. I. Title. II. Series.
  HE151.B757   1997
  388--dc21   97-24731

Copyright © 1998 Addison Wesley Longman, Inc.
All rights reserved. No part of this publication may be reproduced, stored in a retrieval system, or transmitted, in any form or by any means electronic, mechanical, photocopying, recording, or otherwise, without the prior written permission of the publisher. Printed in the United States of America.

1 2 3 4 5 6 7 8 9 10--MA--01 00 99 98 97

*To **my** parents*

Carl B. Boyer

Marjorie N. Boyer

PREFACE

For more than a generation, North American transportation economics has not had a comprehensive textbook accessible to the general public. This book is an attempt to remedy this situation.

The field of transportation economics is now radically different from what it was twenty or thirty years ago. Gone is the predominant concern about regulatory and legal aspects of the field. In its place is a more general aim of understanding the effects of public policies on the transportation sector, communities, and the economy as a whole. In short, the field has been drawn closer to the standard concerns of general economic analysis. At the same time, transportation economics has retained a number of its distinctive characteristics— methods and concerns that are dictated by the nature of the subject matter. This book is an introduction to the distinctive elements of transportation economics, describing how the standard pieces of economic analysis are applied in the transport sector.

Economic analysis and its application to transportation are the central themes of this book. It is not a general introduction to the characteristics of modes of transportation nor a description of business logistics. The consistent focus is on the standard concerns of the economist: demand, costs, and rules for making economic policy.

To ensure that the book is accessible to all, including those who have not had advanced courses in economics, this text is written for an audience that has taken at most the principles of economics course. By studying economic principles of transportation pricing and investment at an accessible level, lawyers, engineers, transportation analysts, and others who have an interest in transport problems can learn the reasoning behind the sometimes opaque arguments made by economic practitioners. There is a great deal of misunderstanding about the logic of economic analysis of transportation. This book attempts to clear up that confusion.

Economic arguments have always been the central focus in the discussion of transport policy. This book is intended to give readers an introduction to the literature on the subject so that they can go further and make up their own minds about the usefulness of the analysis. If the reader disagrees with the analysis offered by the economist, the arguments in this book can be used as a guide for organizing a critique. The chapter endnotes represent a comprehensive organization of the transport economics literature. While many of the arguments in the articles cited in the endnotes will not be accessible to the non-economist, the references do provide a guide to where to look in the literature of transport economics for an elaboration of the ideas presented here.

To avoid the pitfall of doing economic analysis outside a real-world context, whenever possible this book presents economic principles using examples, data, and descriptions from the observable world. Economic principles that are stated without being applied or illustrated are sterile and uninteresting. It is only natural that these examples are derived heavily from the United States since that is where the major readership of this book will have its most extensive experience. This should not, however, suggest that the book is solely about North American transport modes. This book presents both economic theory and the application of the theory in the transportation sector. The introductory chapter, for example, offers examples from Morocco, Switzerland, and Malaysia as well as from the United States. In fact, the first use of a precursor to this book occurred in classes the author taught at the Sino-American training center at FuDan University, Shanghai, China. The techniques of demand estimation, costing, and policy analysis found in this book are universal and generally applicable to the transportation industries around the world.

Those familiar with his work will recognize in the following chapters the influence of James R. Nelson, from whom the author got his introduction to transportation economics when he was an undergraduate at Amherst College. Over the years that the manuscript has been in preparation, it has benefited greatly from supportive advice and guidance from a number of other individuals as well. A debt of gratitude is owed to, among others, the following people who offered their advice on earlier drafts and outlines:

Terrence A. Brown, *Pennsylvania State University—Harrisburg*
Douglas Dalenburg, *University of Montana*
William Dodge, *University of Wisconsin*
Bobby G. Dudley, *Robert Morris College*
Oscar Fisch, *City College of New York*
George Hilton, *University of California—Los Angeles*
Kenneth Small, *University of California—Irvine*
John Spychalski, *Pennsylvania State University*
Helen Tauchen, *University of North Carolina*
Philip Viton, *Ohio State University*
David Webber, *U.S. Coast Guard Academy*
Wesley Wilson, *University of Oregon*
Clifford Winston, *Brookings Institution*

Readers who take exception to what they read in the textbook should not hold the reviewers responsible. The author took most of their advice, but not all. If a wrongheaded statement is found, it likely resulted from ignoring their direction rather than following it.

Kenneth D. Boyer
Michigan State University

CONTENTS

▬ CHAPTER 3

Demand for Freight Transportation   43

▬ CHAPTER 4

The Demand for Passenger Transportation   69

PART II

TRANSPORTATION COSTS   95

CHAPTER 5

Transportation Cost Concepts   97

CHAPTER 6

The Costs of Fixed Facilities   127

▬ CHAPTER 7

Transport Vehicle Costs   151

▬ CHAPTER 8

The Costs of Operating Transport Vehicles   181

PART III

ECONOMIC PRINCIPLES FOR TRANSPORT PRICING   219

▬ CHAPTER 9

Transportation Investment and Disinvestment   221

▬ CHAPTER 10

Efficient Pricing   247

PART IV

GOVERNMENT REGULATION OF TRANSPORTATION   293

1

Why Study Transportation Economics?

Transportation economics is important. As much as 20 percent of economic activity in the United States is directly related to transportation, and transportation has influences far beyond the sector itself. Transportation affects land use patterns and social interaction. Some people blame transportation—in the form of the automobile—for the decline of U.S. cities and the increasingly insular nature of American society. On the other hand, improvements in transportation can also be credited, for example, with helping to increase the standards of living in formerly impoverished Southern states. Good transportation is necessary for a country to be competitive in world markets. With their poor transportation facilities, many developing nations are not capable of participating in world markets because they cannot get to market those goods with which they might have a competitive advantage. Modern transportation facilities allow regions in a country like the United States to specialize in doing what they are good at, that is, trading easily with one another to the benefit of the nation as a whole.

ECONOMICS IS ABOUT COMMON TRAITS

This book is about the economics of transportation. Many people are unsure what economics is and how transportation economics differs from transportation logistics. The field of economics studies how buyers and sellers of goods and services interact with one another, how they are affected by each others' actions, and how their actions affect those outside of their own market. Economics is not about the quirks and peculiarities of individuals, but about the basic underlying forces that cause people and companies to behave as they do. By understanding basic laws of behavior, economists are able to provide advice to governments and businesses on how best to organize economic activity to get the most from available resources.

Students taking their first course in economics are often surprised to find that the field is less practical and more philosophically based than they had expected. This stems from the economist's interest in finding underlying common elements of behavior rather than in dealing with the personalities of individual companies and government agencies. A student of transportation or logistics will need to know about the law covering loss and damage claims, the type of jets that can be used in cross-ocean services, or the frequency of transit bus maintenance. This very practical information about running a transportation business is not the main concern of the transportation economist—in fact, excessive attention to the uniqueness of companies and places distracts from the economist's task of finding what is general and common.

Transportation economics, like all fields of economics, is a combination of statistics, stories, and tools of analysis. The stories about particular companies or people are often the most interesting part of the study, but they serve mainly to illustrate the application of economic principles.

Economists tend to have little experience as entrepreneurs and managers. Thus they do not know, for example, the best techniques an airline should use in trying to increase passenger loads on a particular route. However, through studying airline competition over the years and in many countries, the economist gains a broader perspective than that of a manager who may have more intensive experience but narrower knowledge. Transportation economics studies the general conditions that allow competition to survive and how the degree of competition affects behavior. This information is useful for making broad policy decisions about how (and whether) airline competition should be encouraged. These are the sorts of topics covered in this book; however, if you want to run an airline, you will need to know more about the workings of particular modes and markets than you will read about here.

EXAMPLES OF POLICIES GUIDED BY TRANSPORT ECONOMICS

To say that economists are interested in discovering traits that are common among modes of transport or among users of transportation is not to say that transportation economics is uninterested in practical policy concerning transport. Ultimately, the goal of most transportation economists is to understand the effects of different policies and thus help make sound transport policy. Here are some examples of transport policies that can be shaped using the facts and analyses found in this book.

Truck Taxes

Many American motorists are familiar with placards on the back of over-the-road trucks announcing facts like, "Last year, this truck paid more than $10,000 in taxes." The clear implication is that the fees paid by the owner of the truck are high and that automobile drivers should not complain about the presence of the truck on the highways since it helps to finance the roadway. But is the amount really high? Trucks now pay thousands of dollars per year to the government in the form of fuel taxes and license fees while cars pay only hundreds of dollars. Is this balance correct? Should trucks pay more or less? Does it make a difference if fees for using highways are assessed as an annual fee or if they are charged as part of the price of fuel? Are there other forms of payment that would be better? What benchmarks would one use to evaluate whether the particular truck paid more than its proper share of the roadway costs?

The problem of paying for facilities that are shared by different classes of traffic is perhaps the classic problem of transportation economics. Chapters 9, 10, and 11 describe how to solve problems of financing shared facilities. Part of the answer comes in the form of road damage assessments, which can only be made by engineering evaluations of how rapidly different types of roads crumble with different traffic loads. Economists have no particular expertise in making road life evaluations; but economics can tell you how this information should be factored into the decision on the share of road costs that should be paid by trucks and cars. For example, the basic principle of marginal cost pricing, laid out in Chapter 10, explains why the directly attributable damage costs should be assessed on the basis of the number of miles traveled (as well as where and when), rather than annual fees.

Another part of the answer depends on how decisions are made to construct highways, as discussed in Chapter 11. If the presence of trucks causes these decisions to be made differently, then, at a minimum, these costs must be assessed against the class of traffic whose expected use caused the redesign. But for prices to be subsidy-free, each class of vehicle must pay more than simply the part of the roadway design that has been done with it in mind. Subsidy-free prices are, in fact, not obvious. They depend on a complex calculation of roadway costs under every conceivable combination of classes of traffic. While $10,000 in annual taxes paid to use a tractor-trailer combination on the American highway system may sound like a lot, a closer calculation may well find that it is a vast underpayment.

Straits of Gibraltar Tunnel

Europe and Africa are separated by 18 miles of water. Spain and Morocco are on either side of the Straits of Gibraltar that separate the two continents. Now that the English Channel has been crossed with a new railroad tunnel connecting England with the rest of Europe, proposals have been made to build a similar tunnel between Spain and Morocco. A test bore has already been dug from the African side. As of 1996, the tunnel extended 30 feet through the clay that appears to be beneath the Straits.

Officials in Morocco are trying to raise funds to extend the test bore, and hopefully complete the service tunnel—the first of three planned—all the way to Spain. If all goes well, by the year 2025 northbound trains would speed through one tunnel while trains from Europe to Africa would traverse a second one. The service tunnel would not be used for revenue service, but since it will be unequipped, it would be much cheaper to drill. Current estimates put the price tag for the service tunnel at $384 million and for all three tunnels at $4 billion. Spain and Morocco have offered to put up two thirds of the funds for the service tunnel and have asked the European Union to invest the remaining third.

A certain amount of skepticism about the reliability of financial estimates is warranted. Grand projects like this often have initial price tags that are unrealistically low. For example, the recently completed tunnel connecting England and France had an initial cost estimate of $7 billion, while the final tab came to $13 billion. But even if the cost estimates are reliable, how should one evaluate the desirability of such a project? Should we evaluate the project differently if we are officials of the European Union looking out for the general interests of the public, than as investors whose only interest is the return on their own investment?

The transport economist remains dry-eyed and skeptical when appeals are made based on symbolism: The tunnel, it is argued, will symbolically connect Europe and Africa, uniting two great civilizations. The basic data that economics uses to evaluate a project like this are costs for construction, costs of operation, and the willingness to pay for service. Techniques for using these data in project evaluation form the subject of Chapter 9. From the economic perspective, the grand symbolism of the connection is irrelevant unless there is a willingness to pay for it, especially on the part of potential users. Users, by making decisions in which they themselves have a financial stake, make the most powerful statement about the value of the project. Countries as a whole may be willing to pay for symbolic statements, but the willingness of legislators to spend tax dollars is not considered to be as reliable a measure of value as the sum of toll payments by actual users.

Getting Trucks Out of Alpine Valleys

The Swiss Alps separate Germany and other countries in Northern Europe from Italy to the south. As truck transportation has grown with European prosperity in the last half of the twentieth century, so have complaints from Swiss residents who live near the truck routes. The highways carrying road freight traffic are in narrow valleys which trap noise and exhaust fumes from the trucks. The exhaust fumes react in the atmosphere and cause environmental damage to the delicate forests and pastures of Switzerland.

In 1994, using the direct democracy for which Switzerland is famous, voters in some Swiss cantons decided to close their highways to all international truck traffic beginning in the year 2004. All traffic will, instead, have to be carried on the railroads that parallel the mountain highways. By switching traffic from road to rail, the Swiss hope to reduce both noise and atmospheric pollution.

How should one evaluate the decision of the Swiss? Should similar policies be adopted in the United States? How should one reconcile the fact that the decision of the Swiss voters will benefit those living in mountain valleys while the costs will be borne by those living outside the country?

Economics uses the concept of economic efficiency to reconcile conflicting interests. As discussed in Chapter 14, the key piece of data is the (hypothetical) total willingness of those whose life is improved by banning truck traffic to pay for improvements. As emphasized in that chapter, how to make this calculation is still being refined. It requires understanding the chemistry of pollution as well as how to convert reduced exposure to pollution into measurable units of environmental improvement, and then requires calculating how much the Swiss would be willing to pay for the improvements produced by reduced truck traffic.

The willingness of the Swiss to pay for improvements to their environment will then be calculated against the costs imposed on those currently using the roads for truck traffic. How much more would it cost international shippers to shift their truck traffic to railroads, at least for that part of the journey through the Alps? Answering this question depends on knowing not only the relative costs of truck and rail transportation (the subject of Chapters 6 through 8) but also understanding how shippers see truck and rail transportation as being substitutable. Chapter 3 notes how the casual observer tends to think of truck and rail transportation as being far more interchangeable than do experts in the field. If shippers do not see the two modes as interchangeable at current prices, an estimate will be made to see what apparent cost penalty is associated with using rail rather than truck traffic, or, in other words, how cheap rail traffic would have to become relative to truck movements before shippers were indifferent as to which to use. Economic efficiency criteria would be consistent with the results of the Swiss voter referendum if the willingness to pay for environmental improvements more than offset the cost imposed on the users of trucks.

■ Paying for Docks and Warehouses in Port Klang

Port Klang is the largest port in Malaysia, providing the capital city of Kuala Lumpur access to international shipping services. Port Klang is thoroughly modern with 25 docks for loading and unloading liquid cargoes like palm oil and petroleum, as well as handling dry bulk, roll-on-roll-off and containerized cargoes. In 1994, the port serviced more than 6,000 ships and handled 33.8 million tons of cargo. The facilities were recently privatized, though the pricing of dock services is still regulated by government authorities.

Shippers who move cargoes through Port Klang will use warehouses, dock space, and loading and unloading equipment, as well as the services of stevedores and other port personnel. The harbor must also be dredged by the port authorities and navigation aids need to be installed and maintained. Since all of these services use resources, it is reasonable for the port authority to expect to be paid for the services provided.

The regulated prices charged for using Port Klang have not changed since 1963. During this time, there has been considerable investment in new facilities and a boom in cargoes that move through the port. Through the year 2000, cargo tonnage is expected to continue to grow at 10 percent per year. Is it sensible that port charges should not reflect the increase in demand for port services? How should port charges be structured? What should be the relationship between the charges for using a port and investment in facilities? Does it make sense to charge prices that only pay back investment and operating costs, or are there other principles involved?

Chapters 9 through 11 provide the basic framework for optimal (that is, efficient) transport pricing and investment. The basic tool of efficient pricing is the congestion toll. Congestion tolls and investment patterns are closely interrelated and, under ideal conditions, the optimal price will exactly cover all costs. Where there is a divergence between the goal of efficient utilization of facilities and financial incentives for investment, a second criterion—subsidy-free pricing—is often imposed. How this is done is described in the chapters describing the principles of transport pricing and investment.

■ High-Speed Rail Projects

The Japanese Shinkansen service linking Tokyo and Osaka was the first of the ultra high-speed train line. So successful was the line in attracting passengers that many other countries followed with their own high-speed rail lines. France has several lines whose speeds approach 170 miles an hour. Britain has some 125 mph lines. Germany now has a system of hourly fast trains that use mostly conventional tracks, but is in the process of converting some of the right of way to high-speed dedicated lines. Italy and other European countries have developed their own high-speed rail service, and the continent is making plans to unify the different services.

Notably absent from the list of countries providing high-speed rail transportation is the United States. While the U.S. passenger rail company does provide 100 mph service between Washington and New York, the service is not considered to be in the same class as those overseas.

In the last several decades, several proposals have been made to introduce high-speed rail lines in the United States. California has discussed the idea of building a line between San Francisco and Los Angeles. Florida has considered linking Miami, Orlando, and the Tampa Bay area with new ultra-fast surface transport. Texas has gone as far as to issue a franchise to build a high-speed rail line between Dallas and Houston. There are ongoing discussions of upgrading service between Chicago and several other large Midwestern cities to provide service in the 100–125 mph range. None of the projects has gotten to the building stage, however, and there are persistent and deep doubts about their advisability.

The United States does not have a geography that is favorable to railroad passenger transportation. Cities are too far apart and the population within cities is too dispersed to make current rail passenger transport a serious choice for most travelers. But high-speed rail transport might be different. The 400 miles between San Francisco and Los Angeles, for example, is not very different from the distances in foreign countries where there is a large market for these services. Could such lines in the United States be built and operated at a profit? Is there any economic justification for building the lines if a profit cannot be guaranteed?

The essential factor that has stopped all proposed projects in the United States is traffic projections. New surface transport construction is extraordinarily expensive in terms of land acquisition costs as well as actual construction materials and labor. These costs can be projected with reasonable accuracy. What is unknown is whether enough people will ride the new lines for it to be profitable. The key information that is necessary for making an evaluation is the demand for the service. Techniques for making such an evaluation are discussed in Chapter 4.

In general, demand conditions make high-speed rail projects risky at best. Supporters, however, hope that by offering a new kind of service in areas where none had been seen previously, it will induce the sort of development that will provide the passenger counts necessary to make the lines financially viable. Thus, for example, the argument in favor of the California line depends on the building of new communities around stations far from either Los Angeles or San Francisco—communities that would be dense enough to support rail commutation into the larger existing cities. This three-way dependence among passenger demand, land use patterns, and service is one of the more difficult topics of transportation economics. Chapter 4 describes our current understanding.

▬ Solutions for Traffic Jams

Traffic congestion is one of the most vexing problems facing American urban and suburban areas today. During peak periods, two thirds of the cars on interstate highways are moving at less than 35 miles an hour. Traffic jams are extraordinarily wasteful, causing more than two billion vehicle hours of delay every year. Eliminating traffic jams would allow people more time to pursue productive activities, including leisure. By one estimate, productivity lost to traffic congestion costs the United States more than $40 billion per year.

For many years, the American solution to eliminating traffic jams has been to build new highways. It seems like a logical solution: congestion occurs because there is too little capacity for the number of drivers on the road. What could be a more obvious cure for the problem than to increase capacity? Today, this line of reasoning finds little support. Highways are expensive to build and traffic jams always seem to redevelop after the new capacity is added. That is, additional capacity simply attracts additional traffic.

New technology holds some promise as to how to increase road capacity without road building. By providing real-time information to both the computer that controls traffic lights and drivers in their cars, some traffic engineers hope to induce drivers to choose routes that avoid congested intersections as well as to set the timing of traffic lights to increase the number of vehicles that can go through an intersection each hour.

As promising as information technology is, it cannot solve the problem of traffic congestion. Even if adoption of the technology is able to effectively increase road capacity without new building, it still runs into the problem that in peak periods, traffic on main arterial highways will increase until the speed is equivalent to that on alternate parallel routes.

So discouraging has been the U.S. experience with using capacity additions to solve traffic problems that governments have been eager to try alternatives. One alternative has been to increase capacity and attractiveness of public transit systems. Since the 1970s, there have been modest successes at increasing the ridership in public transportation, but it has had little effect on the problem of automobile congestion.

Transport economists are unanimous in arguing for the pricing of road space as the most efficient way to solve the crisis of traffic congestion. Chapters 8 and 10 describe this process. Exactly how the process will be accomplished is not clear at this point. For example, it is possible that parking charges will be more effective than congestion tolls in discouraging traffic jams. But there is every reason to expect that pricing schemes for highways will be a central feature of any comprehensive plan to deal with the problem of traffic congestion.

▬ International Airline Alliances

In June 1996, American Airlines, the largest carrier of U.S. domestic passenger traffic, proposed a marketing alliance with British Airways, the world's largest air carrier. Under terms of the alliance, the two airlines would be able to issue through tickets to foreign destinations and the passenger would not be able to tell from the ticket which of the two airlines will actually provide service on which leg of the journey. This practice is called *code-sharing* and has been controversial among consumer groups. The airlines would not have a formal merger, but would share revenues on those routes where both airlines have flight operations.

The advantages claimed by the airlines for the alliance come from the fact that each is strong in a different part of the world. British Airways has an extensive route network in Asia, Africa, and Europe. American Airlines has a dense network in the United States and Latin America. Both fly across the North Atlantic. American Airlines can efficiently collect passengers flying from the Western Hemisphere, funnel them through its gateway cities, and deliver them to a limited number of European destinations. When the passengers arrive overseas, they will need to change airlines to proceed to their final destination. Similarly, British Airways can collect passengers in regions where it has a strong presence and deliver them to a limited number of American cities. By combining the two operations in a single code-sharing system, it will appear to passengers that they have the option of single-line service from their home town to almost anywhere in the world.

British Airways and American Airlines emphasize that passengers would have new options for single-line service that were not previously available to them and that this semi-merger should thus seen to be pro-consumer. Consumer advocate groups and competitors are not so sure. In the most recent reporting period, the two airlines together carried 60 percent of passengers across the North Atlantic. Can an arrangement that eliminates competition between two airlines that together have a majority of traffic on a route really be considered to be a benefit to passengers? Competitors of the two airlines have come out against the alliance, fearing that the combination will take traffic away from them. They have demanded increased access to landing rights at the main airport in London as compensation for the added competitive pressure that will be placed on them by the code- and revenue-sharing agreement.

The British Airways–American Airlines combination will require approval of government regulators on both sides of the Atlantic Ocean. How should regulators make their judgment? Evaluating the arrangement requires understanding the sources of network economies. It is often (though not always) the case that operations organized as a hub-and-spoke network will have lower costs than those that are treated as simply a group of single city-pair routes. Chapter 5 shows that one source of these economies derives from the fact that airlines produce service by having passengers share equipment. By having a more extensive network it is possible to use more larger, lower-cost aircraft. It appears, however, that there are limits on the cost savings offered by network operations. Whether a particular mode shows network economies is a matter for empirical investigation. The result of some of these studies is found in Chapter 8.

HOW TO USE THIS BOOK

The examples presented above give a taste for the sorts of topics dealt with by transportation economists. This textbook, in explaining the basic reasoning of the transport economist, follows that of any economics text. The study of demand comes first, followed by costs, then principles for understanding and evaluating the operation of markets, and finally public policy intervention.

Part I consists of three chapters. Chapter 2 describes the basic framework for understanding transportation demand. Since transportation connects many points together, the first task in making a transportation demand study is making sense out of the seemingly infinite number of ways of organizing flows in a transport network into meaningful observations. This is typically done by defining an index of transportation, usually ton-miles or passenger-miles. Chapters 3 and 4 present the frustrations of estimating freight demand and passenger demand using these indices.

Part II deals with transportation costs. The transportation sector uses two different kinds of capital: vehicles and fixed facilities. The first are far more mobile than in most industries while the second are immobile. Fixed facilities also tend to be shared among many different kinds of users and tend to be owned by a different party than owns and operates transport vehicles. Some of the difficulties presented by the unusual nature of transportation operations are described in Chapter 5. This chapter also provides an illustrative example of the sources of network economies. Chapters 6 and 7 deal with the costs of owning the two kinds of transportation capital. Chapter 8 presents the analysis of the costs of operating different modes of transport.

In Part III, the basic principles of transport pricing are presented. The section starts with project evaluation in Chapter 9. This chapter also develops the measure of social surplus that underlies all economic measurements of the benefits of different policies. Chapter 10 describes the basic rule for efficient pricing: What people pay for a service should be equal to the marginal opportunity cost of providing it. This efficiency rule is often assumed to be in conflict with the practical realities of transportation finance. Chapter 11 explains why it is not. Under ideal conditions, marginal cost pricing will lead to financial solvency. When the rule cannot be followed, a close cousin—incremental pricing, derived from the subsidy-free pricing criterion rather than economic efficiency—can be used as a supplement to marginal cost pricing.

The final section of this book deals with current policy issues. Transportation has long been one of the most heavily regulated sectors of the economy. The traditional concern has been the economic power that carriers have over those that use their services. Chapter 12 provides a framework for understanding arguments of economic power in transportation. There is a mismatch between complaints of users, who will use the language of monopoly power, and the economist's evaluation of the subject, in which the problem of monopoly power is assumed to be economic inefficiency. Given the nature of transportation costs, those outside the operation cannot be expected to be able to identify efficient prices. Thus regulation of prices to eliminate the inefficiencies of monopoly power is an impractical exercise.

Price regulation was practiced for more than a century. The results of transport regulation and deregulation are described in Chapter 13. The final chapter treats the more immediate concern with controlling the social cost of regulation. Two aspects have been dealt with extensively and are the core subjects of this chapter: pollution and safety. While it seems unlikely that we will see extensive government controls on market power in the transport sector, increased regulation of automotive safety and pollution are under active discussion. Particularly in the case of pollution-related regulations, efficiency considerations could lead to policy changes that could have profound effects on the transport sector.

On completing this book, the reader should have an appreciation for the similarity of economic conditions in different transportation industries. For example, the economics of Less-Than-Truckload (LTL) motor carriers have strong resemblance to those of scheduled passenger airlines. But economics also dictates that individual modes may have concerns not shared by all. Railroads stand out as unique among the modes of transportation because of the economic conditions under which they operate. By focusing not on individual modes of transport but on common underlying forces that affect all of them, this book offers a framework for analyzing all of the transportation industries.

TRANSPORTATION DEMAND

2

The Source of Transportation Demand

The study of economics starts from the premise that the purpose of economic activity is, ultimately, to satisfy the wants and needs of the people living in the economy. The way people signal their wishes is through their willingness to pay for the goods and services that they consume. How people spend their money gives us some information on their wants. In this chapter, we will review basic statistics on expenditure for transportation and then discuss the basic tools for drawing economic conclusions from those numbers. It turns out that relatively little can be learned from extremely broad expenditure statistics about consumers' desires for transportation and for the services of transportation in producing and distributing the goods that they buy. Finer classifications are needed—at a minimum the division into freight and passenger transportation. These are the subjects of the next two chapters. This chapter presents the basic framework that is used for making the estimates of freight and passenger demands.

EXPENDITURE ON TRANSPORTATION

The left bar in Figure 2.1 shows amounts that U.S. consumers pay to transportation companies. The biggest transportation industry is trucking, followed by airlines and railroads. For-hire

FIGURE 2.1   **Transportation Expenditures in the United States in 1994**

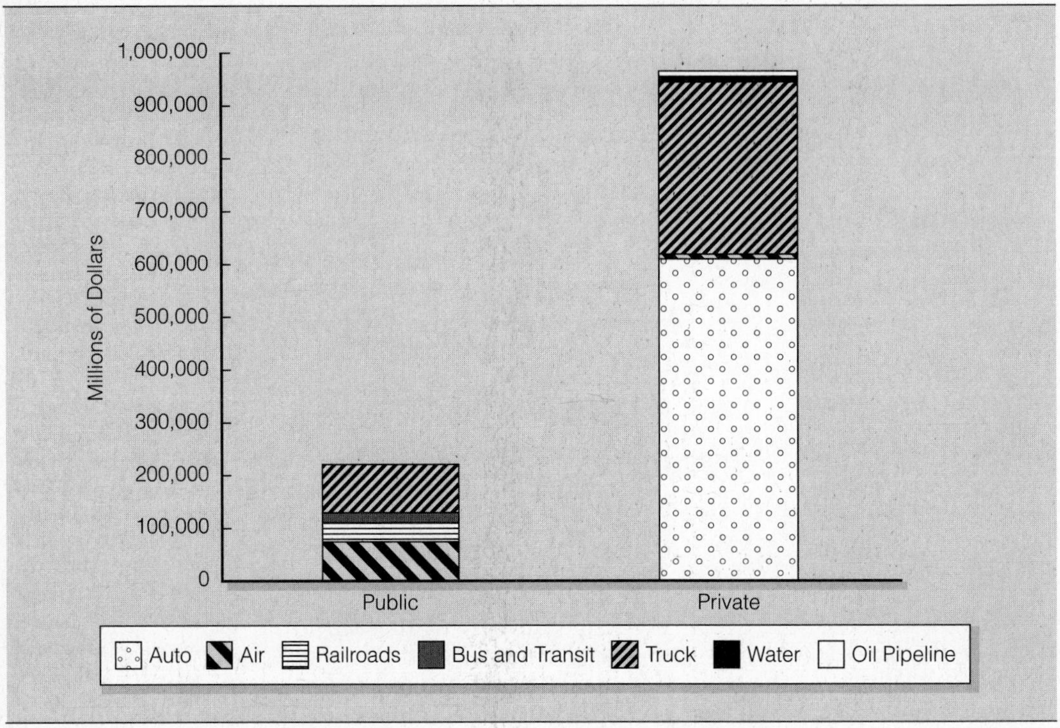

SOURCE: *Transportation in America*, 13th Edition. Private trucking refers to estimated non-ICC authorized.

urban transportation is relatively small in comparison to inter-city transportation. The more than $220 billion spent in the United States on purchasing transportation services in 1995 represented a little more than 3 percent of gross domestic product (GDP).

Looking only at public, or for-hire transportation, misses the important private sector of transportation industries. When one drives a car, flies one's own plane, or carries freight in one's own truck, transportation services are generated, but they do not appear in records as the purchase of transportation. The equivalent to spending on public transportation is the expenditures that private transporters make on purchasing, maintaining, and operating transportation equipment. These amounts are shown in the right bar in Figure 2.1. The annual expenditures for maintaining and operating cars and for purchasing cars are each larger than the total expenditure on all forms of for-hire transportation. Expenditures on automobile transportation are more than ten times that for airline flights.

Private transportation is not only the leading form of passenger transport, but of freight transport also. As shown in Figure 2.1, expenditure on private trucking is larger than expenditures on for-hire trucking, railroads, waterways, and pipelines combined. The close to $1 trillion that Americans spend on private transportation each year is approximately 14 percent of gross domestic product. Combining both private and for-hire transportation, about 17 percent of national expenditures are made on transportation.

While transportation expenditures are large in an absolute sense, and while the United States still spends a larger proportion of its GDP on domestic transportation than many other countries at a similar stage of economic development, spending on transportation is increasing less rapidly than expenditures on other parts of the economy. Figure 2.2 shows that expenditures on transportation in the United States since 1970 have not kept pace with gross domestic product. As a result, transportation expenditures have been dropping as a proportion of all economic activity.

Can one conclude from the observation that the United States spends more on transportation than Germany that Americans have a greater desire for mobility? Can we conclude from the declining relative expenditures on transportation that Americans like traveling less than they did several decades ago? Basic economic theory shows that we cannot. As discussed next, the level of expenditures is affected by price levels as well as demand, and the demand for transportation depends on much more than people's wish for mobility.

FIGURE 2.2   Trends in U.S. Transportation Expenditures and GDP

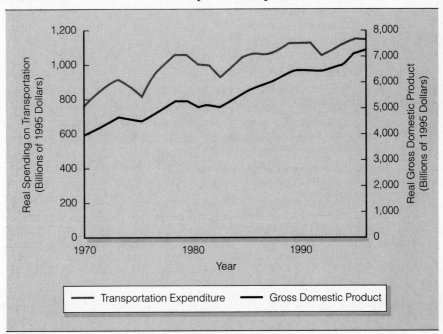

SOURCE: *Transportation in America*, 14th Edition.

DEMAND, ELASTICITY, AND EXPENDITURE

The demand for transportation is the name given to the willingness to pay for transportation services and how that willingness changes as the price or cost of transportation changes. The level of expenditures on transportation gives some information about the demand for transportation, but it does not reveal the important information about how transportation purchases respond to changes in prices. A traffic count is not the same as a demand study. Demand analysis requires an investigation of how consumers make decisions when the price of the service changes.

Those new to the field of economics are sometimes surprised to find that a common word such as *demand* is given a formal definition that is different from everyday usage. The number of gallons of gasoline purchased in a year is sometimes referred to in the popular press as *annual gasoline demand*. The general willingness to spend money to stay healthy is sometimes referred to in the general public as the *demand for health care*. These are contradictory definitions. To avoid logical inconsistencies in analysis, economics uses a very precise definition: Economic demand is the relationship between the quantity of a good or service purchased and the price charged for it. Economic demand is not merely the number of units sold or the general desire to have something. Demand is represented either as a table of numbers showing quantities bought at different prices, or (more commonly) as a downward sloping line in a graph of prices against purchases. Such a graph is shown as the line AA' in Figure 2.3 in which the number of units sold is given by the distance OE and the price per unit is the distance OC. Expenditures like those shown in Figures 2.1 and 2.2 are calculated as the quantity demanded multiplied by price per unit. Graphically, expenditure is represented by the area OCDE in Figure 2.3.

One possible reason that transportation expenditures have not kept pace with spending on other goods and services in the economy is that transport prices have, in general, not risen as rapidly as the prices of other goods and services—in other words, the real price of both passenger and freight transportation has fallen somewhat. This would be represented as a decline in price and a movement down to the right on a demand curve line in Figure 2.3. This representation requires that the vertical axis in Figure 2.3 be scaled in terms of real price—that is, prices quoted in terms of inflation-adjusted dollars. But in order for a decline in real prices to be the explanation for the fall in transportation's share of total expenditure, it must also be the case that the demand for transportation is price inelastic. In other words, a drop in the price of transportation has not been offset by a larger proportionate increase in the quantity of transportation services generated in the economy. Inelastic demands are represented by relatively steep demand curves. If the demand curve is steep, decreasing the price of transportation will lead to a smaller expenditure box. The opposite will be true if demand is elastic (relatively flat.)[1]

FIGURE 2.3   Demand and Expenditure Relationships

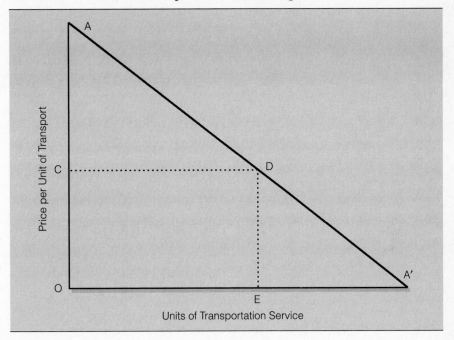

But is it true that the demand for transportation is price inelastic? There is an alternative explanation for the drop in relative expenditures on transportation that does not depend on the inelasticity of demand. It is possible that over the last 20 years the demand has not increased as rapidly in the transportation sector as it has in other parts of the economy. An increase in demand would be represented by a rightward shift of line AA′ in Figure 2.3. Basic economic analysis tells us that increases in demand for a good or service are caused primarily by increases in population, increases in the prices of substitutes or decreases in the prices of complements, or increases in income.[2]

The possibility that there are meaningful, measurable substitutes and complements for transportation is generally ignored (though as discussed in Chapter 4, there is some speculation that improved telecommunications has the promise of decreasing transportation demand). Population has increased by 25 percent over the period, thus pushing the demand curve to the right, but the same force will have affected the demand for all other goods and services. Average real incomes also rose modestly over the period. A possible reason that transportation spending has declined as a percentage of total expenditure is that the income elasticity of demand for transportation is relatively low; in other words, if incomes rise by 1 percent, the demand for transportation shifts to the right by less than 1 percent. If this is the case, however, recent American experience contradicts that in other countries and in other areas, in which increased income led to a greater than proportionate spending on transportation.

What is needed to forecast transportation usage in the future and to make sense out of historical statistics is to estimate the price elasticity of demand for transportation. The following two chapters discuss estimates that have been made for North American freight and passenger transport. In the remainder of this chapter, the framework for estimating demand will be presented. In order to separate all the possible explanations for changes in expenditures, it is important to understand the interaction among the different factors that motivate people to travel and to ship goods and services. With this knowledge, it will be possible to make better measurements of the elasticity of transportation demand with respect to price and income and to identify the other factors that need to be controlled for when making demand estimates.

The framework for understanding what motivates freight and passenger movement is best laid out using numerical examples and simulations. Two such calculations are presented next. The first is the simplest possible example within which transportation is determined by economic forces. It shows the fundamental determinants of transport demand. The second is a more realistic and useful example, but one which is also far more complicated. It shows the multitude of difficulties inherent in estimating the demand for a mode of transportation.

TRANSPORTATION DEMAND IS DERIVED DEMAND: A SIMPLE EXAMPLE

Transportation demand does not exist separately from the economic conditions in the landscape. Transportation demand is said to be derived from demand and cost conditions in the economy as a whole.[3] To illustrate how the demand for transportation is derived from cost and demand conditions, consider Figure 2.4. This figure shows the simplest possible transportation network with a single origin and a single destination. It is most useful to think of Figure 2.4 as representing the path of movements of some commodity—coal, for instance—from a single origin to a single destination. Alternatively, one could think of the origin as the place where vacationers come from and the destination as the place where vacationers go. In order to simplify the analysis and to emphasize the fundamental determinants of transport demand, the figure assumes competitive product markets and does not allow for any other origins or destinations other than the pair shown. Later in this chapter, the complications of including more origins and destinations will be discussed.

Look at Figure 2.4. Immediately below the origin a supply curve is shown. Call this the supply curve of coal. The mathematical form of this supply curve,

FIGURE 2.4   **The Source of Transport Demand**
This diagram shows two cities, A and B. City A produces a commodity with the supply curve shown on the left. After transportation to city B, it is consumed with a demand curve shown on the right. Transportation demand is derived from both the supply curve at A and the demand curve at B.

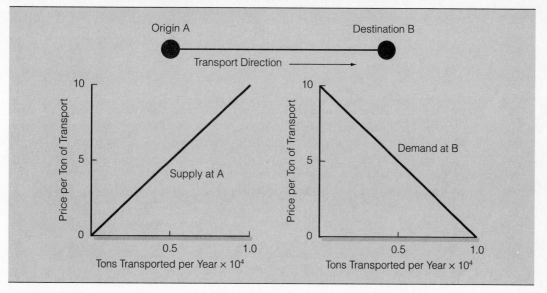

a straight line with an increase of 1,000 units per dollar of price increase at the origin (P_0), is:

$$Q = 1,000P_0 \tag{2.1}$$

The supply curve is shown as upward sloping, the typical shape for a product supply curve; the upward slope corresponds to the observation that at higher prices producers are eager to offer a larger quantity of product on the market. Equation 2.1 states that every dollar increase in the price that producers at the origin get for their goods will increase the number of units offered (Q) by 1,000.

The destination in Figure 2.4 has a product demand curve drawn beneath it. This product demand curve has a downward slope, corresponding to the typical shape of a demand curve. To maintain the simplicity of the example, the demand curve is shown as a straight line. The mathematical form of the demand curve, a straight line with maximum quantity demanded of 10,000 units and a 1,000 unit reduction in quantity demanded for every $1 increase in price, is:

$$Q = 10,000 - 1,000P_d \tag{2.2}$$

Equation 2.2 states that every dollar increase in the price paid by consumers at the destination (P_d) reduces the number of units willingly purchased by 1,000.

The number of tons shipped from the origin to the destination, assuming the markets are competitive, will be determined by the price per ton of transporting coal. The lower the price of transportation, the higher will be the price of coal at the origin, thus encouraging production, and the lower will be the price of coal at the destination, thus encouraging consumption.

The maximum volume of shipments will be made when the price of transportation is zero. When transportation is free, the price of coal at the origin will be \$5 and producers will be induced to produce 5,000 tons. But with transportation free, the same price must prevail at the destination. The demand equation tells us that 5,000 tons will be consumed. Since there is a balance between quantity demanded and quantity supplied, the system is in equilibrium with no tendency of producers to wish to increase production, or demanders to change consumption, or of the coal merchants to change the quantity of coal that is moved from origin to destination.

If the price of transportation rises to \$2 per ton, merchants will no longer be able profitably to purchase coal at \$5 and sell it at \$5.[4] In order to stay in business, a merchant will need to have a price spread between the origin and destination at least equal to the price of transportation. In the example here, a \$2 price of transportation leads to a price at the origin of \$4, a price at the destination of \$6, with 4,000 tons produced at the origin and 4,000 tons consumed at the destination.

In algebraic terms, the demand for transportation combines the product supply curve and the product demand curve through the condition that product price at the origin and destination differ by the price of transportation:

$$T = P_d - P_0 \tag{2.3}$$

Combining Equations 2.1, 2.2, and 2.3 produces the formula for transportation demand:[5]

$$Q = 5,000 - 500\,T \tag{2.4}$$

Table 2.1 illustrates this line by choosing different prices for transportation and calculating the equilibrium quantity of shipments from the origin to the destination. The entire line is graphed in Figure 2.5 (See page 24).

The reader should note that the slope of the demand for transportation curve depends on the slopes of both the product demand and the product supply curves. In the case of passengers, the demand for transportation will depend on both the willingness of vacationers to pay for vacation flights and on the willingness of resort owners to serve vacationers at different room rates. That is, transportation demand can be elastic if either the product demand curve or the product supply curve is elastic enough. This is the sense in which the demand for transportation is said to be derived. It is not independent of

**TABLE 2.1   Calculation of the Demand for Transportation in a One-Origin
One-Destination One-Commodity Problem**

The demand for transportation is read by comparing column 4, "Transportation
Price," with column 1, "Quantity." "Transportation Price" is the difference between
the demand price and supply price at every quantity. The demand price is the point on
the demand curve, Equation 2.2, corresponding the quantity in column 1. The supply
price is the point on the supply curve, Equation 2.1, corresponding to the quantity in
column 1.

Quantity	Demand Price	Supply Price	Transportation Price
5,000	$ 5.00	5.00	$ 0.00
4,500	5.50	4.50	1.00
4,000	6.00	4.00	2.00
3,500	6.50	3.50	3.00
3,000	7.00	3.00	4.00
2,500	7.50	2.50	5.00
2,000	8.00	2.00	6.00
1,500	8.50	1.50	7.00
1,000	9.00	1.00	8.00
500	9.50	.50	9.00
0	10.00	.00	10.00

other economic actions, but is embedded in the sum of decisions made by producers, customers, and individual travelers.

From this simple two-endpoint problem, some of the fundamental factors
affecting transport demand are now apparent. The elasticity of transport
demand, for example, is clearly dependent on the elasticities of demand for and
supply of the goods and services that people want. The demand for transportation can increase (shift to the right) if either the supply curve for goods at
the origin increases or, in the case of passenger transportation, if there has been
an increase in the supply of services at the destination that people travel to get
to. Similarly, if people's demand for those services declines, the demand for
transportation services will also decline. In the same way, if the supply of
goods or services is reduced, so will the transportation demand. The elasticities
of demand for transportation can also be traced back to the demand for goods
and services other than transportation. If the demand or supply curves for
goods and services flatten (become more elastic), so will the demand for transportation.

FIGURE 2.5   The Derived Demand for Transportation
This figure shows the demand for transportation that is derived from the supply
and demand curves shown in Figure 2.4. The curve is derived by subtracting the
supply price from the demand price for any quantity of shipments. It is a
graphical representation of the curve described in tabular form in Table 2.1.

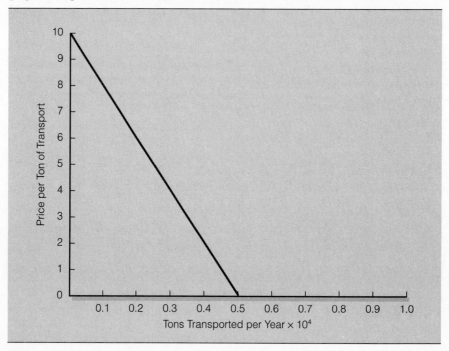

DERIVING TRANSPORTATION DEMAND WITH MULTIPLE MODES, ORIGINS, AND DESTINATIONS

The derived demand example described above forms the basis of transportation
demand analysis. But, unfortunately, this simple problem with one origin and
one destination is not sufficient to model most transportation demand problems. The reason is that in the real world each origin and destination typically
has many available endpoints and modes of transport.

Once a second mode of transportation is introduced, it is possible to analyze factors that influence the substitutability of one mode for another. This is
an important factor in comparing transport modes. To ask whether busses are
an adequate substitute for cars or rapid transit and whether trains can be relied
upon to relieve highways of truck transportation is to ask whether buyers of
transportation services will switch between them depending on relative prices.
The most easily understood measure of substitutability between products or ser-

vices is the cross price elasticity of demand. Cross price elasticities of demand (or simply *cross elasticities*) refer here to the proportionate reduction in use of one mode for a unit proportionate change in the rates charged by the other mode, holding all else constant.[6] If the cross elasticity is greater than zero (that is, a price rise of one mode causes the other mode's traffic to rise), the modes are characterized as substitutes. Negative cross elasticities (meaning that a rise in the price of one mode causes the other mode's traffic to decline) are associated with complementary services. While rail and motor carriers are generally thought of as interchangeable, at least in the case of intermodal service, the two modes are complementary. Thus a finding of a negative cross elasticity is not necessarily an indication of a flawed estimate. As explained in Chapters 3 and 4, in practice it is more efficient to make substitutability estimations by imposing additional restrictions that allow only a partial estimation of the cross elasticity of demand.

As in the previous section, the following example treats transportation demand using the classic economic technique in which prices for transportation are selected and the equilibrium level of transportation services calculated. Then the price of transportation is changed, and the new equilibrium level of transport services calculated. Doing this repeatedly traces out the demand curve for transportation. Unfortunately, once the problem is expanded beyond two endpoints it will be impossible to get an algebraic solution to the problem as we were able to do in Equations 2.1, 2.2, and 2.3. Rather, the problem must be simulated using computers. This is the procedure followed in this section.[7] We will not be able to derive a precise relationship among all the factors that determine the level of transportation in a system, but by solving the transportation equilibrium with many different prices and spatial structures, we will be able to get an idea of how those factors affect the overall level of movement.

To illustrate the factors that affect the demand for transportation if there are multiple modes and multiple endpoints, we will use a stylized structure of geography and a transportation network such as that shown in Figure 2.6. Diamonds represent the location of suppliers and potential suppliers, each with its own upward sloping supply curve; low cost supply areas are shown as larger diamonds than higher cost supply areas. It is easiest to think of supply locations as the position of mineral deposits with the supply curve at each location reflecting the marginal cost of extracting the mineral from the deposits. Demanders and potential demanders are shown as circles. The size of the circle shows the height of its demand curve. Demanders can be thought of as ore processing industries, with locations and processing costs determined by the availability of other inputs.

Every potential demand and supply location is connected by two modes of transportation. A *private* mode of transportation, which one can think of as being private trucking (or in the case of passenger transportation, private automobile), is characterized by costs determined by simple distances: users of private transportation directly between supply position and demand position. There is also what we will call a *public* alternative. The public mode uses sta-

FIGURE 2.6   Structure of a Stylized Transportation Network
Supply areas are represented by diamonds and demand areas by circles. The size
of the diamonds and circles reflects the heights of the supply and demand lines,
respectively. Public transport lines are assumed to be present on all grid lines.
Stations are represented by small squares where grid lines cross. To use public
transportation, a supply or demand area must first access the closest station.
Private transportation is assumed to directly connect the supply and demand
areas, but at higher cost per unit of distance than public transportation.

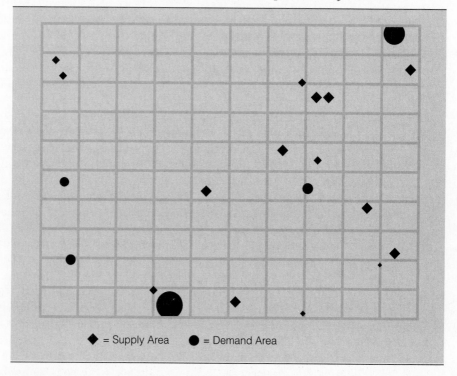

◆ = Supply Area   ● = Demand Area

tions (or ports, freight terminals, or collection yards) and shared vehicles (or
liners or trains) and has a limited route structure. Costs of the public mode are
determined by distance measured along straight line vertical and horizontal distances between stations as well as access costs to the nearest station. Stations are
located where grid lines cross in Figure 2.6. Access costs to the public transport
system are determined by the straight line distance between supply and demand
position and the nearest station.

    For any pair of origin and destination, the choice between the public and
private modes will depend, of course, on the charge per mile of using the mode
of transportation, but also on the degree of circuity in the public mode as well
as on the costs of access. The public mode of transportation is more circuitous

because it does not go directly from one endpoint to the other, but travels on straight line vertical and horizontal routes. This is equivalent to airlines requiring passengers to fly out of their way to hub airports to make connections, or trains traveling on tracks that travel to different stations to pick up passengers for other destinations. If the public mode is faster than the private mode (as is the case in air transport relative to automobile transport), that mode may be chosen even if using it costs more. In general, the public mode will have lower costs per mile, but higher time and access costs. If circuity involved with using the public mode is too large, the cost of using it may be higher than the private mode, even before time and access costs are taken into account.

Finding a transportation equilibrium in a network like that in Figure 2.6 is far more complicated than finding an equilibrium in the two-endpoint system. An equilibrium requires that the price at each supply location is never less than the transportation cost to any demand location; similarly, the price at any demand location must never be higher than the cost of transportation to any supply location. If these conditions did not hold, it would benefit a merchant to arbitrage between the locations, buying in the low price supply location and selling in the high price demand location, thus tending to equalize prices. The solution to such problems is complicated by the fact that one cannot tell in advance which supply locations should be paired with which demand locations. It requires a sophisticated procedure of trial and error, at which modern computers have the advantage. Once the origins and destinations are linked together in the most advantageous way, the basic procedure for finding prices and quantities moving between each supply and demand location will use techniques very similar to those in the two-endpoint problem.[8]

The solution to the spatial equilibrium problem from Figure 2.6 is displayed in Figure 2.7. If a source is connected to a demand destination through the private mode in the equilibrium solution, the two positions are shown as connected by a dotted line. If the equilibrium solution requires the use of a public mode, the origin and location are shown connected to their nearest stations by straight lines representing access; the stations are then connected by dashed lines along paths taken by public transport.

Figure 2.7 shows three active public transport flows and eleven active flows by private transport. All five demand locations are served, but only ten out of the fifteen supply locations are active. For the unused origins, the difference between product price at all destinations and transport costs is greater than the highest point on the supply curve. In other words, given the cost of transportation, none of the unused endpoints offers a sufficiently attractive product to allow it to sell to consumers in the pictured system. A striking feature of Figure 2.7 is the vast number of potential flows that are inactive; only 14 out of the 75 possible flows are active. The active flows are dominated by the private mode of transport. However, the public mode on average has much longer hauls. It should be noted, however, that some of the difference between public and private distances is related to the circuity of the public mode.

FIGURE 2.7   An Example of a Transportation Equilibrium in a Network
This figure shows the flows between supply areas and demand areas that satisfy
the condition that the price at a supply area is never higher than the price at the
demand area minus transportation costs. Flows on the public transport network
are shown by dashed lines connection stations. Straight lines show access between
the stations and a supply and demand area. Dotted lines connecting origins and
destinations that do not follow grid lines show flows by the private mode of
transportation.

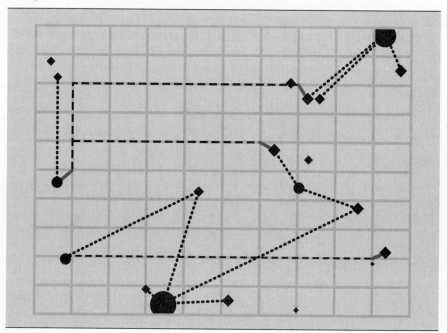

▬ Ton-Miles, Passenger-Miles, and Related Price Indexes

How much transportation is produced in the equilibrium shown in Figure 2.7?
This is a natural question with a deceptively simple answer. To ask the question
says that there is some common element among all of the different flows. We
are asked to combine the flows using this element. In other words, to combine
the flows, an index or aggregator must be defined.

The standard aggregator for combining freight flows is the *ton-mile* or
ton-kilometer. This is the product of the tonnage of the shipment and the distance traveled. The ton-mile has the advantage that it varies both with the
amount of freight as well as with the distance shipped. In this sense, it is a better
measure of the amount of freight transportation than either total tonnage or
total mileage alone.[9] Whether ton-miles is an adequate measure of output of

some particular segment of the transportation industry depends on the question being asked. For example, since it does not vary with speed, the ton-mile measure will not be able to trace changes in service quality associated with some change in policy.

For passenger transportation, the standard measure of output is the *passenger-mile* or *passenger-kilometer*, computed as the sum for all of the services of the number of passengers carried multiplied by the distance traveled. The passenger-mile has the advantage that it treats longer trips and trips with more passengers as having produced a larger number of units of transportation than shorter trips or ones with fewer passengers. As with the ton-mile, however, the passenger-mile measure is not sensitive to service quality; it treats a one-hour stop-and-go local bus run traveling 10 miles and carrying an average of 10 people as equivalent in transportation units to six seconds of operation of a jet airplane carrying 100 people. Whether or not this is a sensible comparison to make depends on the question that one wishes to answer. Just because the passenger-mile index can be constructed for any combination of passenger movements does not mean that the particular combination is meaningful. The same is true of the index used to measure combined freight flows.

The companion price variable to the ton-mile is the *average revenue per ton-mile* (ARTM). It is calculated by computing the total revenue generated by any group of freight services divided by the ton-miles of those services. For passenger transportation, the equivalent price variable is average revenue per passenger mile. Average revenue per ton-mile has an easy interpretation as a unit price of providing the freight services within the group of flows for which the ton-mile index is calculated. Almost invariably, attempts to measure freight demand elasticities have involved relating changes in average revenue per ton-mile (treated as a price variable on a demand diagram) with total ton-miles (assumed to be a quantity variable).

Transport economists are likely to call their groupings of transportation flows *markets*. Sometimes the airline flights from Chicago to New York are called a *market*. Sometimes, one hears about *the market for trucking services*. Neither is a true market in the economic sense, but a grouping of transport services for which an output and price index has been calculated.[10] Transport economists have generally followed the pragmatic principle of adjusting the focus of the analysis, choosing sets or grouping of transportation services based on type (passenger or freight), commodity carried (or passenger travel purpose), endpoints, and direction, depending on the question asked and on the availability of reliable data. Ideal economic markets include only homogeneous outputs which are distinct in both a demand and supply sense from others offered elsewhere.

Despite the fact that private and public transport modes are assumed to be perfectly homogeneous in the example described here, the actual services provided are quite heterogeneous. The substitutability between movements made in the northeastern quadrant of the map in Figure 2.7 and those made in the southwestern quadrant is quite low. The reason is that the level of transportation on a flow in one area is not affected by rates charged in a different area unless they compete for the same customers either directly or indirectly. At the other extreme, however, other transportation into and out of the endpoints of a movement are likely to be sufficiently strong influences on traffic levels between the endpoints that an endpoint pair by itself would not constitute an economic market. This is because product price at each destination and at each origin is determined by all supply and demand curves of active origins and destinations.

Thinking of average revenue per ton-mile as a price per unit of the combined ton-miles is natural. However, ARTM is a price index rather than a price and is sensitive to the changes in the composition of traffic. For example, throughout the 1950s and 1960s, railroads in the United States steadily lost an increasing percentage of their highest priced traffic to trucks. Total traffic expanded over this period, but it was the low price traffic that increased while the high price traffic actually declined. Railroad freight revenue declined. To make up for their lost revenue, railroads increased their charges on all types of shipments, but it did not offset the decline in revenues due to the loss of their high price traffic. Thus, throughout this period, actual railroad rates were rising while the average revenue per ton-mile was declining.[11]

Using the same logic, the index of passenger transportation price is also less than ideal. If the composition of traffic does not change, then ARPM (average revenue per passenger mile) will be an exact measure of changes in prices. But if all prices rise by the same amount and traffic composition does not change, that implies that all types of traffic have the same elasticity of demand. If they did have different demand elasticities, flows would adjust by different amounts, leading to a change in the weighting of the price index. For example, the federal government might want to know what the effect of placing a ten cent tax on jet fuel would be on airline traffic. Since different types of airline traffic have different elasticities of demand, we would expect the composition of traffic to change with an increase in jet fuel costs. If this happened, the actual changes in individual airline fare rates would not be reflected in the change in average revenue per passenger-mile.

The reader may wonder, if these two measures of transportation output and the price of transportation have such difficulties, why not use a better measure? The answer is that there is no better index. Index number complications derive from the heterogeneity of transport services and users, not from the particular index chosen. The extent to which an index correctly reflects changes in its components depends primarily on the extent to which the components respond similarly to outside influences. This puts a limit on the market groupings whose behavior can be accurately analyzed using the standard indexes. For example, does it really make sense to combine local bus and intercity jet service and consider them to be the same service? In some circumstances it would, but in most circumstances it would not.

= Determinants of the Elasticity of Demand for a Mode of Transportation

Estimating the elasticity of demand for a mode of transportation in the system illustrated in Figure 2.7 is a matter of seeing how the index of combined transportation flows changes with respect to prices—that is, what would be the percentage change in tons or ton-miles (or passengers or passenger-miles) carried by a mode if it were to increase its charges by 1 percent. In the simulation presented here, such demand elasticities can be generated by varying the charges of a mode by a constant proportion and solving the new spatial equilibrium problems. Figure 2.8 shows the flows that are generated by reducing the price of the public mode by 20 percent, keeping charges of the private mode at the same level as previously. It is interesting to see how the equilibrium changes in response to the drop in rates. The map shows that there has been some modal switching. Several origin-destination pairs on the western side of the map that had formerly been connected by the private mode are now connected by the

FIGURE 2.8   Transportation Equilibrium with a 20 percent Rate Cut by the Public Mode

This figure represents the same geographic position of supplies and demands as in Figure 2.7. Access costs and the costs of the private mode are the same. The difference between this figure and Figure 2.7 is due solely to a 20 percent cut in rates charged by the public mode.

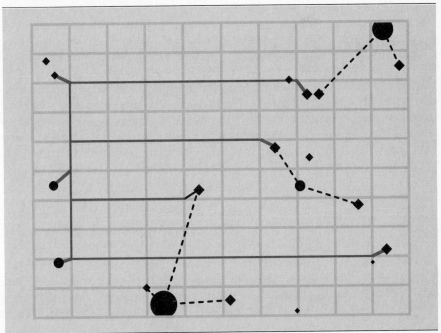

public mode. The dominant changes, however, have been more complex switches in supply and demand regions, with new origin-destination pairs becoming active and others losing all traffic. As a general rule, it is now feasible for more distant locations to reach demand areas.

There are more ton-miles or passenger-miles by the public mode in Figure 2.8 than in Figure 2.7. Part of the reason is visible in Figure 2.8 in the form of new routes that now have traffic on them due to the lower rates. Some of these routes were private mode routes in Figure 2.7, and thus part of the downward slope for the demand curve will come from mode shifting. But the downward slope of modal demands is the result of much more than the choice of mode of transport by any particular pair of shipper and receiver. For example, some routes opened up by lower rates were not previously served by any mode, and there has been an increase in flows on existing routes made possible by the lower rates.

The entire demand for the public mode of transportation is shown in Figure 2.9. It was generated by altering the rates charged by the public mode by small amounts—holding all else constant—and then summing together the distance-weighted flows on that mode. This is the true demand for transportation by the public mode. The true demand curve is not smooth, but slopes down through a series of bumps and valleys. These irregularities are due to the fact that every mode has a limited number of routes that it serves and when a new route is added or one dropped, there will be a discontinuity in the demand relationship.

If the price per mile charged by all modes is zero, all transport will be by the private mode as a means of saving access costs. As transportation gets more costly, at first the only effect is to somewhat reduce flows on all active corridors, with the greatest decreases taking place in the longest movements. As a result, higher costs of transportation pull supply and demand locations towards one another.

In addition to modal shifting, the downward slope of modal demand curves is also affected by the elasticity of overall production with respect to an index of transport costs. This elasticity would be determined by the slopes of the individual demand and supply curves in the same way as in the two-endpoint problem. In addition to the sensitivity of overall production and consumption levels to transport rates and modal switching, another factor that generates the downward slope of modal demand curves is the reduction in the average distance of each unit moved as rate levels rise. The size of market areas shrink as the cost of transportation rises. With extremely high rate levels, there is little overlap among market areas. Despite the fact that higher rate levels increase the proportion of traffic carried by the public mode, the same high rates decrease all demands by limiting the average length of movements.

Readers will note in the following two chapters that our understanding of demand elasticities for different kinds of transportation is at best limited. The reasons are a direct result of the complexity of the adjustments to the transportation equilibrium as prices change. These adjustments are more complex

FIGURE 2.9   True Demand for the Public Mode Generated by the Structure of Product Demand and Product Supply Shown in Figure 2.6

This demand curve was generated by changing the rate level of the public mode, holding access costs and the costs of the private mode constant. Its uneven downward slope is due to changes in pairings of origins and destination in the transportation equilibrium as the rate level changes.

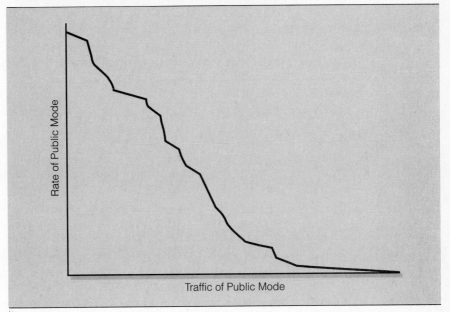

than is typical in most of the economy. For example, transportation demand curves like those in Figure 2.9 are logically irregular in shape with the points of discontinuous change associated with peculiar geography of the transportation map used. This makes it impossible to identify a single elasticity of demand for each mode or a general relationship between rate level and elasticity. Nonetheless, some general results can be derived.

It is logical that the demand for the public mode should be generally more elastic than that for the private mode. This can be inferred from the fact that demand for the private mode can stand much higher rates before all traffic disappears. It also appears that the cross-elasticities of demand for the public mode is higher than the cross-elasticity of demand for the private mode. That is, a one percent change in charges of the private mode of transportation will have a larger percentage effect on the public mode than a similar percentage change in the public mode would have on demand for the public mode. All of these relationships are the result of the cost of access required to use the public mode. Such access costs guarantee that there will be some (primarily short-distance) hauls that cannot be contested by the public mode at any rate level; the inability of the public mode to compete on movements dominated by access costs generates the asymmetry in demand elasticities. To the extent that user costs of transportation are large relative to access costs, however, these results may be reversed.

Factors That Shift Demand for a Mode of Transportation

The example presented above can be used to describe the parameters that determine the modal demand curve. One of the factors has already been discussed: *the prices charged by the other mode.* Another factor is *the per-unit cost of access to the public mode.* Access costs are treated here as proportional to the distance between a user and the closest station. A lower per unit cost of access decreases the cost of using the public mode. Closely related is *the time cost of using a mode.* This cost, neglected in the example presented here, is a non-rate cost of using a mode that rises with the distance traveled by that mode. In the case of automobile and air transport, the time cost of using the private mode is likely to be much higher than that of the public mode, despite the fact that hubbing is likely to give much greater circuity to air transport. A lower cost of time will shift demand curves to the right.

The most important factor determining modal demands is *the spatial distribution of supplies and demands.* Spatial heterogeneity encompasses distances from stations and distances between origins and destinations as well as distances between competing sources of supply or competing demand locations; spatial heterogeneity also defines the circuity of the public mode. Certain spatial patterns are clearly more favorable to the public mode than others—locations of production and settlements near stations obviously reduce the importance of access costs. Greater average separations also favor the public mode since the public mode has the longer movements. Diminished ubiquity will also favor the public mode; decreased ubiquity of supply and demand is likely to increase the average distance of shipment, thus advantaging the mode that specializes in long distance travel—the public mode. (It is interesting to note that in the simulations described above, the public mode is more likely to serve the supplier that has lower average production costs, since it is these low production costs that allow the supplier to ship long distances).

The spatial pattern of supply and demand determines not only the position but also the slope of the modal demand curve. If origins and destinations are dispersed, market areas for each place will be well defined and not greatly affected by transport costs, thus reducing one of the determinants of transport demand and, with it, the elasticity of demand. At the opposite extreme, if origins or destinations are clustered, the elasticity of demand for either mode of transportation is likely to be higher.

LONG-RUN DETERMINANTS OF THE DEMAND FOR TRANSPORTATION

The example just discussed was based on the assumption that factories and consumers were placed at fixed locations. In the short run, this is an appropriate assumption. But in the long run, what determines the location of those supply and demand positions?

History and Geography

Part of the distribution is due to historical accident, weather, the placement of mineral deposits, the location of navigable waterways, and other quirks of geography that are not easily amenable to economic analysis. But not all location decisions are unaffected by the price of transportation. Automobiles are shipped from the upper Midwest because automobiles are manufactured there. But this does not mean that geography determined the demand for transporting new cars. The location of the automobile industry is not due to immovable factors of production. Michigan was the original home of the automobile industry due to some historical accidents (several of the original car builders happened to be born in the state) and due to the central location between sources of steel, wood, and other raw materials and the population of the nation as a whole.[12] As the population of the United States moves increasingly south and west, however, the original location advantages are declining. The newest automobile plants are being built mainly in the middle South, in part to save transportation costs. While the location of manufacturing facilities help determine the demand for transportation, their own location is at least partly determined by the cost and availability of transportation.

When people decide where to live, one of the factors that they take into account is the cost and availability of transportation. The pattern of urban development was determined in large part by the placement of street car lines, and later by bus routes and rail lines. The availability of high quality roads and cheap automobile transportation has reshaped urban areas, allowing suburbs to grow at the expense of core cities. The changing pattern of commuting—now primarily suburb-to-suburb rather than suburb-to-city—has decreased the demand for public transportation and further reinforced the demand for automobile transportation.[13] And yet, even here geography plays a role in determining the demand for transportation. New York City has been able to maintain a substantial proportion of public transit riders among its commuters in part because the shape of the city (long and narrow with many natural barriers to transportation) is not friendly to automobile commuting.[14] The building of new highways and new transit lines is equivalent to altering the geography of a region. This is reflected in the well-known fact that land values change in response to the construction of new transport facilities.[15]

Economic Determinants of Plant Locations

While the influences of history and geography have a large effect on the long-run distribution of demand and supply locations, there are nonetheless some fundamental economic determinants of location. The joint determination of the demand for transportation and the positioning of manufacturing industries and residences is studied in the field of *location theory*. Rather than take places of supply and demand as given, as they are in Figure 2.6, location theory takes a much longer-run perspective than most of economics and tries to predict where the location supplies and demands should be placed, abstracting from advantages dictated by the natural characteristics of particular locations. One of the basic principles of location theory is that weight-gaining manufacturing processes will tend to be located closer to the final market while weight-losing processes will tend to be located closer to the sources of raw materials.[16] (For example, soft drink bottlers will be located close to where the soft drinks are sold, while paper manufacturing plants will be located near the source of wood pulp). But location theory can rarely tell us in which state or county a particular company is likely to locate its warehouses simply by observing transportation rates.[17]

Location theory tells us that, even if a country had the same weather all over, the same fertility of land, the same mineral deposits in all places—in short, if every place had the identical resources as every other place—there would still be a demand for transportation in the long run. At first it seems illogical. If every location can grow its own oranges, mine its own coal, grow its own wheat, and catch its own fish, why would any place wish to trade with any other? The reason is found in the technology of production. For almost all goods and services that the economy produces, on a per unit basis, it is expensive to operate at a very small production level. The tradeoff between production scale economies and transportation costs is shown in Figure 2.10 for the simplest case of production with ubiquitous resources and demand uniformly distributed in a featureless plane. The logic of the shapes of cost curves is developed in Chapter 5. For now it is sufficient to note that average cost curves for production are U-shaped as shown by the lower curve, marked *average production cost*. As a producer's market area expands, average production costs decline due to scale economies in production. The broader the downward sloping portion of the average production cost curve, the more important the scale economies.

As production expands, customers for those goods must be found at locations farther and farther from the production point. The optimal size of operation will be found when the advantages in expanding scale to get lower production costs is counterbalanced by the increased costs of shipping goods longer distances. Without transportation, scale economies would dictate that the optimum size of plant in Figure 2.10 would be x^2. The need to transport larger production runs longer distances to find customers causes the optimal size of the plant to fall to x^1.

FIGURE 2.10   Tradeoff Between Production Scale Economies and Transportation Costs

The average production cost shown in this figure has the classic shape of a region of declining average costs followed by a region of rising costs. The transportation cost curve is generated by the assumption that additional production must be delivered at ever increasing distances and thus higher per unit transportation costs. This combination produces a tradeoff between production cost economies and transportation cost diseconomies. The presence of transportation costs reduces the optimal plant size from x^2 to x^1.

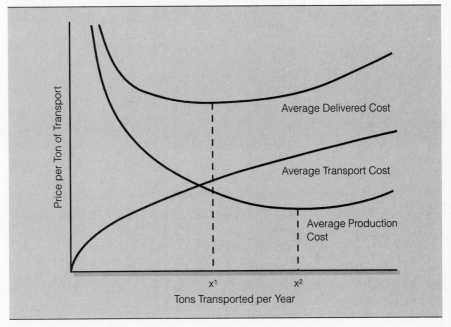

Since there are economies of scale in production of most commodities at least at small output levels, it is inefficient for every town to have its own steel mill, flour mill, carpet mill, etc. The country as a whole can increase its standard of living if towns and regions specialize, producing only a limited number of commodities using factories that are sufficiently large to have low production costs, and then trade with other towns and states for those goods and services that they do not produce. Some economists have found that investments in public infrastructure like transportation facilities have a very high payoff in terms of lifting the overall living standards in the economy—presumably through the mechanism of allowing greater regional specialization and taking greater advantage of production scale economies.[18]

Decreasing the cost of transportation allows greater regional specialization; but increased specialization requires more transportation. In determining locations, regional specialization then acts like the uneven distribution of natural resources in the example given previously. As a practical matter, lower transportation costs will also increase consumer choice and increase the amount of competition in the production of goods and services. If transportation is expensive, scale economies will generally dictate that each city be served by a single inefficiently small company, acting like a monopoly, leaving consumers without a choice. With low cost transportation, consumers can choose between suppliers in different locations. Unfortunately, economists have been unable to model in a usable way transportation that takes place simply to take advantage of competitive opportunities in distant locations. The encouragement to the economy that derives from competition encouraged by improvements in transportation is a benefit that is similarly hard to quantify.[19]

Urban Location Decisions

A tradeoff similar to that in industrial location theory is thought to determine residential location within an urban area. While in the short run urban transportation demand is determined by the location of residences, jobs, recreation areas, shopping centers, and transportation facilities, in the long run all of these locations are variable. The basic theory of urban location assumes that individuals have a tradeoff between three desirable attributes of residence: low travel times, abundant land, and the ability to afford goods and services other than transportation and housing services. Locations with low travel time are desirable, thus bidding up the price of land at those places. Higher land prices make it costly to build houses on large plots. Thus the density of housing will decline from the city center. When choosing residential locations, individuals will then be faced with either low travel times and little land (near downtown), or with high travel times and more spacious plots (distant suburbs).

This tradeoff between travel time and housing density is illustrated in Figure 2.11, which shows travel time and the average number of square feet of land used by residents at different distances from downtown Chicago. At greater distances from downtown, travel times are higher, but because land prices are cheaper, households each use more land than in locations closer to the city center. When transportation costs decrease, the disadvantage of distant locations diminishes. This lowers land values in close-in areas relative to distant areas; in the long run, this brings a change in the settlement pattern, with lower population densities throughout the metropolitan area. This in turn raises the long-run quantity of transportation demanded by residents.[20]

Americans are increasingly choosing to live in very low density suburban and rural areas. These decisions in turn generally lead to more travel and a much greater reliance on automobiles compared with higher density settlements. Given the current structure of costs faced by people making a residence choice, it is hard to argue that the dramatic decline in population densities in this country do not reflect actual preferences. However, there is considerable

FIGURE 2.11   Square Feet per Dwelling and Commuting Time, Chicago 1970

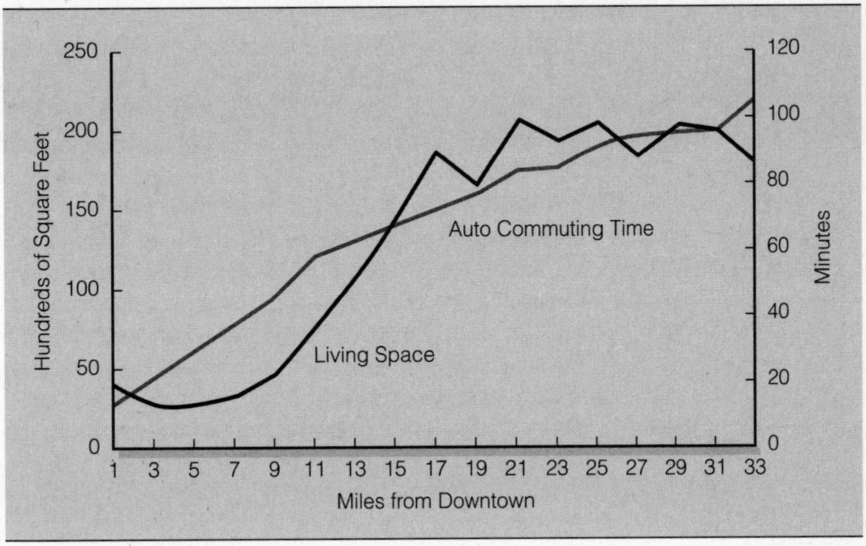

SOURCE: Alex Anas, *Residential Location Markets and Urban Transportation*, (New York: Academic Press, 1982). Data are from Table 4.2.

doubt that those who choose to live in areas of what has been called *urban sprawl* are in fact facing the full cost of transportation and providing services.[21] To the extent that such decisions are made by people who are charged less than the full costs of transportation, an inefficiency will be created. The concept of efficient decision making is covered in Chapter 10. The organization of arguments that those living in urban sprawl do not pay the full costs of their decision is covered in Chapter 14.

CONCLUSION

Analyzing the demand for transportation means finding out how many more (or fewer) ton-miles or passenger-miles of transport are purchased by consumers when the cost per unit falls or rises. Transport demand cannot be looked up in the statistics of how much is transported, but must be analyzed by considering the extent to which transport usage varies with its price. In other words, transport demand analysis tries to sort out the extent to which changes in ton-miles or passenger-miles of transportation are caused by changes in prices and to what extent by other factors. This sort of exercise, examples of which are shown in the next two chapters, requires an analysis of motives for transportation.

Transportation is derived from supply and demand curves in origins and destinations. When there is a single pair of origins and destinations, transportation demand can easily be determined by finding the distance between the supply price at origins and the demand price at destinations for every quantity shipped. Elastic demands for transportation can be generated by combinations of elastic product supplies at origins or elastic product demands at destinations. Anything that shifts supply curves at the origin or demand curves at the destination will shift the demand for transportation.

The presence of multiple origins and destinations makes the analysis of the demand for transportation much more complicated than the simple model suggests. When transport costs rise, a number of things happen simultaneously: Producers produce less, consumers consume less, there is a shift in the preferred mode of transportation, and closer sources of supply are favored. Often these patterns require that there is an extensive re-pairing of buyers and sellers. How each of these factors gets played out is the result of a complex equilibrium in which all buyers and all sellers look for the best options.

NOTES

1. The elasticity of demand for transportation is formally defined as $(\Delta Q/Q)/(\Delta P/P)$ where Q represents the quantity of transportation, P the price per unit of transportation and Δ represents a small change. To simplify the mathematical analysis, elasticity is quoted as the limiting value as the amount of the price change becomes very small.

2. It would be logically possible for a rightward shift of a demand curve to be generated by a decrease in income if transportation were an inferior good. Since there is no evidence that this is the case for transportation as a whole, this possibility will be ignored. In addition, in standard economics, taste is an important determinant of demand.

3. This derivation of transportation demand is based on Samuelson, Paul A. (1952): "Spatial Price Equilibrium and Linear Programming," *The American Economic Review*, Vol. 42, pp. 283–303.

4. The reader will note that the common shorthand of economics is used here, in which competitive forces push profit margins to zero. This zero profit makes allowances for the opportunity cost of all resources used in the transaction.

5. The reader can verify that the equation:
$$Q = 5,000 - 500T$$
can be rewritten with price, the variable traditionally treated as dependent in graphical analyses of markets, on the vertical axis:
$$T = 10 - 500Q$$
This equation is represented in Figure 2.5.

6. In algebraic terms, a cross price elasticity of demand is $(\Delta Q_1/Q_1)/(\Delta P_2/P_2)$ where Q_1 refers to the quantity demanded of good 1 and P_2 refers to the price of good 2.

7. The mathematical treatment of demand in the multi-origin-multi-destination problem is presented in Takayama, Takashi, and George G. Judge (1971): *Spatial and Temporal Price and Allocation Models*, (Amsterdam: North-Holland Publishing).

See also, J.W.B. Guise, "Expository Critique of the Takayama-Judge Models of Interregional and Intertemporal Market Equilibrium," *Regional Studies and Urban Economics*, February 1979, pp. 83–95.

8. T. Friesz, P. A. Viton, and R. L. Tobin, "Economic and Computational Aspects of Freight Network Equilibrium Models: A Synthesis," *Journal of Regional Science* (February 1985), pp. 29–50.

9. A good discussion of the difficulties of different output measures in transportation is found in George Wilson, *Essays on Some Unsettled Questions in the Economics of Transportation* (Bloomington: Foundation for Economic and Business Studies, Indiana University, 1962). See also, Olson, C. E. and Brown, T. A., "The Output Unit in Transportation Revisited," *Land Economics*, August 1972, pp. 280–281.

10. The practical difficulties of defining markets in real-world situations has been dealt with primarily by those applying antitrust law to economics. Among recent contributions are: David, Scheffman T., and Pablo, Spiller T., "Geographic Market Definition under the U.S. Department of Justice Merger Guidelines," *Journal of Law and Economics* 30(1), April 1987, pp. 123–147 and Boyer, Kenneth D., "Is There a Principle for Defining Industries?" *Southern Economic Journal* 50(3), January 1984, pp. 761–770.

11. Task Force on Railroad Productivity, *Improving Railroad Productivity*: Final Report to the National Commission on Productivity and the Council of Economic Advisers (Washington, D.C.: U.S. Government Printing Office, November 1973).

12. James M. Rubenstein, *The Changing U.S. Auto Industry: A Geographical Analysis* (London and New York: Routledge, 1992). See also, J.S. Hekman, "An Analysis of the Changing Location of Iron and Steel Production in the Twentieth Century," *American Economic Review* (September 1978), pp. 123–133.

13. Alan Pisarski, *Commuting in America*, (1987) ENO foundation. The most commonly used model of urban location is that in Richard F. Muth, *Cities and Housing: The Spatial Pattern of Urban Residential Land Use* (Chicago: University of Chicago Press, 1969). The standard model of urban location assumes that jobs are in the city center and that individuals commute inward toward their jobs. The fundamental tradeoff faced by households is between relatively cheaper land at the city's periphery and the lower transport costs that would result from locating closer to the central business district (where land would be more expensive). Bruce Hamilton, "Wasteful Commuting," *Journal of Political Economy*, Vol. 90 (October 1982), pp. 1035–1053. Recently there has been an attempt to reconcile urban location models with the observed commuting patterns. See, for example, Michelle J. White, "Urban Commuting Journeys Are Not 'Wasteful,'" *Journal of Political Economy*, Vol. 96, No. 5 (October 1988), pp. 1097–1110. See also John Yinger, "City and Suburb: Urban Models with More Than One Employment Center," *Journal of Urban Economics,* Vol. 31, No. 2 (March 1992), pp. 181–205. See also Giuliano, Genevieve; and Small Kenneth A., "Is the Journey to Work Explained by Urban Structure?" *Urban Studies*, 30(9), November 1993, pp. 1485–1500.

14. The effect of city shape is explored in Robert M. Solow and William S. Vickrey, "Land Use in a Long Narrow City," *Journal of Economic Theory*, Vol. 3 (1971), pp. 430–447.

15. See, for example, D. Damm, et al., "The Response of Urban Real Estate Values in Anticipation of the Washington Metro," *Journal of Transport Economics and Policy* (September 1980), pp. 315–336; and D.N. Dewees, "The Effect of a Subway

on Residential Property Values in Toronto," *Journal of Urban Economics* (October 1976), pp. 357–369.

16. E.M. Hoover (1948) *The Location of Economic Activity* (New York: McGraw Hill, 1948).

17. Roger W. Schemenner, *Making Business Location Decisions*, (Englewood Cliffs, NJ: Prentice-Hall, 1982). This survey of how businesses make location decisions found that location decisions are affected by labor costs; the degree of unionization; proximity to markets; proximity to supplies and other company facilities; and the quality of life in an area. Different companies were sensitive to these factors to different degrees. For some companies, transportation issues (the proximity factors in his list) were quite unimportant. See also, Robert R. Love, James G. Morris, and George O. Wesolowsk, *Facilities Location: Models and Methods* (Amsterdam: North Holland, 1988), and Edwin S. Mills and John F. McDonald, eds., *Sources of Metropolitan Growth* (New Brunswick, NJ: Center for Urban Policy Research, 1992).

18. Alicia Munnell, "Infrastructure Investment and Economic Growth," *Journal of Economic Perspectives*, Vol. 6, No. 4, Fall 1992, pp. 189–198. Others are far more skeptical that the rate of return to public infrastructure investment is in general higher than that available to private investment. See, for example, Edward M. Gramlich, "Infrastructure Investment," *Journal of Economic Literature*, Vol. XXXII, No. 3 (September 1994), pp. 1176–1196.

19. The difficulty in explaining cross-hauling and quantifying the effects of improved transportation on consumer choice and competition is a central part of the controversy among economic historians on the role that transportation improvements played in U.S. economic development. Robert Fogel, *Railroads and American Economic Growth* (Baltimore: Johns Hopkins University Press, 1964), argues that railroads were not substantially more efficient than the canals that they displaced and so could not have had a major effect on development. Alfred Chandler, *The Railroads: The Nation's First Big Business* (New York: Harcourt, Brace and World, 1965) argues that one of the main developmental benefits of railroads was to break the power of local monopolies—an effect not measured by Fogel.

20. Some attempts to quantify or empirically test this model of urban location can be found in Altmann, J.L. and Desalvo, J.S., "Mills-Muth Simulation Model of Urban Residential Land Use, Tests and Extensions," *Journal of Regional Science*, February 1981, pp. 1–21 and Alperovich, G. "An Empirical Study of Population Density Gradients and Their Determinants," *Journal of Regional Science*, November 1983, pp. 529–540.

21. Downs, Anthony, *Stuck in Traffic: Coping with Peak-hour Traffic Congestion* (Washington: Brookings Institution, 1992).

3

Demand for Freight Transportation

The study of the demand for freight transportation is a study of the current position of the demand curves, their slopes, and how outside factors shift the demand curves to the right or to the left. We speak of demand curves rather than a single demand curve since, as emphasized in Chapter 2, there are no well-defined economic markets for freight transportation. Rather, demand curves are drawn for sets of freight services and there is an almost limitless number of ways of combining freight flows into different groupings, each of which will have its own demand curve.

The broadest aggregate is simply all ton-miles produced in the United States. Figure 3.1 shows that the U.S. economy produces about 3.5 trillion ton-miles of freight transportation every year—more than 12,000 ton-miles of transportation for each individual living in the country. Figure 3.1 shows that the amount of freight transportation in the country has generally paralleled economic development. In recession periods, like 1982 when real gross national product declined, freight transportation decreases. When economic growth is rapid, so is the growth in freight transportation.

Freight transportation has not been sharing in economic growth to the same degree that other sectors of the economy have. While real gross domestic product has increased nearly

FIGURE 3.1   **Ton-miles of U.S. Freight Transportation and GDP**

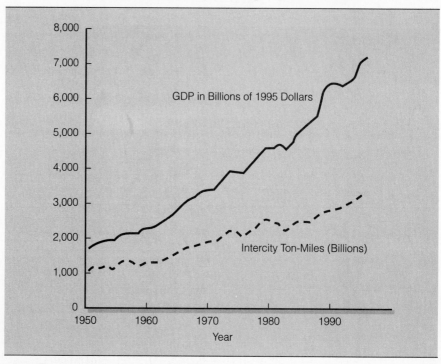

SOURCE: *Transportation in America*, various issues

four-fold since 1947, the amount of freight transportation has increased by less than three times. Put in other terms, while each dollar of real GDP required two-thirds of a ton-mile of freight transportation in 1950, today it requires only half a ton-mile. This decline in the importance of freight transportation in the economy is likely the result of the shift away from heavy industry toward a greater emphasis on light manufacturing, such as micro-electronics, which require little freight transportation, and toward services, which generally require no freight transportation at all.

While the heavy industry sector of the economy has been declining relative to other parts of the economy, it still generates most of the freight in the country. Table 3.1 shows which sectors of the economy generate the most freight. Measured in tons, the oil and coal industries are the largest users of freight transportation. A somewhat smaller quantity of freight is generated by the stone and stone products sectors and by grain and food processors. Lumber, primary metals, and paper are the remaining industrial sectors that generate significant amounts of freight tonnage.

TABLE 3.1   Commodity Classes with Largest U.S. Freight Shipments, 1993

STCC	Description	Millions of Tons	Value ($/Lb)
29	Petroleum and coal products	1,919	0.090
14	Non-metallic minerals	1,827	0.005
11	Coal	1,083	0.010
20	Food and kindred products	860	0.500
32	Clay, concrete, glass, or stone products	798	0.050
24	Lumber and wood products	706	0.090
01	Farm products	653	0.110
28	Chemicals or allied products	551	0.510
Total		9,800	

SOURCE: 1993 Census of Transportation. Does not include pipeline transportation. STCC refers to Standard Transportation Commodity Classification.

The decreasing proportion of freight transport in national expenditure may also reflect the state of U.S. development. In developing countries, freight ton-miles increase two or three times as fast as gross domestic product.[1] The higher the degree of a country's development, the slower the growth of freight transportation compared with the growth of the economy as a whole.

The first half of the ton-mile calculation is the number of tons shipped. The other half is the distance that these goods are shipped. Figure 3.2 shows that the greatest number of tons is shipped locally. The more distant the destination, the smaller the tonnage shipped. The number of tons moving in the U.S. freight transport system more than 1,500 miles is only 120 billion—about 3 percent of the size of the market for local movements. However, the distant hauls are not of trivial importance. Since long-distance movements produce more miles in the ton-mile formula, long-distance transportation still represent a significant percentage of the ton-miles produced by the U.S. transportation system. In fact, Figure 3.2 shows that there are more ton-miles in the 1,500+ mileage block than there are in the under- 50 mile block.

Another way of dividing the total amount of freight transportation in the economy is by the modes that carry it. This is done in Figures 3.3 and 3.4. The left bar in each figure represents the amount of freight transportation in 1950, while the height of the right bars shows the same data for 1995. Railroads in 1995 carried about 40 percent of intercity ton-miles in the economy, an increase in absolute terms since 1950, but a dramatically smaller share of the total than in the earlier period. Oil pipelines and trucks each carry about one quarter of intercity ton-miles; both modes more than doubled their relative shares of the freight market and increased their absolute traffic more than five-fold since 1950. The other major mode of freight transportation, rivers and canals, saw its share of freight traffic increase from 5 percent to 12 percent in the same time.

FIGURE 3.2   **Quantity of Freight in Various Mileage Blocks**

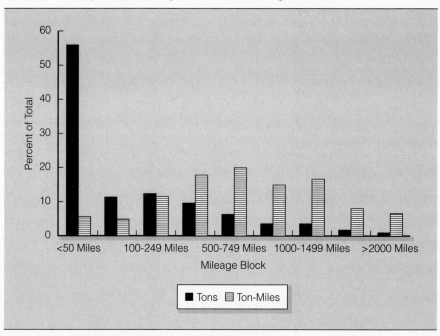

SOURCE: 1993 Census of Transportation, Commodity Flow Survey

The rising share is paralleled by a decline in the share of freight traffic carried on the Great Lakes.

In Figure 3.3, the same information is expressed in terms of tons rather than ton-miles. In these terms, trucks are by far the largest mode of freight transportation, carrying 46 percent of all intercity tons. Railroads are second, with 26 percent, followed by oil pipelines and rivers and canals. Regardless of which share is computed—that of tons or of ton-miles—the railroads share has declined since 1950 while truck shares have risen. Oil pipelines do not appear to be as major a factor in freight transportation when calculated in tons rather than ton-miles. The switch in the relative positions of rivers and canals and Great Lakes shipping reflected in Figure 3.4 is reflected in the tonnage figure as well.

Modes differ in their shares of tons and ton-miles because the average distance that they carry freight is different. By dividing a mode's ton-miles by its tons, we can calculate what the average distance of a shipment is. For railroads, the average shipment moves about 700 miles, a rise from 420 miles in 1950. Trucks specialize in much shorter shipments. The average distance of a an intercity truck movement is more than 250 miles; it was closer to 200 miles in 1950. Oil pipelines, with an average shipping distance of more than

FIGURE 3.3   Ton-Miles of U.S. Freight Carried by Various Modes, 1950 and 1995

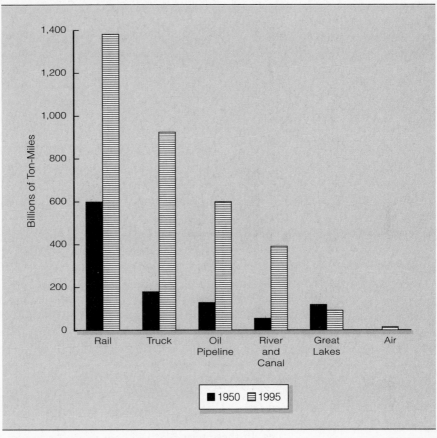

SOURCE: *Transportation in America*, 14th Edition

500 miles, Great Lakes shipments with an average length of 500 miles, and river and canal movements (more than 600 miles, on average) are all long-distance modes.

While modes differ in the average distances of their shipments, they also specialize in the types of commodities they tend to carry. For railroads, coal is by far the largest commodity, with farm products, chemicals, and nonmetallic minerals following. For domestic water carriers, petroleum products are the most important, followed by crude oil, coal, and farm products. Trucks have as their largest tonnage class crushed stone followed by stone, clay, glass and concrete products, food and kindred products, and sand and gravel. None of the modes is absolutely distinct from the others in the type of traffic that it carries, but all modes specialize in markets that do not substantially overlap.

FIGURE 3.4   Tons of U.S. Freight Carried by Various Modes, 1950 and 1995

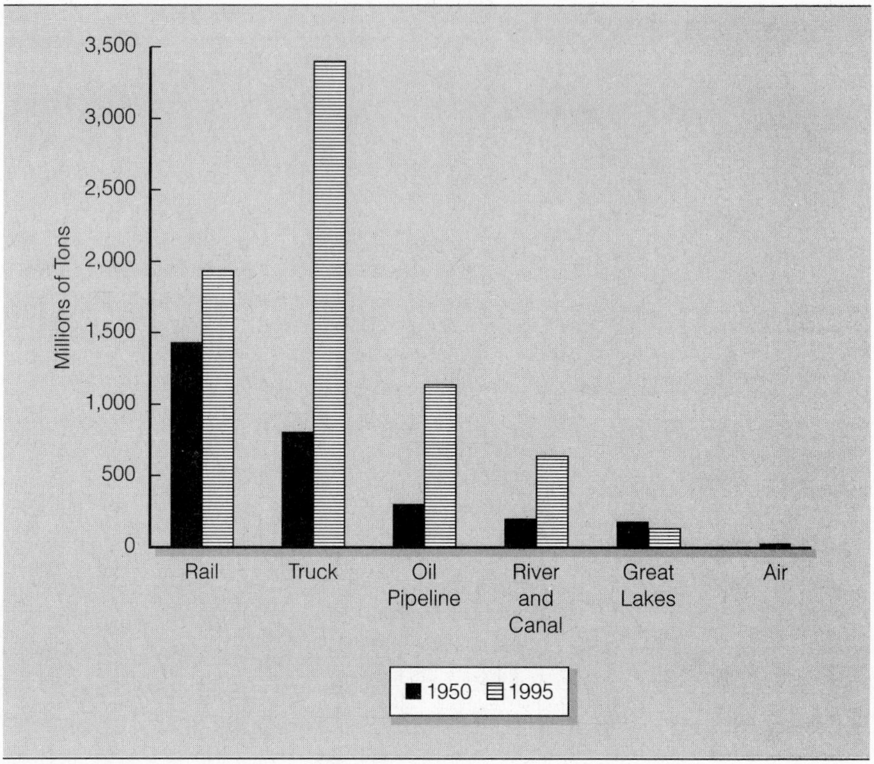

SOURCE: *Transportation in America*, 14th Edition

THE LOGIC OF ECONOMETRIC DEMAND ESTIMATIONS

As emphasized in the previous chapter, the amount of freight traffic listed above are not demands but quantities demanded of freight transportation. Demand is a relationship between the amount of freight transportation and the price paid for it. To discover the true demand for freight transportation is to find out what would happen to freight shipments if the price paid were to change.

Measuring demand is far more difficult than measuring quantity demanded, but is also more important. It is interesting to know the number of tons of dressed chickens shipped from Maryland to New York City in any given week, but by itself the figure is not useful. Imagine, however, that a trucking company wanted to know what the effect on its traffic in dressed chicken would be if it were to raise its rates by 10 percent. Or the government of Maryland might be interested in what the effect on commodity shipments would be if they were to raise the tax on diesel fuel by 5 cents a gallon. Transportation planners might be interested in the effect the routing of shipments might have in slowing traffic on a particular highway. Answers to all of these questions require knowing the slope of some demand curve for freight transportation.

Economics is not an experimental science. If it were possible to run experiments, we could more easily measure the elasticity of demand. We would hold constant all of the other influences on some transportation market and vary price, observing the quantity of traffic, and so trace out its demand curve. Since we cannot run such experiments, all measurements of freight demand elasticities are estimates based on experience in other times or other places with similar conditions.[2]

Time series data is an historical record of prices and quantities in some grouping of services that a researcher is interested in. In addition to average revenue per ton-mile and ton-miles during different years in the past, a researcher will also have a record of values of other variables that affect transportation decisions in the market. The most common control variables are measures of industrial output or income, service quality, and the rates charged for competing modes of transport or competing origins, destinations, or commodities.

Unlike time series estimation, which tries to infer demand elasticities from data that change from year to year, cross-section estimation tries to make sense of prices that are different at a single point in time. To find prices that vary, a researcher will look at other markets that appear to have similar characteristics to the one of interest. In either case, the aim is the same—to observe how changes in prices are correlated with changes in quantities, accounting simultaneously for the influence of other determinants of freight demand.

Econometrics is the tool that is used to measure demand elasticities from either time-series or cross-section data. To understand how econometrics is used to estimate demand curves, observe Figure 3.5. From either cross-section or time-series sources, data have been collected on the quantity of freight transportation, the rate per ton-mile, and the value of a control variable, income. These are plotted in the three-dimensional diagram shown in Figure 3.5. Econometrics is a technique for drawing a plane through the data that most closely matches the data in that figure. The typical result of an econometric estimation will be mathematical equations of this form:

$$Q = 4,000,000 - 23P + 1.5I \tag{3.1}$$

where Q = ton-miles
 P = Price per ton-mile
 I = Income

Equation 3.1 is the mathematical representation of the plane in three dimensions shown in Figure 3.5. If we "hold income constant" at $4,000,000, the

FIGURE 3.5   The Logic of Econometric Curve Fitting
Econometrics finds relationships among variables that best fit the data. Shown here is
the plane that best fits the data points for price, income, and quantity demanded.
Solid points show an observation above the plane. Open circles show observations
below the plane.

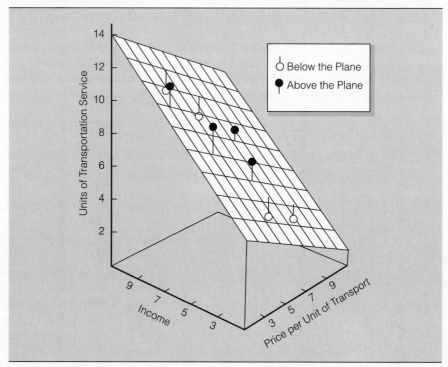

income term of Equation 3.1 will disappear and the constant term will increase
by 4,000,000 × 1.5 or 6,000,000. The equation can thus be rewritten as

$$Q = 10,000,000 - 23P \tag{3.2}$$

which is a linear relationship in the form of a demand curve. By mathematically holding income constant, we have gotten information in the same form
that we would have had we run a controlled experiment. While our data do
not show that income has in fact been held constant in either cross-section or
time-series data, by fitting a multi-dimensional curve (Equation 3.1) and then
taking a two-dimensional slice of that curve (Equation 3.2), econometrics
allows us to make statements about what the data tells us would happen if we
were to hold all variables constant except for price. We can then predict what

quantity demanded would be if we simply move to a different point on the plane, corresponding to the new price and income figures. We can make this prediction, even if there is no experience at all with prices and incomes being at exactly the level of interest.

The validity of such inferences depends critically on the assumption that we know the true underlying relationship between price, income, and quantity demanded. This is called the *functional form*. There is nothing in economic theory that says that demand relationships like those shown in Figure 3.5 must be a flat plane. In fact, the demand curve derived in Chapter 2 had numerous bumps and kinks in it. Unfortunately, econometrics is incapable of fitting highly irregular curves to the data unless the location of the bumps and kinks is already known, and we must settle for using a regular curve that has the same approximate shape as the true demand curve.

The preferred way to choose the shape for the surface fitted to the data is to try to understand the motivations of decision makers. For historical reasons, transportation economics has tended to focus on those who send goods rather than on those who receive them. By focusing attention on only one of the two parties who determine transportation demand, it is possible to employ two standard and very powerful techniques: qualitative choice models and translog derived demand techniques. In a qualitative choice model technique, a purchaser of transport decisions is assumed to make a choice between two modes, say, rail and truck, using a probability based selection rule, where the probability of choosing a mode for a delivery depends on the relative prices of the two modes. For example, a transport purchaser might be seen to select railroads 20 percent of the time if it has the same rate as trucks, but 50 percent of the time if its rates are half those of trucks. This technique is more commonly used in estimating demands for passenger transportation and will be described more fully in the next chapter.

The second econometric technique of general economics that is sometimes used in transportation economics is categorized under the name of *flexible form* or *translog derived demand models*.[3] In these models, demand is seen as the sum of the decisions of a typical purchaser of shipping services. The typical shipper balances the use of rail shipping, truck shipping, labor, and capital to minimize total costs of production and logistics. The higher the price of an input, the less of it will be used. By imposing on the rail/truck purchases the same production relationships that have been found to be generally true among broad input categories like labor, capital, and energy, the translog technique is able to make apparent sense of price/quantity data in freight shipping and produce demand estimates that appear to be quite plausible.

In trying to evaluate the reliability of econometric demand estimates, it is important to remember that estimates of what will happen can never be completely accurate. All econometric measurements are made with some degree of error, and all estimates assume that the variables ignored in the estimation will remain constant when freight rates are changed. If econometric estimates forecast a 5 percent drop in shipments when rates rise by 10 percent, observing that in fact shipments drop by only 3 percent does not mean that the original estimate was wrong. Some other factor, not accounted for in the model, may have shifted; or, sometimes a 3 percent drop and a 5 percent drop will both be within the range of forecasting error. Demand analysis is a matter of estimation, not certainties.

While economists have spent considerable time on evaluating the theoretical properties of different functional forms, the more practical problems in evaluating the aggregation assumptions implicit in the market grouping may be a more important influence on the accuracy of demand estimates. As emphasized in Chapter 2, all demand curves for freight transportation actually refer to some combination of freight flows. The quantity demanded of freight transportation then means the sum of movements of possibly different commodities, in different lot sizes, moving between different end points. As noted in Chapter 2, aggregation is done using the ton-mile index, with its companion price measure, average revenue per ton-mile. As seen previously, one problem with using a price index to define prices is that it can change even when none of the rates has changed merely by changing the composition of the traffic. Some groupings are more susceptible to this problem than others. Of course, if all shippers are charged the same price per ton-mile, then there is no problem: The average revenue per ton-mile equals the price everyone pays. In general, the smaller the price dispersion within a market grouping, the more accurate the demand measurements will be. Another condition that can increase the accuracy of demand measurements is similarity in individual demand elasticities within the market aggregate. If all shippers have demand curves with the same slope, it is more likely that the measured demand curve will have that same slope. The more disparate the slopes of the true demand curves making up the market grouping whose demand is being estimated, the more inaccurate the measurement will be.

As a general rule, investigators trying to measure freight demand elasticities will have more accurate measurements if they work with the smallest grouping of markets for which they have all the necessary data, since narrow market groupings will generally be more homogeneous. However, it is often impractical to work with very narrow groupings. First, data are rarely available that will allow one to measure prices and output at the narrowest level. Second, the researcher's focus of interest is often on policies that affect a broad aggregate of freight transportation movements—for example, increasing wages of all truck drivers at the same time. Knowing the elasticity of demand in very narrow market groups (in which, for example, the wages of truck drivers in competing or complementary markets is held constant) is unlikely to be useful in predicting the effects of broad-based policies (for example, in which the wages of drivers in other markets in fact change simultaneously).

MEASUREMENTS OF FREIGHT DEMAND ELASTICITIES

The broadest market grouping for which economists have tried to calculate market elasticities is for the traffic of a mode of transportation. An early attempt to measure rail elasticities following standard techniques found that the elasticity of overall rail ton-miles with respect to changes in average revenue per ton-mile to be approximately –.6; the corresponding elasticity for truck shipments was –1.8.[4] These figures imply that a rise in rail average revenue per ton-mile of 10 percent would drop rail ton-miles by 6 percent but a similar truck rate rise would lower truck ton-miles by 18 percent. Another study using similar methods and similar data also found that truck demand was much more elastic than rail demand.[5] There is no logical explanation for why truck demand should be so much more elastic than rail demand, and seems to contradict the expectations of Chapter 2. Statistical biases introduced by using such a broad aggregate as all traffic must be suspected as the cause for this surprising result.

Dissatisfaction with the results of direct estimation of the elasticity of demand for a mode's freight traffic led to estimations whose results are strongly restricted by assumptions on the functional form. By restricting the form that demand estimates can take, it is possible to get much more reliable estimates of demand elasticities from limited amounts of data—assuming of course, that the restrictions are correct. A favorite restriction used by researchers is to assume that the overall level of freight traffic is fixed and to calculate that part of the elasticity of demand for the traffic of one mode that derives from switches of traffic to and from other modes of transportation. The other elements of ton-mile generation, changes in the total tonnage generated in the economy and changes in the average distance that a shipment travels, are ignored in these estimations, and assumed to be minor.

The elasticities of total rail or truck traffic implied by these estimates is in the range of –.2 to –.5 if both modes have equal shares.[6] This means that a 10 percent increase in either rail or truck rates would reduce that mode's traffic by 2 to 5 percent, and correspondingly increase the other mode's traffic by the same percentage. By assumption, the larger a mode's share of traffic, the smaller the elasticity will be. In reasonable ranges of market share, rail elasticities will generally be somewhat higher than truck market shares, but still inelastic.[7]

Using more sophisticated techniques, Friedlaender and Spady find that the cross-elasticity of demand between rail and truck shipments is extremely low, while the own price elasticity of demand for each mode is very high: in the neighborhood of –2. This implies that railroads and trucks serve quite distinct markets. If trucking was subject to a 10 percent increase in all prices, the level of traffic would fall by 20 percent, but virtually none of the traffic would be won by railroads. The low apparent substitutability of rail and truck traffic supports findings using more direct estimation techniques. The own price elasticity measurements, by contrast, suggest a much higher sensitivity of transportation to its price than is generally supposed. Logically, since the estimations are based on the assumption of a constant level of output, the reduction in truck or rail ton-miles when a mode raises its rates must derive from an extreme sensitivity of length of haul to changes in rates.[8] An alternate explanation is that the elasticities have been mismeasured by using a market grouping too broad to support the assumptions used to generate the functional form.

Working with narrower market groupings will ameliorate some of the biases apparently introduced by using wider market groupings.[9] A natural way of limiting the market grouping is to divide by commodities. McFadden, Winston, and Boersch-Supan have investigated mode choice in the shipment of fresh fruits and vegetables, the great majority of which are made by truck rather than by rail.[10] (Note that while "fresh fruits and vegetables" is a narrow class of commodities, it still includes lettuce, tomatoes, cabbage, onions, oranges, grapes, and apples, all of which may have different elasticities of demand for freight transportation. The data set also includes many different origins, destinations, lot sizes, and service quality characteristics. Thus while it is a clear improvement over studies using overly broad groupings, the markets covered are not really homogeneous). A 10 percent increase in rail rates is estimated to decrease the shipper's probability of choosing rail by 3.4 percent, but to increase truck probabilities by only 1.9 percent. A 10 percent increase in truck rates would cause truck shipments to drop by 5 percent and rail shipments to rise by 10 percent. These price elasticities appear to follow the logic of the modal-split analyses that the higher the market share, the lower the price elasticity of demand.[11] In other studies of single commodity transport demands, Oum finds that for Canadian conditions, within the fruits, vegetables and edible foods category, as well as for the metallic and non-metallic products groups, the demand for rail service is elastic. The demand for truck service is inelastic only for fuel oil other than gasoline. While these single commodity estimations are undoubtedly more accurate than broader market groupings, even when the commodity appears to be very well defined, these investigations should still be seen as groupings of transportation markets. Attempts to investigate demand elasticities at extremely fine levels of market groupings generally run into problems of identifying data for non-chosen alternatives.

Demand for Shipments of Hard Red Spring Wheat from North Dakota to Minneapolis and Duluth

An example of a very narrowly defined freight demand estimation is provided by Wilson, Wilson, and Koo.[12] This sort of disaggregate estimation is ideally suited for accuracy of estimation since it does away with the ambiguities associated with heterogeneous products and regions. In their study, the authors collected information from July 1973 to June 1983 on the shipment of hard red spring wheat from points in North Dakota to the main destinations for such products, the mills and shipping docks at Minneapolis and Duluth, Minnesota.

By surveying grain elevators, they developed data on monthly quantities shipped by rail and truck and the average revenue per ton-mile charged by each mode in each month.

The authors were concerned that the prices they collected were not the fixed, predetermined numbers that is assumed by the theory of econometric curve fitting outlined above. Rather, they suppose that each month the railroads set their rates based on the expected reactions of truckers. These rates were then assumed to be fixed for the following month; during that month, truck shipments and rates were assumed to be determined by a competitive equilibrium. The equilibrium price and quantity price and quantity of trucking services was modeled to vary from month to month based on changes in the rail rate and the costs of providing trucking service. Along with predetermined rail rates, the trucking rates, set by supply and demand, are then simultaneously factored into the railroad demand curve to determine the quantity of rail services demanded. With their model set, the authors used econometric curve fitting techniques to find the slopes of rail demand and truck supply and demand curves that provided the best fit to their data.

The results of Wilson, Wilson, and Koo's estimations are presented in Table 3.2. Over the 10-year period from which their data were drawn, the slopes of the rail and truck demand curves yield average elasticity estimates that are higher than those found by other researchers. The truck own elasticity of demand is estimated to be –.73—inelastic, but very close to the elastic region. Rail demand is calculated as being –1.18, clearly on the elastic side of unity. The cross elasticity of rail demand with respect to the truck rate is found to be extraordinarily high, +2.3, while truck demand is not found to be nearly as elastic with respect to rail rates. Following rail deregulation in 1980, all of the own price and cross-price elasticities are measured to be larger than previously. The truck demand curve in particular is found to be amazingly responsive both to own price (an elasticity of –13.4) and the price of rail transport (a cross-price

TABLE 3.2   Price Elasticity Estimates for Shipments of Hard Red Spring Wheat from North Dakota to Minneapolis and Duluth

	Average Value		Post–1980	
	Rail Rate	Truck Rate	Rail Rate	Truck Rate
Truck Demand	0.70	-0.73	8.29	-13.4
Rail Demand	-1.18	2.30	-1.46	2.54

SOURCE: William W. Wilson, Wesley W. Wilson and Won W. Koo, "Modal Competition and Pricing in Grain Transport," *Journal of Transport Economics and Policy*, Vol. XXII, No. 3 (September 1988), pp. 319–337.

elasticity of +8.29). Rail demand, by contrast, is estimated to have only slightly higher own and cross-price elasticities.

The estimates may, of course, be incorrect. The study was carefully done, and there is no reason to assume that the authors made an error in their data analysis. But like all econometric analysis, the validity of the results depends critically on the correctness of the functional form that the authors have used, and there is no direct way to be sure that they have the correct form. If prices are not set in the way that they assumed, their estimates will be mismeasured. In most scientific research, we expect to see others try to replicate the exercise with different models or data to see if the same results are obtained; in transportation economics, however, the difficulty of obtaining data generally precludes replication.

Assuming that these results are correct, what can one learn from these estimates? The estimated elasticities are much higher than previously reported results for other commodities in other places. Does that mean that the elasticity of demand for rail and road transportation is higher than previously supposed, or does it mean that demand elasticities for transportation of hard red spring wheat from North Dakota to Minnesota is higher than for other commodities in other places? Both are possible. Since freight transportation is so strongly determined by geography and the shipping characteristics of individual commodities, there is every reason to expect that there will be some situations in which demand is very price responsive and the authors may have found one.

There is no general organizing scheme that leads one to have definite expectations about relative demand elasticities of particular shipping situations. Thus the estimated demand elasticities for shipping hard red spring wheat from North Dakota to Minnesota cannot be used to make inferences about price responsiveness in other shipping situations. Each situation is unique and thus generally uninteresting. Are the demand elasticities for that commodity in that region still as high today as they were in 1973–83 when the authors collected their data? There is nothing that allows us to make a credible prediction. Unless one is a shipper or carrier in the northern Great Plains, there is really no reason to care. A challenge for transportation economics in the coming years is to develop an organizing scheme for allowing transferring of information of price responsiveness made in one area to others that should be reasonably similar.

OTHER FACTORS AFFECTING FREIGHT DEMAND

The quantity demanded of freight transportation is affected not only by rates charged but by other factors as well. We can use the models of Chapter 2 to show us what those other factors should be. In the models, buyers and sellers of products are linked by a transportation equilibrium in which the difference in prices of goods in producing and consuming regions is no greater than the cost of transportation. This is because it is the ability to profitably ship goods from a producing to a consuming area that will cause goods to be transported. If the price of vegetable oil is $1.00 per gallon in a consuming area, the price in a producing area is $0.90 per gallon and the shipping cost between them is $0.05 per gallon, there will be traders who will take advantage of the price differential and transport vegetable oil from the low-price area to the high-price area. The change in the quantity of oil that can be profitably shipped depends on the slopes of the product supply and demand curves. Thus, logically, the demand for freight transportation will shift whenever the product supply curves shift or the product demand curves shift.

Any factor that shifts the supply curve of goods in a producing area will shift the demand curve for freight transportation. A supply curve for any commodity is a representation of the marginal costs incurred by producers. It will be useful to consider *supply* as referring to the costs of producing and loading goods into the carrier's vehicles. Changes in any cost—wages in the producing area, fuel costs, or freight handling costs—shift the product supply curve and thus the demand curve for freight transportation.

Inventory carrying costs will also affect the costs of producing and loading in the producing area. Since all freight transportation requires vehicles, the size of the vehicle compared with the rate of production will determine the size of the inventory that a shipper must hold before it is economically justified to send a shipment.[13] The larger the vehicle, the larger the size of the lot that a shipper must hold before making a shipment. The larger the shipment size, the more important are the factors that determine the cost of holding inventories. For example, an increase in interest rates will have a larger effect on the demand for transporting boat-load sizes of shipments than they will for truckload shipments. One of the most important advantages that motor carriers have over other modes of freight transportation is the inventory holding cost savings that result from smaller lot sizes. This advantage is most pronounced when the freight is of high value. Table 3.1 shows the value per ton of some selected commodities. The commodities that have a high value are generally those where truck shipments dominate.

Using the same logic that identified factors that shift product supply as determinants of transportation demand, another factor affecting the demand for freight transportation is shifts in product demand in the consuming regions. Again it will be useful to think of demand as a relationship between quantity demanded and the cost of the good including costs of removing the good from the carrier's vehicles. In a parallel to factors that shift the product supply curve, reductions in unloading costs will cause an increase in the demand for freight transportation.

One factor affecting product demand that has received considerable attention recently is inventory holding policies for partially finished goods in manufacturing. Japanese factories are organized with extremely low inventories of incoming semi-finished parts.[14] Under a just-in-time organization of production, transportation vehicles are unloaded directly into the production line. The main advantage claimed for this procedure is that holding low inventories of semi-finished parts simplifies quality control supervision and improves the overall quality of output.

Standard inventory models, which treat the cost of using a mode of transportation as determined by the average number of days in which inventory is held up in transit, cannot explain the apparent advantages of just-in-time production policies. In order to be able to use just-in-time policies, the arrival of semi-finished parts must be regular. If a shipment of parts arrives later than scheduled, it will prevent the entire production line from operating; if it is early, it will have to be placed in inventory. But reducing inventory is the goal of the production scheme. For manufacturing firms using just-in-time production policies, a premium is placed on transit-time reliability. An increase in the number of firms in a consumption area using such policies will cause the demand for reliable modes of transportation to shift to the right and cause the demand for the services of unreliable modes to shift to the left. The main beneficiaries of this change have been motor carriers—it has caused railroads to lose some freight.

The discussion to this point assumed that the rate charged to transport goods is the only cost that a trader will incur. If there are non-rate costs to transportation, there will be a smaller quantity demanded of freight transportation. Non-rate transportation costs are thus one of the factors that will shift the demand for freight transportation curve. If the non-rate costs of transportation are $0.06 per gallon and the freight rate is $0.05, a trader will not find it profitable to ship between a producing region where the price is $0.90 per gallon and a consuming region where the price is $1.00 per gallon. An increase in non-rate costs will shift the demand for freight transportation to the left.

The focus of most analyses of non-rate costs is the cost of tying up inventories in transit.[15] Transportation invariably takes time and, to shippers, time is money. Goods in transit represent an inventory just as much as if the goods were stored in a company's warehouse. If a truck carries 20 tons of cargo valued at $5,000 per ton and interest rates are 10 percent per year, each day in transit will cost the owner of the goods in transit approximately $27.00 in interest costs alone. The significance of such inventory interest costs will be determined by the prevailing level of interest rates in the economy, by the value per ton of the good, and the speed of the freight service. The higher the value per ton, the more important is foregone interest on the value of the cargo in transit. Some cargoes are perishable, some easily damaged, and some more likely to be stolen. While some loss and damage insurance is contained in the charge paid for freight transportation, the shipper may believe him or herself not fully compensated by loss and damage claims procedures. Under these conditions, changes in expected loss and damage will be a further non-rate cost of carrying goods and thus a factor that shifts the demand for freight transportation.

It is often claimed that the demand for rail traffic has decreased and the demand for truck service has increased due to the increasing quality of truck transportation. It is impossible to confirm or deny this assertion since the word *quality* is not defined in economics—that is, quality can be defined in so many different ways, that it is not a useful concept.[16] Different modes of transportation do have different characteristics. One shipper will value those characteristics differently from another. To one, equipment availability is the essential feature of service quality; to another it will be the ability to reliably track where shipments are at any time; to a third it will be speed of transportation; to another it will be reliability of transit times. Some shippers may consider courtesy of the sales force to be the essential element of service quality.

Several shipper surveys have been published in which the users of freight transport services are asked to rank in importance characteristics of a carrier.[17] Unfortunately, these surveys do not solicit information that is useful to an economist. Knowing, for example, that for 30 percent of shippers speed of shipment is the most important determinant of choice of carrier, does not tell us how much an increase in speed would shift the demand curve. Knowing that to some percentage of shippers price is ranked third in importance is of no help to us in determining what the elasticity of demand for the service is.

In order to determine the sensitivity of freight transport demand to changes in service characteristics, econometric models require data in which these characteristics change. Sufficient data must be available to control for other factors affecting quantity demanded as well—notably prices charged. In general, such data are not available and are not meaningful at the aggregate level at which most freight demand analyses are carried out. When data on service characteristics are available, it is logical to use them as controls in estimates of demand elasticities. For example, one could imagine estimating equations like 3.1 with service characteristics replacing income. Then, by specifying a value for price, it would be possible to distill an independent effect for service characteristics in a manner similar to the way Equation 3.2 was derived from Equation 3.1. In this way, information on the elasticity of freight demand with respect to service characteristics can sometimes be found in econometric estimates of the sensitivities of freight demand to prices.

Several of the econometric analyses of mode choice have tried to determine the relative importance of speed or reliability as a factor shifting the demand curve. Oum, using Canadian data, found that the speed and reliability of rail shipments had no significant effect on demand for either rail or truck demands, but truck speed and reliability had a large effect on both rail and truck demands.[18] McFadden, Winston, and Boersch-Supan did not try to measure reliability, but in their study they too found that both rail and truck shipments of fresh fruits and vegetables were highly sensitive to the mean transit times of truck shipments but were relatively insensitive to rail travel times.[19] This finding is, perhaps, due to the fact that rail average transit times are much longer and that a significant portion of rail traffic is not sensitive to transit times.

CHANGES IN FREIGHT DEMAND RESULTING FROM CHANGES IN MARKET AREAS

It is convenient to think of factors that shift the demand curve for transportation as divided into those that shift demand curves at a destination, those that shift supply curves at an origin, and non-rate costs of handling freight between the shipper's loading dock and the receiver's unloading facility. But this is strictly correct only if there is a single origin and destination. As emphasized in Chapter 2, when there is more than one mode and there are multiple sources of supply and many destinations, the supply and demand curves at any pair of endpoints is no longer sufficient to define the demand for transportation. When a rate rises on a particular link, it may occur that a totally different source of supply becomes viable or that a supplier finds that it is more economical to sell into a different market than previously had been optimal.

For example, the demand for transportation of potatoes from Maine to New York also depends on the supply of potatoes in Idaho. The supply of potatoes in Idaho helps to determine the price of potatoes in New York, and thus the profitability of shipping from Maine. Even if no potatoes were shipped from Idaho to New York, transport service providers deciding on rates to charge would have to take into account the availability of the alternative source of supply. Given the speed with which market links can be added and broken in transportation, the demand for service should be seen as being determined not only by the supply and demand curves of existing users of a link, but also by potential users.

When one considers very broad groupings of transport services, shifts in demand can occur apparently at random as the composition of the aggregate changes. One possible way that this occurs is through changes in the distribution of production locations. For example, in an attempt to introduce a form of just-in-time production, American automobile makers have been shifting the sources of parts supply closer to their assembly plants. This has been done by increasing the percentage of their parts that are bought from nearby suppliers and reducing the percentage from distant suppliers. This has the effect of reducing the demand for the transportation of automobile parts since each part travels, on average, fewer miles.

In general, a rise in transportation costs will tend to cause sellers to look for closer markets and for buyers to look for closer sellers, thus reducing the amount of transportation performed. For example, between 1960 and 1995, the real (1995) revenue per ton-mile for rail traffic in the United States dropped from about 7 to 2.5 cents. This, along with other factors affecting the economy (notably, changes in the trucking market) resulted in a 37 percent increase in the average distance that a rail shipment moves. Thus it appears that a major determinant of the elasticity of demand for freight transportation is the extent to which the average distance of shipments rises or falls with rate levels.

All of economic analysis simplifies the world to make it understandable. Unfortunately, in the field of freight demand the abstraction that has been used is one that has been borrowed directly and uncritically from general economics in which spatial issues, like distance of shipment, are not easily handled. This has made the world appear unnecessarily complex and more subject to random shocks than would be the case if estimating models used an explicitly spatial view of the world like that described in Chapter 2. Much more work needs to be done in order to evaluate the extent to which the sensitivity of the distance of shipment is an important determinant of the demand for freight transportation. It may be the case, for example, that the primary response of shippers to higher freight rates will be neither mode switching nor general increases in decreases in quantities shipped, but rather a lengthening or shortening of supply lines. As this is written, we simply do not know.

WHY ARE THERE SO FEW FREIGHT TRANSPORT DEMAND ELASTICITY ESTIMATES?

Recent papers in the *Journal of Transport Economics and Policy* surveyed all published estimates of price elasticities of demand for freight transportation.[20] The number was not large: Fewer than 100 were found. Given the importance of demand measurement to public policy and to transportation economics in general, the small number of freight demand elasticity estimate seems odd. There are, however, some very good reasons for the sparseness of freight demand estimates. Following are some explanations provided by the authors to explain the scarceness of results.

Data Availability

Econometric estimate of freight demand cannot be carried out without good data on quantities shipped and on prices charged for those shipments. Unfortunately, neither of these figures is likely to be available except in unusual circumstances. Lawnmower manufacturers do not publish the number of units they ship from their factories to each location for fear that their competitors could use this information to find out who their best customers are and then focus their marketing efforts on those customers. Quantity figures are generally confidential unless gathered through a government census or reporting programs that are part of economic regulation. As transportation regulation has ebbed, so has statistical data reporting.

Price information is, except in the case of regulated shipments, also confidential. For example, if a carrier and shipper have negotiated a price for a shipment, neither will wish other shippers or carriers to have this information: shippers do not want their competitors to know what they are paying for transportation for fear that the competitor will negotiate a lower rate and carriers do not want rates published for fear that other customers will demand an equally low rate. Just as an automobile dealer does not print a daily register of the prices that each customer paid for each car sold, so the actual transportation rates that are charged are generally secret.

Sometimes, the relevant data are not merely unavailable, but do not even exist—that is, it is not simply secret, but no one knows what it is. For example, one of the important determinants of the demand for truck transportation for some commodities is the rate that would be charged by a railroad if the rail option were chosen. But if the option is not chosen, no rate will exist for this option. If approached by a shipper, the railroad could calculate what rate it would be willing to offer (subject to bargaining with each shipper), but if no shipper asks, the railroad will not make the calculation. This is an especially serious problem for attempts to estimate demand elasticities for individual commodities on individual routes.

Non-Random Price Setting

The econometric technique for separating the influence of price changes from those of other factors determining the quantity shipped is based on the assumption that the prices negotiated between the carrier and shipper are determined independently of the quantity shipped and the elasticity of demand for shipping it. But since transport rates are in general negotiated between shipper and carrier, this assumption is likely to be invalid. Moreover, a shipper may use rail in those circumstances in which rail service is ideally suited and truck shipment in other circumstances; the rate negotiated with the railroad may reflect these circumstances. But the researcher, trying to estimate the sensitivity to prices of the division of total shipments between truck and rail, will be unable to tell from the raw statistics that railroads were chosen due to unusual conditions. But if both the rate and the quantity may be the result of an abnormal circumstance, then econometric estimates that ignore that fact will be biased.

In another example of the difficulties presented by non-random rate setting, Wilson, Wilson, and Koo in their analysis of wheat shipments from North Dakota assumed that there was a non-random pattern to the rates charged for trucks and rails. To make sense of their data, they assumed that the rates charged responded in a very specific (and economically logical) way to changes in rail car availability and the costs of providing rail and truck service. But the model that they chose may not have been the correct one and may have contributed to the extremely high elasticities that they estimated.

The Complexity of the Problem

Econometric estimates depend on fitting simple surfaces or curves to the observed data. For example, in Figure 3.5, a linear relationship was assumed between quantity, price, and income. But as shown in the example in Chapter 2, transportation demand curves are anything but regular. While they have a general downward slope, they are quite kinky, with kinks occurring whenever a shipper is indifferent between one transport option (mode, destination, etc.) and another. So simple curve fitting techniques are unlikely to be accurate, even under ideal conditions.

It is possible, as suggested previously, that part of the apparent complexity of the problem may be due to incorrect modeling; alternative approaches may make the world appear to act more predictably and rationally than it has appeared in previous work. Whether the other impediments to econometric demand estimation will permit the estimation of new modeling techniques is at this point unknown.

Transferability

Perhaps the most difficult problem for transportation demand estimation is in deciding when estimations made in one situation can be applied in others. This was noted previously in the discussion of the remarkably high demand elasticities measured for the shipment of hard red spring wheat from North Dakota to Minneapolis and Duluth.[21] Should these estimates be assumed to be valid for all rail shipments of any commodity? For all grain shipments by any mode of transport? Is the information generally valid at least for wheat shipments, even if between Kansas and the Gulf of Mexico?

In principle, estimates of transportation demand elasticities are valid only for that bundle of commodities from which the data were drawn. However, if nothing could be learned about the sensitivities of traffic levels to price in other, similar groups of transport services, there would be little reason to perform or to publish demand estimates for narrow groupings—for example, fresh fruits and vegetables shipped from Arizona and California. The only parties interested would be the handful of decision makers actually involved with making pricing and shipping decisions for that flow. The fact that they are published implies that the researchers assume some transferability of results.

The reader should note that just because measurement of freight demand elasticities is difficult or impossible does not mean that the concept of freight demand elasticities is not useful. Demand elasticities do exist, even when they cannot be measured, and they must be taken into account in pricing transport services and making transport policy. Often sensible policy can be made without precise formal estimates of demand elasticities; those with years of experience in the transport sector or those who follow transport statistics often have a reasonable idea of what transport demand elasticities probably are and will make decisions based on those hunches. Of course, better estimates will allow better decisions, and for that reason there is continuing work on techniques of demand estimation. The difficulty of measurement should be taken as a challenge rather than as a reason to ignore the topic.

CONCLUSION

The study of freight demand is the study of the sensitivity of the quantity of freight shipments primarily to the prices charged, but also to other factors. Demand analysis takes place not in classical markets but in groupings of commodity-origin-destination flows. There is in principle a limitless number of ways that individual freight shipments could be grouped. Groupings may be made with an eye to the particular question being asked—for example, what effect will an increase in fuel taxes have on truck traffic—or on the basis of minimizing the influence of distortions introduced by the use of indexes of price and output. The second principle calls for combining freight markets that have similar prices and similar demand conditions.

The broadest market grouping is all freight shipped in the country. The main determinant of demand in this grouping is the level of GDP. A change in the composition of output in the U.S. economy has meant that freight transportation has been growing less rapidly than the economy as a whole. Most freight is generated by the energy sector and by agriculture, lumber, metal, and paper manufacturers. Most tons move relatively short distances, but long-distance transportation still accounts for a significant number of the ton-miles produced by the U.S. freight transportation industries. Railroad ton-miles have grown slowly in the last 40 years, but have declined as a proportion of all freight traffic. Trucks are the main beneficiary of the slow growth of rail traffic. River and canal traffic has also shown rapid growth.

At the risk of oversimplifying an extremely complex and fragmented group of markets, the following represents a tentative conclusion on similarities among demand studies: The primary determinant of the demand for transportation services is the level of economic activity. For the majority of commodities in the majority of shipping distances there is little inter-modal competition and thus the cross-elasticity of demand between, say, rail and truck, is close to zero in these situations. For these commodities and shipping situations, the primary responsiveness of shipping quantities to prices charged comes from expanding or contracting total production and consumption at shipment endpoints of changing origins and destinations for shipments, with higher rates causing goods to be shipped shorter distances on average. For those commodities and distances where there is inter-modal competition, the elasticity of demand for rail traffic is higher than that for truck traffic, though in each case, the overall demand elasticity is probably less than one.

It is easier to describe those factors that affect the demand for freight transportation than to measure the influence of those factors. The demand for freight transportation is derived from supply conditions in producing areas and demand conditions in consuming areas. The elasticity of demand for freight transportation is higher when either demand or supply for the commodity being carried is highly responsive to price. Any factor that shifts the demand or the supply of the product curve will shift the demand for transportation between the supply area and the demand area. The most commonly mentioned factors shifting product demand curves are consumer incomes and tastes and the prices of closely related commodities. The factors affecting product supply are primarily production costs. Non-rate transportation costs will affect both product supply and product demand curves as well as the willingness of traders to ship between the two areas. The easiest non-rate cost to analyze is the cost of borrowing money to cover inventory involved in transportation. In many situations, however, this will greatly understate the true non-rate cost of using transportation.

Remarkably few freight demand studies have been carried out and thus much of what we believe we know about the elasticity of demand for freight services is based on conjecture. Part of the reason for the unsatisfactory state of freight demand results from decreasing data availability as modes become increasingly deregulated. Other problems stem from the inherent complexity of the spatial setting within which demand is derived and from the fact that prices for individual shipments are not predetermined but set based on market conditions—conditions that the researcher is trying to measure. But the major problem with freight demand studies is that of transferability. Since there is no overarching framework unifying the study of freight demand, each study is a separate exercise with little apparent applicability outside of the particular group of flows whose data is analyzed. Without understanding the transferability of results—an understanding that must surely come from modeling the geographical setting that generates the demand for transportation—even when data are available, the results of demand estimation seem narrow and uninteresting.

NOTES

1. Hans A. Adler, *Economic Appraisal of Transport Projects* (Baltimore: The Johns Hopkins University Press, 1987), p. 1.
2. Non-econometric techniques can also be used to simulate freight transportation demand. These operations-research based methods do not in general have as their primary focus the estimation of the sensitivity of freight flows to prices in particular economic markets. An overview of these techniques is found in Teodor Gabriel Crainic, "Operations Research Models of Intercity Freight Transportation: The Current State and Future Research Issues," *The Logistics and Transportation Review*, June 1987, Vol. 23, No. 2, pp. 189–206; see also Harker, Patrick T. and Friesz, Terry L., "Prediction of Intercity Freight Flows, II: Mathematical Formulations," *Transportation Research-B*, Vol. 20B, No. 2, pp. 155–174, 1986.
3. As representative of this technique, see Oum, T.H. "A Cross-Sectional Study of Freight Transport Demand and Rail-Truck Competition in Canada," *Bell Journal of Economics*, Fall 1979 pp. 463–482.

4. A. L. Morton, "A Statistical Sketch of Intercity Freight Demand," *Highway Research Record*, No. 296 (Washington, D.C.: Highway Research Board, 1969), quoted in George W. Wilson, *Economic Analysis of Intercity Freight Transportation* (Bloomington: Indiana University Press, 1980).

5. Haskel Benishay and Gilbert Whitaker Jr., "Demand and Supply in Freight Transportation," *Journal of Industrial Economics*, 14 (July 1966), pp. 243–263.

6. Richard C. Levin, "Allocation in Surface Freight Transportation: Does Rate Regulation Matter?" *Bell Journal of Economics*, Spring 1978, Vol. 9, No. 1, pp. 18–45; Kenneth D. Boyer, "Minimum Rate Regulation, Modal Split Sensitivities and the Railroad Problem," *Journal of Political Economy*, Vol. 85, No. 3, June 1977, pp. 493–512.

7. While the great majority of single mode work on freight transportation has investigated the relationship between railroad and truck transportation, some work has been done on other modes. See, for example, Hayuth, Y., "Freight Modal-Split Analysis of Air and Sea Transportation," *Logistics and Transportation Review*, December 1985, Vol. 21 No. 4, pp. 389–402. Logsdon, C., et al. "Estimation of Demand for Truck-Barge Transportation of Pacific Northwest Wheat," *Logistics and Transportation Review*, March 1983, Vol. 19 No. 1, pp. 81–89. Winston, Clifford, "A Multinomial Probit Prediction of the Demand for Domestic Ocean Container Service," *Journal of Transport Economics and Policy*, September 1981, Vol. 15, No. 3, pp. 243–252.

8. Ann Friedlaender and Richard H. Spady, "A Derived Demand Function for Freight Transportation," *Review of Economics and Statistics*, LXII, No. 3 (August 1980), pp. 432–441.

9. See Patricia Buckley and M. Daniel Westbrook, "Market Definition and Assessing the Competitive Relationship between Rail and Truck Transportation," *Journal of Regional Science*, Vol. 31, No. 3 (August 1991), pp. 329–346.

10. Daniel McFadden, Clifford Winston, and Axel Boersch-Supan, "Joint estimation of Freight Transportation Decisions under nonrandom sampling." *Analytical Studies in Transport Economics*, Andrew Daughety, Ed. (Cambridge: Cambridge University Press, 1985), pp. 137–157.

11. Tae Hoon Oum "A Cross Sectional Study of Freight Transport Demand and Rail-Truck Competition in Canada," *The Bell Journal of Economics*, Vol. 10, No. 2, (Autumn 1979), pp. 463–482. Other work on single-product estimates of modal freight demand elasticities includes Daughety, A. F. and Inaba, F.S. "An Analysis of Regulatory Change in the Transportation Industry." *Review of Economics and Statistics*, Vol. 63 (1981), 246–255. See also Oum, Tae, H. and Taylor, A.J., "A Comparison of Functional Forms for Freight Demand Models Using Canadian Inter-Regional Flow Data," *Research for Tomorrow's Transport Requirements*, Proceedings of the World Conference on Transport Research, Vancouver, British Columbia, Canada, May 1986 (Vancouver: Centre for Transportation Studies, University of British Columbia, 1986), pp. 1782–1804.

12. William W. Wilson, Wesley W. Wilson, and Won W. Koo, "Modal Competition and Pricing in Grain Transport," *Journal of Transport Economics and Policy*, Vol. XXII, No. 3 (September 1988), pp. 319–337.

13. The relationship between vehicle size and optimal reorder points is studied in queuing theory and business logistics. An application of such theory is found in Inaba, F. S. and N. E. Wallace, "Spatial Price Competition and the Demand for Freight

Transportation," *Review of Economics and Statistics*, Vol. 71, No. 4 (November 1989), pp. 614–625.

14. See, for example, Bagchi, P.K., Raghunathan, T.S., and Bardi, E.J., "The Implications of Just-in-Time Inventory Policies on Carrier Selection," *Logistics and Transportation Review*, December 1987, Vol. 23 4, pp. 373–384.

15. Blauwens, C. and Vun de Voorde, E., "The Valuation of Time Savings in Commodity Transport," *International Journal of Transport Economics*, February 1988, Vol. 15, No. 1, pp. 77–87.

16. See Chow, G. and Poist, R.F., "The Measurement of Quality of Service and the Transportation Purchase Decision," *Logistics and Transportation Review*, March 1984, Vol. 20, No. 1, pp. 25–43.

17. See, for example, Wilson, F.R., Bisson, B.G., and Kobia, K.B. "Factors that Determine Mode Choice in the Transportation of General Freight," *Transportation Research Record 1061* (1986), pp. 26–31.

18. Tae Hoon Oum, "A Cross Sectional Study of Freight Transport Demand and Rail-Truck Competition in Canada," *The Bell Journal of Economics*, Vol. 10, No. 2 (Autumn 1979), pp. 463–482.

19. Daniel McFadden, Clifford Winston, and Axel Boersch-Supan, "Joint Estimation of Freight Transportation Decisions under Nonrandom Sampling," *Analytical Studies in Transport Economics*, Andrew Daughety, Editor (Cambridge: Cambridge University Press, 1985), pp. 137–157.

20. Tae Hoon Oum, W.G. Waters II, and Jong Say Yong, "Concepts of Price Elasticities of Transport Demand and Recent Empirical Estimates," *Journal of Transport Economics and Policy*, Vol. 26, No. 2 (May 1992), pp. 139–154; and P.B. Goodwin, "A Review of New Demand Elasticities with Special Reference to Short and Long Run Effects of Price Changes," *Journal of Transport Economics and Policy*, Vol. 26, No. 2 (May 1992), pp. 155–169. See also, Zlatoper, Thomas J. and Ziona Austrian, "Freight Transportation Demand: A Survey of Recent Econometric Studies," *Transportation*, Vol. 16 (1989), pp. 27–46.

21. Wilson, William W., Wesley W. Wilson, and Won W. Koo, "Modal Competition and Pricing in Grain Transport," *Journal of Transport Economics and Policy*, Vol. 22, No. 3, September 1988, pp. 319–337.

4

The Demand for Passenger Transportation

Like freight transport, passenger transportation is a heterogeneous group of services, some provided publicly and some privately. Whenever outputs are not homogeneous, there will be problems in defining what you mean by a total output or total quantity demanded. As described in Chapter 2, the standard procedure in such circumstances is to define an index of output. In freight transportation, the standard output measures are ton-miles and, less frequently, tons of freight transport. The two companion indexes for passenger transportation are the passenger-miles generated in a year or the number of passenger-trips.

Figure 4.1 shows that U.S. passenger-miles has more than quadrupled since 1950, far exceeding the rate of growth of population. This increase comes from two sources: Each person is taking more trips and the trips taken tend to be longer than they had been. The average person traveled 3,300 miles in 1950 but traveled about 9,000 miles in 1995.

The increase in the amount of passenger transportation has been accompanied by a shift in the composition of the services making up the passenger-mile index. From the perspective of total trips, the quantity of passenger transportation demanded per person has grown less rapidly. As noted in Chapter 2, the most important division in passenger transportation is

FIGURE 4.1   Passenger-Miles and Population in the United States

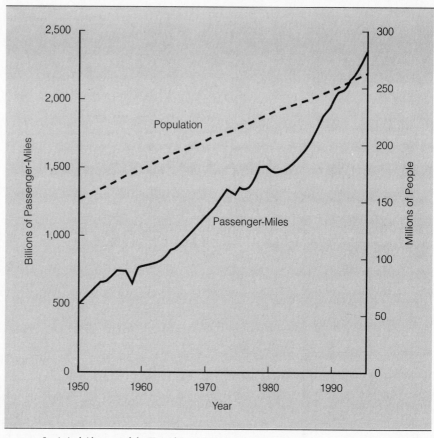

SOURCES: Statistical Abstract of the United States; *Transportation in America*

between private and public transport. As shown in Figure 4.2, private transportation is by far the more important of the two. Purchased passenger transportation amounts to about $100 billion per year. This is only about one-sixth of the total spent on purchasing, maintaining, and driving automobiles. Of the amount spent on public passenger transportation, about 35 percent was for urban transportation (local busses, transit, etc.), about 55 percent for domestic intercity transportation (almost all of it air travel), and about 10 percent for international travel (again, almost all of it air travel).

Figure 4.1 shows there has been an unquestionable overall increase in the quantity demanded of passenger services, measured in passenger-miles. This does not, of course, mean that demand for passenger service has increased. In

**FIGURE 4.2   U.S. Passenger Expenditure, 1995
(Billions per Year)**

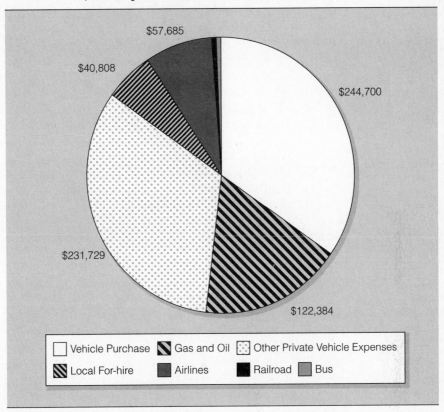

SOURCE: *Transportation in America*, 14th Edition

economic terms, an increase in quantity demanded can result from a decrease in the price of the service, an increase in demand, or both. An increase in demand would imply that for reasons outside the passenger transport sector—consumer incomes or tastes for travel are the main factors studied—consumers now wished to consume more passenger transportation services than they had previously. In order to disentangle the causes for the increase in passenger-miles, we will have to be able to trace what has happened to prices.

This turns out to be not so simple, however. The dominant mode of transportation in the United States is the private automobile, and people do not charge themselves a price for driving their own cars. Instead, they incur the costs of buying, owning, and driving cars. In the case of private transportation, demand is redefined to mean the relationship between quantity demanded and the cost incurred rather than the price paid for a service.

The process of calculating costs will be discussed in Chapter 5. A few comments are useful here: The gasoline used for a trip is, of course, a cost of making the trip. But there are many other costs of operating a car that does not vary with mileage; insurance is the most obvious, but also a large part of the original purchase price represents a cost that does not vary with the number of trips or with the annual driving mileage. Costs that do not vary with the use of the car must be ignored when computing the price of making a particular type of trip; but when determining the demand for automobiles and thus the demand for overall automobile transportation by a household, these costs must be included.

Aggregate data for broad classes of travelers is much more likely to be available than data referring to either individuals or to homogeneous subgroups, and sometimes it is possible to make useful conclusions from aggregate data. For example, Table 4.1 shows that for a period of about 30 years, the expenditure per passenger-mile in the United States was approximately constant

TABLE 4.1   Passenger-Miles and Expenditure in the United States, 1960–1995

Year	Real Passenger Expenditure (Millions of 1995 Dollars)	Passenger-Miles (Billions)-	Real Cost per Passenger Mile (Real 1995 Dollars)
1960	312	781	0.40
1970	449	1,181	0.38
1975	533	1,355	0.39
1980	625	1,468	0.43
1981	627	1,469	0.43
1982	599	1,490	0.40
1983	629	1,524	0.41
1984	674	1,577	0.43
1985	697	1,636	0.43
1986	685	1,724	0.40
1987	708	1,807	0.39
1988	737	1,877	0.39
1989	741	1,936	0.38
1990	735	2,034	0.36
1991	677	2,069	0.33
1992	696	2,143	0.32
1993	720	2,197	0.33
1994	735	2,286	0.32
1995	727	2,363	0.31

**FIGURE 4.3   Shifts in the Aggregate Demand Curve for
                          Pasenger Transportation**

Since the expenditure per unit of passenger transportation did not change while the
amount of passenger transportation consumed increased between 1960 and 1986, it
would appear that the demand for passenger transportation shifted to the right
between those two years.

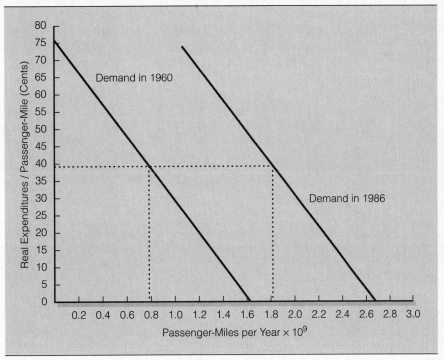

at about 40 cents (measured in 1995 dollars). Since the price of passenger
transportation has been approximately constant while the quantity of passenger-miles generated by the economy increased over that period, it seems clear
that there has been an increase in the demand for passenger transportation
during that time, as illustrated in Figure 4.3. It does not appear to be simply a
case of a movement along the demand curve. Since the end of the 1980s, however, there has been a significant decline in the price per passenger-mile that
consumers pay. Such price movements may enable us to better estimate the elasticity of passenger demand in the future as more data accumulate. However, as
in the case of freight transportation, the first step toward improving the accuracy of demand estimates is to break down the flows into groups that have a
higher degree of homogeneity. The first division made here is that between private and public transport.

THE DEMAND FOR PRIVATE TRANSPORTATION

The demand for automobile transportation is generally treated as being determined jointly as the product of the decisions of how many cars to own and how many miles to drive each car. The most basic determinant of the demand for automobile transportation is the number of cars that a household owns. In all countries in the world, there has been a steady increase in number of cars per 1,000 population. Figure 4.4 shows that the United States has always had a larger number of cars for its population than other countries. Figure 4.4 appears to show that automobile holdings per capita have stagnated between 1988 and 1992. However, this neglects the strong movement in the United States to replace automobiles with minivans, sports utility vehicles, pickup trucks, and other passenger vehicles that are technically classified as trucks. If these passenger vehicles were added in, the United States would show the same continued rise in passenger vehicle holdings per capita that is seen throughout the world.

FIGURE 4.4   Trends in Automobile Ownership in Several Countries

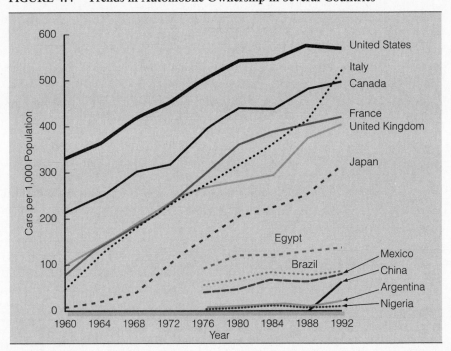

SOURCE: American Automobile Manufacturers Association, *World Motor Vehicle Data*, various issues

The most important determinant of driving demand is income, and its effect is predominantly through automobile ownership rather than through the number of miles driven. The elasticity of miles driven with respect to income, holding the number of cars constant, is less than .1. This means that it would take more than a 10 percent increase in household income to raise the number of miles driven by 1 percent.[1] By contrast, the elasticity of automobile ownership with respect to income is considerably higher—about 0.8—meaning that in the long run a 10 percent increase in income will increase the number of automobiles owned by about 8 percent.[2]

In contrast to the responsiveness of automobile demand to incomes, the elasticity of automobile driving to the cost of driving is quite low and involves complex adaptations as different elements of the cost of driving change.[3] For example, a rise in the price of new automobiles appears to decrease new car purchases but lengthen the life of old cars; the elasticity of overall automobile holding to the price of new cars is virtually zero.[4] Drivers appear to adjust to higher gasoline prices not by driving less but by switching to more fuel-efficient automobiles.[5] Thus while the elasticity of demand for gasoline with respect to the price of gasoline is significantly different from zero, the responsiveness of the number of miles driven to the price of gasoline is close to zero.

Other factors that determine the demand for automobile driving are more difficult to evaluate. It is logical to assume that an increased availability of high-quality highways would make driving more attractive, but studies that confirm this logic are missing. Even more difficult to quantify are effects of changes in urban structure on automobile demand. When offices relocate from the center of an urban area to suburban areas, there is a greater reliance on automobile transportation but each trip to the office is shorter than it was before.[6] The net effect of changes in urban structure on driving is unclear. As discussed below, the availability of public transportation is a significant determinant of the amount of commuting, but in many circumstances, so powerful is the attraction of private transportation that even free public transport would not significantly persuade people to switch.

Private Air Transportation

The other private mode of passenger transportation is private air travel. Unlike automobiles, airplanes are used solely for intercity travel. Nearly as many intercity passenger-miles are produced by private aircraft as are carried on American railroads—about 10 billion per year, or about 0.4 percent of total intercity passenger miles. Private air transportation has been declining in importance, both relatively and absolutely. In 1980, private airplanes flew about 15 billion, or 1 percent of all intercity passenger-miles. This decline occurred at the same time that commercial aviation passenger-miles nearly doubled.

The decline in private air passenger-miles demonstrates that the advantages of private transportation are not insurmountable. Unfortunately, little is known about the determinants of the demand for private air transport. It is logical to assume that the decline in private air traffic is related to the drop in real prices for public air transport, but this has not been confirmed by published studies. Another factor thought to have caused the decrease in private air miles is the liability costs that private aircraft manufacturers have faced, leading to higher costs and decreased availability of small planes.

THE DEMAND FOR URBAN PUBLIC TRANSPORTATION

Except for taxicabs, public passenger transportation is characterized by vehicles carrying multiple passengers. The economic advantages of combining different demands in a single vehicle generally calls for public transportation to be scheduled, meaning that passengers cannot be transported at exactly the time that they wish. Most public transportation has the additional disadvantage of a limited number of destinations. In almost all cases, passengers use private trips (perhaps walking) as an adjunct to the use of public transportation. The fact that public transport does not carry passengers where they want to go at exactly the time they wish to go makes it less attractive than private transport. In order to induce passengers to use public transport it must have some compensating advantages—cost, speed, or comfort. Much of the literature on the choice between private and public transportation concerns the circumstances under which public transportation can overcome these benefits of private transport.

Between 1947 and 1970 the usage of urban public transportation declined precipitously, losing more than half of its ridership. There was a reduction in the number of passengers and in the percentage of commuters using public transportation in every metropolitan area in the United States.[7] Between 1970 and 1980, ridership rose again. Table 4.2 shows that since 1980, public transportation ridership has been stable at about 8.5 billion trips—approximately the same level as 1965. Urban transportation in the United States remains overwhelmingly dominated by private automobile traffic.

The increasing usage of automobiles for urban transportation is a trend seen not only in the United States but in all countries of the world and closely parallels the increase in automobile ownership in different countries. Several foreign countries have actively tried to switch commuters from private automobiles into public transit.[8] With rare exception, these attempts have not succeeded. The general consensus is now that as long as parking is plentiful and expressways uncrowded, commuters who own cars cannot be persuaded by standard pricing mechanisms to use public transportation for the trip to work.

While as a general rule public transportation has not been successful at attracting new passengers, a few urban areas in the United States have been successful at retaining public transit ridership. Table 4.3 shows that, among met-

TABLE 4.2   Trends of U.S. Transit Passenger-Trips (Millions)

Calendar Year	Light Rail	Heavy Rail	Commuter Rail	Trolley Bus	Motor Bus	Total
1980	133	2,108	280	142	5,837	8,567
1981	123	2,094	268	138	5,594	8,284
1982	136	2,115	259	151	5,324	8,052
1983	137	2,167	262	160	5,422	8,203
1984	135	2,231	267	165	5,908	8,829
1985	132	2,290	275	142	5,675	8,636
1986	130	2,333	306	139	5,753	8,777
1987	133	2,402	311	141	5,614	8,735
1988	154	2,308	325	136	5,590	8,666
1989	162	2,542	330	130	5,620	8,931
1990	175	2,346	328	126	5,677	8,799
1991	184	2,172	318	125	5,624	8,575
1992	188	2,207	314	126	5,517	8,501
1993	188	2,046	322	121	5,381	8,217
1994	203	2,206	338	118	5,402	8,435

SOURCE: *APTA Transit Fact Book*, 1995 edition. Total includes demand response and other categories. 1994 figures preliminary.

ropolitan areas with a population of 1 million or larger, New York, Chicago, Washington, Philadelphia, and San Francisco have succeeded in attracting more than 14 percent of commuters to public transportation. At the other extreme, Oklahoma City has fewer than 2 percent of commuters using public transport. The difference in transit percentages is largely explained by the concentration of employment in the central business district. Wherever employment is widely dispersed, it is impossible for public transport to attract a significant number of riders.[9] On average, 6.5 percent of U.S. commuters take public transportation, 13 percent use carpools, and 73 percent drive to work in their own cars.[10]

Without the availability of public transport, the concentration of employment in the central business district is impossible. There is thus a simultaneous relationship between the concentration of employment and the use of public transport. The effect of public transportation on the economic health of the central business district has been widely discussed; it appears that only the availability of heavy rail rapid transit has any significant effect on the economic health of the central city in a metropolitan region.[11] However, cities differ in their economic bases and some types of employment (manufacturing, for example) are less amenable to concentration than others.

According to an estimate based on a survey of a 100 cities around the world, on average, the price elasticity of demand for public transit is about –.45,

TABLE 4.3   Commuting Patterns in the Fifty Largest U.S. Metropolitan Areas

Metropolitan Area of Residence	Total Workers	Means of Transportation (%)					Travel (Minutes)
		Drive Alone	Carpool	Public Transport	Other		
U.S. TOTAL METROPOLITAN	91,515,002	73.0	12.9	6.5	7.6		23.2
Los Angeles-Long Beach, CA	4,115,248	70.1	15.5	6.5	7.9		26.5
New York, NY	3,798,814	30.7	8.9	47.3	13.1		35.3
Chicago, IL	2,888,784	63.8	12.0	17.1	7.1		29.1
Philadelphia, PA-NJ	2,280,559	67.8	11.9	11.6	8.7		24.8
Detroit, MI	1,931,153	83.4	10.1	2.4	4.1		23.7
Washington, DC-MD	2,214,350	62.9	15.8	13.7	7.6		29.5
Houston, TX	1,576,078	75.7	14.6	4.1	5.5		26.4
Boston, MA	1,488,501	65.8	9.8	14.2	10.2		24.5
Atlanta, GA	1,481,781	78.0	12.7	4.7	4.6		26.0
Nassau-Suffolk, NY	1,303,936	73.0	10.0	11.4	5.7		30.0
Riverside-San Bernardino, CA	1,079,948	74.6	17.2	0.8	7.4		27.7
Dallas, TX	1,312,173	77.6	14.0	3.2	5.3		24.6
San Diego, CA	1,230,446	70.9	13.8	3.3	12.1		22.2
Minneapolis-St. Paul, MN-WI	1,307,624	76.0	11.2	5.3	7.5		21.1
St. Louis, MO-IL	1,144,336	79.7	12.0	3.0	5.2		23.1
Anaheim-Santa Ana, CA	1,278,661	76.8	13.7	2.5	7.0		25.5
Baltimore, MD	1,191,813	70.9	14.2	7.7	7.2		26.0
Phoenix, AZ	996,495	75.0	14.4	2.1	8.5		23.0
Oakland, CA	1,034,364	68.6	13.2	9.1	9.1		27.2
Tampa-St. Petersburg- Clearwater, FL	914,711	78.8	13.3	1.5	6.4		21.8
Pittsburgh, PA	881,624	70.7	12.9	8.5	7.9		22.6
Seattle, WA	1,037,749	72.8	11.6	7.4	8.2		24.4
Miami-Hialeah, FL	887,996	72.4	15.6	5.9	6.2		24.8
Cleveland, OH	823,684	77.7	10.5	6.2	5.5		22.6
Newark, NJ	901,453	70.9	12.4	10.0	6.7		26.2
Denver, CO	843,070	75.6	12.6	4.4	7.5		22.7
San Francisco, CA	853,948	56.3	12.2	19.5	11.8		25.9
Kansas City, MO-KS	771,309	79.9	12.5	2.1	5.5		21.4
San Jose, CA	796,605	77.7	12.3	3.0	7.0		23.3

TABLE 4.3   Continued

Metropolitan Area of Residence	Total Workers	Drive Alone	Carpool	Public Transport	Other	Travel (Minutes)
Sacramento, CA	685,945	75.2	13.7	2.4	8.7	21.8
Cincinnati, OH-KY-IN	678,121	78.6	11.6	4.3	5.5	22.4
Milwaukee, WI	690,002	76.7	11.0	5.2	7.1	20.1
Norfolk-Virginia Beach-Newport News, VA	698,999	72.7	14.1	2.2	10.9	21.6
Columbus, OH	677,859	79.5	11.4	2.7	6.4	21.2
Fort Worth-Arlington, TX	664,433	80.9	13.5	0.6	4.9	23.0
San Antonio, TX	569,149	74.6	14.8	3.7	7.0	21.9
Bergen-Passaic, NJ	649,697	71.7	11.9	9.3	7.0	24.7
Ft. Lauderdale-Hollywood-Pompano Beach, FL	588,089	79.7	12.8	2.1	5.4	23.0
Indianapolis, IN	624,971	79.7	12.9	2.1	5.3	21.9
Portland, OR	615,587	72.6	12.5	6.0	8.9	21.8
New Orleans, LA	514,726	70.9	15.3	7.3	6.5	24.4
Charlotte-Gastonia-Rock Hill, NC-SC	604,856	78.8	14.5	1.8	4.8	21.6
Orlando, FL	557,448	78.1	13.3	1.5	7.1	22.9
Salt Lake City-Ogden, UT	479,338	76.3	14.0	3.0	6.7	19.8
Middlesex- Somerset- Hunterdon, NJ	545,739	77.5	10.5	6.4	5.6	26.3
Rochester, NY	481,467	77.7	11.6	3.2	7.5	19.7
Monmouth-Ocean, NJ	453,204	76.5	12.1	5.3	6.1	27.1
Nashville, TN	495,717	79.1	13.8	1.7	5.3	22.7
Memphis, TN-AR-MS	448,237	78.2	13.6	2.8	5.4	21.6
Buffalo, NY	432,883	76.3	11.4	5.4	7.0	19.7

SOURCE: 1990 Census of Population, STF3C. Other category includes motorcycle, bicycle, walked only, worked at home, and all other means.

meaning that a 10 percent increase in fares reduces ridership by 4.5 percent.[12] However, this figure falls with prices. So powerful is the attraction of private transportation that if transit fares were to be eliminated completely, only about 50 percent more passengers would be carried relative to the number when full fares were charged. Estimates of the worldwide responsiveness of transit ridership to service frequency on average are +0.45 percent. North American cities, however, tend to have far lower residential densities than in other parts of the world, thus favoring automobile travel.[13]

The elasticity of demand for particular services may be quite different from the average elasticity. For example, a recent estimate of the demand elasticity of ridership on a suburban Philadelphia rapid transit line was –0.23, meaning that a 1 percent rise in fares would lead to a 0.23 percent drop in passengers. The same study found that closing a station reduced ridership by 2.4 percent and that transit ridership was increased 0.1 percent for a 1 percent increase in gasoline prices; ridership was also sensitive to the tolls on an automobile bridge on a route paralleling the transit line.[14] As with any statistical study, the authors were able to estimate only the effects of those factors that have changed significantly over the period of their study. They were thus not able to separate the influence of the most important determinant of the demand curve for public transportation in any urban area—car ownership, for which income is a close proxy. Increasing geographical concentration of residences and employment will also increase the usage of public transportation.[15]

The results of a study of Boston transit ridership over the decades of the 1970s and 1980s are shown in Table 4.4. Real income was found to have a negative influence on transit ridership as wealthier people tend to drive rather than use transit. With an estimated income elasticity of –0.715, the actual 44.5 percent increase in real incomes over the period were predicted to have decreased ridership by 30.1 percent. This influence was more than offset by three others, however. There was an 8.3 percent increase in employment in downtown Boston over the period, thus leading to a predicted 12 percent increase in ridership. Despite the fact that demand is measured to be quite inelastic with respect to both real fares and service quality, dramatically lower real fares on the transit lines combined with improved service quality (measured by vehicle-miles), to make a 23 percent increase in ridership. The net effect was predicted to increase ridership by 11.9 percent—almost identical to the actual increase of 12 percent. It is interesting to note that the estimated Boston price elasticity of demand of –0.23 is the same as the estimate for a different line in Philadelphia, and both are much lower than the world-average estimates discussed previously. It is possible that U.S. conditions are sufficiently different from those in the rest of the world that public transit demand elasticities here are in general lower than those overseas.

Urban planners are interested in the extent to which improvements in the service quality of public transit will shift the demand curve. As in all of economic analysis, the answer to this question requires that one first define *quali-*

TABLE 4.4   Determinants of Boston Transit Ridership, 1970–1990

Variable	Estimated Elasticity	Actual Change in Variable (%)	Estimated Influence on Ridership (%)
Real Income	−0.715	+44.5	−30.1
Boston Employment	+1.75	+8.3	+12.7
Transit Fares	−0.234	−42.4	+12.1
Vehicle-Miles	+0.358	+38.3	+10.9

Source: Gomez-Ibanez, Jose, "Big City Transit Ridership, Deficits, and Politics: Avoiding Reality in Boston," *American Planning Association Journal*, Vol. 62 (Winter 1996), pp. 30–50.

ty, a characteristic that has too many meanings to be useful. In the Boston study, service quality was measured by vehicle-miles, but this is far from the only measure. What is clear is that the demand for public transit can be increased by reducing in-vehicle travel time and access, waiting, and transfer times. It is often found in mode choice studies that out-of-vehicle time is more important than in-vehicle time. More difficult to quantify are such qualitative and attitudinal variables as comfort, reliability, and safety.[16]

As noted previously, about 13 percent of American workers use carpooling for the journey to work, a percentage that is slowly declining. This is twice the number that use public transportation.[17] Carpooling is in some ways a private mode of transportation, and in some ways public. Compared to driving oneself, carpooling lengthens journey times and requires members to adhere to more rigid schedules; some commuters also feel that it reduces privacy. If high quality transit service is available, the schedule inflexibility of carpooling makes it less convenient than public transportation. Depending on the circumstances, it can be either more or less expensive and either faster or slower than public transportation. Carpooling is always less expensive in terms of out-of-pocket costs than driving alone. Like public transportation, physical relationships within the metropolitan areas have an important effect on the use of carpools. The ideal combination of concentration for the use of carpools is relatively long-distance commuting to a central business district with concentrated employment and difficult parking.

There are no estimates of the price or income elasticity of demand for carpooling. However, the population that is likely to carpool—those with few vehicles in the household, a long-distance commute, and low need for flexibility in departure times—are sufficiently uncommon as to lead researchers to assume that the demand for carpooling is inelastic with respect to cost and service characteristics. Since the availability of automobiles in the household is strongly related to income, it is reasonable to assume that the income elasticity of carpooling would be negative.[18]

PASSENGER FACILITY DEMAND FORECASTING

The main focus of passenger demand studies has been on forecasting the usage of facilities not yet built. It is here where demand studies are most useful since mistakes cannot easily be undone.

Consider the problem of a transit bus operator, for example. The operator knows that ridership is affected by the fare level, service frequency, running times, service hours, community population, unemployment rates, etc. The operator will not generally make a formal demand study of the effects of these factors, but by continuously experimenting, monitoring, and adjusting service and fare levels, the operator can achieve as good or better results than those offered by formal demand studies. For example, if a transit operator sees that ridership is increasing on a route, he or she can easily add another bus to accommodate the increase in demand. If the operator believes that demand is inelastic, it is possible to temporarily put an experimental fare surcharge on some routes to see whether revenue is increased; if consumer resistance to fare increases is higher than expected (i.e., demand elasticities are higher than expected), the surcharges can be removed. One great advantage that transit bus operators have over fixed guideway systems is that mistakes have no long-term consequences and thus service and fare experiments can be undertaken with little cost.

Investments in fixed transit facilities—new expressways, new rapid transit lines, etc.—are, by contrast, much riskier. A subway line that does not attract the ridership that is expected cannot be moved to a new route or sold to another city. In a literal sense, the investment is sunk. Whenever future actions are costly and limited by today's actions, it is important to get as much information as possible about the effects of different decisions.

In the past, demand studies for particular facilities were often misused as the sole or primary determinant of the decision to invest in a facility. A government agency would forecast that at some point in the near future a facility would become congested; the forecast of congestion was then used as a justification for expanding the facility. There are two things wrong with this logic: It fails to account for the sensitivity of demand to prices that governments charge for the use of their facilities and it assumes that it is optimal to have no congestion in transport facilities. Neither of these conditions is economically justified, as explained in Chapter 9. While transport planners no longer use traffic forecasts as a strict signal that a facility should be expanded, understanding the demand for facilities is still a critical component of transportation planning.

The procedure for estimating the demand for the use of some transport facility, like a stretch of highway, is the same as that for calculating demand for a particular aggregate of transportation markets. In principle the standard econometric methods for fitting a plane to price, income, and quantity data could be used. As with most transportation demand estimates, however, it turns out that facilities demand estimates are most efficiently estimated using indirect methods in which a general understanding of the decision-making process used by demanders guides a choice of statistical model. These methods are especially useful for forecasting demand for facilities not yet built.

Following standard economic principles, the focus of transportation demand estimates is on the behavior of the individual household. Members of a household are assumed to have the following choices to make:

1. How many trips to make during a week.
2. What destination to choose for each trip.
3. What mode of travel to use.
4. Which route between the origin and destination to use.[19]

Once a researcher has estimated how a traveler makes these choices, it is possible to calculate the number of trips that an individual will take between, say, Washington National Airport and the Silver Spring Metro stop using the Washington Metro Red line: Simply add together individual demands to get an overall demand for using that facility.

Data for estimating urban demands are generally based on surveys of drivers or passengers.[20] These data allow fully disaggregate estimating procedures—something almost never permitted by data availability in freight transportation or inter-city passenger transportation.[21] With fully disaggregate estimations, there is no problem of trying to infer how changes in the price and quantity indexes relate to actual changes in prices paid and actual amounts shipped on individual flows. The price an individual pays is unambiguously defined and the amount of transportation that an individual undertakes is similarly defined.

The problem with all disaggregate estimations, however, is one familiar in statistics as the sampling problem: how to weight the data that you do have to get information about the full population. To accurately estimate demands for a transport facility, one must know not only how each individual in the data sample will react to a change in price or income, but also the size of the population of which each individual is assumed to be representative.

The four-part classification scheme for urban transportation choices is used to organize the mathematical analysis of the disaggregate data. All such organizing schemes involve a simplification of reality. The primary simplification used in urban transportation analysis is to assume that each of the four choices are made sequentially. If an individual is assumed to make all of the choices simultaneously, the alternatives would be impossibly numerous. This simplification of sequential choice makes the problem mathematically tractable.

Trip Generation

Trip generation models are generally simple linear functions of the socioeconomic characteristics of households. Most empirical studies of trip generation reveal that person-trip production is influenced mainly by income and car ownership (which is itself primarily a function of income).[22]

Trip Distribution

While trip generation can easily be rationalized as consistent with economic models of households maximizing their own well-being, trip distribution models are not as easily justified. Without understanding the economic geography of an urban area it is difficult to understand why individuals choose different destinations for their trips. Unless one knows where in an urban area the major shopping centers are, one will not be able to understand why certain destinations are chosen for shopping trips.

An indirect method that has long been used to deal with trip generation and distribution is the so-called *gravity model*.[23] Using an analogy from physics, the gravitational attraction of two objects, the gravity model predicts that the number of trips between any two origins and destinations will be distributed according to the formula:

$$t_{ij} = \alpha A_i B_j c_{ij}^{-\sigma} \tag{4.1}$$

where t_{ij} = number of trips taken between origin i and
                        destination j
            A_i = number of total trips taken from origin i
            B_j = number of total trips taken to destination j
            c_{ij} = distance between i and j or a measure of cost of
                        transportation between them
α and σ = parameters whose values are estimated
                        for each particular city.

In the formula for gravitational attraction from physics, $\sigma = 2$; that is, the attraction between two objects decreases with the square of the distance between them. Some estimations of transportation demands have found values of σ that are in fact close to 2, thus enhancing the analogy of transportation demand to gravity. In its simplest form, the gravity model says that trips between any pair of localities will increase with the product of the total trips generated at those places and decline with the square of the distance between them. While this formula seems to have remarkable explanatory power in predicting traffic levels not only for urban transportation but also for intercity transport, it is not based on the theoretical foundation of standard economic models of individual behavior.[24] Economists feel uncomfortable using what they consider to be "ad hoc" models if they are not derived from models of individuals maximizing their own well being.

Mode Selection

Most work on urban transportation has focused on the third of the individual's decisions: which mode of travel to take. When mode choice models are applied with individual household data, it is possible to employ discrete choice methods like logit or probit analysis.[25] These models use data on actual choices between modes to forecast how likely it would be that an average household, facing particular costs of using them, would choose one mode or another. The probability range is logically bounded at zero and 1, and thus it makes sense to assume that the probabilities are insensitive to relative costs at both very high and very low costs of one mode relative to another. There will then be a critical cost ratio where the sensitivity of modal choice is the highest. Finding this critical ratio and the sensitivity of mode choice at that point is the focus of logit and probit models.

As noted above, the most important element of mode selection is the number of automobiles owned by a household. Income, the age of an individual and his or her role in the household, household size, profession, and residential location are all factors that will shift the modal split curve. The relative costs of using a mode, measured on the horizontal axis of the modal split curve, depend primarily on in-vehicle travel time, access, waiting and transit times, travel cost, and such attitudinal and difficult-to-quantify variables as comfort, reliability, and safety. The latter group of variables is an attempt to put a name on ignorance—the fact that standard economic models cannot easily explain the overwhelming preference for automobiles over public transportation for most urban trips.

▬ Route Selection

Route selection models are particularly important for facilities planning. Route selection models have borrowed from the traffic engineering literature. A city's transportation network is modeled and traffic generated in the previous three steps is assigned to different traffic lanes following the principle that people choose routes to minimize their own travel time. Traffic assignment turns out to be a difficult process to model, particularly because travel facilities can become congested. When congestion occurs, an individual's choice of route will depend on all others' decisions, thus requiring that the problem be solved simultaneously for all travelers. Route selection models have been criticized for having a particularly simple and deterministic approach to individual behavior—minimize travel time—as opposed to the much richer specification allowed by economist's preferred model specifications.

A general dissatisfaction with non-economic justifications of some of the four-part process of describing urban traffic demands and with the assumed sequential nature of the choice has led to an attempt to develop the demand for using particular facilities within a general framework of economic choice.[26] In this approach, the theory and mathematics of mode choice are used for all parts of the travel choice. Each destination-mode-route combination is considered as a separate economic good; the consumer's choice is how much of each good to consume. It is not yet clear whether this theoretically-appealing generalization of travel choice will be successful at improving travel demand estimates.

THE DEMAND FOR INTERCITY PASSENGER TRANSPORTATION

As with urban transportation, the main competition in intercity passenger transportation is between automobiles and public transport. The automobile is also the dominant mode of intercity transportation, with a market share equivalent to that in urban transportation. However, intercity automobile traffic has been decreasing as a percentage of all intercity travel over the last 20 years. Figure 4.5 shows that the reason for the decline in market share is the dramatic rise in airline traffic. The other modes in Figure 4.5 show stable level passenger-miles over the past 25 years.

Intercity passenger transportation is no more homogeneous an output than is urban passenger transportation. Intercity passenger transportation,

FIGURE 4.5   U.S. Intercity Passenger Traffic of Different Modes, 1970 and 1995

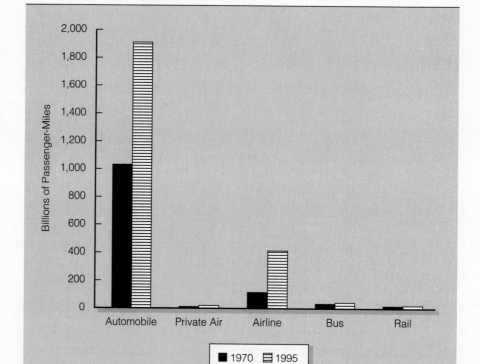

SOURCE: *Transportation in America,* 14th Edition

especially air transport, is even more differentiated than urban transport, as reflected in the widespread use of differential pricing by public transport sellers. Whenever sellers engage in differential pricing, it is impossible to define a single price for the service being sold. Whenever prices cannot be properly defined, the demand estimates will be inaccurate. The problem of price discrimination in air transportation became most acute after deregulation. Before that time, there were several studies of the responsiveness of aggregate passenger traffic to average prices and incomes.[27] While there is general agreement that the income elasticity of demand for the average air passenger is significant and positive, there is no such agreement on whether on average the price elasticity of demand for air travel is large or small. An estimate by Grayson puts the elasticity of demand for air travel at –0.62.[28] Estimates of the average run from –2.5 at one extreme to several markets which seem to have positive elasticities.[29] Positive price elasticities mean that higher prices attract more passengers—something that is illogical for markets like air service, which have positive income elasticities.

One reason that price elasticity estimates of the demand for air travel have varied so much is the varying levels of price discrimination across markets and over time. The statistical analyses have tried to discover differences in traffic levels based on changes in the average fare level; but the changes in fare level are determined primarily by the pattern of discounts offered to different classes of passengers. For example, airline deregulation led to a surge in airline traffic, a decrease in average fare levels, and an increase in airline revenues. The combination of decreased fares and increased revenues is generally a sign that demand is elastic with respect to fares. However, average fares declined primarily due to an increasing proportion of travelers flying with discounted tickets. An attempt to separate the effect of fare level from the level of discounting found an insignificant effect of fare level on traffic levels.[30]

As with all transportation demand exercises, the way to improve demand estimates is to disaggregate traffic into groups within which fare movements and responses to those movements can be assumed to be relatively homogeneous. One such disaggregation is by trip purpose. According to the National Personal Transportation Survey, most travel is not for business, but rather for vacations, visiting friends or relatives (VFR), or other family, personal, social, or recreational reasons.[31] The results of the 1990 survey are shown in Figure 4.6. Automobile trips dominate as the preferred mode of transportation for all trips. Air transport has a significant share of business travel, but even here automobiles carry more than 50 percent of business transportation.

Another way of describing the market for passenger transportation is to divide trips by distance. The great majority of trips are taken close to home. As shown in Figure 4.7, automobile trips are predominantly short-distance. Bus and train travel have similar percentage breakdowns to automobile, with approximately one-half of all trips being taken in the short distance range. By contrast, airline trips have the opposite distance profile, with the fewest trips

FIGURE 4.6   **Purpose of Long-Distance Passenger-Miles**

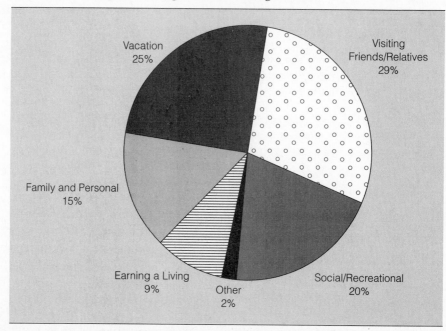

SOURCE: U.S.D.O.T., 1990 National Personal Transportation Survey. Long-distance travel is defined as trips more than 75 miles in length.

being taken in the close range, and the largest percentage of trips being taken to more distant destinations.

It is usually believed that the price elasticities of demand for business travelers are lower than for VFR and vacation trips. Recent estimates by Morrison and Winston confirm this. For vacation travel, they estimate that the average market elasticity of automobile vacation travel with respect to automobile cost is –0.955; for bus it is –0.694; rail has an elastic demand of –1.2, while the elasticity of demand for vacation air travel is –0.378. Elasticities of business travel are somewhat lower: –0.7 for auto; –0.3 for bus; –0.57 for rail; and –0.18 for air.[32]

Approximately 10 percent of all airline trips are international. Both because international air traffic tends to move in more well defined corridors and because international air transport is more closely regulated than other forms of passenger transportation, there has been some active work on the demand for international air passenger transportation.[33] This work, too, indicates that there is a great deal of variation in demand elasticities both across markets and within markets. Straszheim finds that first class air traffic on North Atlantic routes is price inelastic, but all other types of traffic is quite price elastic. He esti-

FIGURE 4.7   Distance Profiles of Passenger-Miles of Different Modes

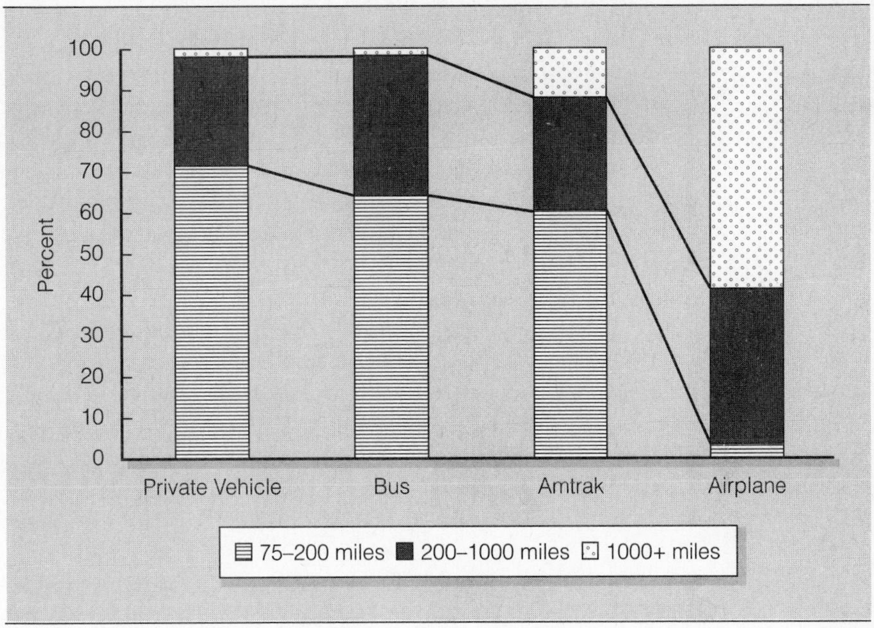

SOURCE: U.S. D.O.T., 1990 National Personal Transportation Survey

mates that for travelers flying on the cheapest international air tickets, the price elasticity of demand is –2.7. The air traffic with the highest income elasticity of demand is short-haul leisure travel. Long-haul business traffic has the lowest income elasticity of demand.[34]

CONCLUSION

Like freight transportation, passenger transportation should be seen as a collection of interrelated but distinct services. Demand analysis starts with the identification of a group of transportation outputs in whose behavior one is interested.

The major division in passenger transportation, as in freight transportation, is between private and for-hire services. The fastest growing sector of passenger transportation is airline service, but the great majority of passenger transportation in the United States is still private automobile traffic.

Since private transportation is not bought and sold, it has no market price. To estimate demand curves for private transportation, economists redefine the concept of demand to be a relationship between the cost of automobile trips and the number of trips taken. While this shift in perspective from price per unit to cost per unit seems logical and sensible, the change in perspective is more problematic than appears on the surface. One must decide on how to divide costs into fixed and variable portions and which portion is appropriate for each demand grouping that one is considering. When calculating the costs of private transportation, one must also include an allowance for these implicit costs in addition to the explicit costs of operation. The calculation of these costs is the subject of the next section of this book.

The demand for automobile use depends primarily on the number of automobiles in existence. The number of automobiles held per capita has been rising in every country in the world; the United States has more cars per capita than any other country. Automobile holding is determined primarily by changes in income. The cost sensitivity of driving enters primarily through changes in the structure of automobile holding and in the type of trips taken. The elasticity of automobile trips with respect to the cost of driving is close to zero.

Competition between private and public transportation is easily divided into urban and intercity modes. Ridership of urban transit modes declined through about 1975, but has recovered slightly since then. Attempts to switch commuters from cars to public transportation have not generally been successful. The worldwide average price elasticity of demand for public transit has been estimated to be about –0.45. Service quality elasticities are estimated to be about +.45. Elasticities may be lower in the United States. The ability of individual cities to attract riders to transit systems is determined primarily by residential density. In very low density cities and suburbs, public transit tends to have low demand.

The majority of effort in estimating passenger demand has been directed towards studies designed to guide investment in facilities like highways, bridges, or new transit lines. These studies often use survey data; having responses of individuals allows use of more sophisticated methods than are used in other branches of demand studies where only aggregate data are available. The disaggregate studies assume that travelers make a series of sequential decisions: how many trips to take, where to go, what mode to use, and what route to take. The sensitivity of each of these choices is estimated and the results aggregated to get the effect on the entire traffic of the proposed facility.

The main competition with the automobile for intercity travel is with the airplane. In this group of markets, public transportation has been gaining ground over the private mode. Estimates of the elasticities and determinants of the demand for airline traffic have been erratic, probably due primarily to the airlines' use of discriminatory pricing policies. Discriminatory pricing policies are profitable if the market can be broken down into groups that have different demand elasticities. Studies confirm that business travel has the lowest demand elasticities while vacation travel has the highest.

NOTES

1. Hill, Daniel H., "Dynamics of Household Driving Demand," *Review of Economics and Statistics*, Vol. LXVIII, No. 1 (February 1986), p. 140. Much of the literature on the demand for automobile usage has been done as a step in the calculation of the elasticities for the demand for gasoline or for automobiles. On the demand for gasoline see, in addition to the paper by Hill: Archibald, Robert and Robert Gillingham, "A Decomposition of the Price and Income Elasticities of the Consumer Demand for Gasoline," *Southern Economic Journal,* Vol. 47, No. 4 (1981), 1021–1031; Berzeg, Korhan, "Demand for Motor Gasoline: A Generalized Error Components Model," *Southern Economic Journal* 49 (Oct. 1982), 462–471; and Wheaton, William C., "The Long-run Structure of Transportation and Gasoline Demand," *Bell Journal of Economics*, Vol. 13, No. 2 (Autumn 1982), pp. 439–454.

2. Wheaton, William C., "The Long-Run Structure of Transportation and Gasoline Demand," *Bell Journal of Economics*, Vol. 13, No. 2 (Autumn 1982), p. 442. An extended discussion of techniques for estimating automobile demand is found in Train, Kenneth, *Qualitative Choice Analysis: Theory, Econometrics, and Application to Automobile Demand* (Cambridge: MIT Press, 1986). A good survey of recent work on the demand for automobiles and its relationship to the demand for driving is in Mannering, Fred L. and Kenneth Train, "Recent Directions in Automobile Demand Modeling," *Transportation Research B*, Vol. 19B, No. 4, pp. 265–274 (1985). There is no completely general treatment of the joint decision among numbers of vehicles, type of vehicles, and the number of miles to drive each vehicle.

3. Mannering, Fred and Winston Clifford, "A Dynamic Empirical Analysis of Household Vehicle Ownership and Utilization," *Rand Journal of Economics*, Vol. 16, No. 2 (Summer 1985), pp. 215–236.

4. Pindyck, R., *The Structure of World Energy Demand* (Cambridge: MIT Press, 1979).

5. Hill, Daniel H., "Dynamics of Household Driving Demand," *Review of Economics and Statistics*, Vol. LXVIII, No. 1 (February 1986).

6. Daniels, P.W., "Transport Changes Generated by Decentralized Offices," *Regional Studies* Vol. 15, No. 6 (1981), pp. 507–520.

7. Hendrickson, Chris, "A Note on Trends in Transit Commuting in the United States Relating to Employment in the Central Business District," *Transportation Research-A*, Vol. 20A, No. 1, pp. 33–37 (1986).

8. The best known example of such policies is in Singapore. See Spencer, Andrew H. and Lin Sien Chia, "National Policy Toward Cards: Singapore," *Transport Reviews*, 1985, Vol. 5, No. 4, 301–323. The U.S. experience is described in Button, Kenneth J., "Road Pricing—an Outsider's View of American Experiences," *Transport Reviews*, 1984, Vol. 4, No. 1, 73–98.

9. Hendrickson, Chris, "A Note on Trends in Transit Commuting in the United States Relating to Employment in the Central Business District," *Transportation Research-A*, Vol. 20A, No. 1, pp. 33–37 (1986).

10. Bureau of the Census, *Annual Housing Survey*; quoted in Izraeli, Oded and Thomas R. McCarty, "Variations in Travel Distance, Travel Time and Modal Choice Among SMSA's," *Journal of Transport Economics and Policy* (May 1985), Vol. XIX, No. 2, pp. 139–160.

11. Webster, F.V., P.H. Bly, R.H Johnston, N. Paulley, and M. Dasgupta, "Changing Patterns of Urban Travel: Part II, Public Transport and Future Patterns of Travel" *Transport Reviews*, 1986, Vol. 6, No. 2, pp. 129–172. Wilson, George W., "Economic Analysis of Transportation: A Twenty-Five Year Survey," *The Transportation Journal* (Fall 1986), pp. 33–44 believes that the importance of transportation on urban development has been exaggerated.

12. Webster, F.V., P.H. Bly, R.H Johnston, N. Paulley, and M. Dasgupta, "Changing Patterns of Urban Travel: Part II, Public Transport and Future Patterns of Travel," *Transport Reviews*, 1986, Vol. 6, No. 2, pp. 129–172. For a recent estimate, see Voith, Richard, "The Long Run Elasticity of Demand for Commuter Rail Transportation," *Journal of Urban Economics*, Vol. 30, No. 3, November 1991, pp. 360–372.

13. See Annas, A., *Residential Location Markets and Urban Transportation: Economic Theory, Econometrics, and Policy Analysis with Discrete Choice Models* (New York: Academic Press, 1982) and Izraeli, Oded and Thomas R. McCarty, "Variations in Travel Distance, Travel Time and Modal Choice among SMSA's," *Journal of Transport Economics and Policy* (May 1985), Vol. XIX, No. 2, pp. 139–160.

14. Doe, Masayki and W. Bruce Allen, "A Time-Series Analysis of Monthly Ridership for an Urban Rail Rapid Transit Line," *Transportation*, Vol. 13, No. 3 (1986), pp. 237–270.

15. These conclusions can be drawn from trip generation tables for individual metropolitan areas. A good discussion of such tables is found in Kanafani, Adib, *Transportation Demand Analysis* (New York: McGraw-Hill, 1983). See also Webster, F.V., P.H. Bly, R.H. Johnston, N. Paulley, and M. Dasgupta, "Changing Patterns of Urban Travel: Part II, Public Transport and Future Patterns of Travel," *Transport Reviews*, 1986, Vol. 6, No. 2, pp. 129–172 and Izraeli, Oded and Thomas R. McCarty, "Variations in Travel Distance, Travel Time and Modal Choice Among SMSA's," *Journal of Transport Economics and Policy* (May 1985), Vol. XIX, No. 2, pp. 139–160.

16. See Kanafani, Adib, *Transportation Demand Analysis* (New York: McGraw-Hill, 1983), Chapter 6.

17. A comprehensive discussion of carpooling is in Teal, Roger F., "Carpooling: Who, How and Why," *Transportation Research*, Vol. 21A, No. 3, pp. 293–314 (1987). See also Kostyniuk L., (1982) "Demand Analysis for Ridesharing: State of the Art Review" *Transportation Research Record* 876, 17–26; and Oppenheim, N., (1979) Carpooling: Problems and Potentials *Traffic Quarterly*, 33, 253–262.

18. Teal, Roger F., "Carpooling: Who, How and Why," *Transportation Research* Vol. 21A, No. 3, pp. 293–314 (1987) notes that there are important differences among types of carpools. Ride only and family carpools are associated with low income and lack of vehicles. Rideshare carpools, toward which much of public policy has been directed, are not associated with low income, but are determined more by length of commutation and concentration of employment.

19. Kanafani, Adib, *Transportation Demand Analysis* (New York: McGraw-Hill, 1983). A fifth element is sometimes added: At what times to make these trips. For recent work on this element, see Kenneth A. Small, "Trip Scheduling in Urban Transportation Analysis," *American Economic Review*, Vol. 92, No. 2 (May 1992), pp. 482–486.

20. Recent work has attempted to get information on choice sensitivities from travelers' stated preferences among different attribute combinations that modes might possess. See David Henscher, "Stated Preference Analysis of Travel Choices: The State of Practice," *Transportation*, Vol. 21 (1994), No. 2, pp. 107–133.

21. Two exceptions to the statement that disaggregate data are unavailable elsewhere are Winston, Clifford, "A Disaggregate Model of the Demand for Intercity Freight Transportation," *Econometrica*, Vol. 49, No. 4 (July 1981), pp. 981–1006 and John B. Lansing et al., "The Demand for Intercity Passenger Transportation," *Quarterly Journal of Economics*, Vol. 75, No. 1, pp. 87–95, 1961.

22. For a review see Webster, F.V., P.H. Bly, R.H. Johnston, N. Paulley, and M. Dasgupta, "Changing Patterns of Urban Travel: Part I, Urbanization, Household Travel and Car Ownership," *Transport Reviews*, 1986, Vol. 6, No. 1, pp. 49–86.

23. A complete discussion of the gravity model is found in Erlander, Sven and Neil F. Stewart, *The Gravity Model in Transportation Analysis—Theory and Extension* (Utrecht: VSP, 1990).

24. Some of the disputes in the appropriateness of gravity models for the trip generation element of urban traffic demand are found in Horowitz, Joel L., "Travel and Location Behavior: State of the Art and Research Opportunities," *Transportation Research-A*, Vol. 19A, No. 5/6, pp. 441–453; Sen, Ashish, "Research Suggestions on Spatial Interaction Models," *Transportation Research-A*, 19-A, No. 5/6, pp. 432–435; and Smith, Tony E., "A Threshold Model of Discretionary Travel Behavior," *Transportation Research-A*, Vol. 19A, No 5/6, pp. 465–467, Nov.–Dec. 1985. See also Barnard, P.O., "Modeling Shopping Destination Choice Behavior Using the Basic Multinomial Logit Model and Some of its Extensions," *Transport Reviews* (1987), Vol. 7, No. 1, pp. 17–51.

25. These methods are described in Moshe, Ben-Akiva and Steven R. Lerman, *Discrete Choice Analysis: Theory and Application to Travel Demand* (Cambridge: MIT Press, 1985).

26. The general problem of transport modeling is covered in Ortuzar, Juan de Dios and Luis G. Willumsen, *Modeling Transport, Second Edition*, (New York: John Wiley, 1994).

27. Examples are Morrison, Steven A. and Clifford Winston, "An Econometric Analysis of the Demand for Intercity Passenger Transportation," *Research in Transportation Economics*, Vol. 2, pp. 213–237; Verleger, P.K. "Models of the Demand for Air Transportation," *Bell Journal of Economics and Management Science*, Vol. 3, No. 2; Ippolito, Richard A., "Estimating Airline Demand with Quality of Service Variables," *Journal of Transport Economics and Policy*, Vol. XV, No. 1, January 1981, 7–15; Anderson, James E. and Marvin Kraus, "Quality of Service and the Demand for Air Travel," *The Review of Economics and Statistics*, Vol. LXIII, No. 4, November 1981, 533–540; Abrahams, Michael, "A Service Quality Model of Air Travel Demand: An Empirical Study," *Transportation Research-A*, Vol. 5, pp. 385–393.

28. Grayson, Alan (1982), "Disaggregate Model of Mode Choice in Intercity Travel," *Transportation Research Record*, 835: pp. 36–42. Grayson also estimates the own cost elasticity of automobile usage at –0.08; for bus travel at –0.32; and rail travel at –0.37.

29. Jung, J.M. and E. T. Fujii, "The Price Elasticity of Demand for Air Travel: Some new Evidence," *Journal of Transport Economics and Policy* (September 1976), pp. 257–262; Verleger, P.K., "Models of the Demand for Air Transportation," *Bell Journal of Economics and Management Science*, Vol. 3, No. 2, 1972.

30. John R. Meyer and Clinton Oster et al., *Deregulation and the Future of Intercity Passenger Travel* (Cambridge: MIT Press, 1987), Appendix B.

31. U.S. Department of Transportation, Federal Highway Administration, *1990 NPTS Databook*, October 1994. An alternative data source, the National Travel Survey (NTS) conducted by the U.S. Travel Data Center, shows a much larger proportion of business trips. The difference is probably due primarily to a difference in the definition of business travel which the NPTS equates to travel incidental to earning a living and the NTS defines as travel whose purpose is "business, convention, seminar or meeting."

32. Morrison, Steven A., and Clifford Winston, "An Econometric Analysis of the Demand for Intercity Passenger Transportation," *Research in Transportation Economics*, Vol. 2, pp. 213–237. A recent attempt to estimate the demand for railroad passenger service between single city pairs in Britain is found in A.D. Own and G.D.A. Phillips, "The Characteristics of Railway Passenger Demand," *Journal of Transportation Economics and Policy* (September 1987), pp. 231–253.

33. Several of these studies are summarized in Kanafani, Adib, *Transportation Demand Analysis* (New York: McGraw Hill, 1983) and in Doganis, Rigas, *Flying Off Course: The Economics of International Airlines* (London: George Allen and Unwin, 1985). See also, Agarwal, V. and W.K. Talley, "The Demand for International Air Passenger Service Provided by U.S. Air Carriers," *International Journal of Transport Economics*, February 1985, Vol. 12, No. 1, pp. 63–70; and Straszheim, M.R., "Airline Demand Functions in the North Atlantic and their Pricing Implications," *Journal of Transport Economics and Policy*, Vol. 12, No.2, 1978, pp. 179–195.

34. Estimates are from Doganis, Rigas, *Flying Off Course: The Economics of International Airlines* (London: George Allen and Unwin, 1985).

TRANSPORTATION COSTS

5

Transportation Cost Concepts

The term *supply and demand* is almost synonymous with the study of economics itself. It is more accurate, however, to describe economics as *the study of demand and costs*. The concept of costs is more general than that of supply. Supply, like demand, is a relationship between market price and a quantity—the quantity that all producers of a good or service would be willing to offer to the market. As a concept, supply is valid only when sellers cannot affect the prices that the market has set for their goods or services. This occurs when firms are in perfect competition. To speak of *supply* to imply that suppliers are perfectly competing against one another—a condition that usually does not hold. When firms have supply curves, the supply curve is identical with a particular kind of cost curve. But all firms have cost curves, regardless of whether they are in perfectly competitive markets. So if we understand transportation costs, we will understand transportation supply.

THE FUNDAMENTAL CONCEPT OF COSTS: OPPORTUNITY COST

Economics defines the *cost* of an action as the value of other opportunities that one gives up by taking the action. The cost of producing a good or service is found in the resources consumed in production: the land, labor, and capital that are unavailable for producing some other good or service because they were used to produce a transportation service. The idea that the cost of producing a good or service can be measured in terms of what is given up is the concept of *opportunity cost*; it is sometimes also called *real cost* to emphasize that costs of an action are properly measured not by money spent but by the things that one can't do because of the action. The opportunity cost of using a tanker to carry a load of gasoline from Texas to Virginia is value of the trip that the ship can't make because it is tied up on that run; the opportunity cost of taking a vacation in Yellowstone Park is measured by the attractiveness of the other options for a vacationer's time and money; the opportunity cost of building a pipeline is measured by foreclosed options from the funds spent and land used by the line.

The basic procedure used to make a dollar calculation of opportunity costs has three steps. First, one makes a list of all inputs used to produce a service or group of services. If the services were not produced, what factors of production and how much of each would be saved? The second step in the calculation of opportunity cost is to determine where the saved resources would be best used. Some labor might stay in transportation, some might produce other things. Much of the equipment might stay in transportation and might increase the level of service on alternative routes or for different passenger classes or commodities. The third and final step is to put a dollar value on the increased production of goods or other services made possible by freeing resources from their use in transportation. The increase in value of other goods and services that would result from a decrease of production of some group of transportation services is the opportunity cost of producing those transportation services.

Opportunity Costs and Expenditures

Students who are first introduced to the idea of opportunity costs generally consider it to be unwieldy and unnecessary. To find the cost of a service, why not simply check how much a transportation company spent to produce the service? For example, why not find out how much a tanker company paid for the fuel, crew, and supplies to carry the load of gasoline from Texas to Virginia and call that the cost of making the trip? The reason is that no one—not the tanker company, its customers, or the government tax collector—treats direct expenditures as a complete list of costs. The ship itself, for example, represents a valuable asset to its owner and using it to carry gasoline in one direction represents a sacrifice of using the asset in other profitable opportunities. Even if it owns its ships rather than leases them, a shipping company will make decisions on where to sell and what cargo to carry as if it had to pay someone else for use of the ship.

■ Sunk Costs and Undervalued Assets

Sometimes a producer has to make a payment for using a resource that has no opportunity cost after it is put in service. This payment is a *sunk cost*. A good example is a railroad embankment. While a railroad company must pay to create a level roadway, the result has no scrap value. In order for the land to be used in its next best use, the embankment may have to be removed. It thus has no opportunity cost, and any payment made to create it is a sunk cost—the name given to the unrecoverable portion of an investment. The dominance of transportation expenditures by sunk costs strongly affects the analysis of the sector.

While the presence of sunk costs makes opportunity costs lower than direct expenditures, it is possible for opportunity costs to be greater than expenditures. This occurs when equipment is used whose value has appreciated since the transportation company originally purchased it. Aircraft have in the recent past been bought and sold for an amount far greater than their original purchase price. The opportunity cost of using an airplane is not affected by the original cost of the plane but by what an airline gives up today to use it as part of its current fleet. By using the plane, an airline gives up the opportunity to profit from the sale or lease of a valuable piece of equipment. The opportunity cost of the plane is thus related to its value in the used equipment market. In the early 1990s, the prices of used aircraft dropped dramatically, thus reducing the opportunity cost of running an airline and attracting new entrants into the airline industry.

■ Implicit Costs and Shadow Prices

In its pure form, the principle of opportunity cost appears to be hopelessly impractical. While it would be laborious, it is in principle possible to make a study of exactly which people, which pieces of equipment, and which items of right-of-way would become idled if we curtailed some transportation service or group of services. But how can anyone know for certain where people who lose their jobs in a service reduction would find work? How can one guess how much the value of production would increase elsewhere if land, labor, and capital freed from use in some transportation service were to be deployed in other places?

The answer is that one cannot. Opportunity cost is an ideal concept, and actual calculations will never be ideal. But is useful to have an ideal so that we can judge the extent to which our actual measurements fall short and so that we can evaluate alternative methods of measuring costs.

In practice, the principle of opportunity cost is introduced by modifying lists of expenditures in two ways: First, where an input is used but no payment was made, an estimate will be made of how much it would have cost to purchase a similar input. The usual situation when this occurs is when a company owns an asset. The opportunity cost of using an owned asset is an *implicit cost*. The second occasion when opportunity cost and expenditures differ is when the amount paid for the use of an input is different from what it would have fetched on the open market. In that case, an adjustment will be made. The opportunity cost of the labor, for example, would probably be listed as the same as the amount paid to labor unless there is some reason to believe that the wage paid to labor was distorted. For example, distortions may arise from union contracts that provided higher than competitive wages, from abnormal unemployment rates among former airline workers, or from unusual shortages of skilled airline labor. If there were distortions, the economist would place a shadow price on the input—i.e., mark up or mark down the expenses paid for labor by a proportion that represents an estimate about the degree of distortions.[1] The use of shadow price rules of thumb is a way to introduce the principle of opportunity cost into expenditure accounts.

The opportunity cost principle is especially useful in studies of the costs of private transportation. People who drive to a local convenience store pay out of their pocket only a fraction of the opportunity cost of making the trip. The trip takes time away from doing other things, for example. In calculating the cost of making the trip, economists will attribute to drivers a sum equivalent to the value of their time. While they do not consciously charge themselves to drive, drivers do behave as if they recognize the costs of their time behind the wheel. So firm is economists' belief that people make transport decisions using the opportunity cost rather than simple expenditures that the transportation choices that people make has been used to calculate a cost of time outside the transport sector as well.

External Costs

Externalities occur whenever someone other than the producer and user of the transportation service are affected by the act of transportation. Externalities are sometimes called *third party effects*. An *external cost* is a cost that is not borne by either the buyer or the seller of the service—it is imposed on a third party. The cost is created either by additional amounts of resources that others must pay to maintain their standard of living or a diminished value of the resources that they own.

Whether a cost is considered to be external or internal depends on the perspective taken. In a factory, for example, if my activity interferes with your ability to make products, I have imposed an external cost on you. But from the point of view of the factory as a whole, it is perfectly normal to expect that increasing production will, beyond some point, lead to a loss of productivity of workers. This loss of productivity would represent an increase in (internal) costs of production, but would not be an external cost on those outside the plant.

In a similar manner, the most prevalent external cost in transportation—traffic congestion—is internal to the sector as a whole. When traffic becomes congested, it slows down, thus requiring other drivers to spend more time to complete their trips. My decision to drive increases the amount of time that you must spend on your own transportation. My driving decision thus imposes an external cost on you. Similarly, automobile traffic can congest truck traffic. So, from the perspective of a different group of transport services, the costs of traffic congestion are external.

Other external costs of transportation are noise, air, and water pollution. As drivers, we do not pay for the use of the air that our motors consume; the quality of the air that we return to the atmosphere is obviously worse than that our motors take in. Since our decision to drive harms other people and we have not compensated them for their diminished enjoyment, we have imposed an external cost on them. Transport vehicles use approximately 65 percent of petroleum consumed in the United States and are a major source of air pollution. Noise pollution around airports or diminished water quality after oil tanker spills are all examples of external costs of using transportation. Chapter 14 contains a discussion of measurements of the external costs of transportation.

Traffic safety issues also may involve external costs. To the extent that people are injured or inconvenienced in transportation accidents—through exposure to toxic chemicals when a tank car derails, or being killed by a drunk driver—and to the extent that these costs are not reimbursed to the person injured, an external cost of transportation is created. The external cost of traffic safety is also discussed in Chapter 14.

Transportation may impose a range of more subtle and controversial external costs. It is sometimes argued that the use of imported petroleum in automobiles weakens national defense by making the nation vulnerable to an embargo of imported oil. If this argument is correct, it is another example of an external cost of driving. Military preparedness is one of the arguments that has been given for subsidization of the U.S. merchant fleet. It has also been argued that the use of automobiles for urban travel worsens the quality of city life by isolating citizens and preventing the creation of traditional urban communities. If citizens value the type of communities that public transportation facilitates (something that is by no means clear) and if my use of an automobile causes me to withdraw from the community with a resultant decrease in your satisfaction with your living situation, the costs of driving must be increased by an amount related to the external costs imposed on you by my decision to drive.

The importance of external costs of transportation is one of the areas of greatest controversy in transportation economics. The traditional assumption in the field has been that external costs are small in relation to direct costs. There is a growing body of opinion, however, that concludes that external, or *social costs* of transportation are sufficiently important as to require explicit governmental policy to deal with these costs. These issues are discussed in Chapter 14.

TRANSPORTATION COST CLASSIFICATIONS

In economics, factors of production can be classified in various ways. The best known classification is that of *land* (natural resources), *labor* (the human input into production), and *capital* (all forms of equipment, buildings, and other items produced to aid production of other items). Another classification is of productive resources into fixed inputs and variable inputs. A *fixed input* is a resource whose level of use cannot be altered within a specified time period; a *variable input* is one whose level of use can be altered to suit a firm's needs during the same period. *Fixed costs* are costs paid to fixed inputs and *variable costs* are costs associated with the use of variable inputs.

In transportation economics, it is useful to make a further distinction between two types of capital: fixed facilities and vehicles. With a few exceptions, the operating costs of *fixed facilities* tends to be negligible, with almost all costs independent of use levels. *Vehicle operations costs* tend to be substantial, however. This leads transportation costs to be divided into three main categories: fixed facilities ownership costs, vehicle ownership costs, and vehicle operating costs. These three cost categories are the subjects of the next three chapters respectively. Fixed facilities, often referred to as infrastructure, are immobile pieces of capital. The cost of creating fixed facilities is usually sunk. Vehicles, precisely because they are mobile, can be shifted from market to market according to current demands; the costs of owning transportation vehicles is not sunk.

Different modes of transportation vary not only in the extent to which their costs are concentrated within each of the three categories, but also in the extent to which costs are fixed and variable within those categories. In addition, they vary in the extent to which payments made by users are fixed and variable. A commuter who buys an unlimited use bus pass has made a fixed payment for use of a service most of whose costs are variable. By contrast, drivers pay for highways—most of whose costs are fixed—through taxes on fuel, which vary with the amount of driving done; a fixed cost is paid as a variable charge. Regardless of the nature of the system of user charges, the fixity of costs depends on the extent to which inputs vary as the level of output changes.

Fixed Facilities Costs

Every mode of transportation has fixed facilities. Railroads use tracks, stations, and yards. Trucks use roads and terminals. Airlines use the air traffic control system and airports. Ocean vessels use ports. Automobiles use roads and parking lots. In some cases, the owners of the fixed facilities also provide the transportation services. In most cases, the owners are different from those who provide the transportation. According to the principle of opportunity costs, the identity of the owner and user makes no difference to cost calculations. The costs of fixed facilities is measured as the resources that are unavailable for other economic activities, because fixed facilities are used for transportation.

Fixed facilities ownership is not an activity that consumes resources. Transportation activities take place on fixed facilities but the fixed facilities themselves—with a few exceptions, like pipelines and cargo handling facilities—are not active. However, the placement and maintenance of fixed facilities for their use by transportation is an activity. Retaining waterways as transportation routes implies foregone activities. The preservation of fixed facilities for transportation is in a real sense a costly activity. We can quite properly ask what the value of foregone activities is for roads and railways that are retained in their current uses rather than abandoned or converted to other uses.

Fixed facilities are costly to construct, but after they are constructed, much of the cost becomes sunk. Sunk costs, as noted above, do not enter into the calculation of opportunity costs. The principle of opportunity cost states that a facility's cost is the value or resources that could be saved if it were not used for transportation. To illustrate, consider the cost of roads. Some of the costs of a highway owner are clearly fixed: If a road were abandoned for use by motor vehicles, maintenance crews would no longer be needed to keep the grass cut on the shoulders; the state police would not be needed to patrol the highway; winter ice would not need to be melted with road salt. But what about maintenance to the road surface? Roads periodically need repaving. Abandoning the roadway would save repaving and repair costs when those would have become necessary; but the date at which repaving and repair would be necessary is likely to depend on the amount of traffic on the road. To some extent, the costs of owning a highway are attributable to the amount of traffic using it and thus are treated as a cost of operations. The cost of operating transport vehicles is covered in Chapter 8.

▬ Vehicle Costs

Pipelines constitute the one mode of transportation that does not use vehicles. In all other cases, transportation requires both vehicles as well as fixed facilities. The second main classification of transportation costs is the cost of owning transportation vehicles—airplanes, railroad rolling stock, taxies, busses, trucks, barges, and ships.

In contrast to fixed facilities, the cost of purchasing transport vehicles is not sunk. Transport vehicles are made to move people and goods and themselves in the process. Since they are movable, they can be switched from market to market with ease. There is thus little difficulty in identifying the opportunity cost of owning a vehicle—it is the amount that the highest bidder would be willing to pay to use your vehicle. The annual cost of owning a car that is worth $10,000 in the used car market (in addition to insurance, minimum maintenance, and obsolescence) is equal to the annual amount that an individual would have to pay to borrow $10,000. The idea that the annual cost of using vehicles is measured by an interest rate applied to the value of the vehicle in the used market is explained more fully in Chapter 9.

The mobility of transport vehicles means that it is easy to organize a market for used equipment. Where vehicles have a predictable life—either in years or in mileage—the opportunity cost of vehicle ownership can be approximated by subtracting depreciation allowances from the original cost of the vehicle. Using the definition of fixed and variable costs, to the extent that vehicles have a useful life determined by years, that cost of vehicle ownership is fixed; if the life of a vehicle is determined primarily by the amount that it is used, vehicle ownership costs are primarily variable. In the case where the life of a vehicle is predictable from neither time nor usage (airliners are a good example), the opportunity cost of vehicle ownership cannot be determined by applying a depreciation allowance to the original cost of the vehicle; in this case the used vehicle market is the only source of information on vehicle ownership costs. Vehicle ownership costs vary greatly from mode to mode, as discussed in Chapter 7.

The Costs of Operation

The two main costs of operations—labor time and fuel—both vary with the level of use of the vehicle and thus are, by definition, variable costs. The cost of operating a transportation vehicle is sensitive to the way in which it is used, and in particular to the vehicle speed. There is a speed which will minimize fuel use per mile for any vehicle; labor costs per mile decline with speed. Speed, in turn, is determined in large part by traffic levels. Traffic congestion slows speeds, thus raising the opportunity cost of labor time required to complete the trip.

Traffic slowdown occurs when fixed facilities become congested, but vehicle stocks can become congested in the same economic sense. If an airline finds that its traffic rises more rapidly than it expected, it can reschedule its flights to get more passenger-miles out of its existing fleet. But this rescheduling may require that the aircraft be kept in the air for more hours per day than they were designed for or routed by more circuitous routings than would be optimal in order to accommodate the pattern of demand increase. This economizing on the scarce factor of production by increasing use of the variable factors of production, fuel, and labor, will cause variable costs of operation to rise. Another way of describing the process is to say that increases in the variable factors of production are congesting the fixed factors.

In addition to the direct costs of fuel and labor, traffic operations require a support staff of dispatchers, reservation clerks, flight attendants, marketers, and personnel administrators. The costs of hiring this support staff and of materials they use is treated as an indirect cost of vehicle operations. Whether this indirect cost is a fixed or variable cost of operations depends, by definition, on whether the costs vary with the level of operations. Chapter 8 discusses estimates of the costs of vehicle operation.

THE SHAPE OF ECONOMIC COSTS

Despite its unusual three-way cost classification, transportation economics uses much of the framework of standard economic cost analysis. Of course, since standard economic analysis was not developed with an emphasis on the distinction between fixed and mobile capital or on enterprises which operate in many markets, it is not surprising that the cost analysis of transport economics is somewhat different. Nonetheless, it is important to understand the basic economic cost concepts, since that is the foundation of transportation cost analysis.

Standard economic cost analysis starts with the production function underlying the creation of a good or service. Production functions—the relationship between inputs and outputs—have been found to have the same general shape regardless of the industry or output. If output increases more rapidly than inputs, all inputs increasing by the same proportion, the production function is said to be characterized by *increasing returns to scale*.[2] A production function is used in standard economic analysis to identify the inputs necessary to produce a given level of output. A cost function is simply the relationship between a level of output and the dollar value of the inputs needed to produce the output.[3]

Whether or not the production function of an industry shows economies of scale is one of the most important pieces of information that economists look for in describing an industry. The sources of scale economies are generally assumed to be technological; ships, for example, can have their capacity doubled without doubling the amount of material that is used to construct them. But large organizations are often subject to *diseconomies of scale*. Economics is far less precise about the possible source of such scale diseconomies, but they are generally assumed to arise not from technology but from management:

> The larger organizations, with more layers in the vertical and vastly wider spread in the horizontal lines of authority and communication introduce friction and inertia that make for slower responses, less sense of urgency and responsibility, less individual initiative, and more of what are known as bureaucratic tendencies.[4]

When an industry's scale is locked into place, a different set of cost considerations are introduced. With the operation already in place, there are some inputs, those that are fixed, that will not need to be expanded. The curve marked MC in Figure 5.1 has the general shape of the unit cost of expanding or contracting the size of the operation and is given the name of *short-run marginal cost curve*. Production theory predicts that if there are fixed inputs, there will come a point beyond which increasing the variable inputs will increase output at slower and slower rates. This point is the famous *point of diminishing returns* to the variable input. Beyond the point of diminishing returns, payments to increasingly large levels of the variable inputs push up the unit cost of expanding production and the MC curve will be positively sloped. The unusually high expenditures on variable inputs to expand production will also cause *average variable costs*, marked AVC on Figure 5.1, to rise along with marginal cost.

Two other lines that generally appear on economic cost diagrams are those marked AFC and ATC. AFC represents *average fixed cost*, which must decline continuously as output expands. (If it did not, then the costs that it represented would not be fixed). ATC, the short-run *total cost curve*, represents a relationship between service levels and the value of all resources that would be used in the short run. It is constructed by adding together average fixed costs and average variable costs.

The names *long-run cost curve* and *short-run cost curve* are, in fact, misleading. There is no number of months or years that will separate a long run

FIGURE 5.1   The Shape of Standard Economic Cost Curves
For most industries, short run cost curves have the shapes shown above. Average Fixed Cost declines for all output levels. Marginal Cost rises beyond the point of diminishing returns to the variable input and pulls the Average Variable Cost curve toward it. The U-shape of the Average Total Cost curve is due to the sum of the AFC curve and the AVC curve.

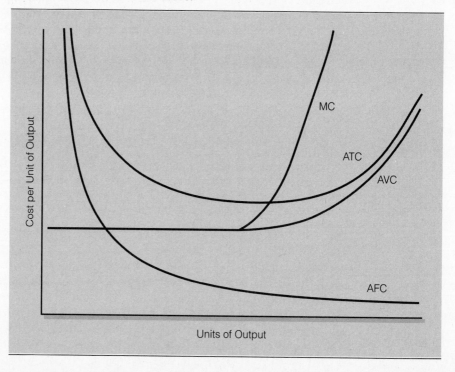

and a short run. The actual distinction is between deciding on a scale of the firm when starting out fresh (or abandoning the entire operation) and deciding on a scale of the firm when the company is already in operation. It is logical to think that a firm which is already in operation could more quickly change its scale of operation; but after many years, a company's plant and equipment may have all been replaced and employees retired and replaced with new ones so that the company has, in effect, made a long-run decision about the size of the firm in the process of making a series of short-run decisions.

The Effect of Lumpy Facilities

When the principles of economic costs outlined above are applied to the transportation industries, some modifications become necessary. The first of these alterations derives from the fact that transport facilities investments tend to be *lumpy*. Lumpiness refers to the fact that increments to transport capital must be made in discrete sizes determined by technological conditions rather than cost minimization.

The lumpiness of transport-fixed facilities investment have several important theoretical and practical implications for transport investment and pricing. Because of this, the concept of a long-run cost curve becomes difficult to interpret in transportation economics. Figure 5.2 shows a pair of short-run marginal cost curves, marked AB and CD; and two average total cost curves corresponding to two different sizes of transportation fixed facilities, labeled EF and GH. The larger the size of the facilities, the larger the traffic level will be that minimizes the average total cost of using the facilities. At traffic levels lower than that marked J, it will be cheaper to use the smaller facility, and at higher levels the larger. The bold scalloped shaped curve marked EJH is the closest that transportation economics can come to a long-run average cost curve. Its irregular shape is due to the lumpiness of facilities sizes.

An often neglected implication of the lumpiness of transport-fixed facilities investment is that it is impossible to define unambiguously the economies of scale of a transport service. Transport economists have generally focused their attention on the initial declining section of the minimum average cost curve. This region derives from the technological constraints that railroads must be built with size sufficient to handle modern railroad cars or that bridges be built sufficiently long to reach both ends and sufficiently strong to handle modern truck weights; that is, as one designs a facility, there is a point below which reducing traffic levels will not alter the design specification of the facility. In this region, additional traffic can be handled with no change in the facility and (assuming no congestion), the average cost of the facility per unit of traffic will decline—thus making it appear that there are economies of scale. This characteristic does not extend to the entire range of production possibilities, however.

FIGURE 5.2   The Effect of Lumpiness on Average Cost Curves for Transportation-Fixed Facilities

When facilities can be built only in limited numbers of sizes, the long-run cost curve becomes the scalloped-shaped figure corresponding to the minimum ATC of each of the short-run cost cureves. This is shown as EJH. At traffic levels below J, it is less expensive to build and use the smaller facility. At traffic levels above J, the larger facility should be used.

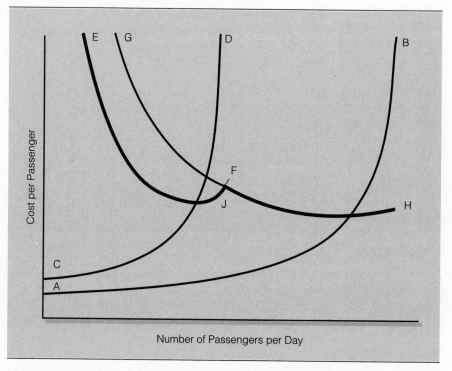

Modes of transport differ greatly in the extent to which lumpiness of investment causes difficulties for economic analysis. In general, the smaller the importance of fixed facilities and the smaller the proportion of fixed facilities costs that are sunk, the less important facilities lumpiness will be. For example, less-than-truck-load (LTL) trucking lines are able to enter a new area by using leased fixed facilities or, sometimes, by using *drop lots* instead of terminals in a new area. That is, LTL terminal facilities are not lumpy like railroad lines or waterway locks. A company does not need to put at risk any investment funds before it determines whether or not there is a market for its service. This enables the industry to be far more aggressive in soliciting new traffic and far more likely to be able to attract investment funds from lenders.

A SIMPLE EXAMPLE OF TRANSPORTATION COSTS

To illustrate how standard economic cost curves can be adapted to transportation markets, consider the Black Mesa and Lake Powell Railroad in northern Arizona. The Black Mesa and Lake Powell Railroad is isolated from the rest of the American railway system. The system consists of 78 miles of electrified track connecting a coal mine and a power plant, three locomotives, and 77 coal cars. The cars shuttle back and forth carrying coal from the coal mine on one end of the line to the power plant on the other end, then return empty to pick up another load. The railroad provides a single service—coal transportation from mine mouth to power plant—to a single customer, using a single type of equipment. Since the line is isolated, it does not lend or borrow equipment from other railroads. It is, in short, atypical of the type of transportation services that we see in the United States today; its operation is more like that of a very long conveyor belt within a factory than that of a railroad company.

Short-run cost curves for the Black Mesa and Lake Powell (BM&LP) can be drawn easily using the guidelines of economic theory. The curves will look exactly like those in Figure 5.1. The Black Mesa and Lake Powell railroad cost $55 million to construct in the early 1970s and had an expected life of 35 years. The original cost is, of course, partly sunk in the embankments and power pylons that line the tracks. However, it is possible that the value of locomotives, coal cars, and the scrap value of salvageable parts has risen over the years so that total salvage value of the investment is today greater than $55 million. An amount related to the current value of the rolling stock, track, property, and equipment can be treated as a fixed cost of operating the system, with fuel and labor expenses counted as variable costs. Spreading the fixed cost over the ton-miles of coal carried in a year will trace out the AFC curve in Figure 5.1.

The single trainset that uses the tracks on the BM&LP makes three round trips per day. Round trips take an average of 6 hours, 40 minutes: 1 hour and 45 minutes to load, 2 hours and 40 minutes for the trip from the mine to the power plant, 30 minutes to unload, and 1 hour and 45 minutes for the return trip. To increase output, the railroad would add more round trips per day. While it is probably possible to get a fourth round trip per day by speeding operations (using fuel at an inefficiently high rate and paying workers to man the train at all shifts during a day), speeding operations to allow a fifth round trip per day may require speeds that are impossible to achieve given the current engineering of the railroad and equipment. The fact that increased labor and fuel expenditures can lead to higher output causes the short-run cost curves in Figure 5.1 to have the classic property of rising marginal costs as capacity is approached. As the physical capacity of the line and trainset are approached, the marginal cost is treated as going to infinity. Output can then be increased only by expanding the physical capacity of the system, presumably by adding a second train set. Anything that increases the investment in line would cause the short-run cost curves in Figure 5.1 to shift to the right.

The fact that the Black Mesa and Lake Powell Railroad can be described in terms of the classic economics cost curves is the result of the operation being unlike most transport systems. Since vehicles cannot be used on any other route, they can be treated like fixed capital; and the fact that there is only one service produced by the system means that there is none of the complexity of shared facilities and network economies that are so common to transportation economics.

NETWORK ECONOMIES

Examples of transportation operations that can be analyzed as simply as the BM&LP are rare. Unfortunately, realistic operations do not usually make the best examples for illustrating the basic principles. For that it is best to use a much simpler system, like the stylized and completely hypothetical one shown in Figure 5.3. Using this system, we will explore how the presence of shared facilities in networks produces its own peculiar economics. Figure 5.3 is intended to show the position of cities connected by airline service. To keep the

FIGURE 5.3   A Map of Cities in a Hypothetical Airline System
Cities E,F, and G are on a north-south line, 100 miles apart. Cities D,B, and A are also on a north-south line 100 miles apart. Cities H, F, B, and C are on an east-west line. Cities H and F are 100 miles apart. Cities B and C are also 100 miles apart. Cities F and B are 700 miles apart. Lines show system connections with a hub-and-spoke system.

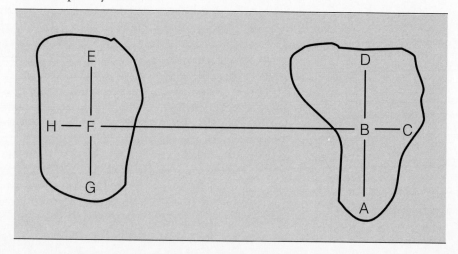

example simple, we will assume that all airline traffic is between cities on the right side of the map and cities on the left side.

Network economies refer to the reduction in unit costs in a network as economic activity expands. To generate unit costs, we must assign traffic flows between each pair of cities. This was done by picking populations for each city at random and then using the gravity model described in Chapter 4 to convert populations and distances to daily passenger flow. Table 5.1 shows the number of passengers traveling each way between each pair of cities per day. The system carries a total of 2,226 passengers, 1,113 of whom fly from east to west and 1,113 fly from west to east. The heaviest traffic flow is between A and E, where 173 passengers fly each day in each direction. The lightest traffic flow is between the relatively small (and distant) cities labeled B and G, where demand is only 16 passengers per day in each direction.

One of the essential features of transportation services is that they take place within networks. Another feature is that there is limited flexibility in the size of the equipment that can be used. Such lumpiness in vehicle size can generate network economies, as the following example shows.

Airlines have a variety of different sizes of aircraft to satisfy demands. To keep our example simple, we assume that there are only two kinds of airplanes that can be flown: a large size airplane with 150 seats and a flying cost of 10 cents per seat-mile; and a small size airplane with 20 seats and a cost per seat-mile of 20 cents. Costs are the same regardless of whether a seat is occupied or not. There is, however, a cost of $5.00 per passenger for each airport at which a passenger lands.

It is important to recognize that the costs listed above are quite incomplete; they are intended to represent operating costs of an airline company only. They do not include fixed facilities costs, the costs of owning aircraft, or costs of travel borne by the passenger. How to account for these other elements of transportation costs is the subject of Part III of this text.

An airline that chooses to serve each city pair with direct flights will find that the least cost type of aircraft will depend on the number of passengers on a route. Column 4 of Table 5.1 shows calculations of the minimum cost type of aircraft that should be used on each route. Direct flights between A and E would be made with large airplanes, while those between B and G can be satisfied with a single daily flight of a small aircraft. As shown in Table 5.1, if all flights were direct, there would be a total of 29 flights per day in each direction at a cost per passenger-mile of 18.7 cents. Of the 29 flights, 8 would be made with large planes and 21 with small planes. Load factor (the percentage of all sets that are occupied) would be 69.3 percent. The combination of excessive use of small aircraft (with high costs per seat-mile) and poor load factors make direct flights an expensive way to satisfy demands.

All modes of transportation use the principle of shared facilities to lower the costs of service. Facilities sharing is the main source of difficulties in analyzing transportation costs. In our example, the way that the airline could

TABLE 5.1   Comparing the Costs of Direct and Network Services

City pair (1)	Passengers per Day (2)	Non-Stop Service			Hub and Spoke Service		
		Direct Miles (3)	Minimum Cost Equipment (4)	Cost of Service (5)	Miles Through Hub (6)	Minimum Cost Equipment (7)	Number of Stops (8)
From City A							
to City E	173	728	2 large	$22,705	900	3 large	2
to City F	80	707	1 large	$11,007	800	3 large	1
to City G	56	700	3 small	$ 8,680	900	1 large	2
to City H	141	806	1 large	$12,798	900	3 large	2
From City B							
to City E	55	707	3 small	$ 8,760	800	3 large	1
to City F	24	700	2 small	$ 5,720	700	8 large	0
to City G	16	707	1 small	$ 2,908	800	1 large	1
to City H	43	800	3 small	$ 9,815	800	3 large	1
From City C							
to City E	142	806	1 large	$12,803	900	3 large	2
to City F	63	800	1 large	$12,315	800	3 large	1
to City G	43	806	3 small	$ 9,890	900	1 large	2
to City H	114	900	1 large	$14,070	900	3 large	2
From City D							
to City E	67	700	1 large	$10,835	900	2 large	2
to City F	28	707	2 small	$ 5,797	800	2 large	1
to City G	18	728	1 small	$ 3,002	900	1 large	2
to City H	50	806	3 small	$ 9,925	900	2 large	1

Total One-Way Passengers: 1,113	Non-Stop Service	Hub-and-Spoke Service
Total Connections	29	42
Total System Cost	$161,030	$121,530
Total Seat-Miles	1,240,497	1,065,000
Total Passenger-Miles	859,063	968,400
Cost/Passenger-Mile	$.187	$.126
Load Factor	.693	.897

Source: Results of a simulation. Cities shown in Figure 5.3 were assigned populations at random between 0 and 999999. Demands were generated as 1/5000 of the product of the populations divided by the square of the straight-line distance between them. Two types of aircraft are assumed: a 20-seat plane with costs equal to 20 cents per passenger-mile and a 150-seat plane with costs equal to 10 cents per passenger-mile. The simulation also assumes a $5.00 per passenger cost for every airport at which a passenger lands. For direct service, the cost of providing all service by large planes or by small planes was calculated as the minimum number of craft necessary to serve the demand multiplied by $15 per mile for large planes and $4 per mile for small planes plus airport costs; the number and type of planes for the least cost service is shown in column 5 and the cost of providing the lesser cost service is shown in column 6. For service through hubs, the simulation assumes that all flights travel through hubs at B and F. The number and type of craft that minimizes total cost for given demand is shown in column 7. The number of connections is the sum of columns 4 and 8 respectively. Load factor is the total number of passenger-miles divided by the total seat miles.

share facilities is to operate with a hub-and-spoke system rather than direct flights. In our example, airports at B and F are chosen to be hub airports. Under a hub-and-spoke system, all passengers between city A and cities E, F, G, and H can be consolidated on the same aircraft which would be routed to city B. There, traffic from B, C, and D could be consolidated on the same flights to F. At F, traffic would be broken down again and passengers routed to their destinations. Traffic consolidation still takes place even in the distribution phase of transport, however, since the flight to each destination carries passengers from all of the origins.

Traffic consolidation justifies the use of larger aircraft. Column 7 in Table 5.1 shows that a traffic system that operated as a hub-and-spoke system would use large airplanes exclusively. All of A's transportation needs could be satisfied with three daily flights to hub B; C would also have three flights, while D would see two flights. There would be eight flights daily between B and F and six flights distributing passengers beyond hub F. The average cost of serving a passenger in this system is 12.6 cents per passenger-mile—far less than the 18.7 cents per passenger-mile cost of serving demands through direct flights. The total cost of providing service in the entire hub-and-spoke system is $121,530, which is $39,500 less than the $161,030 daily cost of providing service in each direction using direct flights.

The cost saving of producing transport services in a network rather than a system of direct service derives from two sources: serving passengers with large aircraft (which are less expensive per seat-mile) rather than smaller ones and increasing the number of seats that are filled on each flight. In this example, serving demands through a hub-and-spoke system increases the systemwide load factor from 69 percent to more than 89 percent.

The comparison of serving transportation markets with direct rather than hub-and-spoke system shows why most transport systems are provided within networks rather than as companies serving individual city-pair markets. Networks allow customers from different markets to be consolidated in the same vehicles, justifying larger vehicles that are cheaper (per passenger) to operate and providing higher load factors within each of the vehicles. Counteracting these benefits, however, are two others. In our example, they are higher hub costs and longer mileages. By moving from a service based on direct flights to a hub-and-spoke system, the total number of passenger-miles increased from 859,063 to 968,400—a 12 percent increase in mileage. Also, since passengers making connections increased their use of airports, hub costs increased by $5.00 per passenger connection. With traffic levels listed in Table 5.1, the advantages of consolidating traffic outweighs the cost of longer distances and higher passenger terminal costs. As is shown below, however, it need not be the case that hub-and-spoke systems are cheaper to operate than direct flights.[5]

Cost per passenger-mile calculations from Table 5.1 can be used to develop cost curves for transportation. Transportation economists would like to produce cost descriptions that parallel those in other industries—for example, being able to draw a cost diagram like Figure 5.1 for some service would make it easier to describe its costs. But transportation companies almost always operate within a network, consolidating a variety of different types of traffic within the same facilities. There is no unique output measure (and therefore, no unique cost per unit of output) when an enterprise produces multiple services. The natural solution, the same one as was used in Chapter 2, is to define output as an index—passenger-miles or ton-miles.

As we saw in Chapter 2, using a traffic index as a measure of output causes a number of ambiguities for economic analysis. The source of the problem is that how costs respond to an increase in passenger-miles is sensitive to exactly where the increase in passenger-miles came from. One possible way that passenger-miles could increase in our example is changing all traffic flows by a common percentage. For example, doubling the passenger demands would increase the number of flights in a hub-and-spoke system from 22 to 41. Since the service is entirely by large aircraft both before as well as after the doubling of traffic, the only cost consequences derive from a change in the capacity utilization which allows a doubling of traffic without doubling flight equipment. The cost per passenger-mile drops from 12.6 cents to 11.8 cents. The decrease in cost per passenger-mile as all demands increase in the same proportion has been called an *economy of density*. Economies of density can also be described as economies of hubbing, economies of networking, or economies of traffic consolidation. Such economies are based in the fact that when traffic increases in a network, not all pieces of the network—vehicles or fixed facilities—need be increased proportionately.

It is not always cheaper to serve customers through hubs rather than direct flights. For example, if the number of passengers in Table 5.1 is multiplied by a factor of 10, it would be cheaper to serve each location by direct flights rather than by hubbing. While network operations would have higher load factors (as they always will), traffic is sufficiently high that each route can support large aircraft on direct flights. The saving of passenger-terminal costs and shorter mileages more than make up for the lower load factors of direct flights. The total system cost of the hub-and-spoke system is higher than the total system cost for direct service, despite the fact that the cost per passenger-mile is the same in both cases. In this case, the fact that hub-and-spoke systems cause an increase in the number of passenger-miles makes the comparison of direct versus network service by measuring cost per passenger-mile misleading; the hub-and-spoke system has higher load factors and saves on airport costs, but the increased mileage that passengers travel outweighs those advantages. Whether individual transportation demands are more cheaply met by direct service or service using shared facilities depends on the tradeoff between high facility usage with low costs per unit against the costs of consolidating traffic and increased mileages.

FIGURE 5.4   Cost per Passenger-Mile for Proportional Increases in Traffic

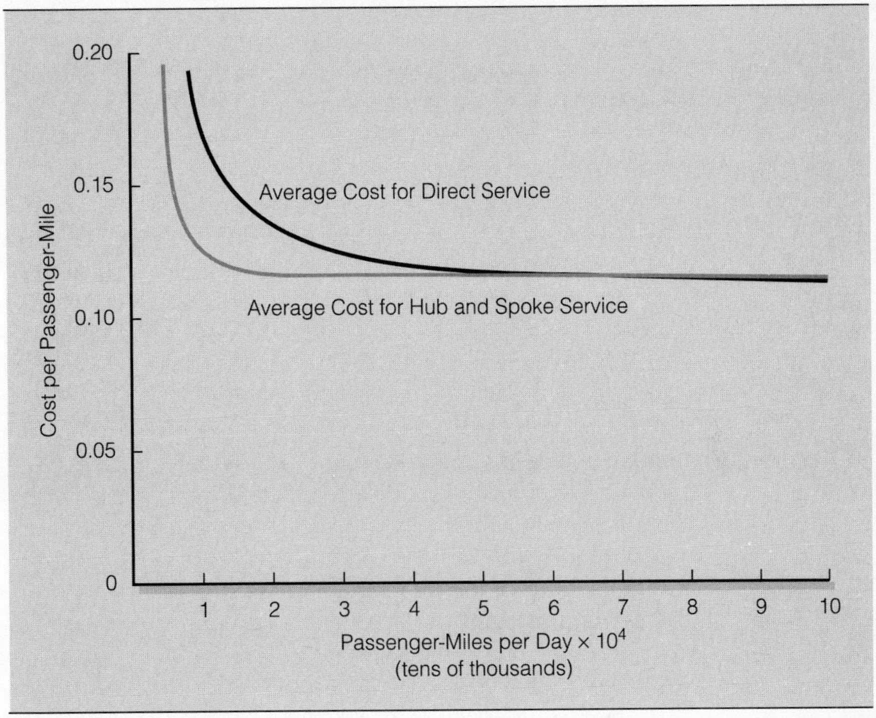

SOURCE: Based on calculations described in Table 5.1 and multiples of traffic in that table. The declining shape of each curve reflects economies of density in the network, regardless of whether service is provided with direct flights or with hub-and-spoke service. Except at very large traffic levels, it will be less expensive to provide service using hub-and-spoke operations.

Passenger-miles and cost per passenger-mile for direct and for hub-and-spoke service drawn from Table 5.1 and multiples of traffic in that table are graphed in Figure 5.4. Curves for both direct and hub-and-spoke service are downward sloping, indicating economies of density for both kinds of service. The hub-and-spoke systems' density economies are especially pronounced at small levels of traffic.

While our example has been based on airline service, it can be used to understand network economies in other modes of transportation. In all cases, network economies exist only when consolidating traffic allows a saving on per-unit facilities costs. Railroad economies arise because consolidating traffic allows running longer trains with a smaller crew per freight car; and consolidating traffic between different locations on the same line permits saving on track costs. Less-than-truckload carriers have network scale economies because they consolidate small shipments while truckload carriers are less likely to have network economies because they do not do any traffic consolidation. But for each mode of transportation, network economies may not be inexhaustible. In each case, it is an empirical question whether economies exist. Some estimates are provided in Chapter 8.

The Cost of Expanding a Network

The concept of economies of density is not meaningful in industries other than those with network technology. Density economies are not true scale economies since scale economies are based on increasing all inputs to accommodate an increase in output, and some of the resources used are described by the size and nature of the network. Measuring scale economies in network services requires that the size of the network be altered when output is altered. Unfortunately, there is no good measure of the size of a network. One could count service mileage or stations as a measure of network size, but since each network is geographically unique, when it is expanded, the cost consequences will be different depending on where the new link goes. Cities differ considerably in size and in production specialization in addition to geographic position.

For example, consider two possible ways for expanding the network described in the previous example. Figure 5.5 shows two new cities, J and K. City J is close and to the right of the right-hand cluster of cities in Figure 5.3, while city K is farther away and to the left of the same cluster of cities. Both cities are medium sized, with a population of 500,000. Obviously, city J would be better served by the existing hub-and-spoke system than would city K, since residents of city K would have to travel in the wrong direction to reach the initial hub. Simulations using the method described in Table 5.1 confirm that city J is a good match for the existing network. If city J tried to service itself outside of the network using direct service, it would cost $33,539 per day (the sum of all the costs of all direct services from J). But including city J in the network increases the total network cost from $121,530 to $141,877 per day, for a difference of $20,347. Including the new city in the network reduces the average cost per passenger-mile from 12.6 cents to 12.4 cents. The same forces of improved equipment utilization through consolidating different kinds of traffic will pull city J into the network since the airline operating the network will be able to easily underbid an operator outside the network.

City K is a different case however. Simulations show that an operator that decided to serve city K with direct flights, bypassing the network, would incur costs of $40,475. If the network operator tried to serve K through hub B, total system costs would increase from $121,530 to $175,412, or $53,882. It would be cheaper to serve K outside the network than within it. In this case, there are no network economies since city K is not geographically suited to be served by the network. However, if city K were very small—for example, 50,000 people— the calculation would be different. There would then be so few passengers that

FIGURE 5.5   A Map of a Hypothetical Airline System with Possible Service Extensions

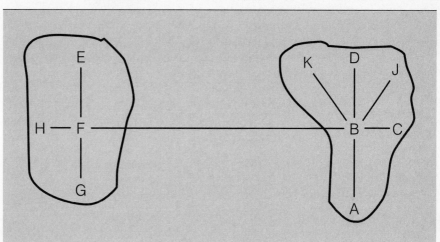

See Figure 5.3 for position of original cities. City J is 100 miles east of city D and 100 miles north of city C. City K is 200 miles west of city D. Lines show system connections with a hub-and-spoke system.

it would be efficient to join the network despite the fact that the city is not in an ideal location. The cost of direct service, $9,242, is far greater than the $5,459 increase in network costs due to the inclusion of city K. Whether there are economies due to increasing the size of the network clearly depends on the nature of the network addition: It is inherent in the economic geography of the service region and not necessarily in the mathematics of networks.

Despite the logical difficulties in defining scale economies within service networks, economists have tried to measure the effect of simultaneously increasing traffic flows and either network mileage or service points; some authors have referred to a decline in the cost per passenger-mile or per ton-mile as the network expands and traffic expands by the same proportion as an *economy of size*. Others have referred to it as an *economy of scale*. In our simulation, whether a researcher would find economies of scale would depend on which city, J or K, was added to the network.

The cost of adding a new service is generally referred to as the *incremental cost* of the service. Incremental cost divided by passenger counts is the *average incremental cost* of a service. One way of identifying whether there are scale economies in a particular network is to compare average incremental cost with the average cost of serving all passengers. If average incremental cost is less than average total cost, there are scale economies in the network.

Marginal and Average Costs in a Network

While there are limitless ways to bring about a change in ton-miles or passenger-miles in a network, researchers have devoted their attention to studying only three of them. Two of the three have already been discussed: increasing the size of the network (measured in mileage or service points) and increasing the density of the network (increasing all traffic proportionally). The third common focus of cost studies is the effect of increasing one flow only, holding all other flows constant. For example, in the original network of Figure 5.3, we could calculate the consequences of doubling the traffic from A to H, holding all other traffic constant. The effect of this would be to increase the number of flights by one, increase passenger-miles in the network from 968,400 to 1,095,300, and increase the total system cost from $121,530 to $137,145. The increase in system cost of increasing one flow divided by the increase in passenger-miles can be thought of as the marginal cost of serving passengers on that route. In this case, the marginal cost of serving passengers between A and E is 12.3 cents per passenger-mile. This cost is less than the average cost of serving all passengers in the system of 12.6 cents per passenger-mile.

It is not just traffic between A and E for which the marginal cost will be below the average systemwide cost. The same will be true of all traffic flows in Figure 5.3. That is, for every type of traffic, marginal cost is below average network costs. The reason is found in the network economies of traffic consolidation, load factors, and economies of large sizes of equipment. The fact that marginal cost is less than average cost is sometimes taken as an indication of scale economies or that service networks are natural monopolies. The example here shows that the effect of these economies extends to traffic levels beyond 1,000 passengers per day, despite the fact that the factor driving the calculation (the lower cost on the larger aircraft compared with the smaller one) is exhausted at 150 customers. This is due to the sharing of lumpy facilities by many markets and the increase in average load factors available in a larger network. However, as noted above, network economies can be exhausted and at high traffic levels, network bypass becomes economically justified. While large networks clearly have advantages over direct service at small traffic levels, it is not clear that these advantages continue to be present for large scales of operations—this is a question that must be answered with empirical investigations. Some studies on this point will be described in the next three chapters.

Cost Traceability

The average incremental cost of offering transportation to a group of customers—for example, passengers between points A and H—has been calculated in the previous section as the change in operating costs incurred by the transportation group if a new service is offered (or old one dropped) divided by the passenger-miles using the service. Incremental cost differs from marginal cost in that the former refers to the per-passenger cost of adding a new service, while the latter refers to the cost per passenger-mile of increasing output without changing the services offered in the network.

Let us now consider the case of one more passenger being carried in the system. For example, imagine taking the traffic pattern described in Table 5.1 and increasing traffic on AH by only one passenger. Since the flights from A to H were not fully booked, there is no increase in flights necessary to accommodate only one extra passenger. The only cost to the network of increasing traffic by this one passenger is $15.00 worth of airport costs, which divided by the 900 miles traveled in the network, yields a marginal cost of adding one passenger-mile on AH of 1.7 cents, far below the 12.6 cent average cost per passenger-mile in the system.

Whenever marginal cost is less than average cost, there is a problem of *cost traceability* in the system. By this is we mean that the sum of costs that an individual user imposes on the transport company—his or her marginal cost, as calculated above—will not equal the total costs of the operation. There appear to be some phantom costs paid by the airline to its flight crew, ground personnel, and fuel suppliers that cannot be traced to the decision to fly of any of its customers. The same relationship sometimes appears in the transportation literature under several other names; for example, problems of roadway costing or adding-up problems. In all of these cases, if individual users are only responsible for the costs that they cause the network, it appears as if there are some costs for which no one is responsible. In the case of service networks, the whole of the cost is likely to be greater than the sum of the parts. In the example presented, total cost will be greater than either the sum of marginal costs that users impose on carriers or the sum of incremental costs of services used by customers.

Non-traceability of costs occurs whenever the average cost of service declines as the amount of service increases. It can arise from improvements in load factor and equipment size when output in a network expands, as in the simulation in this chapter. It can also arise from the lumpiness of fixed facilities described previously in this chapter; the need to make roadways of a minimum strength or the need to make railroad tracks of standard width, will each cause total costs to rise less rapidly than output, at least for low traffic levels.

Transport economics is dominated by problems of cost traceability. The standard techniques for dealing with the problem are outlined in Chapters 9–11.

Economies of Scope

Another source of difficulties in assigning cost responsibilities comes from the prevalence of back-hauls in some modes. Consider, for example, the Black Mesa and Lake Powell Railroad. If asked to determine how much it costs to move a ton of coal from the mine mouth to the power plant, one would be tempted to measure the cost of hauling coal by considering only the fuel and labor costs of carrying a loaded car from the mine to the power plant—this, after all, was the form in which the question was asked. But this would be inaccurate, since every loaded car must be returned empty to the coal mine before it is ready to carry another load. The loaded run and the back-haul of the train comprise a logical cost unit since production of one requires production of the other. Two goods or services which are inevitably produced in fixed proportion are called *joint products* and the cost of producing a joint product is called a *joint cost*. There are techniques for efficiently pricing the two halves of a joint product, as we shall see in Chapter 10, but as an element of strict cost finding, it is illogical to assign the cost of making a vehicle round trip to one direction or another.

The concept of joint costs has other uses in transportation economics in addition to describing the costs of back-hauling equipment. For example, the fact that one additional passenger from A to H had a marginal cost of 1.7 cents per passenger-mile could be traced to a form of joint costs. When one seat-trip is produced in the large aircraft considered above, inevitably 149 other seat-trips must be produced simultaneously. Since they are produced in fixed proportion they are a joint product. There will be a well defined cost of producing the joint product—all 150 seat-trips—but it is impossible to identify the cost of a single seat-trip. As shown in the simulation, the influence of the joint cost of aircraft operation is to produce an uneven, but generally downward sloping relationship between passenger-miles and average cost per passenger-mile.

Even fixed facilities can be interpreted in some cases as subject to joint costs. Consider, for example, the case of uncongested road capacity. The capacity is available 24 hours per day. One could think of road capacity during each hour as being a 24-part joint product. It is illogical to ask what the cost of building a road for use between 3:00 and 4:00 p.m., since this service is not provided unless the service is also provided during the other 23 hours of a day. Roadway costs are thus joint between inbound commuters, outbound commuters, shoppers, trucks, cars, and motorcycles. Only when the roadway becomes congested does the provision of road capacity cease to be a joint product.

It is tempting to apply the logic of joint products to the cost of hauling each car on a 50-car train, but this is not the same situation. The reason is that trains can be of different lengths. It is not technologically necessary that trains be exactly 50 cars in length. It is, then, not necessary that 49 other car-trips be generated every time one car-trip is made. Since the proportion between different types of car-trips can be varied, we say that the cost of hauling a train is a *common cost* to each of the cars in the train. While the presence of common costs causes the same sort of practical difficulties in assigning cost responsibility to individual users, the economics of common costs is fundamentally different from that of joint costs. In the case of common costs it is possible to identify the additional cost—however small—of hauling each car in the train; in the case of joint costs, it is logically impossible to identify the cost of producing one particular part of the joint product.

An umbrella term used to describe a variety of conditions that occur frequently in transportation economics is to say that transport is subject to economies of scope. This term, recently developed by Baumol et al., describes situations in which it is less costly to produce two services, or groups of services, within the same enterprise rather than in different firms.[6] *Economies of scope* covers a wide variety of situations from hubbing economies to joint costs and common costs.

MEASURING OPPORTUNITY COSTS

The prevalence of multi-product producers, the importance of scale economies, sunk costs, joint and common costs, and the dual types of capital—fixed facilities and vehicles—make transportation cost measurement especially interesting and challenging. Under these conditions, the standard methods used by accountants to identify the costs of a product or service are particularly unreliable.

Accounting Cost

Accounting costs are related to expenditures made for inputs used to produce a good or service. As an example, consider the procedure used by Department of Transportation (DOT) accountants to identify the cost of transportation services. The DOT allocates as many expenditures as possible to individual railroad or trucking services. These expenses are called *out-of-pocket costs*. The remaining expenses of a transportation company that cannot be allocated to particular services are grouped together as an overhead and then divided among all the services that a railroad or trucking company produces to create a *fully distributed cost* of a service.[7]

Out-of-pocket costs are sometimes seen as direct or allocable costs and are sometimes thought of as equivalent to marginal costs. This is misleading, however. Out-of-pocket costs make no allowance for congestion costs, for example; the cost measure is not intended to track the rise or fall of costs as the scale of a service increases or decreases. At best it should be seen as average variable cost at the current level of operations. Even this, however, is misleading since it does not evaluate inputs at their opportunity costs and ignores the complications of sunk, joint, and common costs.

Fully distributed costs, since they contain an allowance for overhead expenses, are sometimes taken to be equivalent to average total costs of a service. This analogy is even more unsatisfactory than the equation of out-of-pocket costs with marginal cost. One reason is that the total costs of a transportation company may not bear much resemblance to the total expenses. This is due to the presence of sunk costs or payments for the use of inputs that do not match their opportunity costs. A second reason is that any particular service is likely to use only a small fraction of all of the inputs of a transportation company. For example, a container shipped from Long Beach to Chicago will traverse a small fraction of the railroad company's tracks. To put all track costs of the company into a group and then allocate them arbitrarily to all traffic does not correspond with the concept of a fixed cost of producing a particular service. Any transportation company produces a variety of transportation services. The opportunity cost of producing those services is the value of the resources saved if those services were not produced. Fully-distributed costs do not approximate this concept.[8]

▬ Econometric Costing

Perhaps because of a general dissatisfaction with the ability of accounting costs to match opportunity cost in transportation, railroads were among the first industries whose costs were studied with econometric methods. Statistical methods were used as early as the 1920s to show that railroad costs were more variable with the level of output than were previously thought. Railroad costs are still being used as a testing ground for new econometric techniques.[9]

Econometric costing techniques use as data the total expenditure for some class of traffic and then try to explain the expenditure by correlating it with the price of inputs and mix of traffic outputs. The technique of econometric costing entails the same curve-fitting that was described in Chapter 3. In the simplest case, an econometric costing exercise might use this sort of estimating form:

$$C_i = \alpha + \beta Q_i + \sigma W_i + \tau F_i + e_i \tag{5.1}$$

where:

C_i = Total expenditure on some class of traffic at point i
Q_i = Amount of traffic within some class at point i
W_i = Wage paid to labor at point i
F_i = Price of fuel at point i
ε_i = Influences unexplainable by other factors at point i.

If there is a record either over time or in different places of similar traffic being subjected to different levels of traffic, wages, and prices of fuel, the researcher can determine an independent effect on costs of an increase in traffic, removing the influence of prices of variable inputs. The way that this is done was described in Chapter 3: Equation 5.1 can be thought of as a plane in four dimensions and β as the slope of that plane in the Q dimension. The value of the coefficient β shows how much costs would rise if output were to increase by one unit. It thus is a measure of marginal cost.

It is probably not a very accurate measure of marginal cost, however. Since β is constant for all levels of Q, the estimating form 5.1 assumes that the marginal cost curve is simply a horizontal straight line at a height given by the value of β. But the reasoning in the previous section tells us that beyond some point, opportunity costs of traffic will rise. In order to allow for the likely shape of cost curves, the estimating form will have to be modified. The standard modification is to estimate a cost curve that is derived from the relationship between costs and productivity.[10]

The main problem that econometric cost estimates have had to deal with is that the estimating forms are developed for disaggregate data while all econometric estimations of transportation costs to date have been applied to aggregate data—for example, estimating the costs of railroad operations as a whole. These extremely aggregate estimations are useful for deciding whether a mode of transportation is subject to increasing returns to scale, but are not useful for a variety of more interesting cost calculations. For example, the data requirements of econometric investigations have not yet permitted the calculation of transport costs at a level that would be useful for assisting railroad companies to judge the relative profitability of different kinds of traffic. For this purpose, accounting costs are still used, with modifications, despite the limitations on the usefulness of the costs discussed previously. Chapter 8 describes the results of a variety of econometric cost estimates.

CONCLUSION

Economic costs are opportunity costs. The opportunity cost of providing a transportation service is measured by the dollar value of forgone alternatives. One place where opportunity costs differ from expenditures is in sunk costs. Payments made to dig a canal are sunk since the cost cannot be recovered in the future if it is decided that the canal was a mistake in the first place. If costs are sunk, there is no opportunity cost to using the facility other than expenditures to maintain and operate it. Another place where opportunity cost differs from expenditures is where assets have appreciated in value since first put in service. For example, the airline fleet is today more valuable than the sum of total expenditures paid to aircraft builders. The opportunity cost of using an airliner depends on its current value, not on its original cost.

Transportation economics divides costs into three groups: the cost of owning fixed facilities, the costs of owning vehicles, and operating costs. Fixed facilities costs are generally sunk and are made to serve narrow parts of the total transport market. For example, a road built on the northside of Denver is much more likely to be used by northside residents than those on the south side of the city. In most transport systems, some fixed facilities will be idle at the same time that other fixed facilities are congested. Vehicle investments, by contrast, affect all vehicle users in the system. Since vehicles can be moved around to places where they are most needed, the value of the vehicle stock will rise and fall with systemwide demands. Direct operating costs are, at a minimum, fuel and labor time. However, indirect costs—track maintenance or airline reservation departments, for example—can be larger than direct operating costs.

Extremely simple transportation systems can be described using classic economic cost curves. Since transport systems provide multiple services to many different types of users, standard cost curves need to be adapted to transportation. Transport systems generally serve multiple markets due to economies of density in a network. Density economies arise from the savings of consolidating different types of traffic going in the same general direction. Since there are economies per seat-mile in the size of aircraft, or lower costs per barrel-mile as the diameter of pipelines rises, or a minimum capacity of railroad track, there will generally be some economies of traffic consolidation and so a transportation company will wish to use its equipment to serve multiple types of users.

Cost curves cannot be easily described in transportation networks. Each network is geographically unique and therefore will have different costs. To make cost analysis tractable, transport economists investigate an aggregate cost relationship between the ton-miles (or passenger-miles) and cost per ton-mile (or passenger-mile) in a transport system. This relationship should be seen as an average cost of serving a transport system; the costs of serving individual users may vary greatly from averages computed in this way.

Economies of traffic density is defined as a declining cost per ton-mile (or passenger-mile) as all types of traffic in a network increase proportionally. Economies of traffic density arise from economies of shared facilities. A transport network with higher traffic levels can use larger vehicles and expect to have a higher load factor, both of which will lead to lower costs. At very high traffic levels, however, economies of density may be exhausted or even reversed so that operating outside a network becomes a less expensive means of operations.

The same factors that generate economies of density may also produce economies of network size. However, the geographic positioning of potential new parts of network must be compatible with the existing network for there to be economies in expansion. Scale economies in networks occur when a proportional expansion in traffic levels and network size lead to a lower cost per ton- or passenger-mile.

On average, incremental and marginal costs in transportation networks decline as service levels rise. Usually, they are less than average cost for the network as a whole. This leads to the problem that costs are non-traceable. When costs are non-traceable, airlines or trucking companies must charge more than marginal cost to recoup the expenses of operating their networks.

The inability to theoretically identify who is responsible for which costs in transportation networks is compounded in practical application of cost analysis by the inability of expenditure accounts to reflect opportunity costs. Econometric costing can sometimes be used to help increase cost traceability, but it often suffers from overly aggregate data.

NOTES

1. The term *shadow price* comes from linear programming, where it represents the increase in the value of the objective that could be achieved by a 1-unit relaxation of the constraint. The concept has been adopted by planners to refer to adjustments to market values necessitated by non-market constraints. Shadow prices are extensively used in cost-benefit analysis of transport projects in developing countries.
2. Economies of scale are said to exist when:
$$f(\lambda Q) > \lambda \bullet f(Q)$$
Where Q is a vector of inputs, $f(Q)$ is a production function and is an arbitrary positive constant. In words, this says that scale economies exist when increasing all inputs by 1 percent increases output by more than 1 percent.
3. In formal terms, a cost function is defined as:
$$C(Q) = \Sigma w_i x_i$$
where x_i is the cost minimizing level of input i and w_i is the respective per-unit opportunity cost. According to duality theory, x_i is determined solely by the production function and input prices. Input prices are generally assumed to be exogenous to the firm.
4. Kent Healy, *The Effects of Scale in the Railroad Industry* (New Haven: Yale University Press, 1961).
5. The choice of direct flights versus hub-and-spoke systems may have broader effects than those noted in this chapter. See, for example, Fujii, Edwin, Eric Im, James Mak, "The Economics of Direct Flights," *Journal of Transport Economics and Policy*, Vol. 26, No. 2, May 1992, pages 185–95.
6. See Baumol, William J., John C. Panzar, and Robert D. Willig, *Contestable Markets and the Theory of Industry Structure* (New York: Harcourt Brace Jovanovich, 1982).
7. A good description of methods for computing carrier costs is found in Talley, Wayne K., *Transport Carrier Costing*, Transportation Studies series, Vol. 9, (New York; London; Tokyo and Camberwell, Australia: Gordon and Breach Science, 1988.)
8. See Ronald R. Braeutigam, "An Analysis of Fully Distributed Cost Pricing in Regulated Industries," *Bell Journal of Economics*, 03, 1980, pp. 182–196.
9. Classics are Borts, George H., "The Estimation of Rail Cost Functions" *Econometrica* 01, 1960, pp. 103–131 and Griliches, Zvi, "Cost Allocation in Railroad Regulation," Bell Journal of Economics, 03, 1972, pp. 26–41.

10. An estimating form for cost functions that is very flexible but consistent with standard theoretical expectations about the shape of production functions is the translog, generally estimated in this form:

$$lnC = a_0 + a_1 \bullet (lnQ) + a_2 \bullet (lnQ)^2 + a_3 \bullet lnW + a_4 \bullet (lnW)^2 + a_5 \bullet lnF + a_6 \bullet (lnF)^2$$
$$+ a_7 \bullet (lnQ) \bullet (lnW) + a_8 \bullet (ln\,Q) \bullet (ln\,F) + a_9 \bullet (ln\,F) \bullet (ln\,W)$$

where C, Q, W, and F are as described in Equation 5.1 and ln refers to the natural logarithm of the expression. The estimating form is, in principle, capable of dealing with multiple types of transportation service simply by adding more terms on the right-hand side of the equation. However, increasing the number of terms on the right-hand side of the equation increases the number of terms required for estimation exponentially. The flexibility of the translog cost function is offset by the complexity of the estimating form. The complexity of the form makes it *data hungry*, that is, it requires considerable numbers of observations to estimate the parameters of a translog cost function. This makes it impractical to use in many of the situations where it would be most useful.

6

The Costs of Fixed Facilities

Fixed facilities is the name given to the immobile part of transportation facilities. There are two important consequences of the inability to take up and move roads, canals, and airports. First, fixed facilities are dedicated to particular geographic markets. Investing in fixed facilities does not increase capacity uniformly in the transport system as a whole but in only a part of it. Second, investments in fixed facilities are sunk. The combination of sunkness and dedication of capacity to a limited set of markets means that investment and pricing decisions made about fixed facilities tend to be quite different from those made about vehicles.

This chapter will focus on the differences among transport modes in the importance of fixed facilities costs as a proportion of their total costs. Modes also differ in the extent to which they are expanding or contracting. As will be emphasized in Part III of this book, if a mode is expanding, additional tools are available to apportion financial costs among individual users.

HIGHWAYS

There are few places in developed countries that are not accessible by road. Adding together every interstate highway, mountain road, and city street, the United States has approximately

3.9 million miles of roads. New road mileage is being added at the rate of approximately 0.1 percent annually. Most of this mileage is in local roads that are used for access rather than intercity transportation. Intercity transport generally uses the system of federal aid highways. Figure 6.1 shows the locations of these roads. The roads form a tight web, with each population center connected with every other with a nearly direct route.

Highway quality is more variable than is the quality of fixed facilities of other modes of transportation. While all roads can be used by automobiles, only the strongest highways are designed and built to be used by heavy trucks. In the future, roadways may become more diverse as electronic controls are embedded in some of them. Electronics are currently being developed to take over guidance from drivers, to give information to drivers on their current position, and to help drivers avoid accidents.[1] When these electronics become available, they will not be available on all roads. Regardless of the character of the roadway, however, the economic principles of roadway costing are the same.

Highway Expenditures

Local highways are administered by municipal, county, and township governments. Intercity roads are administered by state governments.[2] While the federal government provides some assistance, actual highway expenditure is made by state and local governments. Highways rank third in state and local budgets; only education and public welfare get a larger share of funds.

Table 6.1 shows categories of expenditures on highways made by all levels of government. Of the more than $90 billion spent in 1995, approximately half went for the capital expenditures of right-of-way purchase and engineering, new construction, reconstruction, major widening, resurfacing, restoration, rehabilitation, and bridge work. Of capital expenditures, approximately two-thirds went to state-controlled (i.e., major) highways and about a third went for improvements or construction of local roads. The other half of government expenditures on roads are principally maintenance (24 percent), policing (8 percent), and administration (8 percent). While most construction funds are spent on new intercity highways, most maintenance expenses go to local roads.

It is useful to compare the size of expenditures on fixed facilities in road transportation with other costs of highway modes. The amount spent on roads each year is less than the amount spent on gasoline and oil and is less than half of the amount spent on new and used cars. The amount spent is one-third of the costs paid by shippers for truck transportation. It is about 10 percent of the amount spent on all aspects of highway transport.

Expenditures are not the same as economic costs, as discussed in Chapter 5. An economic cost is the value of the resources used in production of highway services were they to be used in their next best alternative use. Chapter 5 explained how to operationalize the concept of opportunity cost: Start with expenditures and then ask whether there is reason to believe that expenditures diverge from alternate values. There are two situations under which this might

TABLE 6.1   U.S. Expenditures on Highways, 1995

	Capital Outlay (In Billions of Dollars)
State administered highways	30.550
Locally administered roads	12.115
Unclassified roads	.432
Total Capital Outlay:	43.097
	Maintenance
State administered highways	10.359
Locally administered roads	14.052
Unclassified roads	.071
Total Maintenance:	24.455
Administrative and miscellaneous	8.332
Highway police and safety	7.977
Bond interest	3.982
Total direct expenditure	87.843
Bond retirements	4.661
Total Disbursements:	**92.504**

SOURCE: Highway Statistics, 1995, Table HF-10

occur. One is that the amount paid for resources used in the provision of high-ways is different from that amount that would be paid for those resources in their next best alternative use. This is not usually considered to cause problems for transport analysis: As long as the governments pay a fair market value for the land used to make highways, buy materials and machines in free markets, and pay workers what is necessary to induce them to work on the highways, expenditure and opportunity costs are likely to be about the same.

The second situation when there is a divergence between expenditure and cost is a greater problem: Roads which are already in place occupy land and thus there is an opportunity cost to the existence of roads; but governments, since they own the land, do not charge themselves to use the land. Thus road costs may be understated. Since roads and parking lots cover as much as 30 percent of many cities, the opportunity cost of land tied up in highway transportation may be substantial. On the other side, however, construction costs return bene-fits over many years, yet are often charged in the year in which they are made. This tends to overstate the annual cost of roadway ownership. In addition, much of roadway costs are sunk, and any allowance for sunk costs will overstate opportunity costs. Without any clear guidance on whether highway expenditures overstate or understate opportunity costs, we will take $90 billion as a reason-able approximation of the annual costs of roadway ownership.

FIGURE 6.1   Major Transportation Facilities of the United States

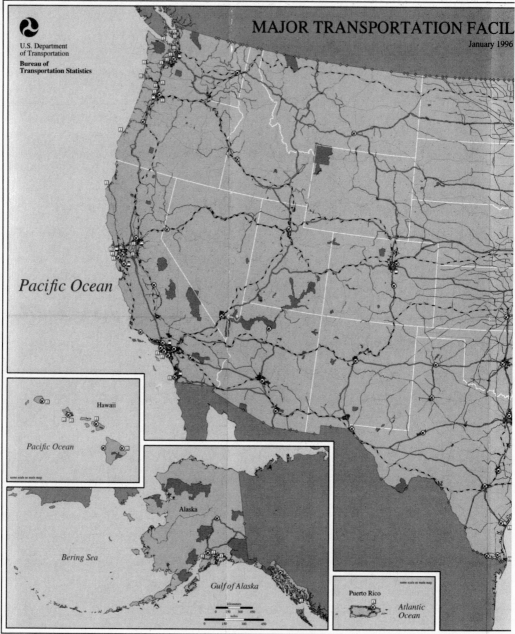

SOURCE: Courtesy of Metro-North Railroad and Parsons Brinckerhoff Quade and Douglas, Inc.

FIGURE 6.1   Continued

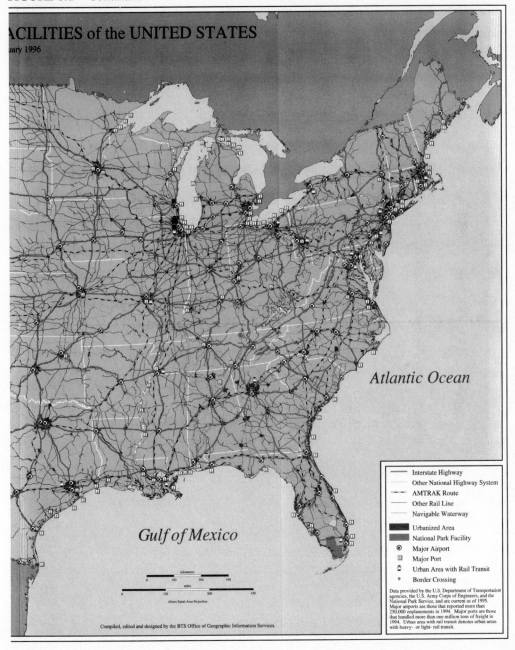

ACILITIES of the UNITED STATES
uary 1996

Atlantic Ocean

Gulf of Mexico

	Interstate Highway
	Other National Highway System
	AMTRAK Route
	Other Rail Line
	Navigable Waterway
	Urbanized Area
	National Park Facility
⊗	Major Airport
	Major Port
	Urban Area with Rail Transit
◆	Border Crossing

Data provided by the U.S. Department of Transportation
agencies, the U.S. Army Corps of Engineers, and the
National Park Service, and are current as of 1995.
Major airports are those that reported more than
250,000 enplanements in 1994. Major ports are those
that handled more than one million tons of freight in
1994. Urban area with rail transit denotes urban areas
with heavy- or light- rail transit.

Compiled, edited and designed by the BTS Office of Geographic Information Services.

The Effect of Traffic Level and Mix on Highway Construction Costs

Three major costs of highway ownership—capital, maintenance, and policing—will vary with traffic levels and mix. Exactly how these costs vary has been the subject of repeated studies.[3]

If traffic levels on a new stretch of highway are expected to be light and to consist solely of passenger cars, a highway can be engineered differently than if it must carry heavy trucks. The American Association of State Highway and Transportation Officials (AASHTO) has made some engineering estimates of the required pavement thicknesses depending on axle loads, the type of soil on which the roadway is built, the desired condition of the roadway at the end of its lifetime, and the region of the country in which the roadway is to be built. For a given desired condition of the roadway at the end of its design life, the heavier the expected traffic load, the thicker the roadway must be. Traffic, of course, comes in various forms—cars, buses, trucks, and other vehicles. AASHTO engineers found that the damage done by heavier axle loadings increased exponentially. This means that the number of heavy trucks on a roadway will have a far greater effect on pavement thickness decisions than the number of cars, despite the fact that many more cars generally use roads. However, roadway strength also increases exponentially with thickness; thus doubling the effective traffic load does not double pavement costs.

Pavement width also varies with traffic mix. In order to accommodate wider vehicles like trucks and busses, highway officials will build wider roads. According to the Department of Transportation, the added design costs of thicker pavements and wider lanes to accommodate trucks amount to 50 percent of the costs of new pavement.

Bridges require a minimum amount of structural strength merely to hold up the weight of bridge parts. Beyond this, bridges need to be strengthened to support the weight of vehicles using it. Bridges used by buses and heavy trucks must be designed with more strength—and thus higher costs—than they would be if they were designed to be used solely by cars. According to the Department of Transportation, about 40 percent of bridge construction costs are the result of their design to be used by trucks.

Finally, the grades with which roadways can be built depend on the stopping and climbing power of the vehicles using the highway. To keep traffic moving smoothly, roadways cannot be built more steeply than will permit vehicles to maintain a normal cruising speed. In general, this means that roadways can be built more steeply if they are to be used only by vehicles which have powerful motors relative to their weight. Again, use by heavy trucks causes roadways to be built more expensively than they would be for car traffic alone. According to the Department of Transportation, about 20 percent of road grading and drainage costs are due to design differences to accommodate trucks.

Not all roadways have been designed and built to accommodate heavy loads. Roads built for heavy traffic represent a minority of the highway mileage, although a majority of construction expenditures. Once a road has been designed and built to accommodate heavy traffic, however, the cost has been sunk. That means that actual use of the road by the traffic for which it was designed does not increase costs to the road builder. Changing the traffic level or mix will not save any of the construction or design costs of the highway. In this sense, after the cement has dried, construction costs are no longer economic costs of operation of the highway authority. Part III of this book will discuss tools for highway finance that take into consideration the fact that heavy trucks cause highways to be built differently than they otherwise would be.

The Effect of Traffic Level and Mix on Highway Repair Costs

While bridges do not wear out with use (unless there is a catastrophic overloading), highway surfaces do. On average, a bituminous highway surface lasts about 12 years; a Portland cement highway lasts about 25 years. Some deterioration is independent of traffic levels; some is simply due to weather. Expenditures for resurfacing, restoration, rehabilitation, and reconstruction (so called 4-R costs) of roadways is a second way in which the actions of highway users affect the costs of the highway authority.

All major highways carry a mix of traffic from motor cycles to trailer trucks. The main (and most controversial) finding of the AASHTO road tests described previously is that the damage done to a roadway rises with the fourth power of the weight on an axle. This means that a typical heavy truck wears out pavement at a rate equivalent to about 5,000 automobiles. A truck loaded to 100,000 lbs. does four times more damage than one loaded to 80,000 lbs. The thicker the pavement, however, the less damage any vehicle will cause.[4]

The effect on costs of the highway authority due to pavement damage of different classes of vehicles depends on the interaction of heavy vehicles and automobiles, and differs with pavement thickness and even weather. According to the Department of Transportation, between 40 and 90 percent of repair costs of highways should be paid by trucks, depending on the method used to calculate costs.[5]

The roadway authority bears most costs of roadway rehabilitation. Some, however, can be shifted to vehicle users by delaying rehabilitation; the form of these costs is slower traffic, increased fuel use, and additional repairs required on vehicles. The extent to which other vehicles are affected by roadway conditions depends on the speed with which repairs are made to the roadway.[6]

Non-Assignable Costs

Not all of the costs of roadway ownership are affected by traffic levels or traffic mix. Some roadway maintenance must take place even if the road is not used at all. Minimum strengths of bridges need to be maintained even if they were not expected to carry any traffic. Some roadway grading needs to be done regardless of the traffic load. There is a minimum thickness of highway that is required if any vehicle is to use a roadway. These costs represent about half of the expenditures made by highway authorities. They are non-assignable or in the language of Chapter 5, non-traceable costs. This means simply that they are costs that could not be saved if traffic were to be removed from a highway. They are genuine opportunity costs in the sense that they are costs that could be saved if the roadway were to be abandoned as a roadway.[7] If the roadway continues to be maintained without traffic, however, the roadway authority still is faced with these non-traceable costs.

Non-traceability of costs has more sources than the need to make facilities with minimum strengths, as noted in Chapter 5. In general, there will be a non-linear and non-separable relationship between roadway expenditures and travel of different vehicle classes. To the extent that individual cost responsibilities sum to less than the total cost borne by the highway authorities, non-linear cost relationships can cause the identical type of non-traceability problems as are caused by minimum strengths and sizes of facilities.

Some of the most interesting and important economic problems in transportation are how to deal with these non-assignable costs of operating fixed facilities. This is one of the central topics of Part III of this textbook. It is worth noting at this point that one reasonable-sounding approach is invalid: charging each vehicle class only for the additional strengthening above that which would be required by the next-most damaging class of vehicles. If this were valid, heavy trucks would be charged only the additional cost of roadway strengthening that is not charged to light trucks. Light trucks would be charged for the cost of roadway strengthening above that required for automobiles, etc. If this logic were followed to its logical conclusion, cars would pay only for additional strengths not required for motorcycles, and the entire initial surfacing cost would be charged to bicyclists—clearly illogical as well as unworkable.

RAILROADS

Railroad tracks are privately owned in the United States. In most cases, the tracks are owned by the same company operating the rail service. This contrasts with highways, which are publicly owned. It is also counter to the practice in most of the world where rail operations are publicly provided and tracks publicly owned. Unlike highways, railroad tracks do not provide ubiquitous access. The combination of private ownership and the lack of access to any location in the country is the primary distinguishing characteristic of rail transportation compared with motor transport.

The map of transportation facilities in Figure 6.1 shows the location of major railroad lines currently operating in the United States. Maps of major highways and railroads show a strong resemblance to one another. It appears that roads and railroads follow approximately the same routes and should be close competitors with one another, but the maps are deceiving. Railroads provide intercity transportation; roads are used for both intercity transportation as well as locational access. One reason for the advantage of road transportation apparent in the demand studies described in Chapter 3 is that the access function can be efficiently combined with intercity transportation.

The apparent blanketing of the country by railroads implied by Figure 6.1 is misleading in another sense as well. The U.S. railroad map is composed of a very small number of private systems. While railroads do exchange traffic with one another, the amount of traffic interchange is rapidly declining. Railroads have the right to refuse to carry goods from an off-line source of supply in competition to one that they do serve. The ownership of railroad tracks by their operators also leads to some circuitous freight traffic routings that would not be used if tracks were owned by all companies in common. Passenger trains, unlike freight trains, will switch tracks between different owning companies if it provides a better routing because passenger trains are not operated by the track owning companies, but by a national entity, Amtrak.

In the highway system, a significant portion of the capital budget is devoted to new construction; at least until recently, railroad systems have been shrinking in length. Figure 6.2 shows the length of the U.S. railroad system since 1940. The size of the railroad network reached a maximum shortly after the turn of the century and has been contracting ever since. The rate of abandonment accelerated after 1980, with railroad track being abandoned at the rate of approximately 2 percent of track miles per year. Except for a short line built for access to a coal mine in Wyoming in the 1970s, no significant new railroad construction has taken place since 1920.

The fact that the fixed facilities in the railroad industry are shrinking rather than expanding is important for comparing railroad and truck costs. As will be discussed in Part III, some portion of the design and construction of highway facilities can properly be attributed to different classes of traffic by investigating how the presence of different classes of traffic causes the engineering design of a roadway to be different from what it would be in the absence of such traffic. The railroad system, however, was designed for a very different traffic mix than today's loads. When railroads were built, more than half of the traffic was passenger trains. Today, passenger traffic accounts for less than 3 percent of the railroad business. Also, when the system was built, passenger and freight traffic was centered in the industrialized northeastern part of the country. As population and economic activity has moved south and west, the northeast has become the area with the most redundant trackage.

The current traffic in the railroad system has no effect on the map of the existing system except through abandonment decisions. If the system were to be recreated today, it would probably look quite different; it would have much wider tracks, would not enter the downtown areas of cities, and would be

FIGURE 6.2   Trends in U.S. Railroad Mileage

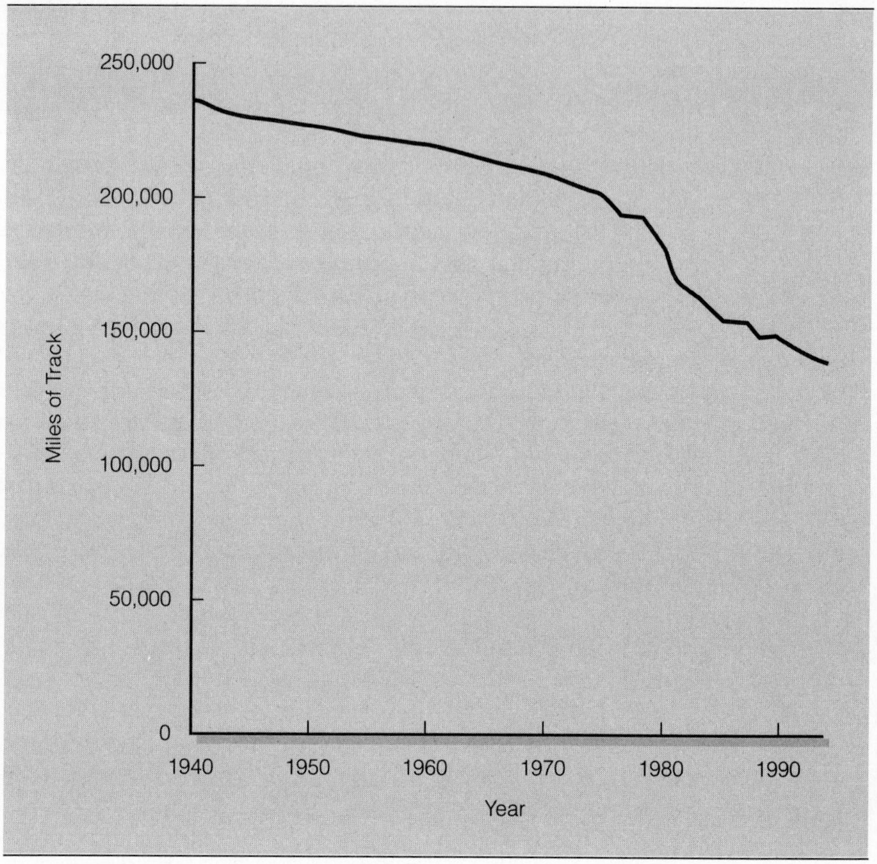

SOURCE: *Transportation in America*, various issues

built for the slower speeds of freight trains rather than fast passenger trains. It is also clear that if the country were choosing to build the railroad system anew, a far smaller network would be put in place. One reason that railroads are abandoned is that technological advances in traffic control and car design have allowed the capacity of the railroad system to grow without increases in the amount of track.

The U.S. railroad industry values its track and structures at approximately $54 billion, less some depreciation. This amount, however, is based on the original costs of investment in the railroad system. The costs of construction, engineering, and design of the railroad system are fully sunk. Eliminating the use of the railroad system by passenger and freight trains will not save any past construction costs. The cost that can be attributed to using railroad fixed facilities is simply the opportunity cost of the land and structures used by the track network and the maintenance costs caused by use of the tracks by railroad trains. Of course, where facilities are modified to accommodate new equipment (for example, raising clearances to allow the use of double-stack container trains), these expenses are properly considered opportunity costs of fixed facilities ownership.

Measuring the Cost of Fixed Railroad Facilities

The economic measure of the cost of using railroad fixed facilities for railroad transportation is the total amount per year that other users would be willing to pay for the use of the railroad fixed facilities. As we shall see in Chapter 9, one common technique for calculating this figure is to multiply the going interest rate in the national economy by the market value of railroad property. While there are economic principles to guide the choice of an interest rate, it is impossible to calculate the value of railroad property from published accounts. Part of the reason relates to a change in railroad accounting in 1983 from retirement, replacement, betterment accounting to depreciation accounting. But a more important reason is that the value of railroad fixed facilities in financial accounts is based on the cost of creating railroads, while the economically correct measurement of the cost of using the fixed facilities is based on what non-railroad users would be willing to pay for the abandoned property.

The other cost of using railroad fixed facilities—annual upkeep expenses—is much easier to measure. Since railroad expenditures for labor, machines, fuel, and raw materials are ongoing, maintenance expenditures are likely to be quite close to the economic costs of the activity. In 1995, railroads spent about $25,000 per mile of track on maintaining way and structures. At approximately 17 percent of all operating expenses, outlays on fixed facilities is a much larger proportion of railroad expenses than are roadway costs compared to expenditure on highway transportation. In this sense, railroad transportation is more fixed-facilities intensive than highway transport.

Since railroad fixed facilities are owned by the same companies that use the tracks, the cost that traffic imposes on tracks has been treated as an internal business calculation of railroad companies. While railroads may have undertaken studies similar to the AASHTO tests for attributing highway costs to levels of different kinds of road traffic, the studies have not been made public. Little is known outside of railroad engineering departments about the determinants of the extent to which railroad traffic levels change the level of required maintenance expenditures. It seems reasonable to expect that some part of maintenance expenditure is related to traffic levels and some is due simply to weather and other factors independent of use levels.[8] More is known about the timing of maintenance expenditures. Prior to the conversion of railroad accounting to depreciation accounting, there was an incentive to do extensive maintenance during profitable years and to defer maintenance during financially difficult periods. Railroads in the 1970s were known for having extensive amounts of deferred maintenance and unsafe track and operations due to poor earnings. The prosperity resulting from deregulation in 1980 and the conversion to standard accounting seems to have eliminated incentives to defer maintenance and have made maintenance expenditures more consistent.[9]

AIR FACILITIES

Aircraft do not use fixed guideways the way railroad trains or highway vehicles do. They are technically capable of flying in any direction and taking any route between two points. In practice, however, commercial aviation is limited to government-determined air traffic corridors. The air traffic control system sets up the equivalent of a network of fixed facilities for the airline industry. The combination of the air traffic control system and the airports that are used to load, unload, and transfer passengers and freight make the airline industry more fixed facilities-intensive than initial appearance would indicate. Like highway transportation, however, the fixed facilities are provided by governments, thus making the individual companies in the industry appear to have very low fixed facilities costs.

The Air Traffic Control System

The Federal Aviation Administration maintains a system of about 150,000 miles of high-altitude jet routes in the contiguous 48 states; it also maintains a system of about 200,000 miles of low altitude routes not suitable for jets. These routes are controlled from 24 air route traffic control centers and 684 traffic control towers. The air corridors are not the property of individual operators. While airlines do have different regions and routes in which they are strong, this specialization is not based on ownership of rights of way as it is in the railroad industry.

Civilian air traffic control expenditures by the federal government are $4.8 billion annually. This expenditure is about 2 percent of total expenditure on civilian passenger and freight air transportation. Comparable figures for other modes of transportation are much higher.

The great majority of expenditures by the Federal Aviation Administration for their air traffic control function consists of salaries. Since labor is mobile, labor costs are generally considered to reflect opportunity costs more accurately than do capital expenditures. Annual expenditure on the air traffic control system is thus likely to be a reasonably accurate estimate of the costs of airline guideways.

There are no publicly available studies detailing how air traffic control expenditures change with traffic levels. A minimum amount of equipment and personnel must be available simply to keep air lanes open. On the other hand, since each air traffic controller can only control a limited number of aircraft, much of the costs of operating the fixed facilities must be considered variable with respect to traffic levels. We will treat the majority of fixed facilities expenses in the airline industry to be variable.

▬ Airport Expenses

There are more than 18,000 airports in the United States, but almost all of these have short, unlit, unpaved runways. Only 250 airports have runways over 10,000 feet long; long runways are required for operating large jet aircraft. Another 384 airports have runways between 7,000 and 10,000 feet.

Airports are owned and operated by states, municipalities, or agencies set up by local governments to operate airports. Annual government expenditure on airports is about $12 billion. Of this amount, approximately $2 billion is provided by the federal government in grants to the states and for expansion of runways and control equipment. The remaining $10 billion of airport expenditures are made directly by the state and local airport authorities.

Airport authorities are nonprofit institutions that set the prices for their services to match their expected expenditures. Large airports have a larger proportion of their expenses in terminals and a smaller proportion associated with runways. In general, about 28 percent of airport expenses are associated with runways and landing areas; terminal areas including parking account for 57 percent; the remainder is associated with hangars and other leased or operating areas.[10] Landing fees, which average 2 percent of airline revenues, and rental revenues for counters, gates, and hangars provide most of the revenue of the airport authorities; parking fees and concession fees from restaurants and other services are the other major source of airport revenues. If revenues fail to cover expenditures, airline landing fees are raised until expenses are covered.

The land used by airports is generally not correctly accounted for in calculating airport costs. Airport bonds are generally paid off after 25 or 30 years, after which no opportunity cost of using land and buildings as part of the airport is charged to the users of the airport. This, combined with the fact that inflation has pushed up land and building costs, means that old airports have apparently lower costs than new airports. There are no publicly available estimates of the extent to which airport expenses underestimate the economic costs of using airport facilities for transportation. Since airports tend to be in prime urban locations and to use tracts of land that could be converted to industrial or commercial uses, the opportunity costs of airports must be considerably higher than the expenses listed in their accounting books.[11]

There are economies of scale in runways: One four-runway airport is less expensive than two two-runway airports. Counterbalancing these economies are diseconomies of terminal size: As a terminal expands, access to the increasing numbers of gates becomes more and more difficult. The optimal size of an airport must be based on the tradeoff between runway economies and terminal diseconomies.[12]

Airline relations with airports are not based on spot market transactions but on long-term contracts; airlines sign long-term leases on counter, gate, and terminal space and airlines guarantee the bonds that airport authorities sell to finance expansion. Existing airlines thus tend to have the best locations in an airport. Existing airlines also have a stake in future expansion plans that might allow more competition or facilitate their own flight arrangements. This is especially important at those airports which are used to capacity. Airports do not currently have a mechanism for efficiently dealing with congestion and depend on direct negotiations to limit the number of flights during peak periods. Airlines generally wish to increase capacity by less than airport authorities wish to do in order to limit possible new competition.

The low fixed facilities costs of the airline industry and the public ownership of the airports should make for easy entry. Entry is far more difficult than is generally supposed, however, in part because of the long-term leases through which fixed facilities are financed.[13] Some leases between airport authorities and airlines allow tenant airlines to veto expansions in capacity that would be necessary to allow new entry. Limited capacity and preferences given to incumbents have raised substantial barriers to entry by new airlines.

WATER TRANSPORT

Water transportation uses two kinds of fixed facilities: channel improvements and port facilities. Ocean transportation tends to use primarily port facilities while domestic water transport is affected more by decisions on channel improvements.

Channel Improvements

There are three kinds of non-ocean going water transportation in the United States: (1)coastal shipping, along the Gulf Coast from Texas to Florida and along the Atlantic Coast from Florida to Virginia; (2)river and canal shipping, the vast majority of which is on the Mississippi River and its tributaries, and to a far lesser extent on the Columbia-Snake River system; and (3)Great Lakes and St. Lawrence Seaway shipping. The location of waterways in Figure 6.1 does not bear much resemblance to that of railroads or highways. Those modes have had fixed facilities placed in a position to connect the major population areas of the nation. Water transport, by contrast, has its channels placed primarily by the chance of nature. We have the same basic map of navigable waterways that we had at the Civil War.

Wholly new waterways are not generally constructed in response to economic demands. From 1970 through 1982, the mileage of U.S. waterways stood at 25,543; this number was increased by 234 miles to 25,777 in 1983 to reflect the completion of the Tennessee-Tombigbee Waterway. The minimum navigation depth of most U.S. waterways is 9 feet. A few of the lightly used secondary rivers are 6 feet. No major new increases or decreases in waterway mileage or depths are anticipated in the near future.

The correct test for calculating the economic cost of a facility is the value of the facility in its next best alternative use. In the case of domestic waterways, the cost of waterways is correctly measured as the increase in the value of the economy's resources that the public would experience if they were no longer used for transportation. Rivers would continue to flow regardless of whether there are barges floating on them, and thus there is little to be gained by not using them for transport. There is a cost only to the extent that we could increase our enjoyment of waterways by not using them for transport, or if we could enjoy other things with the savings of waterway expenses.

One obvious expense that could be saved if rivers and canals were not used for transport is the maintenance expenditures on the waterways (the dredging to keep the channels open), as well as the operating expenses of the locks on the waterways. Placement and maintenance of navigational aids could be saved, as could rescue systems for sailors. In the Great Lakes and upper Mississippi, ice breaking expenses necessary to keep the channels open for navigation at the beginning and end of the season could also be saved.

A less obvious cost of using rivers and canals for navigation is the external cost that is imposed on alternative users of the water resource. In some circumstances, water levels are kept higher or lower than they would be kept if it were not for the transport uses of a river or lake. Property owners on shorelines complain about soil erosion caused by high water levels maintained for navigation as well as damage caused by ice breaking to support navigation. The operation of towboats in shallow water increases the turbidity of the water. Navigation sometimes interferes with recreation or with commercial fishing. Some observers of the great floods of the Mississippi in 1993 claimed that the channelization of the river for the benefit of shipping intensified the extent of flooding. River channelization to stabilize and deepen shipping channels also has the effect of reducing wildlife habitat.

None of these external costs is included in the standard calculation of the costs of maintaining waterways in navigable condition. The U.S. government spends approximately $1.7 billion per year to construct and maintain navigable waterways and to maintain navigation through U.S. ports. Waterways differ greatly in required maintenance and construction costs per mile, and it is thus misleading to sum together appropriations made by congress to improve and maintain waterways and divide by the length of U.S. waterways to develop an average cost per mile. As described in Chapter 9, the most recent major waterway construction project, the Tennessee-Tombigbee waterway, has been extraordinarily costly in terms of expenditure per mile as well as expenditure per ton of cargo transiting the canal.

The major demand for navigation expenditure now and in the near future is for replacement and expansion of dams and lock facilities. As river traffic has expanded, congestion has occurred. Most of the locks and dams on the system are now about 50 years old, the age at which they were designed to be replaced. Like railroads, the facilities used by the domestic waterway transporters were designed for an older technology. Unlike railroads, waterway facilities will generally be updated in the future to adapt to improvements in shipping technology.

The economic principle of opportunity cost says that capital expenditures to improve waterways in the past are not current costs of navigation. However, improvements that are required either because of deterioration of old navigational aids, through lack of capacity, or adoption of new technologies are costs that should be attributed to navigation. Treating the $1.7 billion annual federal expenditure as the cost of navigation facilities, we find that fixed facilities costs are 60 percent of the $2.8 billion annual revenues of inland waterways carriers or about 30 percent of the $5.8 billion combined annual revenues of coastal and inland waterway carriers. If most expenditures are made for navigational aids in inland waterways, the waterway industry would be one of the most fixed-facilities intensive transport industries. Moreover, since fixed facilities costs of waterways are not fully paid for by the water freight industry, it is possible that fixed facilities costs can be more than 100 percent of the revenues of carriers.[14] These percentages vary greatly depending on which stretch of waterway is being considered.

Port Costs

Other than navigational aids, the main fixed facilities used by water transportation are port facilities. While ports number in the hundreds, only a few are equipped to handle containerized cargo. Many of the ports have specialized equipment for handling bulk commodities. The most important bulk commodities requiring specialized equipment are grain, coal, ore, petroleum, and liquefied gasses.

While harbor and channel expenditures are made by the federal government, most expenditures for port facilities are made by port authorities that are created by state and local governments. State and local expenditures for the year 1995 were approximately $2 billion. Considerably more than one half of rivers/harbors fixed facilities expenditures each year are devoted to ports and less than half of expenditures are made for channel development.

As with airports, most of this expenditure does not come from the pockets of state and local taxpayers but is financed through long-term leases of port facilities. As is also the case with airports, ship operators lease space in public ports for their own use. A dwindling minority of companies that load and unload ships at public ports are independent of the shipping lines that use the ports. As is the case with other modes of transportation, maritime shipping companies are trying to maintain control of transportation for as much of the trip as possible; operating their own terminals at public ports is one means for extending such control. In addition to the long-term lease payments that shipping companies pay to the port authorities for use of on-shore facilities, the federal government has recently imposed a tax of 4 cents for every $100 paid by users to port authorities to recover some of the costs of keeping harbors open.

Port infrastructure expenditures cover docking equipment, loading and unloading equipment, and warehousing space. Technological development in loading and unloading ships—particularly the almost complete conversion of non-bulk cargo handling to containerization—has required increased amounts of land for storage of cargoes. This in turn has led to a shift of ports away from the traditional city-center locations to areas at the edge of metropolitan areas. Modern cargo handling has reduced the requirement for sheds at ports and increased the amount of specialized equipment for loading and unloading ships.

Most expenditure on port facilities is made for deep-draft ships. The amount spent annually on ports is approximately 15 percent of the annual expenditure on international ocean shipping or about 12 percent of the sum of expenditures on international and deep-draft coastal shipping. Deep-draft shipping appears to be somewhat less fixed facilities-intensive than railroads or shallow-draft shipping, but much more fixed facilities-intensive than highways or airlines.

PIPELINES

Pipeline transportation is the one mode that does not use vehicles. The operator of the fixed facilities provides the transportation directly. Many of the interesting and important problems of transportation economics concern the relationship among fixed facilities operators, vehicle operators, and their customers. Since, unlike other transportation modes, it does not use vehicles, and since ownership patterns in the industry often integrate the transportation, production, and marketing functions, pipelines have received less attention from transportation economists than have other modes of transport.[15]

The map of U.S. pipelines does not look like at all those for rail, highway, and air modes, reflecting the fact that pipelines are not a general mode of transportation. They are narrowly limited both in type of cargo and in geographical reach. With rare exception, pipelines carry only three types of commodities: natural gas, crude oil, and petroleum products (primarily gasoline and fuel oil). They connect producing fields (or landing ports) and consumers. The geographic placement of pipelines is determined by the location of petroleum and gas deposits and by centers of population. The general direction of flow in pipelines is from southwest to northeast, following the geographic pattern of production and consumption.

There are approximately 450,000 miles of pipeline in the United States. This is more than the total of railroad and waterway lengths combined. The largest number of pipeline miles are used to move natural gas. The remainder are used to move liquids—either crude oil or petroleum products. Unlike railroads, there has been no steep decline in the mileage of pipelines in the United States. Petroleum products pipelines carry different commodities in the same pipe, separated by devices called pigs. Pigs are also used to separate products moved for different shippers. The mixing of products in pipelines is one of the main technical and regulatory problems since it produces the problems of cost nontraceability for shared facilities that were discussed in Chapter 5; the same problems are not found in crude pipelines or natural gas lines where there is greater product homogeneity.

Pipeline costs are dominated by construction outlays. The construction costs are almost evenly divided between materials (pipe and equipment) and labor. Land costs for pipelines are minimal—generally around 3 percent of construction costs. One reason that land costs are such a minor part of pipeline costs is that pipelines are underground and after placement, the surface of the land can generally be used normally without regard to the existence of the pipeline underneath.

The costs of pipeline construction will vary with the diameter of the pipe, the length of the pipeline, and the type of terrain through which it is built. Longer pipelines are somewhat cheaper per mile to build than are shorter ones. Pipeline construction costs increase with the size of the pipe, but costs do not rise as rapidly with pipe size as does the throughput of the pipe. A recent 10-mile 36-inch pipeline in Nebraska cost $675,000 per mile. A 17-mile 20-inch pipeline in Illinois and Indiana cost $954,000 per mile. In 1994, the average cost of a pipeline built on dry land rather than in the Gulf of Mexico or other body of water was $650,000 per mile. Compressor stations cost on average $1,227 per unit of horsepower.[16]

After a pipeline has been constructed, the main operating cost is fuel for running compressors and pumps to keep the liquid or gas moving through the pipeline; the only other substantial cost is labor to operate the compressor and transmission stations. These costs are very small in comparison to original construction costs. The ratio of fixed costs to total costs is by far the highest in the transportation industries.

Pipelines do not have a useful life that can be measured in years. Pipelines are designed to last for as long as the deposit they were built to tap. Construction costs of pipeline facilities are genuinely sunk. In this sense, the opportunity cost of fixed facilities in pipeline transportation are greatly overestimated by calculations based on the construction costs of the pipeline. If a line were not used for transportation, it has no alternative use. But, like highways and unlike railroads, pipelines are still being built, and the new construction unquestionably requires drawing resources away from alternative uses. Unlike the railway system, if the pipeline network in the United States did not exist, it would undoubtedly be recreated in much the same form that exists today. The existence of the pipeline system saves the economy the cost of recreating it, and in this sense, current construction costs approximate the fixed cost of using the pipeline system.

Pipeline technology is often described to new students of economics to illustrate the concept of scale economies. In fact, as noted in Chapter 5, the geographically dispersed nature of transportation markets makes the concept of scale economies difficult to define. Nonetheless, we could ask the question: How much would it cost to increase the rate of transportation of crude oil from a specific origin to a specific destination, holding constant the flows between all other origins and destinations that use the same pipeline? Logic, mathematics, and experience dictate that the costs should look approximately like those in Figure 6.3. Three curves are shown. Curve AA represents the minimum cost of increasing flow rates in the short run which we take to mean without any increase in pipe or equipment. Curve BB shows the minimum cost way of increasing flow rates in the intermediate run which we take to mean increasing the number and size of compressors and other equipment, but not building the line anew.[17] Curve CC shows the technologically minimum way of increasing the flow rate if the entire pipeline could be reengineered and constructed to accommodate the increase in flow; we can think of this as the long run.

With given pipe diameter, increasing the flow rate requires increasing the speed of flow in the pipe, which in turn means increasing the amount of fuel used to operate compressors and pumps. The rising part of curve A is the result of increased fuel used to push the crude oil in the pipe more quickly. The resistance in the pipe makes it impractical to increase flow rates substantially simply by making the pumps work harder. A more fuel efficient means for increasing flow rates would be to add more pumping stations. This is shown in curve B, which dips below curve A beyond flow rate X^*. If building anew, however, the pipe size can be optimized to the flow rate. Small diameter pipe has the advantage of a lower construction cost per mile and less difficulty of mixing in product pipelines. Larger diameter pipelines have the distinct advantage of lower construction cost per unit of throughput and less resistance to flow in the pipeline. These advantages are reflected in a lower cost of curve C beyond flow rate X^{**}. The downward slope of curve C is often described as showing economies of scale in pipeline transportation.[18] If *scale economies* are taken to mean that it is cheaper to build and operate one large diameter pipeline rather than two smaller diameter lines covering the same route, pipelines are clearly subject to economies of scale. Unquestionably, however, pipelines are far and away the most fixed facilities-intensive mode of transportation.

FIGURE 6.3   Costs of Pipeline Transportation
The unit cost of expanding pipeline transportation depends on how it is done.
Curve AA shows the unit costs of expanding throughput by using more fuel to
operate compressors. Curve BB shows the costs of expanding by adding
additional equipment. Curve CC shows the costs of expanding by building anew.
The downward slope of CC reflects economies of scale in pipeline construction.

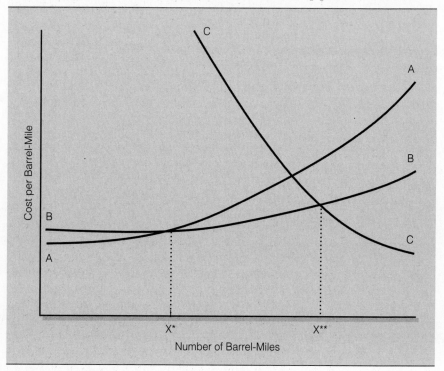

CONCLUSION

Fixed facilities in transportation consists of physically immobile pieces of transportation capital. Fixed facilities are generally sunk and dedicated to geographic markets.

The greatest amount of capital tied up in transport facilities is in the
nation's highways. Highways are unique among transport modes for providing both a right of way for inter-city transportation as well as for local
access. Inter-city highways are provided by state governments, but with considerable financial support derived from federal motor fuel taxes. About

$90 billion per year is spent on highways—less than 10 percent of all amounts spent on highway transportation. Since highways are continuously being expanded, renovated, and maintained, most annual highway expenses must be considered ongoing economic costs of fixed facilities used for cars, trucks, and buses.

Some of the most contentious issues in highway costing is in determining the cost responsibility of each class of users. Both highway construction and highway maintenance expenditures do vary with the level of traffic. Highways are engineered differently depending on their expected usage levels by different classes of vehicles. Highways that are designed to accommodate heavy trucks must be constructed with lower grades, thicker pavements, and wider shoulders than highways designed solely for automobiles. The use of highways by heavy trucks also makes highways deteriorate much more quickly than they would if used only by automobiles. Allocating the costs of fixed facilities to individual users has been a perennial theoretical and empirical problem in transportation economics. The difficulties are especially acute in the case of highways, where only a fraction of costs are traceable.

Railroads are more fixed facilities cost-intensive than are highway modes. Railroads are unusual among transport modes in that the rights of way connecting cities are owned and maintained by the same company that operates the transport vehicles. The railroad network is shrinking and, unlike the case of highways, the relevant economic issues relate to how rapidly the network should shrink and which parts of it should be abandoned first. (Due to technological improvements in freight cars and locomotives, however, the railroad system continues to increase the amount of freight it hauls, even as the network shrinks). Today's railroad network was designed and built for a very different geographic distribution of population and a different industrial base. A railroad system designed for current conditions would be quite different from the one used today.

All previous expenditure on track and structures should be considered a sunk cost, not affecting the current cost of fixed facilities. This does not mean, however, that the cost of railroad facilities should be considered minor. Railroads occupy valuable pieces of land—resources that could be turned to other uses if it were abandoned for use by railroads. In addition, most costs attributed on railroad accounts to fixed facilities is for maintenance of tracks. Track maintenance accounts for approximately 17 percent of all railroad expenditures. In comparison, expenditures for highway maintenance and construction are only 10 percent of all highway costs.

Airlines appear to use no fixed facilities at all. In fact, however, they do: The air traffic control system operated by the Federal Aviation Administration is a fixed facility in the same sense as highways and railroad tracks. It costs approximately $4.8 billion to operate, an amount that is almost as large as annual expenditures to maintain railroad tracks. However, since the airline industry is much larger than the railroad industry and since the costs of the air traffic control system are shared with the military branch of government, right-of-way costs are small for commercial airlines.

Airport expenses are the other cost of fixed air facilities. Airports are operated by local port authorities, though the expenses are paid by airline landing fees and space rentals under terms of long-term leases between airline companies and port authorities. The contracts signed between airport authorities and airlines tend to make it difficult for new airlines to offer attractive service at existing airports. Often, the long-term contracts used by the airport authority to fund airport development give existing airlines a veto over expansions that would be necessary to allow for significant new airline entry. So, despite the fact that fixed facilities costs of airlines are small, they have a major effect on airline competition.

Ocean transport shares many of the characteristics of air transport. The main fixed facilities of ocean transport are ports and channel improvements. Port facilities are financed very much like airports: State or local port authorities develop the facilities under the guarantees of long-term contracts signed with ship owning companies. The annual expenditure on port development, while smaller than airport expenditures, represent a much larger percentage of total costs of shipping companies.

Pipelines are the one mode of transport that do not use vehicles. Pipelines have been used as a classic example of economies of scale. As in all network services, it is difficult to confirm or reject this belief since the measurement of scale is problematic. Pipelines are, however, unquestionably the most fixed cost-intensive mode of transportation.

NOTES

1. For an overview of the current status of developments in intelligent highways, see The Congress of the United States, Congressional Budget Office, *High-Tech Highways: Intelligent Transportation Systems and Policy* (Washington, U.S. Government Printing Office, October 1995).

2. For a more complete discussion of the topics of highway finance, see Davis, M. Grant, and William A. Cunningham, *A Primer on Highway Finance*, Lanham, Md. and London: University Press of America, 1994. For the European perspective, see Papaioannou, Rodolfos and Dinos Stasinopoulos, "The Road Transport Policy of the European Community," *Journal of Transport Economics and Policy,* Vol. 25 No. 2, May 1991, pp. 203–208.

3. The literature on optimal pavement design has been written almost exclusively from the engineering perspective. See American Association of State Highway Officials, "The AASHO Road Test," *Highway Research Board, Special Report No. 73* (Washington, DC: National Academy of Sciences, 1962); American Association of State Highway and Transportation Officials, *AASHTO Guide for*

Design of Pavement Structures, Washington, 1986; also U.S. Department of Transportation, Federal Highway Administration, *Final Report on the Federal Highway Cost Allocation Study* (Washington, DC: U.S. Government Printing Office, May 1982). For a recent economic report on road costs, see Kenneth A. Small, Clifford Winston, and Carol A. Evans, *Road Work: A New Highway Pricing and Investment Policy* (Washington: Brookings Institution, 1989).

4. Small, Kenneth A. and Clifford Winston, "Optimal Highway Durability," *American Economic Review*, Vol. 78, No. 3 (June 1988), pp. 560–569 claim that the AASHTO tests were based on incorrect statistical analysis. When they reanalyzed the AASHTO data, they found that highway damage is more closely related to the third power of axle loading rather than the fourth power.

5. U.S. Department of Transportation, Federal Highway Administration, *Final Report on the Federal Highway Cost Allocation Study* (Washington, DC: U.S. Government Printing Office, May 1982), pp. D20–D21. For a recent assessment of whether heavy trucks pay the costs of the damage that they cause, see Vitaliano, Donald F. and James Held, "Marginal Cost Road Damage User Charges," *Quarterly Review of Economics and Business*, Vol. 30, No. 2, Summer 1990, pp. 32–49.

6. David Newbery has calculated that under some conditions, efficient prices will not include an assessment to take into account the effect of roadway damage on other users. See Newbery, David M., "Road Damage Externalities and Road User Charges," *Econometrica*, Vol. 56, No. 2 (March 1988), pp. 295–316. See also Newbery, David M., "Cost Recovery from Optimally Designed Roads," *Economica*, Vol. 56, No. 222, May 1989, pp. 165–185.

7. The concept of road abandonment is not as fanciful as it seems. Some parts of the U.S. rural road system is overbuilt in the same sense as railroads. For an analysis, see Hamlett, Cathy A. and C. Phillip Baumel, "Rural Road Abandonment: Policy Criteria and Empirical Analysis," *American Journal of Agricultural Economics*, Vol. 72, No. 1, February 1990, pp. 114–120. For an analysis of alternative mechanisms for providing rural road service, see Deller, Steven C., David L. Chicoine, and Norman Walzer, "Economies of Size and Scope in Rural Low Volume Roads," *Review of Economics and Statistics,* Vol. 70, No. 3, August 1988, pp. 459–465.

8. Using aggregate data, the ICC claims that maintenance of the way expenditures are about 45 percent variable with traffic levels and 55 percent fixed. See Denver D. Tolliver, "Economies in Density in Railroad Cost Finding: Applications to Rail Form A," *The Logistics and Transportation Review*, Vol. 20, No. 1. The proportion of total costs that are fixed and variable must, of course, be sensitive to traffic levels. Railroad fixed costs are also discussed in Chapter 8.

9. See Wood, Wallace R., "Discretionary Spending and Railroad Costing Bias," *Logistics and Transportation Review,* Vol. 21, No. 2, June 1985, pp. 99–114.

10. Howard, George P., ed., *Airport Economic Planning* (Cambridge: MIT Press, 1974).

11. Walters, A.A. "Airports: An Economic Survey," *Journal of Transport Economics and Policy* 12 (May 1978), pp. 125–160. See also Dienemann, Paul F. and Armando M. Lago, "User Taxes and Allocations of the United States Airport and Airway System Costs," *Journal of Transport Economics and Policy*, 10 (January 1976) and O'Connor, William E., *An Introduction to Airline Economics, 2nd Ed.* (New York: Praeger, 1982). Doganis, Rigas, *The Airport Business* (New York and London: Routledge, 1992).

12. Walters, A.A., "Airports: An Economic Survey," *Journal of Transport Economics and Policy* 12 (May 1978), pp. 125–160.

13. Golaszewski, Richard, "Aviation Infrastructure: A Time for Perestroika?" *Logistics and Transportation Review,* Vol. 28, No. 1, March 1992, pp. 75–101. The standard claim that fixed facilities costs are low for entrants has been challenged by a recent survey. The authors have calculated minimum investments in ground facilities for new airlines and found that they are substantial in comparison to other costs of airline operations. See R.V. Butler, and J.H. Huston, "How Contestable Are Airline Markets?" *Atlantic Economic Journal,* Vol. 17, No. 2 (June 1989), pp. 27–35.

14. A tax on fuel used by ship owners is expected to cover a portion of the annual construction costs of navigation aids in the future. Maintenance and operation of the waterways will continue to be funded from the national treasury.

15. A good source of information on the pipeline industry is the annual OGJ Report on the industry in the *Oil and Gas Journal.* See also Hansen, John A., *U.S. Oil Pipeline Markets: Structure, Pricing, and Public Policy* (Cambridge: The MIT Press, 1983).

16. All figures from True, Warren R., "U.S. Interstate Pipelines Ran More Efficiently in 1994," OGJ Report, *Oil and Gas Journal* (November 27, 1995), pp. 3958–3964.

17. There is a second type of intermediate cost curve: Since the liquid or gas being transported enters and leaves the pipeline at different places, there may be short stretches that are the bottlenecks and the capacity of the whole system can be increased by double piping particular stretches rather than rebuilding the entire system. Another form of intermediate cost curve could be drawn for minimizing total costs allowing for increases in pumping capacity as well as a limited amount of new pipeline construction.

18. Since the volume of a cylinder increases with the square of the radius, a doubling of diameter will result in a quadrupling of the amount of oil that it will deliver. Actually, the increase is greater because the inner surface friction per unit is also lessened as diameter increases. Since surface area increases in proportion to diameter, the steel required will increase much more slowly than capacity; other elements of costs behave similarly. In an old estimate, pipeline transportation was found to have a cost function that is homogeneous of degree 2, meaning that:
$$C(\lambda Q^*) = \lambda^2 \bullet Q^*$$
Such cost curves have rapidly decreasing average costs as output increases—the characteristic of scale economies. See Leslie Cookenboo, Jr., *Crude Oil Pipelines and Competition in the Oil Industry* (Cambridge: Harvard University Press, 1955).

7

Transport Vehicle Costs

All modes except for pipelines use vehicles to transport passengers or freight. This chapter describes the costs of owning vehicles used by each of the modes of transportation. A discussion of the cost of operating transport vehicles is covered in Chapter 8.

Vehicle leasing companies directly bear the costs of vehicle ownership, but not vehicle operation. Individuals or companies who own and use their own vehicles combine the costs of vehicle ownership and vehicle operations. In this chapter, transport operations will be analyzed as if owners and operators were separate parties with separate costs.

Vehicle owners bear three main costs: (1) vehicle depreciation; (2) the costs of tying up investment funds in vehicles; and (3) vehicle maintenance. Modes of transportation vary considerably in the importance of each of these three factors, in the ease with which each is calculated and in the tradition of considering maintenance to be a cost of vehicle ownership or operations.

FIXED AND VARIABLE COSTS OF VEHICLE OWNING

Vehicles wear out due to a combination of chronological age and amount of use. The reduction in value of transport vehicles, which results from age or use, is called *depreciation*. Some vehicles have become technologically obsolete before they are physically worn out. If vehicles wear out due to age more rapidly than due to use, depreciation costs are a fixed cost of ownership. This is because the time at which the vehicle needs to be replaced is independent of level of use. If vehicle lives can be measured in miles, or take-offs and landings, depreciation is a variable cost of ownership; variable costs of ownership are often easier to analyze as a cost of vehicle operation.

In some cases, appropriate maintenance appears to allow transport vehicles to be capable of being kept in service indefinitely; their life is then determined by technological obsolescence or by normal attrition due to traffic accidents. If vehicle lives can be predicted by either age or use, the year-to-year drop in value can be predicted and a depreciation allowance calculated in advance. If vehicle lives are unpredictable, the year-to-year change in value of used vehicles will not have a close relationship to depreciation allowances. In fact, the value of such equipment can increase from year to year. In those cases where the value of used equipment is not predictable from annual depreciation allowances, vehicles have no calculable costs of depreciation.

All modes of transport have vehicle costs that can be traced to the value of investment funds tied up in the vehicle stock. These costs are determined by values in the used vehicle market. An airline fleet with a value of $1 billion has an annual implicit interest cost of $100 million, assuming that interest rates in the economy are 10 percent per year. Even if an airline owns rather than leases its aircraft, it must treat implicit interest costs on the value of its aircraft as a cost of owning the planes; if it does not, it will not make sensible business decisions. This point is further discussed in Chapter 9.

In almost all modes of transport, there is a cyclical pattern to demand. During harvests, for example, the demand for rail cars is higher than at other times of the year. During periods of peak demand for petroleum, there is a much larger market for the services of oil tankers than otherwise. The cost of vehicle services for making individual trips is determined by the overall market for using a type of vehicle. In those cases where vehicle owners lease their services by the trip, the opportunity cost of using a vehicle can be clearly read by the figure on the freight invoice—it is the amount that was necessary to pay a vehicle owner to induce him or her to provide capacity in one transport market instead of another. In the typical situation where vehicle owners do not trip-lease, there is a similar definition of the cost of using a vehicle to make a particular trip, but the amount will not be listed in any public records. In this circumstance, economists must impute a vehicle cost to the particular trip. How to do this is described in Chapter 10.

Some annual maintenance is required on transport vehicles regardless of the amount that they are used. These are fixed costs of vehicle ownership. The maintenance costs that depend on the level of use of a vehicle are, by definition, variable costs. As with depreciation costs, it is sometimes easier to calculate variable maintenance costs as an operating cost instead of a cost of vehicle ownership. Depending on the form in which cost statistics for each mode of transportation are collected, maintenance costs will in this chapter sometimes be considered to be a cost of vehicle ownership and thus discussed in this chapter; in the other cases, maintenance costs will be considered an operating cost and discussed in the next chapter.

AUTOMOBILES

Exactly what is a private passenger transportation vehicle is no longer certain. Increasingly, trucks, vans, and recreational vehicles are being used in situations where automobiles had been used in previous years. The stocks of automobiles held by American consumers, businesses, and governments continue to rise each year, as shown in Figure 7.1. But since the number of trucks and other non-automobile vehicles on the highway used for personal transportation has been rising more rapidly than the number of automobiles, the true rate of

FIGURE 7.1   Privately and Publicly Owned Automobile Registrations in the United States

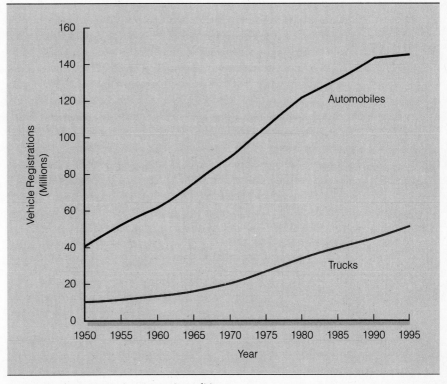

SOURCE: *Transportation in America*, various editions

increase of personal passenger vehicles has been even steeper than that shown in Figure 7.1. As noted in Chapter 4, the stocks of passenger vehicles in the United States and in every country around the world has been increasing more rapidly than the nation's population.

Like any population, the number of automobiles in the United States depends on the rate of births and deaths, or in automotive terms, on production and scrappage. The U.S. automobile stock has been increasing because more cars are produced each year than are scrapped. A great deal of attention has been given to the determinants of the "births" decision. Automobiles were the subject of some of the very earliest of the econometric studies of the demand for a commodity. Econometricians were able to determine that, in accordance with economic theory, the demand for automobiles was sensitive to consumer incomes and the price of automobiles as well as the price of complements—primarily petroleum products. As noted in Chapter 4, consumer income is by far the most important determinant of the demand for automobiles.

But of equal importance to the size of vehicle stocks is the decision on when to terminate the life of a car. This is a much less glamorous subject, with data found not in dealers' showrooms but in registration records; vehicles are assumed scrapped when they fail to appear among state motor vehicle authorities' records. Vehicles are scrapped on a predictable schedule. Figure 7.2 shows the number of vehicles in three cohorts that survive in each year of its life. An accelerating number of vehicles disappear each year until, because there are fewer and fewer cohort members, there is a decline in scrappage rates (measured as a percentage of the number of vehicles originally built).

Scrapping an automobile is an economic decision; scrappage rates respond in predictable ways to the price of new cars (substitutes for used cars) and to the cost of fuel and repairs (complements to used cars). In periods of economic recession, households reduce their rate of scrappage and they reduce the rate of purchases of new automobiles. The age of the automobile fleet on the highways thus increases in recessionary times and decreases during more prosperous periods. During periods when the price of new cars rises more rapidly than the rate of inflation, households tend to hold their cars longer. Throughout all economic conditions, however, the stock of automobiles in the possession of U.S. households has continued to expand.

Any driver knows that the stock of automobiles is not homogeneous. Cars differ not only in age—the factor that is emphasized in the calculations of the economic life of a car—but also in size and characteristics. About 30 percent of new car sales are classified as small, 45 percent are middle, 12 percent large, and 13 percent luxury cars.[1] Over the last decade, the percentage of small cars has decreased while the shares of middle and luxury cars have increased. The heterogeneity of the automobile stock means that it is possible for households to adjust vehicle holding to changing economic circumstances without the adjustments being apparent in the total vehicle stock figures. For example, a

FIGURE 7.2   Survival Rates of Automobiles, 1975–1985

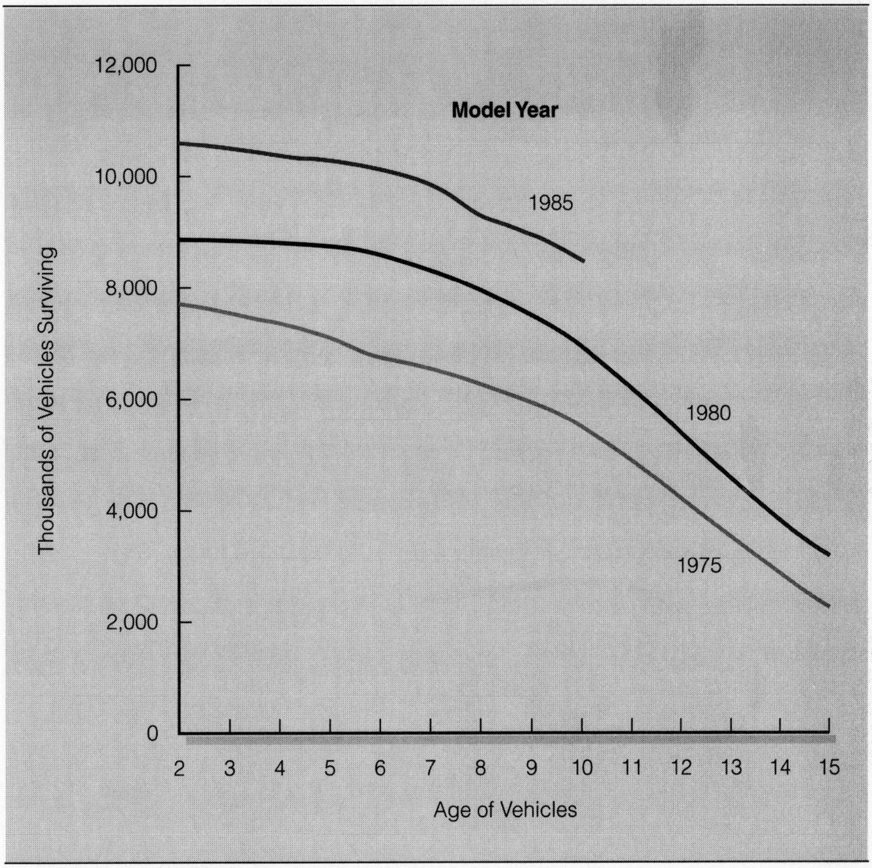

SOURCE: American Automobile Manufacturers Association, *Motor Vehicle Facts and Figures*, 1988 and 1995 editions

household may adjust to changing gasoline prices not by buying more or fewer cars but by buying larger or smaller cars. Many households own multiple vehicles and can adjust to fuel prices by changing the proportion of driving done in large and small vehicles in their possession.

The Costs of Purchasing and Owning Automobiles

The largest expense of driving is associated with purchasing and owning an automobile, rather than driving it. Figure 7.3 displays the expenses that an average automobile owner faces for each car owned. Of the $4,130 average annual fixed cost of owning a new car, $211 are paid for license and registration fees—an amount that clearly does not depend on the amount of driving done, and is thus a fixed cost. Insurance costs do vary somewhat with the amount of driving that the insurance company predicts the car will be used for, but the great majority of the expense is also a fixed cost. In Figure 7.3, all of the expense is considered to be a fixed cost. But by far the largest fixed cost of owning an automobile involves the purchase and finance of the automobile.

In 1995, the average price of a new automobile was about $20,000. The annual depreciation expense of driving a car is measured as the amount by which its value decreases over the year. Most automobile depreciation is due simply to age—a 10-year-old car is worth less than a new car, regardless of the miles on the car. However, used car price books indicate that the price of used cars decreases approximately 5 cents per mile for every mile that a car is driven above the normal 12,500 miles that most cars are driven each year. The "non-use based depreciation" amount in Figure 7.3 is computed by subtracting $625 from the reported depreciation figures to account for the decrease in value associated with the amount that the average car is driven. Non-use based depreciation accounts for about 60 percent of the total annual fixed cost of owning a new car.

Approximately 70 percent of all new car buyers finance their purchase by borrowing. The amount that those consumers need to pay per year to use the borrowed funds is a fixed cost, and is listed in Figure 7.3. However, the 30 per-

FIGURE 7.3   Annual Fixed Costs of Maintaining an Average 1995 Automobile

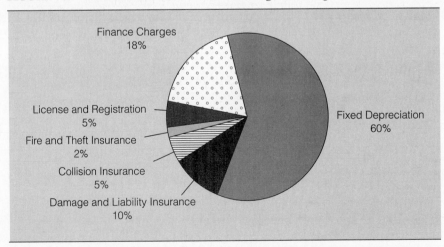

SOURCE: Motor Vehicle Manufacturers Association: Motor Vehicle Facts and Figures, 1995, p. 58. Adjustment to depreciation charges based on reduced vehicle value of $0.05/mile and average annual mileage of 12,500.

cent of buyers who do not borrow to make their purchase have also given up something to buy the car—the foregone earnings that they would have received had they kept in a bank the money that they spent on the car. This implicit interest is no less a fixed cost of owning a car than is the amount of interest that one must pay on a loan. Since Figure 7.3 is based on expenditures rather than economic principles, an allowance for the opportunity cost of funds of those people who do not borrow to buy a car is not included. The $4,130 annual fixed cost of owning a new car is likely to be somewhat underestimated.

Figure 7.4 shows the fixed cost of owning the entire nation's private automobile stock. Rather than estimate depreciation, Figure 7.4 treats the cost of automobile purchases as the sum of all automobile depreciation. This is a valid procedure if all automobile demand is for replacing old automobiles and if automobiles are replaced at a constant rate. (If all cars wore out in 10 years, and one tenth of the cars needed to be replaced every year, the annual purchases of automobiles would be the same as the sum of the depreciation—one-tenth of

FIGURE 7.4   U.S. Consumer Expenditures on Automobile Fixed Costs (Millions of Dollars)

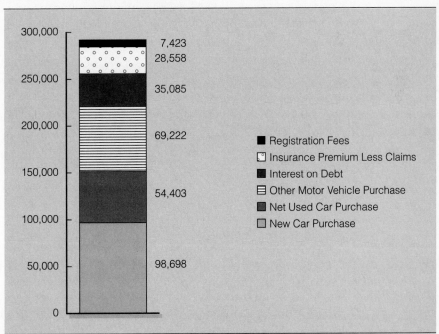

SOURCE: Motor Vehicle Manufacturers Association: Motor Vehicle Facts and Figures, 1995. *Transportation in America*, 14th edition.

each car—for all cars). Figure 7.4 also calculates insurance costs as net of claims made against insurance companies, greatly reducing the fixed cost associated with insurance.

When expenditures for the fixed cost of owning automobiles is summed for all households, the magnitude of these costs is seen more clearly. Approximately $222 billion is spent by consumers each year on purchasing motor vehicles used for personal transportation. Consumer expenditure on cars by itself—ignoring expenditure on other motor vehicles—is more about three times the size of annual expenditures on highways. The total annual cost of owning automobiles is shown in Figure 7.4 to be approximately $300 billion. This is more than half of all expenditures that consumers make on all forms of transportation. The fixed cost of owning vehicles is a substantial part (about 7.6 percent) of all household expenditures. The cost of private automotive transportation is clearly dominated by the fixed costs of owning vehicles.

TRUCKS

It is easy to speak of the trucking industry, but in fact it would be more accurate to refer to the trucking industries. Truckers are united only in that they use trucks and public highways to produce their services. However, the types of equipment that they use and the types of services that are provided are far more diverse than in any other branch of transportation.

The Diversity of Trucks and Truckers

There were approximately 60 million trucks on the road in the United States in 1992, but all but 5 million of these vehicles were pickups, panel trucks or vans, utility vehicles or station wagons—the sort of vehicles that are used primarily for personal transportation. It would be an unusual definition of a trucking industry that included these vehicles as part of the capital of the industry. The remaining vehicles are a mixture of platform trucks, refrigerator vans, livestock trucks, wreckers, garbage haulers, dump trucks, and concrete mixers along with the basic enclosed van that we think of as being the classic over-the-road truck. Figure 7.5 shows that, excluding pickups, panel vans, utility and station wagons, the sectors using the largest number of trucks are construction and agriculture. For-hire trucks account for about 16 percent of all trucks used primarily for freight hauling. Most trucking is not done by the trucking industry but by companies providing their own trucking services as part of a business unrelated to transportation.

The sorts of trucks used by the for-hire trucking industry tend to be different from those used by industries which do some trucking as part of another business. The intercity for-hire industry uses mostly enclosed vans. The for-hire

FIGURE 7.5   1992 Truck Usage Pattern

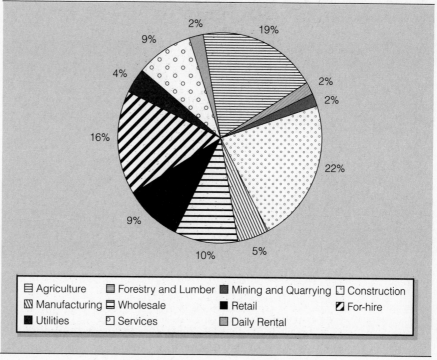

SOURCE: U.S. Bureau of the Census, *Truck Inventory and Use Survey*, 1992

industry is the largest user of standard vans, but still only one-third of standard vans are used by the for-hire industry. The remaining highway vans are used by private shippers for their own use. The for-hire industry is the largest users of heavy trucks (those between 60,000 and 80,000 lbs.), long trucks, and combinations. But the for-hire industry is in every case less than one-half of the total users of these vehicles. Most of the trucks that compete with railroad transport and which affect highway maintenance and construction are operated by non-trucking companies.

Like automobile stocks, the number of trucks on the highway at any time depends on both the number of trucks purchased in any year and the number of trucks that are scrapped. In Table 7.1, attention is limited solely to those trucks that are likely to be used by the over-the-road trucking industry and private truckers who provide services for themselves that are similar to the for-hire industry—heavy trucks and their constituent parts, tractors and trailers. There are approximately three trailers for every tractor unit, reflecting both the fact

TABLE 7.1   U.S. Sales and Stocks of Heavy Tractor-Trailers

Year	New Heavy Truck Sales	New Trailer Sales	Registered Tractors	Registered Trailers
1982	75.8	103.9	1,193.1	3,202.3
1983	81.6	117.7	1,240.3	3,127.8
1984	137.7	213.9	1,100.3	3,241.3
1985	133.6	175.1	1,150.3	3,413.3
1986	112.9	169.2	1,121.8	3,367.5
1987	131.2	180.1	1,134.9	3,484.2
1988	148.4	186.5	1,182.7	3,557.9
1989	145.1	181.5	1,237.1	3,717.1
1990	121.3	149.1	1,240.3	3,606.2
1991	98.7	122.4	1,236.1	3,607.8
1992	119.1	165.3	1,278.8	3,801.9
1993	157.9	185.7	1,288.8	3,906.2
1994	185.7	227.8	1,315.0	4,121.0

SOURCES: American Trucking Associations, *American Trucking Trends*, 1995 Ed., and *Transportation in America*, various editions. New heavy truck sales refer to trucks with gross vehicle weight over 33,001 lbs.

that a tractor may under some circumstances haul more than one trailer at a time, and also the fact that trailers may be left for loading and unloading with the tractor being unhitched to pick up another load. Like all transportation equipment, the pattern of orders for tractors and trailers is erratic. The recent low point of heavy truck sales was 75,800 units in 1982; the recent high was 185,700 in 1994. Trailer sales have not been quite as erratic, generally varying between 100,000 and 200,000 units over the same period. The average price of a tractor-trailer combination in 1994 was $127,000, of which approximately $16,000 represented the value of the trailer and approximately $111,000 was the cost of the tractor. Trailers have a longer expected life than tractors. The median life of a heavy truck is 12 years.

The Costs of Owning Trucks

The heterogeneity of trucks and the diversity of truck users makes it difficult to identify a meaningful cost of owning trucks. The cost of owning a pickup truck is obviously less than the cost of owning a heavy truck. A heavy truck purchased for $100,000 and financed for 12 years at 10 percent interest would require annual payments of $14,676. Trucks are used much more intensively than automobiles, with economic lives measured in miles rather than years. Thus depreciation, some of which is included in the estimate of the annual pay-

TABLE 7.2   Estimated 1994 Truckload Trucking Costs (Based on a Single 48' Truck Unit)

	Cents per Mile	Cents per Loaded Mile	Cents per Ton-Mile	Percent of Total
Labor[1]	39.5	43.8	2.3	35.5
Equipment[2]	38.3	42.5	2.2	34.3
Fuel	18.8	20.8	1.1	16.8
Overhead[3]	5.5	6.1	0.3	4.9
Other costs[4]	9.7	10.8	0.6	8.7
Total	111.8	124.1	6.5	100.0

SOURCE: L. Lee Lane, "Innovation in Trucking: Advanced Truckload Firms," unpublished paper at Association of American Railroads, Intermodal Policy Division. Figures updated from original 1986 calculations to 1994 using producer price index.

[1]Labor includes driver wages, paid time off, and fringe benefits.

[2]Equipment includes original purchase price, depreciation and amortization, vehicle parts, and tires.

[3]Overhead is a markup that includes salaries, paid time off, fringes for all employees other than drivers, general supplies and expenses, communications and utilities, expenses for all non-transportation equipment and buildings, and miscellaneous expenses.

[4]Other costs include federal and state user charges and insurance.

ments, should in most cases be treated as a variable cost of ownership or as an operating cost.

Within the trucking industry, there is increasing specialization of firms into those that carry truckloads and those that solicit LTL (less-than-truckload) traffic. The costs of carrying these two types of traffic is quite distinct. Truckload carriers do not need terminals. J.B. Hunt, a truckload firm, has more than 80 percent of its corporate assets in vehicles. By carefully choosing their customers, specializing in truckload traffic, balancing loads in both directions, using non-union labor, and using new equipment that requires little maintenance, truckload carriers have been able to achieve costs per ton-mile that are close to railroad costs. Table 7.2 shows an estimate by the Association of American Railroads on the costs of such truckload firms. Equipment costs are listed as 34.3 percent of total trucking costs for such firms.

Carriers like J.B. Hunt are still a relatively small part of the trucking industry. More typical of the main bulk of trucking firms is Yellow Freight Systems, a company that gets most of its revenue from less-than-truckload shipments. Such shipments are inevitably much more expensive to handle than truckload movements since they require terminals where partial loads can be consolidated and broken down on either end of the main part of the haul. Because of the added fixed facilities and additional labor to handle less-than-truckload shipments, it is predictable that vehicle costs would be a smaller percentage of

TABLE 7.3   Operating Expenses and Value of Property for Two Trucking
              Companies

Operating Expenses

	Yellow	J.B. Hunt
Salaries, wages, and employee benefits	$1,918,406	$ 457,567
Operating expenses and supplies	433,789	237,831
Operating taxes and licenses	110,004	26,422
Claims and insurance	76,953	50,707
Communications and utilities	41,046	14,822
Depreciation	133,970	130,265
Purchased transportation	142,295	362,989
Total Operating Expenses	**$2,856,481**	**$1,280,603**

Value of Operating Property

	Yellow	J.B. Hunt
Land	141,134	17,313
Structures	613,530	50,962
Revenue equipment	897,426	1,050,986
Other operating property	214,475	65,547
Gross operating property	1,866,565	1,184,808
Less accumulated depreciation	989,281	375,798
Net Operating Property	**877,284**	**809,010**

SOURCE: Annual Reports, Yellow Freight System (1994 fiscal year) and J.B. Hunt (1995 fiscal year)

total costs. That is what is shown in Table 7.3, which displays amounts from the income statements and balance sheet for Yellow Freight Systems. Total expenses of the firm during 1994 were $2.8 billion, of which about $1.9 billion were salaries. Fuel and other supplies were a little more than $.4 billion.

Yellow Freight estimates that their tractors have a useful life of 3–5 years; trailer depreciation lives are 6–8 years. (Used equipment is normally sold to others, however, and will remain on the road several years more). The company uses about $900 million worth of operating equipment. To replace this equipment over a 5-year cycle, the firm should budget approximately $180 million. This is approximately 6 percent of the total costs of the company. Even if insurance and claims (an amount that will surely vary with the level of use of the equipment) is treated as a cost of owning equipment, vehicle costs for this LTL firm, will be considerably less than 10 percent of total expenses.

PUBLIC TRANSIT

While several U.S. cities have rail-based transit systems, most cities are served only by bus systems. As shown in Table 7.4, motor buses and demand response vehicles (mini-buses, municipal taxis, or limousines) comprise more than 80 percent of all vehicles owned by transit companies. Rail vehicles account for about 15 percent of the fleet. With the exception of commuter rail cars, which are not being replaced as rapidly as they wear out, the purchases of new vehicles shown in Table 7.4 are approximately sufficient to keep constant the average age of transit vehicles shown in the last column of the table. Buses appear to have approximately the same life expectancy as private automobiles. Rail vehicles are considerably more durable.

When vehicles are being replaced at a steady state, the annual expenditure on the vehicle stock is an accurate measure of the accumulated depreciation of the vehicles. To get a complete measure of the cost of owning transit vehicles, one would have to add the opportunity cost of funds tied up in car stocks and the non-use based amount of maintenance done on them. Unfortunately, none of these statistics can be estimated from publicly available reports. Part of the reason is the absence of an active market in used transit vehicles. In the absence of such a market, we are forced to rely on accounts such as those shown in Table 7.5. Vehicle maintenance expenditures are approximately 20 percent of total transit system operating costs for all kinds of vehicles. Much of this amount must be considered to be related to use and is thus a cost of operating vehicles rather than owning them.

Most vehicle ownership costs are hidden from view since capital expenditures for transit systems are financed by grants from the federal government

TABLE 7.4   Characteristics of U.S. Transit Vehicle Stocks, 1994

	Number of Vehicles	Number of New Vehicles	Average Age of Vehicles
Motor bus	67,492	5,418	8.9
Rail rapid transit	10,138	55	18.9
Light rail	1,054	72	20.9
Trolley bus	877	36	12.5
Demand response	31,872	na	4.0
Commuter rail	4,517	8	18.8
Total	118,589	5,628	

SOURCE: American Public Transit Association, *Transit Fact Book*, 1994–96 editions. Totals are larger than the sum of individual items due to the inclusion of other minor categories of transit vehicles (e.g., ferry boats). New demand response vehicles are included in motor bus category. Average age of vehicles refers to 1993.

TABLE 7.5   Cost Profiles of Different U.S. Public Transit Modes, 1993

Type of System	Vehicle Operations Costs	Vehicle Maintenance Costs	Total	Maintenance Costs as Percent of Total
Motor bus	$3,503,919	$1,424,461	$ 6,359,200	.22
Rail rapid transit	781,603	586,202	3,101,600	.19
Streetcar	60,122	42,764	157,800	.27
Trolley bus	56,563	19,836	98,200	.20
Demand response	84,528	12,855	176,100	.07
Commuter rail	400,233	272,290	1,640,300	.17
Total	$4,980,940	$2,384,743	$11,747,500	.20

SOURCE: American Public Transit Association, *Transit Fact Book*, 1994–95 edition

which are matched to varying degrees by grants from state and local governments. In 1994, total transit capital expenditures amounted to $5.598 billion, of which a little under half came from the federal government. Of that amount, fixed facilities expenditure (primarily heavy rail and commuter rail) accounted for about 50 percent while rolling stock expenditures were about one quarter. There was $611 million spent on new buses, while about $300 million was spent on new rail cars. Since capital costs are covered by grants, there is no allowance on the account books of public transit systems for the opportunity cost of funds spent on transit vehicles. The wisdom of the division of capital spending between buses and rail has been questioned by advocates for the poor who note that buses are heavily used by lower economic groups while commuter rail is patronized heavily by wealthier groups. However, no mode of public transportation covers its total expenditures and thus, to the extent that there is an economic justification for the maintenance of such services, it must be found in non-market influences that the presence of the services has on the broader community; it is possible that different modes will make different contributions to such non-marketed attributes like air quality and the social vitality of downtown locations.

RAILROADS

Railroads use two kinds of vehicles: locomotives and cars. The primary technical advantage of railroads over road transportation is that a single locomotive can pull many cars, thus economizing on crew and fuel costs.

FIGURE 7.6   **Trends in U.S. Railroad Rolling Stock**

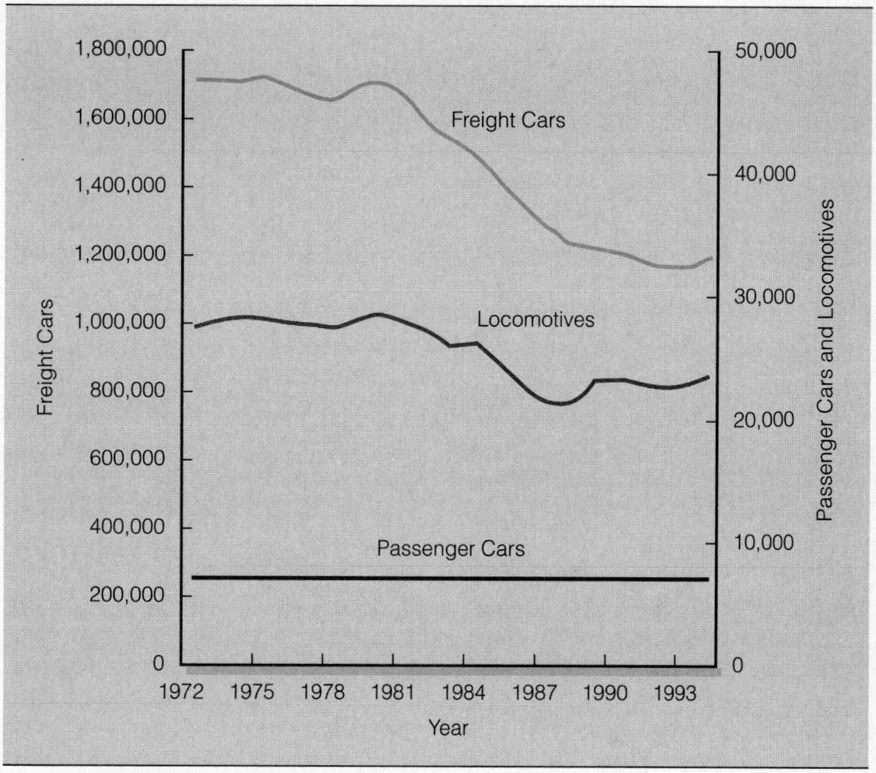

SOURCE: *Transportation in America*, various editions

▬ Railroad Vehicle Stocks

The number of locomotives used by U.S. railroads has declined drastically in the past decade. As shown in Figure 7.6, the locomotive stock declined from about 28,000 during the years before 1982 to a current level of about 22,000. This decline was due to a combination of gradual scrapping of locomotives as they reached the end of their useful life and a huge drop in production of locomotives beginning in 1981. Figure 7.7 shows that the number of locomotives produced in the mid-1990s was a small fraction of those produced in the late 1970s.

The drop in locomotive stocks occurred while the actual amount of railroad freight ton-miles was increasing. Deregulation caused railroads to operate many fewer, but longer and heavier freight trains on track that permitted higher operating speeds. Higher operating speeds means that locomotives can pull more trains per day. Fewer but longer and heavier trains means that the

FIGURE 7.7   U.S. Railroad Equipment Purchases

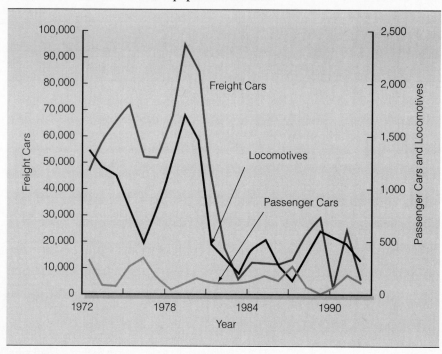

SOURCE: *Transportation in America*, various editions

same number of locomotives can produce more ton-miles. The new locomotives that were purchased are also more powerful than the locomotives they replaced. A train that required four old locomotives can be pulled with three of the modern engines.

Figure 7.6 shows that there has also been a decline in the number of freight cars. The reasons for the decline are also the same—changes in operations has allowed increased quantities of freight to be transported with less equipment. Since new cars need less maintenance, they are available for use more days per year. Having fewer cars tied up in slow trains on branch lines has increased utilization in the same way that it has improved locomotive use. The new freight cars are also larger, meaning that more freight can be handled with fewer cars. As smaller cars are retired and larger cars purchased, the average size of the freight car fleet has risen, offsetting part of the decline in the number of freight cars.

Not all types of freight cars have been declining. Table 7.6 shows that the largest number of railroad freight cars are hopper cars. Covered hoppers are primarily used to carry grain while open hopper cars are used for coal. These types of cars have shown the smallest decline in numbers. The increase in capacity of new equipment is most pronounced with hopper cars. Box cars are used primarily to carry manufactured commodities. These goods are being increasingly moved by truck, and rail shipments are more frequently made using intermodal equipment.

One of the strongest movements in rail cars fleets has been toward car owning by independent car companies, shippers, and smaller railroads. Table 7.6 shows that Class 1 railroads (the largest companies and those with the familiar names) now own only half of their own freight cars. For certain kinds of equipment (e.g., tank cars and covered hoppers), virtually all of the equipment is owned by parties other than the railroad providing the transportation service.

Intermodal equipment has traditionally meant trailers on flatcars for domestic shipments and containers on flatcars for import and export commodities. Rapid technological change in this sector has altered this tradition. There has been an increasing trend of both domestic as well as international freight toward double-stack containers. By stacking two standard containers on top of one another and carrying them on specially-designed flatcars, railroads have been able to greatly improve handling and lower the costs of inter-modal movements substantially below that of competing truck transportation. In

TABLE 7.6   Types of Railroad Freight Equipment Owned by U.S. Railroads and Other Parties, 1994

Type	Class 1 Railroads	Other Railroads	Car Companies and Shippers
Box Cars	104,568	33,113	26,333
Plain Box	17,970	11,836	17,884
Equipment box	86,598	21,277	8,449
Covered hoppers	148,611	11,076	152,223
Flat cars	78,217	62,581	44,292
Refrigerator cars	27,326	3,834	2,568
Gondolas	92,342	15,014	49,272
Hoppers	133,302	14,636	39,927
Tank cars	1,056	36	198,226
Others	5,508	2,153	2,521
Total	590,930	86,120	515,362

SOURCE: *Railroad Facts*, 1995 edition; Association of American Railroads

many parts of the country, this technology requires modification in roadbed or clearances, however. Another innovation that has attracted modest interest is the hauling of modified truck trailers with railroad wheels directly behind a locomotive without the use of a flat car.

The decline in passenger service stabilized with the creation of Amtrak in 1971. The passenger car fleet that was in existence in 1971 was created for a much larger number of railroad passengers; the fleet also did not provide the amenities that the traveling public has become accustomed to while flying on airlines. Amtrak scrapped unneeded cars, rebuilt some to meet more modern standards of comfort and reliability, and purchased a limited number of new cars.

Problems of Railroad Equipment Interchange

Railroads have historically had a problem of poor equipment utilization. In 1985, the average railroad car carried 13.67 loads; in other terms, the average freight car picked up a new load once every 3.8 weeks. But car utilization is improving. By 1994, the average car was loaded 19.5 times per year or once every 2.7 weeks.[2] As a result, railroads have produced increasing numbers of car-miles even as the size of the rolling stock has continued to decline.

The railroad industry has been hampered in its attempt to improve car utilization by the necessity of equipment interchange. By one estimate, 70 percent of railroad car-miles in the mid 1970s involved movements that began on one railroad and terminated on another.[3] The requirement that equipment be interchangeable has hampered innovation in railroad equipment since changes in car standards require approval of competing carriers. It has also limited the ability of individual railroad companies to control the utilization of equipment. As described in Chapter 13, the movement of cars while not on home tracks has been governed by regulations that were made with goals other than that of maximizing efficiency. One railroad might have a plan to improve equipment use but be unable to implement it because it would be opposed to government regulations.

If all railroad tracks were owned by a single company, there could be a substantial improvement in equipment utilization since the problems of equipment interchange would be eliminated. To the extent that the recent railroad mergers have reduced interchange, they should have helped with improving rates of car usage. Some types of cars—intermodal equipment and tank cars— are owned by pool operators rather than individual railroads. For example, Trailer Train has used the ability to dispatch intermodal equipment to the point of greatest need. This has allowed it to raise its equipment use to more than 50 loads per year. The principle of equipment pooling should, in theory, always improve car use by increasing the likelihood of running full rather than empty.

■ The Cost of Owning Railroad Equipment

Freight cars cost approximately $50,000 each; locomotives more than $1,000,000. For two reasons, it is difficult to determine what part of railroad costs is attributable to equipment costs. First, equipment purchases, as noted previously, are extremely erratic, ranging from 1 to 4 percent of the total fleet in recent years. Second, the techniques of financing purchases tends to hide the true costs of equipment.

Table 7.7 shows expenditures of U.S. railroads on rolling stock and on tracks and structures. There has been a distinct shift away from spending on

TABLE 7.7   Capital Expenditures of U.S. Railroads, 1973–1994

Year	Total Capital Expenditure (millions)	Rolling Stock Expenditure (millions)	Rolling Stock as Percent of Total Capital Expenditures	Roadway and Structure Expenditures (millions)	Roadway and Structure Expenditures as Percent of Total
1973	$1,342	$ 893	66.5%	$ 449	33.5%
1974	1,565	1,038	66.3	527	33.7
1975	1,790	1,303	72.8	486	27.2
1976	1,725	1,175	68.1	550	31.9
1977	2,290	1,540	67.2	751	32.8
1978	2,738	1,883	68.8	855	31.2
1979	3,325	2,285	68.7	1,039	31.3
1980	3,621	2,346	64.8	1,275	35.2
1981	2,855	1,521	53.3	1,334	46.7
1982	1,975	713	36.1	1,262	63.9
1983	2,761	455	16.5	2,306	83.5
1984	3,744	806	21.5	2,938	78.5
1985	4,423	956	21.8	3,458	78.2
1986	3,601	693	19.2	2,938	80.8
1987	2,971	657	22.1	2,314	77.9
1988	3,681	1,027	27.9	2,654	72.1
1989	3,709	1,171	31.6	2,538	68.4
1990	3,640	996	27.4	2,644	72.6
1991	3,437	1,068	31.1	2,369	68.9
1992	3,610	874	24.2	2,736	75.8
1993	4,177	1,382	33.1	2,795	66.9
1994	4,885	1,734	35.5	3,152	64.5

SOURCES: Association of American Railroads, *Railroad Ten-Year Trends*, various editions, and *Railroad Facts*, 1995 Edition. Data before and after 1983 are not comparable due to a change in methods of depreciation.

equipment beginning in 1981 corresponding with the major decline in equipment purchases. At approximately the same time there was a major increase in spending on roadway and structures, thus changing the percentage of capital spending on equipment from two-thirds to one-quarter.

The figures in Table 7.7 show only capital expenditures on equipment. Under traditional equipment financing methods, equipment was purchased for railroads by banks; the railroad paid off the equipment obligations over 15 years. Recently, more equipment has been purchased by non-railroads. Such equipment expenditures are not shown in Table 7.7, but will be listed as an expense in railroad company accounts. Equipment expenditures for railroads have averaged approximately 25 percent of total reported railroad expenses. Since some equipment expenditures are made by shippers and other non-railroad interests, it is reasonable to treat 25 percent as a lower bound of the proportion that equipment expenses represent of total railroad costs. The true figure is probably greater than 30 percent.

SHIPS, BOATS, AND BARGES

There are four different kinds of maritime freight transportation in the United States, each with its own type of craft and its own cost structure. In order of expenditure on the type of transport, they are: (1) ocean-going transport (almost exclusively export-import trades); (2) coastal trade; (3) inland river and canal operations; (4) Great Lakes/St. Lawrence Seaway sailings. Inland river and canal transport is made with shallow-draft vessels while the other three types of water transport generally use deep-draft ships. While both forms of water transport share the advantages of being able to transport large quantities of freight with very little motive energy, the costs of owning each type of craft is sufficiently different as to be treated separately.

Deep Sea Ships

Deep sea ships are designed to handle dry bulk cargoes (grain or coal, for example); liquid commodities (crude oil or products); or containerized traffic. Containerized traffic in turn can be carried in fully cellular ships (which are designed to carry only containers), roll-on/roll-off (sophisticated ferries), or semi-cellular (a hybrid of bulk and container ship). The standard measure of the size of a container ship is the number of 20-foot equivalent units, or TEUs that it can carry. Modern container ships can carry several thousand TEUs. For bulk carriers, a common measure of size is deadweight tonnage or the carrying capacity of the ship measured in long tons.

Ocean shipping of U.S. imports and exports is carried on a fleet of ships which serve the world's ports. There is a U.S. merchant marine which serves coastal trades and some international trade, but for most purposes, U.S. deep sea transportation should be seen as using part of the world fleet of ships; it is the size of the world ship fleet, rather than the U.S. merchant marine, that determines what shippers must pay for maritime transportation. Figure 7.8 shows that there has been nearly a doubling in the size of the world fleet of deep-draft ships over the last 20 years. This has paralleled the increase in the amount of international trade. While there has been a steady increase in "other vessel types" (which includes general cargo, general cargo/passenger, refrigerated cargo, container, and roll-on/roll-off ships), there has been an erratic increase in the size of the fleet of oil tankers, corresponding to the large rise in the price of oil in the late 1970s and the collapse of oil prices in the 1980s. At the beginning of the period, oil tankers comprised 39 percent of the world fleet while ore and dry bulk carriers represented 24 percent of the ships. In 1993, the two kinds of ships were each 31 percent of the total. In both the first and last years of the table, other vessel types were about 38 percent of the total.

Deep sea ships are custom made for buyers who generally have particular routes and services for which they intend the vessels. Modern ships, which are

FIGURE 7.8   The World Shipping Fleet, 1972–1993

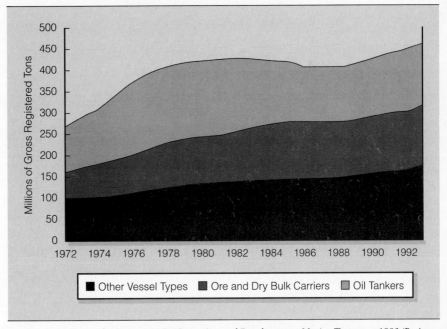

SOURCE: Organization for Economic Co-Operation and Development, *Marine Transport 1993* (Paris: 1995). Figures are for ships of 100 gross registered tons and over.

generally constructed in shipyards in other countries, can cost $100 million or more. Since each ship is constructed to specifications, a shipping company can order ships that are exactly the right size for the service on which they will be used. Very large ships have lower operating and construction costs per unit of capacity than smaller ships. The same principle that is credited for economies of scale in pipeline diameters also affects ship construction costs: Capacity is determined by volume, whereas construction costs tend to be roughly proportional to surface area. Econometric costing exercises find that ship construction costs are subject to the "two thirds power rule," meaning that ship costs are proportional to ship size raised to a power of 2/3.[4] While there are important economies in construction of large vessels and clear but less important economies in operation of large ships, these are counterbalanced by the lower frequencies that are required to fill large ships and by the lengthened port time necessary to load and unload large ships. The average size of new ships has been affected by the price of fuel, the opening and closing of cargo routes, and the changing importance of speed.

Ships have very long and unpredictable lives. Unlike automobiles, where the past pattern of scrappage can be used to estimate the expected lifetime of a new car, the ocean-going ship industry has over the last three decades seen a rapid increase in the size of the fleet with relatively little scrappage of the new vintage of ships.[5] When ordering new ships, a life of 20 years is often assumed, but most ships will survive much longer.

Table 7.8 shows estimates for three different bulk carriers delivered in 1991. By far the largest cost element for this form of deep-draft shipping is the cost of paying off the loan used to buy the ship. For the smallest of the three ships, the annual capital cost represented 44 percent of total annual costs. For the largest ship, it was 69 percent. Some portion of maintenance and insurance costs should probably be considered vehicle costs as well. In any case, vehicle ownership costs for deep draft bulk shipping represent the highest percentage of total costs of any mode of transportation.

The long and uncertain life of ships means that depreciation is relatively less important as an element of ownership costs than the opportunity cost of funds tied up in the fleet. The long life of the fleet and uncertain future demand for shipping services means that the value of the shipping fleet is constantly changing and may bear little resemblance to the original cost of constructing the ship. As explained in Chapter 11, when the demand for shipping services is high, using a ship on any particular route requires bidding the services of the ship away from another route for which it is suitable; when the demand for shipping services is relatively low and there are plenty of vessels available, the opportunity cost of using a ship may be quite low. The opportunity cost of ships is reflected in the value of used ships.

The prices of used ships, and hence the opportunity cost of owning them, is extremely volatile. When there is a glut of ships, ship ownership costs will be far less than those shown in Figure 7.8; a change in market conditions can lead ship ownership costs to be far higher. In July 1996, the rental rate for a stan-

TABLE 7.8   Projected Annual Costs for Three Bulk Carriers

Description of Ship and Projected Use			
Size of ship	25,000 tons	65,000 tons	120,000 tons
Cost of building ship	$ 17,000,000	$31,700,000	$ 59,000,000
Commodity	grain	coal	iron ore
Loading port	U.S. Gulf	Virginia	Brazil
Discharge port	Japan	Japan	Rotterdam
Voyage miles	14,400	13,000	10,000
Days at sea per voyage	44	41	31
Days in port per voyage	8	6	6
Voyages per year	6.7	7.4	9.5
Fuel oil (metric tons per voyage)	960	1,220	1,480
Diesel oil (metric tons per voyage)	105	120	115
Cost Calculation			
Manning	$ 611,000	$ 592,000	$ 633,000
Maintenance and repair	276,000	320,000	428,000
Stores and lubricating oils	189,000	272,000	317,000
Insurance	247,000	288,000	390,000
Administration	131,000	128,000	150,000
Fuel costs	1,140,675	1,576,200	2,382,125
Annual capital costs	2,100,000	4,438,000	9,436,000
Total Annual Costs	$4,694,675	$7,614,200	$13,736,125

SOURCE: Lane C. Kendall, *The Business of Shipping*, 5th ed. (Centreville, MD: Cornell Maritime Press, 1986 p. 356). Fuel costs calculated using $150/metric ton for fuel oil and $250/metric ton for marine diesel oil.

dard liner making a transatlantic round trip was $8,621 per day. In recent years, this figure has varied greatly depending on market conditions.

Inland River and Canal Boats

Modern river boats bear little resemblance to the paddle wheel steamboats described by Mark Twain. The vast majority of all shallow draft operations use a tow of barges pushed by a large towboat. Each towboat is capable of handling 20 or more barges, lashed together so that they are maneuverable as a single craft. Tows are generally too long and too wide to pass through locks. They are disassembled, often into groups of nine barges, for passage through locks, and then reassembled beyond to continue the trip. The average barge can hold 1,400 tons of freight—far more than an average rail car's 70 tons, or a standard truck's 40-ton gross weight limit. A standard tow can move as much freight as many ocean-going ships.[6]

U.S. barge fleet numbers about 30,000 dry vessels and 5,000 tankers. In 1994 there were 5,210 towboats or tugs. Large towboats have a purchase price of approximately $700,000 and barges cost about $500,000. Table 7.9 lists a breakdown of expenditures by seven towing firms in the late 1970s. Assuming that insurance, depreciation, and maintenance expenses are all costs of vehicle ownership (and subtracting the cost of towing by others to avoid double counting), vehicle ownership costs in barge transportation are approximately 30 percent of total expenses. As with deep-draft vessels, barges and towboats are long-lived and subject to periodic gluts and shortages. The fleet increased rapidly during the 1970s and then abruptly stopped growing in the early 1980s. An

TABLE 7.9   Costs of Inland Water Transportation

Costs Attributable to Towboat Operations	Percent
Wages and fringe benefits	13.78
Insurance	2.86
Depreciation of boat	2.78
Maintenance	4.88
Fuel	16.03
Lubricants	0.69
Other	4.04
Towing by others	13.73
Costs Attributable to Barge Operations	
Insurance	2.06
Depreciation on barge	8.17
Maintenance	4.59
Other	1.01
Port Costs	
Shifting/fleeting	12.60
Cargo Costs	
Cleaning and cargo insurance	3.10
General and Administrative Costs	9.68
Total	100.00

SOURCE: National Transportation Policy Study Commission, *National Transportation Policies through the Year 2000, Final Report*, June 1979. Figures are for seven firms surveyed by the Interstate Commerce Commission, in Suspension Board Case No. 68652 dated November 3, 1978.

overcapacity in barges and towboats reduced their value and with it the proportion of transportation costs represented by vehicle ownership. For a period of several years in the mid-1980s barge building stopped. By the 1990s, barge construction had resumed.

AIRLINES

As is the case with ocean shipping, the cost of aircraft ownership is determined by the world market for aircraft. Aircraft are distinguished by engine type (piston or jet), by seating capacity, and range. The very largest aircraft can seat as many as 600 people and can fly up to 8,000 miles without refueling. In 1994 there were 18,342 fixed wing aircraft in commercial service in the world. Of these, approximately 7,000 were part of fleets of U.S. air carriers. The largest number are in the short-range category. The segment with the highest value—and the one that is increasing most rapidly—is the long-range high capacity category dominated by the Boeing 747.

There is an active market in used aircraft; the price volatility in the used aircraft market is similar to that in the market for used ships, and for similar reasons. As with ships, aircraft are very long-lived pieces of equipment with a useful life that is not accurately predicted either by age or by use. The value of aircraft increases when the demand for flying increases anywhere in the world. The value of the aircraft fleet decreases when demand falls.

In the late 1980s, the world aircraft industry anticipated an increasing rate of orders due to the growth of airline passengers, a decreasing tolerance of the noise of an older generation of jets, fears for the safety of older planes, and, eventually, the replacement of aircraft that have come to the end of their life as passenger planes and, following the standard pattern, are converted to use as freighters. This expectation of increased demand bid up the value of used aircraft and created long delivery queues for the world's aircraft builders. However, in the early 1990s, the market crashed as the expected increases in traffic volume did not materialize and as the financial condition of U.S. airlines prevented them from following through on aircraft orders. This drastically dropped the price of used aircraft and swept away the order backlog at manufacturers.

In 1996, a new 747–400 had a list price of $156 million. At that price, an airline must earn more than $100 per day per seat simply to pay off a 20-year loan used to buy the aircraft. The expense of new aircraft has encouraged airlines to make increasing use of leasing companies who buy aircraft directly from the manufacturer and charge users by the day to operate the planes. Approximately 79 percent of operating assets of U.S. airlines is represented by the value of flight equipment (the remainder being various types of ground equipment and buildings).

TABLE 7.10   1996 Value and Operating Expenses of Various Used Aircraft

Aircraft Type and Year of Manufacture	Number of Units in U.S. Fleet	Expected Hours per Plane per Year	Value of Plane in 1996 ($Million)
767-300 (1991)	105	4,655	$ 55.3
MD-11 (1995)	28	4,635	90.1
747-400 (1992)	33	4,950	105.0
737-300 (1990)	426	3,895	23.9
727-200A-17 (1978)	443	3,155	2.5
A320-200 (1992)	92	4,012	33.1
Brasilia (1991)	89	3,181	4.7
Metro IIIA (1986)	22	2,812	1.0
Dash 8-100 (1992)	23	3,032	6.0

SOURCE: Calculated from Aircraft Values and Aircraft Operating Data presented in various 1996 issues of *Air Transport* and then divided by annual block hours per plane in fleet; this figure was then compared with reported total direct costs to *World*. Annualized projected 5-year depreciation rates and a 10 percent interest rate was applied to reported aircraft value calculate the last column.

There is some disagreement about the length of the economic life of an airplane. Some aircraft have been made technologically obsolete by changes in fuel prices and the rapid improvement in fuel economy made over the last decade by aircraft designers. The design life of aircraft is between 20 and 30 years; however, the previous generation of propeller aircraft has been kept in service indefinitely through increased maintenance, and the U.S. industry has assumed that the same will be true of the current generation of aircraft. Several incidents of partial disintegration of aircraft in flight and a cluster of accidents of older aircraft have cast doubt on the validity of the assumption that economic lives of aircraft are longer than their design lives. European aviation administrations limit commercial passenger service to aircraft younger than 25 years. The U.S. Federal Aviation Administration disagrees and sees no reason to assume that older airplanes are any less safe than newer ones.

An indication of the importance of aircraft ownership costs is shown in Table 7.10, which displays 1996 values for nine different kinds of used aircraft. Aircraft values vary with age and with size. For the most modern large aircraft, depreciation and interest allowances account for about a third of the sum of fixed and variable costs. For smaller commuter planes, which tend to be more fuel and labor intensive, this figure is less. Smaller aircraft tend to spend more hours per year on the ground, and thus the fixed cost of equipment needs to be spread over fewer expected operating hours. The long distance 747–400 by contrast spends more than half the hours in the year flying passengers. As with any used equipment, owners trade lower fixed costs against higher operating costs. As shown in Table 7.10, a 1978 727 is an especially cheap plane and thus the

TABLE 7.10 (Continued)

Depreciation + Interest per Hour of Operation	Direct Cost per Hour of Operation	Deprecation + Interest as Percent of Total
$1,396	$3,083	31
2,071	4,397	32
2,267	6,603	34
916	1,830	33
123	2,231	5
399	1,900	17
185	514	26
43	531	8
283	851	25

fixed costs of owning the equipment is very low—only 5 percent of the total costs of flying.

CONCLUSION

The costs of owning transportation vehicles (as opposed to using the vehicles or creating roads and railroads to operate them on) is the largest part of transport costs. This is due to the overwhelming importance of automobile transportation in the American budget and to the fact that the automobile ownership costs account for more than half of the costs of automotive transportation. There is six-tenths of an automobile for every man, woman, and child in the United States. The rate of vehicle holdings continues to increase every year as the level of automobile scrappage lags behind the rate of new car purchases.

A rapidly growing share of the population has turned to light trucks for personal transportation and the U.S. industry has been successful at maintaining its dominance of the truck building business. Trucks are an extremely diverse class of vehicles. In the last census of trucks in 1992, 800,000 heavy trucks pulling enclosed vans operated on U.S. highways. These are the basic vehicles of the over-the-road trucking industry, although a majority of these trucks are owned and operated by companies who do not see themsleves as primarily in the trucking business. Most trucking is not done by the for-hire trucking industry but by manufacturers, retailers, or wholesalers carrying their own goods. The diversity of the trucking industry makes impossible a single estimate of vehicle ownership costs. Vehicle ownership costs—making no allowance for the depreciation and maintenance costs of using trucks—range from about 5 percent of total costs for less-than-truckload firms to about 15 percent for truckload companies. If maintenance and depreciation costs are added in, vehicle costs approach one-third of all trucking costs.

Unlike other modes of transportation, the fleet of railroad equipment—both locomotives and cars—is rapidly shrinking. The decline in rolling stock is partly the result of improved equipment utilization following deregulation. It cannot be predicted how far improvements in utilization will allow equipment levels to decline in the future. Currently, rolling stock expenses account for more than 30 percent of total railroad costs.

Deep draft maritime shipping is far more vehicle cost intensive than railroads. By one estimate, between about one-half and two-thirds of the total cost of a voyage of bulk carriers is accounted for by paying for loans (or equivalent implicit costs) used to purchase the vessel. The larger the ship, the larger is capital costs as a percentage of total cost. Ship values can change abruptly, however, depending on supply and demand conditions for the shipping industry, thus making the expenses based on the original cost of the vessel a poor guide of the opportunity cost of owning ships. Shallow-draft shipping, since it is more labor intensive, has a lower percentage of total costs attributable to owning barges and towboats. Approximately 30 percent of shallow-draft shipping costs are attributable to owning, maintaining, and depreciating equipment. This percentage is approximately the same as the truckload trucking industry.

Modern, long-range aircraft tend to have vehicle costs of about one-third of all expenses. Since commuter airlines tend to be more labor intensive, the importance of vehicle costs is correspondingly less. With all transportation equipment, there is a tradeoff between vehicle costs and maintenance expenditures. Older aircraft tend to be much cheaper and thus appear on the books to have much lower vehicle costs associated with their operation.

NOTES

1. AAMA, *Motor Vehicle Facts and Figures*, 1995, p. 20. Note that these figures do not make an allowance for the recent movement toward increasing the use of trucks for personal transportation.
2. Calculated as the total number of carloads in 1985, 19.42 million, divided by the number of serviceable cars, 1.42 million. In 1995, 23.18 million carloads were carried in 1.19 million cars. From *AAR Railroad Facts*, 1995.
3. Harris, Robert G., and Clifford Winston, "Potential Benefits of Rail Mergers: An Econometric Analysis of Network Effects on Service Quality," *The Review of Economics and Statistics*, Vol. 65 (February 1983), pp. 32–40.
4. Jansson, J. O. and D. Shneerson, *Liner Shipping Economics* (London: Chapman and Hall, 1987), pp. 129–130. The authors find that for ships delivered in 1976/77, log(building cost) = -4.236 + .655(log S), where S is the deadweight tonnage of the ship.

5. Pearson, Roy and John Fossey, *World Deep-Sea Container Shipping* (Aldershot, Haunts, England: Gower Publishing), 1983.
6. This description is based on National Waterways Foundation, *U.S. Waterways Productivity: A Private and Public Partnership* (Huntsville, Alabama: The Strode Publishers, 1983).

8

The Costs of Operating Transport Vehicles

The most obvious costs of transport operations are the time of the driver (or crew) who is operating the vehicle and the cost of the fuel. There is no ambiguity about whether the expenditures for transport operations are true opportunity costs. In almost every case they are: the fuel saved by not moving a vehicle could have been used to generate electricity or make plastics; the opportunity cost of the fuel is measured as the value of the electricity or plastics that could have been produced. The time of the crew operating the vehicle might have been used to manufacture some good; the value of labor is what an employer would have been willing to pay the crew to work in the non-transport sector.

The cost of operating vehicles includes more than the obvious costs of fuel and crew time. In Chapter 6, we noted that operating vehicles causes roadways to wear out. In Chapter 7, we saw that the amount of maintenance that needs to be done on vehicles will vary with the level of usage and thus may be treated as a cost of operating vehicles even if the maintenance costs are born by the vehicle owner rather than the vehicle operator. Maintenance is the clearest example of effort by non-operating personnel required to operate vehicles. But every transport operation needs a support staff of non-operating workers like reservation clerks, dispatchers, and lawyers. The required level of this support staff will generally vary with the level of vehicle operations.

THE COSTS OF OPERATING RAILROAD TRAINS

The low rolling resistance of steel wheels on steel rails makes railroad transportation extremely fuel efficient. Railroads produce 360 ton-miles of freight transport per gallon of fuel consumed.[1] Fuel costs account for about 8 percent of railway operating expenses. This is far less than other modes of transportation and is the major advantage of railroads.

The same advantage is not seen in labor costs. The combined cost of salaries and wages, fringe benefits, and payroll taxes accounts for more than 43 percent of railroad operating costs. While the small number of railroad employees who actually ride on freight trains makes it appear that railroads have extremely low labor costs, in fact rail is one of the most labor intensive modes of transport. Labor costs are higher than would be expected in part because vehicle operations require many more support personnel than do other modes of transportation. Track repair crews, yard switching crews, car shop employees, and traffic sales staff are all necessary to keep trains moving. Figure 8.1 shows that only about three-eighths of railroad employees are actually involved with running trains. Most railroaders maintain the roadbed or rolling stock or are involved in general administration.

Another reason for high railroad labor costs is the traditional relationship between rail management and labor, determined in large part by federal law and by union contracts. Railroads employ more workers than would be required for efficient operations and pay them higher salaries than they would be able to earn in other occupations. Railway workers in 1994 earned an average of $69,671 in wages and fringe benefits, compared to $42,728 for Class 1 and 2 motor carriers, $45,812 for airlines, and $45,343 for maritime operators.[2] If railroads paid market wages and were allowed to determine staffing levels by commercial criteria rather than historical requirements, railroads would be a lower cost mode of transport than they are today.[3]

Transportation expenses divided by revenue ton-miles in 1994 was just under 1 cent per ton-mile. The total of all expenses divided by output was a little more than 2 cents per ton-mile. Since some equipment costs, general and administrative, and way and structures cost are traffic sensitive, it is reasonable to assume that the true average variable costs of railroad operations would be somewhere between these two extremes.[4]

The Cost of Individual Movements

The percentages quoted above are for all railroad operations, summing together the costs of short hauls of stone, long hauls of double-stack container trains, and movements of wheat, automobiles, and chemicals. The costs of individual

FIGURE 8.1   U.S. Railroad Employment Levels, 1994

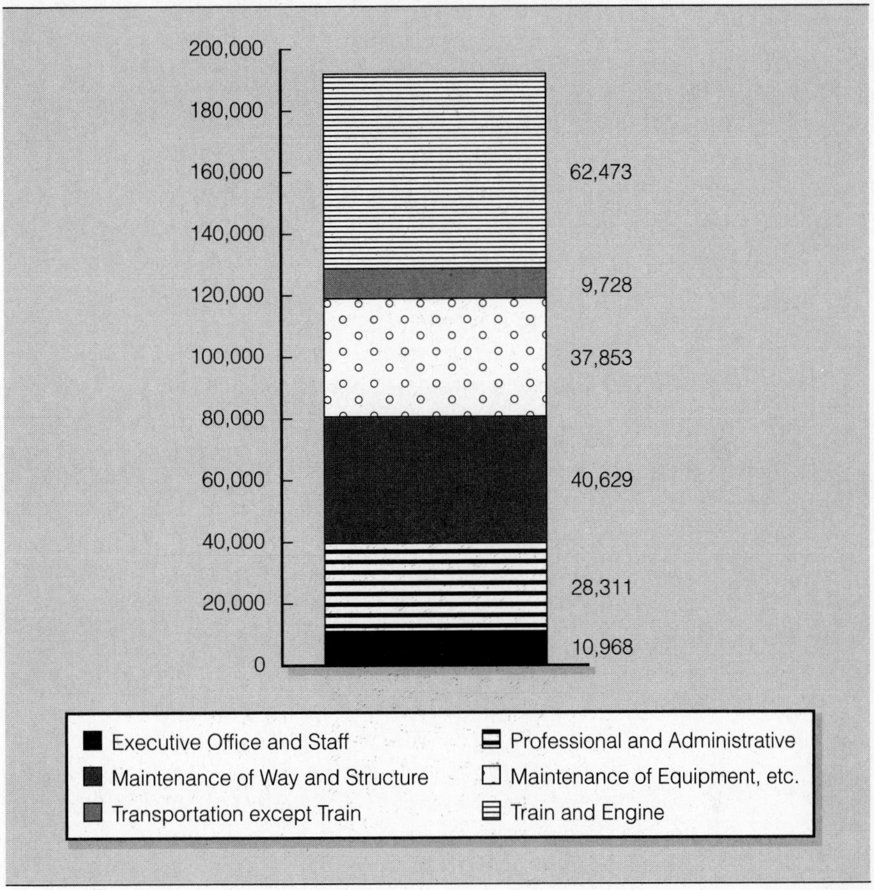

SOURCE: Association of American Railroads, *Railroad Facts*, 1995 edition

rail movements may be much lower or higher than the average for all traffic. Due to the nature of railroad operations, operations costs are much more variable than for other modes of transport. The best known source of the cost variability of individual movements is back-hauling equipment. Railroad cars that have carried a load from a shipper to receiver must be returned to the original location, regardless of whether they are loaded on the return trip or not. The labor associated with moving a loaded car is identical to that needed to move it empty, and the additional fuel cost to moving a loaded car is small. So the economic cost of a shipment loaded into a car that was returning to its original location is much lower than the average cost of generating freight ton-miles. In fact, the cost of returning the car to the original shipper should, under most circumstances, be treated as a cost of making the original shipment. We will return to the question of back-haul costs in Chapter 10.

Back-hauls are not the sole reason that the costs of individual rail movements can vary from the average. Fuel and labor handling costs of moving a ton of rail freight will vary greatly depending on the amount of other freight in a car; on the type of equipment used to handle the freight; on the length of the train in which the car is moved; on the terrain, track quality, and track congestion of the line in which the movement is made; on the number of yards through which a shipment moves and the degree of congestion in those yards; on the size and regularity with which shipments of this type are made; and on many more factors.

More than any other mode of transportation, railroad costs are unpredictable on the basis of a few simple traffic descriptions. A traffic manager can predict with reasonable accuracy the costs of moving a truckload of oranges 1,000 miles knowing little more than whether a return load is available to the trucker. Such is not the case in railroads; in order to estimate what the costs of a shipment would be, a traffic manager would have to know about the railroad operation in great detail. For example, a consultant trying to calculate the cost of shipping iron ore from Mountain Iron, Minnesota to Duluth, a distance of 134 miles, required 6 pages of description of the rail line and more than 100 pages of description of a single train movement in order to justify his calculation. In order to calculate the costs of one movement, it was necessary to detail the train size, car type and size, ruling grade of the track, speed limits, traffic density, train delays, running times, car utilization, other train movements on the tracks, and a description of all yards and terminals that the train would pass through.[5]

Data on the true costs of railroad operations are critical if railroads are to price their operations most profitably and if regulators are to evaluate whether a particular rate is justified. With railroad costs highly variable and railroad pricing specifically targeted to individual flows of traffic, both railroad management and railroad regulators would like to have cost information at the finest level possible—hopefully, at the level of individual car movements. Unfortunately, however, ideal cost data is illusory to hope for—even for railroad management. The cost of making a cost study of a particular car movement would surely be more costly than making the shipment itself.

In place of the detailed engineering studies that would be necessary to determine the cost of making particular freight shipments, government regulators have developed a system based on the systemwide average of performing a limited number of railroad transportation functions. Under the Uniform Rail Costing System (URCS), railroad companies are required to report expenses in a number of categories: running track maintenance, running crew wages, transportation fuel, yard operations, yard locomotive repairs, freight car repairs, and so on. The regulator then found which of several indicators correspond most closely to each of these expenses. Indicators are car-miles, gross ton-miles, locomotive-miles, yard hours, etc. The next step is to determine, on the basis of gross results from all railroads, the amount by which expenses in each category increase as the indicator variable increased; for example, the regulator might determine that on the basis of all railroads' experience, a one-hour increase in yard switching time increased yard expenses by $25.64. The variable cost of making a particular freight movement is then approximated by determining how many yard-hours, tons, ton-miles, road-miles, and so on that the shipment accounted for. The dollars per unit of each item in each category are then summed to produce an approximation to the cost of making the particular movement.[6]

The Cost of Operating All Railroad Services

One reason that URCS fails to identify accurately the costs of particular movements is that it does not properly account for the relationship between traffic levels and costs. As described in Chapter 5, operating costs are likely to rise as the physical capacity of fixed facilities is reached. The cost penalty in high operating rates is assumed to arise from inefficiencies that result from congestion of key tracks and equipment. Congestion causes traffic to slow, increasing the amount of time for which operating labor must be paid to complete a shipment. Congestion will also increase the amount of time for which cars must be hired and thus increase vehicle ownership costs as well. Economists also assume that there is a variety of other subtle cost effects that arise from production bottlenecks when any fixed facility is operated more rapidly than it was designed for. These inefficiencies of excessive use of fixed facilities may be difficult to identify at their source, but will show up at the end of the year in the cost accounts of the firm.

Neither the URCS nor engineering studies are designed to deal with traffic levels other than those that prevailed during the period of the cost study. That is, they are not set up to answer the question, "What will happen to average or marginal costs if traffic expands or contracts?" They are simply intended to determine the current average cost level—a level assumed not to change when traffic levels change. The only way to deal with the question of the relationship between cost levels and traffic levels is to change the perspective to aggregate traffic flows. While the main reason for this change in perspective is practical—data availability—there is a good economic reason for analyzing the relationship between costs and traffic levels using aggregate data. The railroad industry produces many different kinds of services using the same tracks and vehicles. Traffic levels that congest a track will congest it for *all* traffic on that line, not just the traffic that has increased.

Authors who have attempted to estimate the degree to which costs rise or fall with traffic levels have not distinguished between operations costs and total costs including vehicle ownership and the costs of fixed facilities. Including these costs makes the shape of railroad cost curve resemble the one shown in Figure 8.2. Figure 8.2 is drawn for aggregate traffic levels of an individual railroad system. The declining lines marked *average track costs* and *average rolling stock costs* are drawn with the shape of average fixed costs. In

FIGURE 8.2   **The Approximate Shape of Aggregate Railroad Costs**

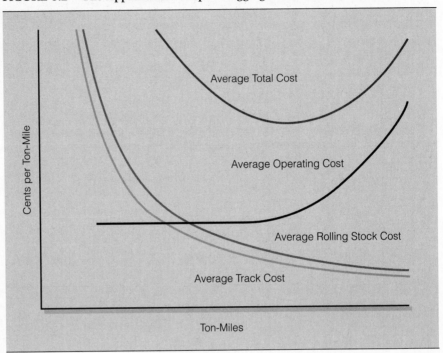

Figure 8.2, vehicle stocks and fixed facilities levels are held fixed, but traffic levels of each traffic type are assumed to increase proportionally. Summing together average vehicle operations costs, vehicle costs, and fixed facilities costs produces the line marked *average total cost*. It has the classic shape that average cost curves have in all of microeconomic analysis. It slopes down initially due to spreading the fixed costs of vehicles and facilities over a larger traffic base and slopes up eventually as the influence of rising average vehicle operations costs at high output levels overcomes the effect of spreading fixed costs of vehicles and fixed facilities.

There is much literature covering econometric estimates of the average total cost curve in the railroad industry. Without exception, railroad cost studies show that railroads operate either in the region at which average total costs are a minimum or in the region to the left. In short, there is no evidence that railroads operate in the region of diminishing returns to the variable inputs: Fixed facilities appear, on average, not to be overused. In one well known estimate, Keeler estimated that cost minimization—which requires that railroads operate in a region in which traffic continuously presses against the limitations of fixed facilities—would require that railroads abandon more than 100,000 miles of tracks.[7]

Economies of Size versus Economies of Density

The concept of economies of scale in multi-service enterprises is based on a hypothetical exercise where all traffic levels are increased by a common percentage—say, 10 percent—and all inputs are adjusted optimally to accommodate the change in traffic levels. As explained in Chapter 5, in the case of transportation enterprises like railroads the concept of scale economies is unworkable since trackage has a geographical description. It makes no sense to increase all tracks by 10 percent to accommodate a 10 percent increase in traffic. A 10 percent increase in trackage would require the extension of a line to a new geographic area (thus increasing the scope of services offered by the company); or double tracking part of one line, in which case some but not all shippers will benefit. A 10 percent decrease in track would similarly require adjustments that would affect some but not all users. The only unambiguous measure of cost responsiveness to changes in traffic levels is one in which trackage is held fixed as all outputs change by a common percentage. As discussed in Chapter 5, this measure is called an economy of density to emphasize that it is not the exact equivalent to the economic concept of scale economies.

The precision of the definitions of cost concepts has not been matched by the precision of measurements of railroad economies of density or size. With the exception of two time-series studies of individual railroads, all railroad cost studies have used cross-section data.[8] In these exercises, the costs of moving a ton-mile of freight on different railroads are compared with the size of the networks, the amount of freight traffic, and various control variables. Despite the fact that railroads differ in their traffic composition and the geographic spread of their networks, the extent to which costs vary with ton-miles of traffic is assumed to be a measure of size economies and the extent to which costs vary with ton-miles per mile of trackage is assumed to be a measure of density economies. They are not, of course, exact measures; theoretically correct measurements would require that all railroads have identical traffic mixes and identical (though somehow larger or smaller) networks; given the data, however, it is probably the best that can be done.

The general conclusion of modern railroad cost studies is that carriers operate under approximately constant returns to size but strong economies of density.[9] In other words, those railroads that have a high traffic per mile of track have low costs while those railroads that have both large amounts of traffic and track will not necessarily be low-cost carriers. Figure 8.3 is a diagram that reconciles the presence of density economies with the lack of scale economies. Both railroad A and railroad B in Figure 8.3 are positioned on declining portions of their average total cost curves; this means that neither railroad has experienced operating difficulties due to capacity constraints on their tracks. Railroad A is larger than railroad B, as evidenced by its higher traffic level (it produces X_A rather than X_B ton-miles) and its higher ATC curve which reflects larger amounts of fixed costs; they both have the same average total

FIGURE 8.3   Reconciling Economies of Density and Economies of Scale

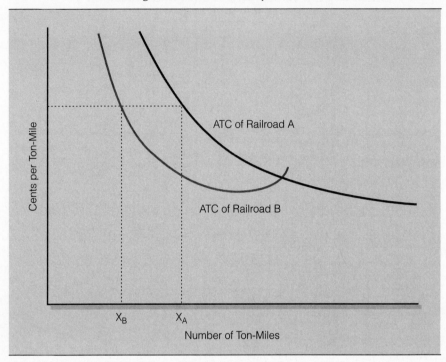

costs despite their differences in size since both of them are operating well to the left of the minimum point on their average total cost curves.

The cost estimates which find density economies but not size economies are based on the total costs of railroad operations including vehicle and track costs, not just vehicle costs. One possible explanation for the economies of density is simply spreading track costs over more traffic. However, since track costs are only about 20 percent of total railroad costs, spreading a fixed cost is unlikely to be the sole explanation for the strong economies of density found by econometric studies. It seems likely that if traffic is more highly concentrated on a few lines, train length can be optimized and improvements like those illustrated in Chapter 5 can be made in operating procedures to allow lower operating costs.

THE COSTS OF OPERATING TRUCKS

Chapter 7 described the diversity of types of trucks. Most trucks are not used by the trucking industry but by individuals and companies providing transportation services for themselves. The cost of operating trucks will, of course, depend on the type of truck and the type of operation in which they are used.

The cost per ton-mile of operating a fully loaded 80,000 lb. van in intercity operations will be a tiny fraction of the cost per ton-mile of providing local pickup and delivery of small packages within a metropolitan area.

The economics profession has focused most of its attention on the for-hire segment of the trucking industry, but private users of trucks operate more trucks and produce more ton-miles of transportation services than the for-hire industry. There is, however, virtual ignorance among economists of the costs of operating private fleets. The profession has assumed that the costs of operating private fleets must be similar to the operating costs of the for-hire industry, where data availability is much better.

Firms that carry general commodities are operationally different from those that carry specialized goods: household goods, heavy machinery, liquid petroleum products, forest products, motor vehicles, building materials, refrigerated goods, etc. It is worth noting that the commodities in which railroads compete most successfully with truckers are those transported by specialized commodity carriers. Carriers of specialized commodities have historically received less regulatory oversight than general commodities carriers. Transport regulation has traditionally distinguished between exempt carriers (primarily haulers of agricultural commodities) who were free from all regulation; contract carriers, who were limited in the number of shippers with whom they could deal, but were otherwise generally free to negotiate rates without government approval; and common carriers, who were considered to be a public utility and were regulated as such. Common carriage obligations required that a trucking company be available to the general public for service at posted and approved rates. Any shipper who was willing to pay the posted price had to receive nondiscriminatory service treatment from the carrier. The lifting of common carriage limitations began in 1980 and by 1994 deregulation was complete. Trucking regulation and deregulation is described in Chapter 13.

▬ Costs of the Truckload and Less-than-Truckload Industries

As noted in Chapter 7, the distinction between TL and LTL motor carriers is important because the operating costs of the two types of operations are quite distinct. Truckload carriers' operating expenses consists primarily of labor and fuel, but some part of equipment maintenance and insurance expenses should also be attributed to vehicle operations. Labor and fuel costs for truckload carriers are about three and one-half cents per ton-mile.

Truckload costs are easy to predict and analyze. There is none of the ambiguity of how much the presence of each freight car has caused the costs of operating a train to change. The only difficulty in analyzing the costs of truckload carriers is how to deal with the cost of an empty back-haul. However, it is uncommon to find truckload carriers returning empty. The use of freight brokers, the willingness to make triangle trips to maximize the proportion of mileage traveled with a load, and occasionally the unwillingness to take a load without a prearranged back-haul all enable the truckload operator to minimize empty mileage. Moreover, the intensely competitive nature of the truckload market should, according to economic theory, ensure that the rate charged will be equal to marginal cost; thus to discover the cost of making a truckload shipment, one only needs to find out what price is being charged for it.

Less-than-truckload operators have many of the same difficulties in defining costs that railroads have. The network structure is also likely to lead to the same form of density economies.[10] TL carriers pick up a load directly from a shipper and deliver it directly to a receiver. A typical LTL movement involves sending a driver around a metropolitan area to pick up loads from various shippers. These loads are taken to a terminal where the freight is removed from the local vehicle and stowed in line-haul trucks going to the metropolitan areas of the different receivers. At the destination terminal, the cargo is handled a second time and loaded into local delivery trucks for final delivery. It is sometimes necessary to warehouse a shipment at a terminal for a brief period of time to wait until a complete truckload is available. If the trucking company does not serve the metropolitan areas of both the shipper and receiver, it will be necessary to interline the shipment, thus causing the freight to be handled one more time.

LTL carriers bear the costs of owning and operating terminals in addition to the costs of owning and operating vehicles. Terminal operations are more labor intensive than hauling goods. Yellow Freight, an LTL carrier whose operating expenses were listed in Chapter 7, spends two-thirds of its operating budget on labor; the average of all motor carriers is less than half and truckload carriers spend only about one-third of their operating budget on labor. J.B. Hunt, a truckload firm, has less than 5 percent of its assets in terminals and other structures; the comparable figure for Yellow Freight is 30 percent.

▬ Econometric Estimates of Scale Economies in Trucking

There has been little controversy over the costs of individual truck movements and little attempt to develop methods for identifying costs at the level at which rates are quoted. Part of the reason is found in the ease of analysis of truckload operations and in the belief of all market participants that the pattern of competitive rates closely matches the costs of providing the services. Less-than-truckload costs, by contrast, are not so easily analyzed. The reason that there has been so little interest in discovering the costs of particular LTL shipments is likely that the rates are not critical to the financial health of the shipper. A grain elevator or coal mine which is likely to ship all of its output to only a single destination may discover that a rate change from 2 to 2.5 cents per ton-mile eliminates all profit of the business. A shipper of greeting cards who ships to many different destinations will not be similarly affected by a change in the rate on a particular 500 lb. shipment from 20 to 25 cents per ton-mile; transportation is a smaller part of the delivered cost of the product, and the costs of non-homogeneous manufactured goods may be more easily passed forward to consumers.[11]

While there has been little interest in costing individual truck movements, there has been intense interest in determining whether there are scale economies in the trucking industry.[12] This interest in the existence of scale economies can be traced to a belief among many industry participants that the existence of scale economies in an industry justified traditional forms of regulation. Truckload shipping does not seem to have the characteristics of industries in which scale economies are important. Capital requirements are very low, and extremely small firms appear to be able to survive and prosper. The same argument cannot be made for LTL carriers. These firms require terminals, coordination among pickup and delivery service, and balancing of loads in multiple directions. LTL carriers must have a sales staff and advertise for traffic. They must have sophisticated communications systems to track shipments and to analyze how best to dispatch loads arriving at the terminals. LTL carriers operate as a network rather than simply as point-to-point transporters; in general, larger traffic levels in networks enable the network as a whole to achieve higher utilization levels, as discussed in Chapter 5. Large carriers should be able to offer more frequent service to the average shipper. Carriers with a large geographic reach are less likely to need to interline a shipment with another carrier to reach its final destination, thus saving the costs of interlining and offering what customers consider a better service. Against these possible advantages, however, are the standard factors that limit the efficiency of all large corporations: It is more difficult to monitor employees in a large company and more difficult to provide incentives for employees to act in the best interests of the company.

Most estimates of trucking scale economies have been made using data from the period before the Motor Carrier Act of 1980. (All cost estimates to date have been for the combined costs of terminals, vehicles, and vehicle operations). As noted above, prior to 1980, most regulated trucking companies were limited to fixed networks and there was less of a distinction between LTL and TL carriers than there is today. In one of the best known studies under traditional forms of regulation, Friedlaender and Spady calculated two different relationships between average cost and the size of the firm, depending on whether or not characteristics of trucking companies' traffic mix are controlled for. In the 1972 sample that the authors use, the largest firms have longer average hauls, heavier average loads, and a larger percentage of truckload traffic. All three of these characteristics are associated with lower operating costs; thus large firms were found to have lower costs than small firms. However, if the effects of the differences in trucking companies' traffic mix is removed and a pure scale effect is measured, the results were reversed. In other words, trucking companies would then be considered to be subject to decreasing returns to scale.[13]

If large trucking companies have heavier average loads as a result of better equipment utilization (in turn due to their ability to consolidate individual shipments), the fact that large truckers have heavier loads should be considered a source of true scale economies; large companies can serve any given customer more cheaply. If, by contrast, large companies specialize in serving shippers who can offer heavier loads or operate in regions that generate heavier loads, the cost advantage of heavy loads should not be considered to be an advantage of scale; large carriers simply happen to serve low-cost customers. Similar arguments are valid for other variations of traffic mix across carrier sizes. In the most recent study of trucking scale economies in the post–deregulation era, Xu, Grimm, and Corsi continue to find that the existence of scale economies depends on which characteristics are controlled for. They note that large trucking companies have longer hauls and greater average load size. Since they believe that these cost-reducing characteristics are the result of firm size, they find that there are strong economies of scale in trucking.[14] These findings can be seen as parallel to those for the railroad industry: Firms with dense operations—that is, with heavy traffic per unit of network size—have lower costs; the geographic reach of the network appears to increase traffic density by increasing the average length of haul and improving equipment utilization.

The Motor Carrier Act of 1980 freed motor carriers to develop their own network and to solicit all kinds of traffic. As noted previously, this had the effect of encouraging specialization by major motor carriers in less-than-truckload traffic, ceding truckload traffic to smaller carriers and to a group of new operators that specialize in truckload traffic. As predicted by studies based on pre-1980 data, trucking companies have scrambled to develop the characteristics of low-cost carriers, in particular by increasing the geographic extent of their service areas. Many regional carriers that were unable to develop national service coverage went bankrupt, while the largest carriers have increased their market share. This can be seen as an indication of scale economies in the LTL trucking industry in the post–1980 period.[15] Another study finds that the major effect of the Motor Carrier Act of 1980 was to allow LTL firms to adjust the average length of haul and the average weight of shipments to levels that allowed them to be more efficient truckers.

In a recent study, a group of carriers that specialize in truckload shipments was found to have gone from a position of showing scale economies before 1980 to showing constant returns to scale following 1980. The authors of the study speculate that, since the technology of the trucking industry did not change substantially, the existence of scale economies depends on regulation rather than the technology of the industry.[16] Regulation, by controlling routes that could be served by trucking companies, had forced truckload operators to operate within a network technology (in which there are scale economies) rather than with a point-to-point technology (in which there are constant returns to scale) which is more efficient for truckload movements. LTL shipments are more efficiently carried with a network technology, and thus removing the limitations on networks enabled the advantages of size to be more clearly expressed in that industry. While not all studies of motor carrier costs show a change to increasing returns to scale for LTL carriers and a change to constant returns to scale for TL truckers in the years after 1980, all studies show that trucking costs declined dramatically following 1980, regardless of the size of the firm.[17] This is due partly to the expansion of low cost non-union trucking operations in recent years.

While it now appears that the LTL trucking industry is subject to some scale economies, it is not clear how far these economies extend—that is, whether they continue to predominate for all sizes of firms (in which case the industry would be considered a natural monopoly), or whether they are exhausted at a smaller output level. A recent estimate by Wang Chiang and Friedlaender suggests that what appears to be an advantage of size is due, in fact, to complementarities of operating various lengths of LTL service within the same firm. They claim that these economies are exhausted at relatively small levels of output. They argue that the long-term development of the trucking industry will not be toward domination of the LTL business by one or a handful of firms, despite the apparent scale economies that exist among trucking companies of current size.[18]

AIR CARRIER OPERATIONS COSTS

Air carriers have an operating technology and cost structure that closely resembles less-than-truckload motor carriers. Like LTL trucking firms, airlines can use publicly provided fixed facilities by paying fees that have the character of variable costs. Like LTL trucking companies, airlines must operate their own equipment maintenance facilities and transfer terminals. They must also be concerned about soliciting traffic and developing routes with the aim of maximizing equipment utilization.

While the cost structure of the industry is similar to the LTL industry, as described below, the size of firms in the airline industry is much larger. An indication is the revenue cutoffs for a carrier to be classified as a *major,* the equivalent of a Class I railroad or motor carrier. To be a major requires $1 billion in revenue, compared to the $5 million for truckers. There are tens of thousands of trucking companies, but fewer than 100 operating airlines. In terms of number of vehicles, however, airlines are much smaller: Most majors operate fewer than 500 airplanes, compared to nearly 10,000 motor units and 20,000 trailers owned by Yellow Freight. The airline industry as a whole is also smaller than the trucking industry: 1995 expenditures on intercity truck transportation were more than $200 billion. The total revenue of domestic air carriers in the same year was about $68 billion.

Flight Operations Costs

According to statistics developed by the Federal Aviation Administration and presented in Table 8.1, the cost of flying aircraft accounts for about 28 percent of the total operating cost of airline companies. Flight operations expenses include the costs of the cockpit crew and fuel for flying the aircraft, but exclude the cost of the flight staff that serves passengers.

TABLE 8.1   **Breakdown of Domestic Air Carrier Operating Expenses in 1994—(Millions of Dollars)**

Expense Category	Amount	Percent
Flying operations	$17,701	28
Maintenance	7,169	11
Passenger service	5,307	8
Aircraft and traffic servicing	10,362	17
Promotion and sales	9,782	16
Depreciation and amortization	3,750	6
General and administrative and other transport related	8,902	14
Total Operating Expenses	$62,974	100%

SOURCE: *Aerospace Facts and Figures*, 1995/96 edition

The largest element of flight operations costs is fuel. As shown in Table 8.2, fuel costs have been highly volatile over the last two decades, rising from 12 percent of total operating expenses to nearly 30 percent and then declining to less than 12 percent in 1994. While aircraft have become much more fuel efficient over the years, the wide fluctuation in the price of fuel has made flight operations the most unpredictable element of total airline costs.

Cockpit staffing is determined by union contract and aircraft technology. Throughout the 1980s, however, wage levels of the cockpit crew declined. The combination of declining crew costs and lower fuel costs reduced flight operations costs over the decade from approximately 39 percent to 28 percent of operating costs. Both numbers represent a considerably smaller percentage than the comparable expenditures for crew and fuel by truckload transportation, though higher than the percentage in railroad operations. As with those other transport modes, however, there are costs of other support personnel that are necessary for an airplane to fly and whose magnitude will vary with the number of flights. Part of maintenance expenditures is one such expense, though some portion of maintenance is necessary regardless of how much an aircraft is flown. Maintenance accounts for approximately 11 percent of airline operating costs. Some portion of traffic servicing and general and administrative costs also vary with the number of flights and so should be treated as a cost of operations.

U.S. airlines in 1994 flew 585 billion seat-miles in domestic operations and incurred operating expenses in domestic operations of $62.9 billion, or 10.7 cents per seat-mile. Assuming that between 30 percent and 40 percent of this is the direct and indirect cost of flight operations, it costs roughly between 3 and 4 cents per seat-mile to fly aircraft in the United States. This proportion rises and falls with the price of airline fuel and the cost of cockpit labor.

TABLE 8.2   Fuel Expenditures by U.S. Air Carriers, 1972–1994

Year	Gallons Consumed (Millions)	Total Cost (Millions)	Fuel Costs per Gallon (Cents/Gallon)	Fuel Cost as Percent of Operating Expenses
1972	10,100.8	$ 1,178.2	11.7	12.1
1973	10,700.4	1,365.3	12.8	12.1
1974	9,565.2	2,333.5	24.2	17.3
1975	9,495.3	2,777.3	29.2	18.9
1976	9,820.8	3,116.1	31.7	19.2
1977	10,282.0	3,729.8	36.3	20.1
1978	10,627.1	4,178.2	39.3	20.1
1979	11,278.1	6,503.0	57.7	24.4
1980	10,874.0	9,769.5	89.8	29.7
1981	10,087.8	10,498.0	104.1	29.3
1982	9,942.1	9,755.2	98.1	27.2
1983	10,214.4	9,073.1	88.8	24.5
1984	11,050.4	9,361.7	84.7	23.8
1985	11,675.1	9,326.7	79.9	22.3
1986	12,643.0	6,995.8	55.3	16.3
1987	13,629.5	7,593.8	55.7	16.0
1988	14,204.8	7,557.2	53.2	14.4
1989	14,103.9	8,472.7	60.1	14.9
1990	14,841.1	11,465.2	77.3	17.6
1991	13,798.4	9,329.5	67.6	14.8
1992	14,172.0	8,907.9	62.9	13.5
1993	14,165.0	8,452.9	59.7	12.7
1994	14,153.4	7,722.7	54.6	11.7

SOURCE: *Aerospace Facts and Figures*, various editions

■ Passenger Service Costs and Load Factors

Passenger service costs are similar to cargo handling costs of LTL truckers. But while the costs of handling cargo are hidden as *terminal expenses* on the books of motor carriers, they are broken out explicitly in airline accounts, as shown in Table 8.1. Passenger service costs are expenses contributing to comfort, safety, and convenience of passengers while in flight. Passenger service costs account for about 8 percent of all airline operating costs, primarily in the form of flight attendants' salaries and meals. These costs are distinct from flight operations costs because if there were no passengers these costs could be saved; the level of these costs varies with the number of passengers on an airplane. These direct passenger service costs amounted to 1.4 cents per passenger-mile.

There are other costs that vary with the number of passengers rather than the number of flights. Among these are aircraft cleaning, baggage handling, gates, reservations, and sales. Aircraft and traffic servicing account for 17 percent of total operating costs and promotion and sales expenses (including reservations and the development of tariffs and schedules) account for another 16 percent of costs. These two cost elements, which can be assigned to the number of passengers flown by an airline during a quarter, though not to the passengers on a particular flight, account for 33 percent of airline costs. Together with direct passenger service costs, they account for 41 percent of airline operating expenses—approximately the same amount as the costs attributable to flight operations. Treating 41 percent of total domestic operating expenses of U.S. airlines as passenger-related produces an estimate of about 6 cents per passenger-mile.

These percentages are for standard airline service, which corresponds closely to LTL trucking service. The equivalent to truckload service in airlines is charter service. Charter companies can operate much more cheaply than scheduled airlines because they have much lower needs for terminals and ground support personnel. Table 8.3 shows estimates published for a new charter service between London and Singapore. Since the service covers solely long-distance flights, fuel costs are a much higher proportion than for most airlines. Since the airline has no reservation system and virtually no ground crew, the indirect passenger service costs are negligible. Aircraft leasing costs—which should be treated as a cost of owning rather than operating aircraft—appear in the table since the airline leases rather than owns its airplane. In this charter service, vehicle operating costs are between 51.5 percent (fuel, other running costs, and crew costs) and 72.3 percent (including maintenance) with passenger costs adding another 6.2 percent of total costs. Flight operations costs are clearly much higher than in standard scheduled service, while direct and indirect passenger service costs are much lower.

The reader will note that flight costs are quoted in terms of cents per seat-mile while passenger costs are quoted in terms of cents per passenger-mile. As noted in Chapter 5, load factor is the ratio of passenger-miles to seat-miles. Load factor, which measures the average percentage of seats that are occupied, can be calculated for individual flights or for a system as a whole. Major domestic U.S. airlines in 1995 had a historically high average load factor of 70 percent. Load factors for individual flights are, of course, much more variable. While load factors of zero (a flight with no passengers) are not unheard of, load factors of 100 percent (a sold-out plane) are common.

Load factor can be thought of as a multiplier that converts seat costs into passenger costs. The higher the load factor, holding all other factors constant, the lower the operations costs per passenger-mile. Many airline operating policies are designed to improve load factors. For example, following deregulation, airlines switched operations from one based primarily on serving city-pair markets to one based on serving a geographic area with one or two stop services through hubs. As shown in Chapter 5, it is in part the higher load factors

TABLE 8.3   Projected Outlays of a London to Singapore Charter
Service

Cost Category	Percent of Total Costs
Fuel	42.8
Aircraft leasing costs	11.6
Insurance	4.2
Maintenance	20.8
Other aircraft running costs	3.0
Personnel costs (crew)	5.7
Passenger costs (catering, etc.)	6.2
Other, mainly administrative costs	5.8
Total	100%

SOURCE: M.E. Beesley, "Commitment, Sunk Costs, and Entry to the Airline Industry,"
Journal of Transport Economics and Policy, May 1986, p. 185. Estimates are for
Autumn 1985.

of operations organized through hubs and spokes that generate economies of
networking.[19]

Charter services tend to have much lower costs per passenger-mile than
scheduled service. The reason is that charter services can be scheduled well in
advance to exactly correspond to predicted demands; charter services can be
canceled if demands are not as high as expected. As a result, load factors near
100 percent can be expected for charter service, rather than the 65 percent
expected for scheduled service. Higher load factors combine with lower ticket-
ing costs to give charter services very low costs.

Scale Economies in Aircraft Operations

LTL carriers are thought to have the opportunity for scale economies due to
improved equipment utilization: A carrier with a lot of traffic can operate with
fewer empty truck-miles or, equivalently, a higher load factor. As described in
Chapter 5, there is a second source of network economies that is available to
airlines: Long distance equipment that seats many people has lower operating
costs per passenger-mile than smaller aircraft designed for short distance use.
For example, a calculation immediately after airline deregulation found that a
737-200 seating 121 and with a maximum range of 1,000 miles had direct
operating costs of 6 cents per seat-mile when used on a 1,000 mile route; a 747
seating 500 passengers had direct operating costs of 3.7 cents per seat-mile
when flown 2,500 miles.[20] Chapter 5 provides an extended example of network
economies that stem from the use of vehicles of multiple sizes.

Trucking companies have traditionally used vehicles that are the maximum size permitted by law for the line-haul portion of a movement, though there has been a recent shift by LTL carriers toward operating pairs of pups, 28-foot vehicles, in place of the standard 40-foot van. The use of pups makes LTL carriers more like airlines, which use a variety of sizes of airplane, matching aircraft to demand on each route. An airline that has a steady and heavy passenger flow on a route has an opportunity to use larger aircraft without sacrificing load factor. There may also be economies of operating terminals so that an airline with considerable traffic into a terminal may be able to process passengers more cheaply than an airline with a lighter passenger count. As in all large organizations, however, scale brings managerial difficulties and with it the possibility of decreasing returns to scale.

It is in general impossible to directly read from accounts the extent to which operating costs will vary with output. Rather, economists rely on econometric analyses of operating costs in which total reported costs are related to changes in output levels and other control factors. The most careful pre-deregulation study done by Caves, Christensen, and Tretheway found that a 1 percent increase in output (overwhelmingly passenger-miles, but also including mail and freight) was associated with a 0.8 percent increase in total costs, if all other characteristics of a system's operations could be held constant: points served, stage length (the distance between takeoff and landings), load factor, and the price of inputs. The authors say that there are economies of operating in the airline industry since costs do not rise as rapidly as output when other factors held constant. *Density economies* are intended to have the same meaning here as they have in the railroad industry: economies achievable by increasing traffic within the limits of a fixed network. Scale economies in the railroad industry were defined in terms of the cost changes when both ton-miles and the size of the railroad network were adjusted by the same amount. Thus Caves, Christensen, and Tretheway define scale economies in the airline industry in terms of costs associated with a 1 percent increase in output and a simultaneous 1 percent increase in the size of the system, the latter measured by the number of points served. According to the authors' calculations, a 1 percent increase in the number of points served causes a 0.13 percent increase in airline costs. The sum of the cost elasticities associated with output and points served is 0.94, which is statistically insignificantly different from 1.0, which would indicate constant returns to scale in the airline industry. Thus they conclude that airlines are subject to the same economic characteristics as railroads: constant returns to scale, but strong economies of density.

It is important to note that while Caves, Christensen, and Tretheway's results are consistent with statistically constant returns to scale, 0.94 is numerically within the range of increasing returns to scale. The authors also found that a 1 percent increase in the average length of a flight segment reduces costs by 0.148 percent and that a 1 percent increase in load factor reduces costs by 2.64 percent. But both load factor and stage length are likely to be affected by the nature of the network and the size of the airline. In fact, one way that large airlines may be able to achieve lower costs is through having higher load factors and flying longer routes. To treat these factors as independent of the size of the airline is to miss one source of scale economies.

Measurements of airline scale and density economies in the deregulated environment are not unanimous on the extent or degree of the cost advantages of size.[21] Even small airline companies are large relative to those in the trucking industry and the largest airlines have been rapidly expanding their networks. Unlike the trucking industry, there is some doubt about the ability of very small airlines to survive in the industry. By 1990, small airlines unaffiliated with others had all but disappeared. By the mid-1990s, there were again a few successes of small-scale entry. It appears that the ability of small airlines to survive in the industry is more dependent on the price of used aircraft and the ability to find gates at airports than inherent advantages of network size.

OPERATING COSTS OF WATER TRANSPORT

The economics of all forms of water transportation—deep-water or inland, bulk or container—is dominated by ship design and particularly by the size of ships and tows. While air transport costs are affected by similar factors (the lower cost of large aircraft is one reason for the apparent economies of density in air transport) other modes of transport have vehicle design limitations that are effectively determined by the size of fixed facilities. Trucks, for example, can typically be no longer than 48 feet long or 102 inches wide; off-road trucks can be, and are, much larger. Railroad car size is determined by the 4-foot 8-inch traditional track width, the curve radius of tracks in place, and the height of bridges and tunnels. Inland water transport have some restrictions on vessel size due to the 110-foot width of locks. Great Lakes boats have a long and very narrow design exactly matching the dimensions of the locks at Sault Ste. Marie. Barges on the Mississippi River system are made 195 feet long and 35 feet wide, allowing a tow of 9 barges to transit a 600×110-foot lock at the same time; tows are usually much larger than this, however, requiring that they be disassembled and reassembled at each lock.

The only technical limitations on deep-water ships is the draft of the vessel compared to the depth of the harbors on the route for which the ship is designed, and these are not usually constraining except for tankers and dry bulk ships. Unique among modes of transportation, ships are custom-made for each customer and can be exactly adapted to the trade for which the ship was intended. The most important decision for the shipping company is how big a ship to order. There are advantages and disadvantages to large ships; shipping companies have the opportunity to trade off the advantages and disadvantages and choose a ship size for each route that is most efficient.[22]

Economies of Ship Size

As noted in the previous chapter, construction costs of a ship rise with ship size according to the *two-thirds power rule*.[23] This rule, which derives from the fact that the holding capacity of a ship is proportional to its volume while the construction cost is proportional to its surface area, states that construction costs rise only two-thirds as fast as the size of a ship. The construction cost per unit of capacity declines apparently without limit.

Operating costs show an even stronger decline per unit of capacity. The reason is that manning is determined by a fixed number of tasks, regardless of the size of the ship. Manning requirements have been declining rapidly due to automation. Other operating costs such as maintenance are much more closely related to ship size. Jansson and Shneerson estimate the elasticity of operating costs with respect to container ship size is equal to 0.43, meaning that a 1 percent increase in the size of a ship results in a 0.43 percent increase in its operating costs. This estimate does not include fuel costs. Fuel costs have an elasticity of 0.72, further suggesting economies of ship size. The fact that fuel costs per unit of capacity decline with the size of the ship is due to the fluid-dynamic principle that the resistance of water does not increase as rapidly as ship size, holding the speed of the ship constant.

Since all three of the determinants of ship costs have elasticities below 1, there seems to be no limit to the advantages of large scale ship operations. Both the average construction cost and the average operating cost per unit of cargo capacity apparently decline without limit as shown by the average ship cost line in Figure 8.4. There is, however, another cost of ship operation: port costs. Port costs, or cargo handling costs, are strongly inclined against large ships. Large ships must spend longer in port to load and unload cargo. Although containerization has greatly speeded cargo handling for non-bulk commodities, the length of time that a ship spends in port is still significant. For conventional liners, a ship may spend more time in port than sailing, and even container ships are in port for 20 to 30 percent of the year.[24] Large ships spend longer in port for the same reason that it takes a large bathtub longer to fill than a small bathtub. A ship that is twice as large will take twice as long to load and unload for any given speed of loading or unloading. Units of cargo can be unloaded somewhat more rapidly from large ships than small ships, but the difference is not significant: A 1 percent increase in ship size will increase cargo handling rates by at most 0.3 percent. A ship that takes longer in port can make fewer roundtrips per year, thus reducing the annual amount of cargo it can carry. Cargoes sufficient to fill a large ship may also not be readily available causing either a decrease in sailing frequency (and thus poorer quality of service) or calls in multiple ports to fill a large ship, thus further worsening the problems of equipment utilization of large vessels. The average handling cost line in Figure 8.4 is rising due to the disadvantages of port time of large ships. Average total cost in the same figure is the sum of the two costs and the lowest point on that curve, X^*, is the optimum size of the ship. The optimum size ship represents a

FIGURE 8.4   The Determination of Optimal Ship Size

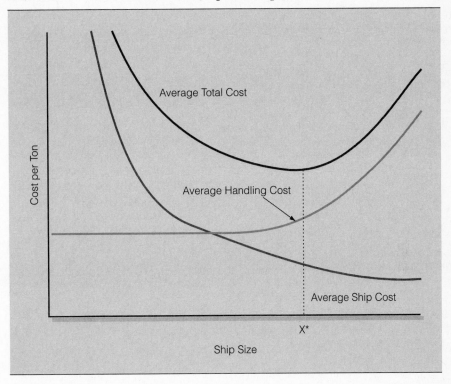

tradeoff between the advantages at sea of large ships and the advantages in port of small ships. Depending on the length of the voyage (which increases the importance of sea costs) and cargo handling costs, a larger or smaller ship is appropriate on a route. Over the last several decades innovations in cargo handling, particularly containerization, have shifted down the average handling curve and shifted the minimum point on the average total cost curve to the right, producing some very large ships.

Since vessel sizes vary considerably, so too does the relationship among the cost categories of shipping companies. Table 8.4 shows cost breakdowns for three different container shippers. Each of the three companies breaks costs down somewhat differently. Two of the three companies include in their cost estimate outlays for getting cargo to and from ports. Fuel costs (listed as bunkers in Table 8.4) range from 8 to 22 percent of total costs. Running costs or vessel costs range from 16 to 24 percent of the total and the sum of the two ranges from 34 to 39 percent of total costs. Port costs are considerable, however. The sum of terminal costs, container costs, positioning, port charges, and cargo-related expenses amounts to 30 to 35 percent of total costs. These costs are for container ships. Port costs for bulk ships are much lower, though even

TABLE 8.4   Cost Structure for Three Different Container Companies (Percent)

Cost Category	Company 1	Company 2	Company 3
Terminal costs	15	21.5	
Transport costs	9	9.6	
Cargo-related costs			35
Container costs	13		
Commissions	5	16.0	
Overheads and promotion		4.8	
Port charges	4	4.8	
Positioning		4.0	
Running costs			16
Vessel costs	24	21.7	
Bunkers	10	8.0	22
Administration	10		4
Other fixed costs	10		
Capital costs			23
Equipment		9.6	
Total	100%	100%	100%

Company 1: Small company operating primarily in trades from Europe to East Mediterranean, South Africa, and Australia; figures assume normal budgeted load factor of 75 percent.

Company 2: Large company operating on North Atlantic; figures assume normal budgeted load factor of 75 percent.

Company 3: Large company operating in Europe/Far East trade; figures assume normal budgeted load factor of 90 percent.

Transport costs are the costs of moving containers from inland points to/from ports.

SOURCE: J.E. Davies, "An Analysis of Cost and Supply Conditions in the Liner Shipping Industry," *The Journal of Industrial Economics*, Vol. XXI, No. 4 (June 1983), p. 420.

bulk ships spend between 10 and 20 percent of their time in port during which the opportunity cost of ship and cargo can quickly mount.

Economies of Fleet Size

The ocean shipping industry is divided into the same sorts of divisions as the trucking industry: Tankers correspond to specialized carriers, tramp carriers are the equivalent of contract carriers, and the LTL trucking industry has its equivalent in scheduled liner services. Just as there are few concerns in the trucking industry about economies of scale in the contract and specialized sectors, among ocean carriers the only concern about scale economies is among liner carriers.[25] There is a strong belief in the industries that scale economies are present and important. The economies are thought to derive from the ability of a ship line with more frequent sailings to attract more cargo and the ability of a carriers with higher cargo levels to justify more frequent sailings. It is claimed that on the North Atlantic, shippers expect at least weekly sailings. Given the time it takes to make a round trip, a company wishing to enter this route must have at least three ships; but these ships are becoming increasingly larger due to improvements in port handling. According to one estimate, it would have required an initial investment of $373 million to buy the five equipped container ships and port equipment necessary to enter the U.S./Far-Eastern trade in 1978; inflation will have more doubled this figure in the intervening years. The belief that these economies of scale exist over the entire extent of the market is used to justify non-competitive rate conferences governing several of the most important world trade routes.[26] The world shipping industry is thus treated by governments as having the potential to develop market power. There are, however, no direct estimates of scale economies in this industry.[27] As this is written, international deep-sea shipping is one of the few transportation industries still subject to tariff filing requirements.

Less attention has been given to the measurement of scale economies among inland water carriers. One estimate from the 1960s, when barges were more intensively regulated than they are today, showed statistically insignificant economies of fleet size.[28] Another estimate, also from the 1960s, showed strong economies of scale in the size of tows (equivalent to finding economies of ship size in deep-draft shipping), and statistically insignificant economies of fleet size.[29] The public concern over the size of scale economies appears most pronounced among scheduled network services; since the inland waterway industry acts like contract carriers, there has been little concern about scale economies in this industry.

AUTOMOBILE OPERATING COSTS

Vehicle operating costs are those costs that vary with the time or distance that the vehicle travels. For most modes of transportation, the most important components of vehicle operating costs are the opportunity cost of the crew and the fuel used to move the vehicle. In some modes of transport, either use-based depreciation or use-based maintenance expenditures are also important as operating costs.

Figure 8.5 shows the real operating outlays per mile of a typical automobile in 1995, 1987, and 1981. Gas and oil is the major operating expense, with maintenance expenditures a distant second. The total operating expenses in 1995 of 10 cents per vehicle-mile make automobile transportation the least expensive mode of transportation, measured in terms of operating expense per vehicle-mile. To the amounts in Figure 8.5 should be added parking and storage fees, washing, and other expenses related to use. The sum of all consumer expenditures on gasoline and oil, tire, tubes and accessories, repair, greasing, washing, parking, storage, and rental in 1994 was $252 billion, or approximately 49 percent of total automobile expenditures in that year. Fuel costs—treated often as the sole operating expense of automobiles—is only 20 percent of total annual expenditures on automobile transportation.

FIGURE 8.5   Real Automobile Operating Outlays, 1981–1995 (1995 cents per mile)

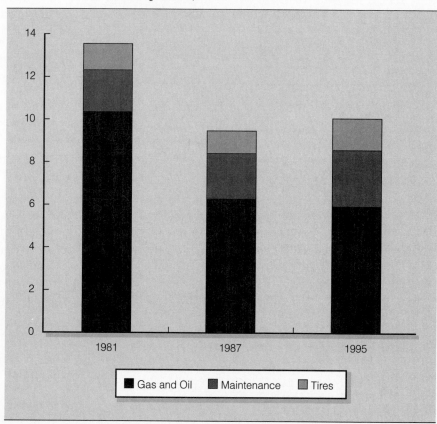

SOURCE: Motor Vehicle Manufacturers Association, *MVMA Facts and Figures*, 1995, p. 58.

Figure 8.5 also shows real cost per mile of operations declined noticeably between 1981 and 1987 as the price of motor fuel fell. There has been a modest increase since 1987 attributed to higher outlays for tires and maintenance expenditures.

Automobile Congestion Costs

Conspicuously missing from the calculation of automobile expenses, however, is an allowance for the cost of crew labor. The reason, of course, is that automobile transportation is private. Outside of a few chauffeured cars, there is no crew and thus no expenditure for labor. This does not, however mean that the driver's time is costless. In Chapter 4, the time cost of driving was assumed to be some proportion of the hourly wage rate of the driver and passengers. The logic is the same as is used to justify all opportunity cost calculations: If the

FIGURE 8.6   The Relationship between Traffic Speed and Traffic Density

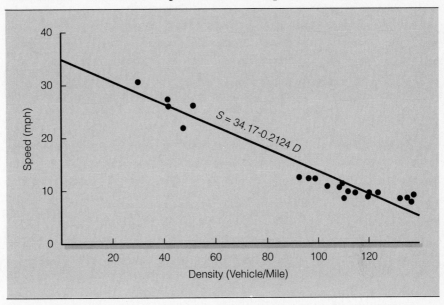

SOURCE: Matthew J. Huber, "Effect of Temporary Bridge on Parkway Performance," in *Highway Research Bulletin* 167, Transportation Research Board, National Research Council, Washington, D.C., 1957, as reproduced in John Baerwald, ed., *Transportation and Traffic Engineering Handbook*, Prentice Hall, 1976, p. 97.

automobile occupants were not driving, they could have used the time to earn income at a rate proportional to their wage rate. The cost of making a trip by automobile thus depends on how long it takes to complete the trip. Trips that are done at high speed are less costly than slow trips.

It is a well-known principle of traffic engineering that the speed of traffic depends on how many cars try to use the road at any time. Since the distance that drivers allow between vehicles increases with speed, when many vehicles crowd on a highway link (reducing the distance between vehicles), the speed of the traffic will naturally fall. Figure 8.6 shows a relationship between traffic density—the number of cars trying to use a piece of highway at any time—and the speed of the traffic on a single piece of highway. The dots in the diagram represent actual observations. The engineer has chosen to approximate the relationship between speed and traffic density as a straight line.[30] The equation of the straight line that best fits the data is given by:

$$S = 34.17 - 0.2124D \tag{8.1}$$

where:

S = traffic speed in miles per hour
D = traffic density in vehicles per mile of highway lane.

TABLE 8.5   The Relationship between Traffic Density and Traffic Volume

Traffic Density (Cars per mile)	Traffic Speed (Miles per hour)	Traffic Volume (Cars per hour)
1	33.96	33.96
10	32.05	320.46
20	29.92	598.44
30	27.80	833.94
40	25.67	1026.96
50	23.55	1177.50
60	21.43	1285.56
70	19.30	1351.14
80	17.18	1374.24
90	15.05	1354.86
100	12.93	1293.00
110	10.81	1188.66
120	8.68	1041.84
130	6.56	852.54
140	4.43	620.76
150	2.31	346.50
160	0.19	29.76

SOURCE: Computed from information in Figure 8.6. Traffic density is chosen and then traffic speed is calculated as: Speed = 34.17 − 0.2124 × density. Traffic volume is speed × density.

This equation says that traffic moves about 34 mph if the roadway is (almost) empty. Each additional vehicle per mile of traffic lane reduces speeds by approximately one-fifth mile per hour.

The simple relationship between traffic speed and density shown graphically in Figure 8.6 and expressed mathematically in Equation 8.1 is the key to understanding the economics of traffic congestion. The more cars that try to use a portion of roadway, the slower traffic will be. Eventually, if more and more cars try to use the roadway, traffic will slow so much that the actual volume of car-trips per hour will decline. This is shown in Table 8.5 in which traffic density is multiplied by traffic speed to produce the volume of traffic that the portion of highway studied in Figure 8.6 can handle per hour. The absolute capacity of the highway is 1,347 vehicle-trips per hour. To operate at maximum capacity, traffic moves at 17 miles per hour; when this happens, the highway will have 80 cars per mile. If more than 80 cars per mile try to use the roadway, the slowing of traffic will more than offset the increased number of cars on the road. When 150 cars try to use a mile of highway, traffic will slow to a little more than 2 miles per hour and only 346 vehicle-trips per hour will be produced.

It is irrational to allow more than 80 cars to use a mile of highway at any time since this actually decreases the number of cars that can be served per hour. But it will probably make sense to restrict the number of cars that can use the highway to fewer than 80 per mile. The reason is that even before the highway reaches capacity, traffic congestion has slowed vehicle speeds and thus increased the opportunity cost of driving time per mile of highway. For example, if the number of vehicles that used the highway could be restricted to 70 per mile, only 23 fewer vehicle-trips per hour would be produced (a reduction of less than 2 percent), but the average speed of all the cars that do make the journey would be increased by 2 miles per hour (approximately a 12 percent increase in speed).

Increasing the speed of traffic decreases the cost of driving. The amount by which costs are decreased depends on the opportunity cost of each vehicle's time. A calculation of the opportunity cost of drivers' time is presented in Table 8.6, which shows the traffic speed and traffic density corresponding to traffic volumes between 1,100 cars per hour and the maximum of 1,374 cars per hour. Reading the first line in Table 8.6, we find that a traffic volume of 1,100 cars per hour for the stretch of highway studied in Figure 8.6 is generated by 44.5 cars per mile traveling at 24.72 miles per hour. At a speed of 24.72 miles per hour, one mile of road is covered in .0405 hours or 2 minutes and 24 seconds. If we assume that the opportunity cost of time of a car's occupants is $10 per hour, it costs the car $10 per hour × 0.04 hours per mile or 40.5 cents per mile in labor time. This amount is listed in column 4 as the average cost per mile of driving. As traffic volumes increase (in column 1), traffic speeds decrease (column 3) and thus the labor cost of driving increases. At the capacity of 1,374 cars per hour with traffic speeds at 17.33 miles per hour, each mile requires nearly 3.5 minutes or 57.7 cents in lost time of the car's occupants.

According to Equation 8.1, each additional car using the highway reduces travel speeds for all vehicles by 0.2124 miles per hour. According to Table 8.6, if traffic flow is 1,370 vehicles per hour, increasing volume to 1,371 vehicles per hour requires increasing traffic density from 75.95 cars per mile to 76.51 cars per mile, thus reducing speeds from 18.04 miles per hour to 17.92 miles per hour. The drop in speed has increased travel costs for each of the 1,370 vehicles by nearly 0.4 cents per mile. The increase in total travel costs of increasing traffic volume from 1,370 to 1,371 vehicles is the sum of the travel costs of the 1371st car (55.8 cents per mile) plus an additional approximately 0.4 cents per mile multiplied by the 1,370 vehicles that were already traveling. This amount is listed in column 5 of Table 8.6 as *marginal cost*. Marginal cost represents the increase in the total time cost of increasing traffic flow by one vehicle per hour.

At small traffic volumes, most of the cost of driving is represented by the cost of the time of the driver and passengers and average cost (the cost that each car incurs) is approximately the same as marginal cost. But as traffic volumes increase and traffic slows, marginal costs begin to diverge from average cost. At extremely high traffic levels, most of the costs of driving are not incurred by the driver and passengers but by occupants of other cars stuck in traffic. For example, at traffic volumes of 1,370 per hour, increasing traffic flow by one more car costs, in total, $5.59. But only 55.8 cents of this is borne by the 1,371st car; the

TABLE 8.6　The Relationship between Traffic Volume and Driving Cost (Assumed Opportunity Cost of Time: $10 per Car-Hour)

Traffic Volume (Cars per Hour)	Traffic Density (Cars per Mile)	Traffic Speed (Miles per Hour)	Average Cost ($/Mile)	Marginal Cost ($/Mile)
1,100	44.50	24.72	0.405	0.654
1,110	45.16	24.58	0.407	0.667
1,120	45.84	24.43	0.409	0.680
1,130	46.52	24.29	0.412	0.693
1,140	47.23	24.14	0.414	0.708
1,150	47.94	23.99	0.417	0.724
1,160	48.68	23.83	0.420	0.740
1,170	49.43	23.67	0.422	0.758
1,180	50.19	23.51	0.425	0.777
1,190	50.98	23.34	0.428	0.798
1,200	51.79	23.17	0.432	0.821
1,210	52.63	22.99	0.435	0.845
1,220	53.49	22.81	0.438	0.872
1,230	54.37	22.62	0.442	0.902
1,240	55.29	22.43	0.446	0.935
1,250	56.25	22.22	0.450	0.971
1,260	57.24	22.01	0.454	1.013
1,270	58.28	21.79	0.459	1.060
1,280	59.37	21.56	0.464	1.114
1,290	60.52	21.32	0.469	1.178
1,300	61.74	21.06	0.475	1.255
1,310	63.04	20.78	0.481	1.348
1,320	64.45	20.48	0.488	1.466
1,330	66.00	20.15	0.496	1.621
1,340	67.73	19.78	0.505	1.840
1,350	69.75	19.36	0.517	2.180
1,360	72.24	18.83	0.531	2.822
1,370	75.95	18.04	0.554	4.969
1,371	76.51	17.92	0.558	5.592
1,372	77.16	17.78	0.562	6.533
1,373	77.98	17.61	0.568	8.213
1,374	79.29	17.33	0.577	13.059

remainder is borne by all other drivers as they are slowed by the last car. As traffic volumes increase, marginal cost and average cost diverge farther and farther until the maximum traffic flow of 1,374 per hour is reached. Since traffic flows beyond this level cannot occur, the marginal cost of increasing traffic flow is undefined, or infinite. Figure 8.7 shows a graph of the data in columns 4 and 5 of Table 8.6.

FIGURE 8.7   Marginal and Average Costs of Driving

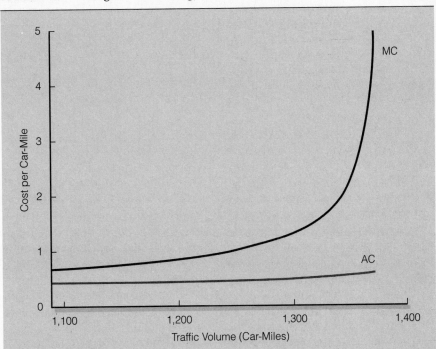

Diagrams with the general shape of Figure 8.7 are used to describe the economics of congestion for any mode of transportation. The economic conditions that generated the figure are valid for virtually any mode of transportation, not just for automobiles. Since the diagram is so widely used in transport economics, it is worthwhile to stop and consider the nature of the problem from which it was drawn. The model assumes a single road with homogeneous traffic (meaning a constant value of time and a constant relationship between traffic density and speed for all vehicles). The lines will change if either the value of time changes or if the relationship between traffic speed and traffic density changes. For example, mountain roads will obviously have very different speed/density relationships, while roads which carry multiple passenger vehicles (perhaps due to carpooling) will have a higher value of time and so higher vehicle operations costs than roads which carry single-occupant vehicles.

While changes in the engineering of the roadway and the value of time of vehicle occupants will shift the cost of driving curves up or down, dropping the assumption of traffic homogeneity changes the shape and interpretation of the cost curves. For example, if there is a mixture of cars, trucks, and buses using the same road, both the marginal and average cost of traffic volume will be different depending on the nature of the marginal vehicle. Moreover, with heterogeneous traffic, there is likely to be *balking* at traffic queues where some vehicles decide to choose an alternate route or mode of transport or the time of day at which a trip is taken. If traffic is heterogeneous, it is logical to assume that the vehicles with the highest value of time will be those who choose alternate routes. Thus, as traffic levels rise, the average value of time of vehicles may fall.[31]

TRANSIT OPERATING COSTS

One of the uses that is made of transportation cost calculations is to compare the cost of one mode against another. When comparing private automobile transport against other types of passenger transportation, the time of the driver and passengers must be handled consistently. One possibility is to calculate the time of bus passengers as a cost of operating buses.[32] Since public transportation is in most cases slower than private transportation, such a procedure will generally find that public transportation is more costly than automobiles.

The alternative procedure is to ignore the time costs of passengers in both modes and to assume that the difference in time costs is a factor that will affect the responsiveness of demand to out-of-pocket costs. This is the procedure followed in most analyses of bus and transit costs. The advantage of this method is that transit expenditures can be analyzed using publicly available accounts. In 1993 the total expenditure of all public transit systems was $16.8 billion, excluding depreciation and payments for purchases of fixed facilities and vehicles. (As discussed in Chapter 7, in most cases, depreciation and debt payment does not properly value the costs of owning transit vehicles since they are generally purchased by a government body other than the Transit Authority). Transit systems produced 3.75 billion bus-equivalent miles of service (adjusting for the greater seating capacity of rail vehicles); the cost of transit vehicle miles was thus $3.73 per bus-mile.

The breakdown of transit expenses for three types of systems is given in Table 8.7. As noted in Chapter 7, whether vehicle maintenance should be treated as a cost of vehicle ownership or a cost of vehicle operation depends on whether the required amount of maintenance varies with the level of use. In bus-only systems, about 50 percent of total expenses are for vehicle operations. Almost all of this goes to pay for fuel, drivers, and dispatchers. Depending on how much of maintenance is treated as a cost of vehicle operation, nearly three-quarters of expenses of bus-only systems can be attributed to vehicle operations. Transit systems that included non-bus operations (usually rail rapid transit) have a very different cost profile. Table 8.7 shows that such systems had a lower proportion of vehicle operations costs and a higher proportion of non-vehicle maintenance. This results from the costs of maintaining tracks and stations that partly offset the lower cost per seat-mile of operating railroad trains. In 1994, operating costs were $5.70 per vehicle-mile for transit buses, $5.20 per vehicle-mile for heavy rail transit, and $12.30 for light rail.

TABLE 8.7 **Breakdown of Operating Expenses for U.S. Transit Systems, 1993**

Expense Category	Multi-Mode, All Areas	Bus Only, Large Cities	Bus Only, Small Cities
Vehicle operations	45.3%	49.2%	54.2%
Vehicle maintenance	17.6	19.0	17.4
Non-vehicle maintenance	13.2	3.3	2.9
General administration	16.7	13.8	17.8
Purchased transportation	7.2	14.7	7.7

SOURCE: American Public Transit Association, *1994–95 Transit Fact Book*, Table 20. *Large city* refers to operating areas with a population of 1 million or more. *Small city* refers to operating areas with populations between 200,000 and 500,000.

Competition among transit operators within a single metropolitan area is uncommon. The reason is that transit services in the United States do not cover costs from passenger revenues. The tradition in the United States is to operate services that require public subsidy as a government firm. An alternative might be to offer subsidies to competing firms.[33] The stability of competition would then depend on conditions of scale economies. There is mixed evidence on the subject. While most studies have found constant returns to scale in public transit, one claims to find scale economies and other diseconomies of scale beyond relatively small sizes.[34]

CONCLUSION

The costs of the crew operating transport services and fuel are the most obvious costs of transportation operations. Some modes of transport have a number of less obvious costs that are indirectly related to transport operations; dispatchers, reservation clerks, and switch operators are all necessary to support traffic operations. Payments made to support staff are fixed or variable costs of transportation operations depending on whether the number of employees is independent of the traffic level or varies with it.

The main cost advantage that railroads have over other modes is the low level of fuel use. However, railroads are a labor intensive mode of transportation due to extremely high levels of support staff necessary to operate trains. Train movement costs are on average between 20 and 50 percent of all railroad expenses. But railroad costs are more variable and more difficult to analyze than any other mode of transport due to the overwhelming importance of joint and common costs. Cost analyses of individual car movements are almost impossible to calculate accurately.

Econometric studies of rail costs have dealt with the aggregate cost of rail shipments. The shift in focus to aggregate shipments gives the researcher the opportunity to discover how traffic levels affect costs. The general conclusion of these studies is that railroads are subject to constant returns to scale but strong economies of density.

In comparison to railroad transport, there appears at first glance no reason to think that trucking is subject to scale economies. The industry appears to be easy to enter and have low capital requirements. However, this is true only of the truckload industry. The trucking sector is splintered into many different segments, each of which has different cost conditions. Most trucking is done by firms engaging in manufacturing or providing non-transportation services. Little is known about the costs of these so-called *private truckers*. In fact, within the for-hire trucking industry it is only the truckload segment of the motor carrier industry that is easy to enter. The largest trucking firms are concentrated in the less-than-truckload segment of the market. Entry into this segment is not easy, since it requires investment in terminals and such support staff as traffic salesmen and warehouse operators. Econometric estimates of costs in the less-than-truckload segment of the market suggest that these carriers have similar cost conditions to railroads: economies of density but no economies of scale. These estimates are based on data from the period before trucking deregulation, however. The rapid consolidation of the industry gives support to the belief in the industry of strong economies of scale.

Airlines are much larger than trucking companies, but have similar cost structures to LTL truckers. Fuel costs are much higher, as are the costs of handling loads. But airlines, like truckers, have to maintain and operate terminals and coordinate their network. Network economies of the form described in Chapter 5 appear to give strong advantages to airlines with large networks. One study of the pre-deregulation airline industry found, as with railroads and LTL trucking, that there are economies of density but not of scale. A study based on more modern data may find that with the freedom to adjust their networks, large airlines do in fact have lower costs than smaller ones.

The cost analysis of water carrier operations is dominated by the tradeoffs between economies of sailing large ships and diseconomies of loading and unloading ships. Containerization, by drastically reducing the time that it takes to load and unload ships, has increased optimal ship sizes. The longer a trade route, the more important sailing cost as a proportion of the total and thus the larger the ship that is economically justified. Short trade routes call for smaller ships with higher sailing costs. The world shipping industry believes that there are economies not only of ship size but also of fleet size; this belief is used to justify the organization of the world's general freight fleet into cartels. The remaining part of the world fleet—dry bulkers and tankers—operate as contract carriers. Just as there is no reason to think that there are economies of scale in the truckload sector of the motor carrier industry, there is little reason to think that there are scale economies in operating bulk and tank ships.

Automobile operating costs appear to be quite a small proportion of the total costs of owning and operating a car. Part of the reason is that the driver's time is not generally assigned a cost. Once the cost of drivers' time is included, it becomes clear that the costs of automobile travel depend strongly on the level of traffic. Since increasing vehicle density on any highway slows traffic speeds, the cost per mile of driving must rise with traffic levels. Marginal costs rise much faster than average costs, since the presence of one more vehicle slows traffic not only for the new car entering traffic but for all others who are already there. Drivers do not take into account the slowing that they impose on others, however. This external cost that drivers impose on one another forms the basis of efficient congestion tolls that are described in Chapter 10.

Accounting for the time of drivers and passengers complicates comparisons between automobile and urban public transportation. Ignoring the costs of passenger time, urban buses are seen to have relatively high operating expenses relative to total costs, while rail-based systems have a much smaller proportion of costs associated with vehicle operations.

NOTES

1. Figures in this section are from Association of American Railroads, *Railroad Facts, 1995 Edition.*
2. *Transportation in America*, 14th edition.
3. For an analysis of the effect of staffing requirements on railroad costs and service quality, see Keaton, Mark H., "Train Crew Size, Crew Cost, and Service Levels for Single Carload Freight Traffic in the U.S. Rail Industry," *Logistics and Transportation Review*, Vol. 27, No. 4, December 1991, pp. 333–349.
4. Note that these are average accounting costs. Average opportunity costs are likely to be lower.
5. Described in McBride, M.E., "An Evaluation of Various Methods of Estimating Railway Costs," *Logistics and Transportation Review*, March 1983, Vol. 19, No. 1, p. 60.
6. For a description of the Uniform Rail Costing System, see McBride, M. E., "An Evaluation of Various Methods of Estimating Railway Costs," *Logistics and Transportation Review*, March 1983, Vol. 19, No. 1, pp. 45–66.
7. Keeler, Theodore E., "Railroad Costs, Returns to Scale, and Excess Capacity," *Review of Economics and Statistics*, Vol. 56 (May 1974), pp. 201–208.
8. See Braeutigam, Ronald R., Andrew F. Daughety, and Mark A. Turnquist, "The Estimation of a Hybrid Cost Function for a Railroad Firm," *Review of Economics and Statistics*, Vol. 64 (August 1982), pp. 394–404; and Braeutigam, R.R., A. F. Daughety, and M. A. Turnquist, "A Firm Specific Analysis of Economies of Density in the U.S. Railroad Industry," *Journal of Industrial Economics*, Vol. 33, No. 1, September 1982, pp. 3–20.
9. Recent econometric studies of North American railroad costs include Friedlaender, Ann F., et al., "Rail Costs and Capital Adjustments in a Quasi Regulated Environment," *Journal of Transport Economics and Policy*, Vol. 27, No. 2, May

1993, pp. 131–152. Keaton, Mark H., "Economies of Density and Service Levels on U.S. Railroads: An Experimental Analysis," *Logistics and Transportation Review,* Vol. 26, No. 3, September 1990, pp. 211–227. Kumbhakar, Subal C., "On the Estimation of Technical and Allocative Inefficiency Using Stochastic Frontier Functions: The Case of U.S. Class 1 Railroads," *International Economic Review,* Vol. 29, No. 4, November 1988, p. 727. Caves, Douglas W., Laurits R. Christensen, "The Importance of Economies of Scale, Capacity Utilization, and Density in Explaining Interindustry Differences in Productivity Growth," *Logistics and Transportation Review,* Vol. 24, No. 1, March 1988, pp. 3–32. Freeman, Kenneth D. et al., "The Total Factor Productivity of the Canadian Class I Railways: 1956–1981," *Logistics and Transportation Review,* Vol. 21, No. 3, September 1985, pp. 249–276. Caves, Douglas W., Laurits R. Christensen, Joseph A. Swanson, "Productivity Growth, Scale Economies, and Capacity Utilization in U.S. Railroads, 1955–1974," *American Economic Review,* Vol. 71, No. 5, Dec. 1981, pp. 994–1002. For the European experience, see McGeehan, Harry, "Railway Costs and Productivity Growth: The Case of the Republic of Ireland, 1973–1983," *Journal of Transport Economics and Policy,* Vol. 27, No. 1, January 1993, pp. 19–32. Filippini, Massimo and Rico Maggi, "The Cost Structure of the Swiss Private Railways," *International Journal of Transport Economics,* Vol. 19, No. 3, October 1992. Gathon, Henry Jean and Sergio Perelman, "Measuring Technical Efficiency in European Railways: A Panel Data Approach," *Journal of Productivity Analysis,* Vol. 3, Nos. 1–2, June 1992, pp. 135–151.

10. See, for example, Walker, W. Thomas, "Network Economies of Scale in Short Haul Truckload Operations," *Journal of Transport Economics and Policy,* Vol. 26, No. 1, January 1992, pp. 3–17.

11. This argument is made in Boyer, Kenneth D. "Equalizing Discrimination and Cartel Pricing in Transport Rate Regulation," *Journal of Political Economy,* Vol. 89, No. 2, April 1981, pp. 270–287.

12. A study showing the variability in marginal costs between different truck shipments is found in Jara Diaz, Sergio R., Pedro P. Donoso and Jorge A. Araneda, "Estimation of Marginal Transport Costs: The Flow Aggregation Function Approach," *Journal of Transport Economics and Policy,* Vol. 26, No. 1, January 1992, pp. 35–48

13. See Friedlaender, Ann and Richard Spady, *Freight Transport Regulation: Equity, Efficiency and Competition in the Rail and Trucking Industries* (Cambridge, Massachusetts: MIT Press, 1981). A criticism of these techniques is found in Daughety, Andrew F., Forrest Nelson, and William Vigdor. "An Econometric Analysis of the Cost and Production Structure of the Trucking Industry," in Andrew F. Daughety, ed., *Analytical Studies in Transport Economics* (Cambridge: Cambridge University Press, 1985).

14. Kefung Xu, Robert Windle, Curtis Grimm, and Thomas Corsi, "Re-evaluating Returns to Scale in Transport," *Journal of Transport Economics and Policy,* Vol. 28, No. 3 (September 1994), pp. 275–286. See also Gagne, Robert, "On the Relevant Elasticity Estimates for Cost Structure Analyses of the Trucking Industry," *Review of Economics and Statistics,* Vol. 72, No. 1, February 1990, pp. 160–164.

15. Keeler, Theodore E., "Deregulation and Scale Economies in the U.S. Trucking Industry: An Econometric Extension of the Survivor Principle," *Journal of Law and Economics,* Vol. 32 No. 2, Part 1, October 1989, pp. 229–253.

16. McMullen, B. S. and L.R. Stanley, "The Impact of Deregulation on the Production Structure of the Motor Carrier Industry," *Economic Inquiry*, April, 1988, Vol. 26, No. 2, pp. 299–316. See also, Christensen, L.R. and J.H. Huston, "A Reexamination of the Cost Structure for Specialized Motor Carriers," *Logistics and Transportation Review*, December 1987, Vol. 23, No. 4, pp. 339–351; and Thomas, Janet M. and Scott J. Callan, "Constant Returns to Scale in the Post Deregulatory Period; the Case of Specialized Motor Carriers," *Logistics and Transportation Review*, Vol. 25, No. 3, September 1989, pp. 271–288.

17. See, for example, Daughety, Andrew F. and Forrest D. Nelson, "An Econometric Analysis of Changes in the Cost and Production Structure of the Trucking Industry, 1953–1982," *Review of Economics and Statistics*, Vol. 70, No. 1 (February, 1988), pp. 67–75; and Harmatuck, D. J., "Short Run Motor Carrier Cost Functions for Five Large Common Carriers," *Logistics and Transportation Review*, September 1985, Vol. 21, No. 3, pp. 217–237.

18. Wang Chiang, J.S. and A. F. Friedlaender, "Truck Technology and Efficient Market Structure," *Review of Economics and Statistics*, May 1985, Vol. 67, No. 2, pp. 250–258. See also Bruning, E. R., "Cost Efficiency Measurement in the Trucking Industry: An Application of the Stochastic Frontier Approach," *International Journal of Transport Economics*, Vol. 19, No. 2, June 1992, pp. 165–186. Harmatuck, Donald J., "Economies of Scale and Scope in the Motor Carrier Industry: An Analysis of the Cost Functions for Seventeen Large LTL Common Motor Carriers," *Journal of Transport Economics and Policy*, Vol. 25, No. 2, May 1991, pp. 135–151. Ying, John S., "Regulatory Reform and Technical Change: New Evidence of Scale Economies in Trucking," *Southern Economic Journal*, Vol. 56, No. 4, April 1990, pp. 996–1009. Grimm, Curtis M., Thomas M. Corsi and Judith L. Jarrell, "U.S. Motor Carrier Cost Structure under Deregulation," *Logistics and Transportation Review*, Vol. 25, No. 3, September 1989, pp. 231–249.

19. See Keeler, Theodore and M. Abrahams, "Market Structure, Pricing, and Service Quality in the Airline Industry under Deregulation," in W. Sichel and T. Gies, eds., *Applications of Economic Principles in Public Utilities Industries* (Ann Arbor: Graduate School of Business Administration, 1981).

20. Bailey, E. E., David R. Graham, and Daniel P. Kaplan, *Deregulating the Airlines*. (Cambridge: MIT Press, 1985), p. 51. One source of lower costs of large aircraft is fuel costs. See Steven A. Morrison, "An Economic Analysis of Aircraft Design," *Journal of Transport Economics and Policy*, (May 1984), pp. 123–143.

21. Brueckner, Jan K. and Pablo T. Spiller, "Economies of Traffic Density in the Deregulated Airline Industry," *Journal of Law and Economics*, Vol. 37, No. 2, October 1994, pp. 379–415. The empirical literature on airline scale economies is surveyed in Antoniou, Andreas, "Economies of Scale in the Airline Industry: The Evidence Revisited," *Logistics and Transportation Review*, Vol. 27, No. 2, June 1991, pp. 159–184. See also Jha, Raghbendra and B. S. Sahni, "Toward Measuring Airline Technical Inefficiency: The Case of Canadian Airlines Industry," *International Journal of Transport Economics*, Vol. 19, No. 1, February 1992, pp. 45–59. Windle, Robert J., "The World's Airlines: A Cost and Productivity Comparison," *Journal of Transport Economics and Policy*, Vol. 25, No. 1, January 1991, pp. 31–49. Mechling, George W., Jr., "Deregulation and the Capacity, Productivity and Technical Efficiency of Equipment of Former Trunk Airlines,"

Journal of Transport Economics and Policy, Vol. 25, No. 1, January 1991, pp. 51–61. Kumbhakar, Subal C., "A Reexamination of Returns to Scale, Density and Technical Progress in U.S. Airlines," *Southern Economic Journal,* Vol. 57, No. 2, October 1990, pp. 428–442. Gillen, David W. Tae Hoon Oum, and Michael W. Tretheway, "Airline Cost Structure and Policy Implications: A Multi-product Approach for Canadian Airlines," *Journal of Transport Economics and Policy,* Vol. 24, No. 1, January 1990, pp. 9–34. Kirby, Michael G., "Airline Economics of 'Scale' and Australian Domestic Air Transport Policy," *Journal of Transport Economics and Policy,* Vol. 20, No. 3, September 1986, pp. 339–352.

22. A useful source on international shipping is White, Lawrence J., *International Trade in Ocean Shipping Services: The United States and the World,* American Enterprise Institute Trade in Services Series (Washington, D.C.: American Enterprise Institute for Public Policy Research; Cambridge, Mass.: Harper and Row, Ballinger, 1988).

23. J.O. Jansson and D. Shneerson, *Liner Shipping Economics* (London: Chapman and Hall, 1987).

24. J.O. Jansson and D. Shneerson, "Economies of Trade Density in Liner Shipping," *Journal of Transport Economics and Policy* (January 1985), pp. 7–22. See also Tolofari, S. R., K. J. Button, and D. E. Pitfield, "An Econometric Analysis of the Cost Structure of the Tank Sector of the Shipping Industry," *International Journal of Transport Economics,* Vol. 14, No. 1, 1987, pp. 71–84; de Borger, B. and W. Nonneman, "Statistical Cost Functions for Dry Bulk Carriers," *Journal of Transport Economics and Policy,* Vol. 15, No. 2, May 1981, pp. 155–165.

25. See, for example, Wayne K. Talley, Vinod B. Agarwal, and James W. Breakfield, "The Economies of Density of Ocean Tanker Ships," *Journal of Transport Economics and Policy* (January, 1986), pp. 91–99.

26. J.E. Davies, "An Analysis of Cost and Supply Conditions in the Liner Shipping Industry," *The Journal of Industrial Economics,* Vol. XXI, No. 4, (June 1983), pp. 417–435 and J.E. Davies, "Competition, Contestability and Liner Shipping, *Journal of Transport Economics and Policy* (September 1986), pp. 299–312.

27. J.O. Jansson and D. Shneerson, "Economies of Trade Density in Liner Shipping," *Journal of Transport Economics and Policy* (January 1985), pp. 7–22. The authors perform a simulation of equilibrium structures of trade routes and discover that while there are economies of density on individual routes, they are not of such a magnitude to make competition impractical.

28. Leland S. Case and Lester B. Lave, "Cost Functions for Inland Waterways Transport in the United States," *Journal of Transport Economics and Policy* (May 1970), pp. 181–191.

29. Charles W. Howe et al., *Inland Waterway Transportation* (Baltimore, Johns Hopkins Press, 1969).

30. Logically, the true relationship between traffic density and speed must be curvilinear and modern analyses show such curves. See John Baerwald, ed., *Transportation and Traffic Engineering Handbook* (Englewood Cliffs, N.J.: Prentice Hall, Inc., 1976), Chapter 7. In order to simplify the analysis, only straight line speed-volume curves will be considered here.

31. For an advanced description of the treatment of *balking* when congestion becomes severe, see Stephen Glaister, *Fundamentals of Transport Economics* (New York: St. Martin's Press, 1981).

32. Herbert Mohring, "Optimization and Scale Economies in Bus Transportation," *American Economic Review*, Vol. 62 (1972), pp. 591–604, argues that this is the logically preferred procedure.

33. For a discussion of private urban transit see Charles Lave, ed., *Urban Transit: The Private Challenge to Public Transportation* (San Francisco: The Pacific Institute for Public Policy, 1985).

34. Viton, Philip A., "Consolidations of Scale and Scope in Urban Transit," *Regional Science and Urban Economics*, Vol. 22 (1992), pp. 25–49. See also Berechman, J., "Costs, Economies of Scale and Factor Demand in Bus Transport: An Analysis," *Journal of Transportation Economics and Policy*, January 1983, *17*, pp. 7–24; and Tauchen, H., F. D. Fravel, and G. Gilbert, "Cost Structure of the Intercity Bus Industry," *Journal of Transportation Economics and Policy*, January 1983, *17*, pp. 25–47. Tauchen et al. also find strong economies of scope among intercity buses, local service, charter operations, and school buses.

ECONOMIC PRINCIPLES FOR TRANSPORT PRICING

9

Transportation Investment and Disinvestment

Economic policy toward the transport sector is primarily concerned with installing and paying for fixed facilities. In all countries in the world, transportation issues are primarily about what kind of transportation assets to invest in and how use of those assets should be priced. This chapter begins the discussion of the central elements of the economic analysis of transport policy by describing the standard tools for evaluating investments. The first subject will be investment in vehicles. Since vehicles investments are not sunk, it is possible to describe investment criteria using the simple curves of basic microeconomics. Fixed facilities investments, by contrast, require the use of forecasting and discounting, a subject described subsequently. The remainder of the chapter highlights the differences between financial and economic criteria for evaluating transport investments.

INVESTMENT AND DISINVESTMENT IN VEHICLES

The opportunity cost of shifting aircraft among markets is small compared with their daily rental rates. This leads to an approximately common price for services in all areas. If there is a single price for all vehicle services, the decision to invest or sell off part of the fleet becomes easy enough to illustrate on a diagram like that shown in Figure 9.1. Figure 9.1 shows unit cost curves for a fleet operator. As shown, fleet costs are dominated by the cost of capital. For reasons described in this chapter, capital costs are calculated as the dollar value of the vehicle fleet multiplied by the opportunity cost of having a dollar tied up in the vehicle fleet. In most circumstances, this can be considered to be a going interest rate in the economy. Average capital costs are represented by a downward sloping line since, with a fixed value of the fleet, increasing the number of days that the vehicles are rented decreases the average capital cost per vehicle-day.

The other costs of vehicle ownership, maintenance, and depreciation, are represented as a horizontal line, rising as the physical vehicle-day capacity of the fleet is approached. The line is upward sloping since, by a costly acceleration of vehicle maintenance, the fleet can be operated more days per year; a second possible reason for the upward slope of the average maintenance and depreciation costs is the possibility of increased depreciation if vehicles are operated more hours than they were designed for.

The sum of average capital costs and average maintenance and depreciation costs is the average total cost of vehicle ownership, as was discussed in Chapter 7. A marginal cost per vehicle-day—the cost of trying to get one more vehicle-

FIGURE 9.1 Profitable Opportunities for Investment in Vehicle Stocks

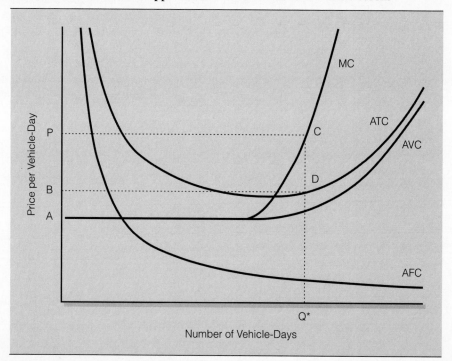

day per month out of an existing fleet—is drawn as cutting through the bottom of the average total maintenance and depreciation cost curve. Mathematically, an average cost curve must be upward sloping when its marginal cost curve is above it and downward sloping when marginal cost is below.

Figure 9.1 shows a price of vehicle services as a horizontal line at the level marked P. This means that the price of vehicle services is not affected by the fleet owner's decisions on how many days of vehicle service to offer to the market. The price of vehicle services is assumed to be set by supply and demand in the national market. The profit maximizing number of vehicle-days to offer is given by the intersection of the price line and marginal cost of vehicle services, listed as Q*. The logic behind this result—one of the most famous rules in microeconomics—is that a fleet owner who offered either a larger or smaller number of vehicle-days would be worse off. If fewer than Q* days were offered, the fleet owner would be foregoing revenue that more than covered costs; beyond Q*, the additional costs of accelerated maintenance and depreciation would not be covered by the revenue received for vehicle use. Thus Q* must be the profit maximizing output. In mathematical terms, Q* is described by the condition:

$$P = MC \tag{9.1}$$

or Price equals Marginal Cost.

At Q*, the difference between average total costs and the price of vehicle services is the per unit profit margin. The area PCDB in Figure 9.1, which multiplies the profit margin PB by Q*, shows the dollar profit per period of the fleet owner. This is *pure* or *economic profit*—that is, profit in excess of the cost of capital. Since the fleet owner is making a profit—and assuming that the owner believes current conditions will continue in the future—he or she is justified in expanding the fleet by purchasing vehicles in the new or used market.[1] Expanding the fleet will bring in revenues in excess of the cost of capital, depreciation, and maintenance.

Disinvesting in Vehicle Stocks

Figure 9.2 is identical to Figure 9.1 except that the price of vehicle service that a fleet owner faces is now lower. This might occur because the national fleet of vehicles expanded too rapidly or because there was a drop in the demand for vehicle services in the area served by the operator. At the price shown in Figure 9.2, the fleet owner is not making an economic profit. While maintenance and depreciation costs are covered, the price of vehicle services does not allow the owner to make a normal rate of return on capital invested in the fleet. This is a signal that the fleet owner should not invest in new vehicles; in fact, the owner should allow the fleet to shrink by not replacing vehicles as they wear out or by selling vehicles out of the market to other operators who can make better use of them.

FIGURE 9.2   Vehicle Stocks Should Be Shrunk Rather Than Expanded

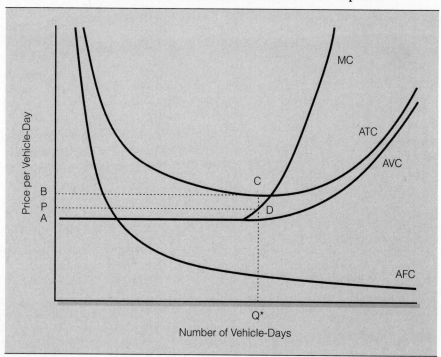

Note that the fleet operator in Figure 9.2 is still justified in operating the fleet since maintenance and depreciation costs are covered and operations do provide a contribution to overhead costs; the appropriate responses are to lengthen maintenance cycles and to scrap vehicles when they need major repairs. Only if the price of vehicle services falls below the average cost of maintenance and depreciation should the owner mothball the fleet and wait for better times. In mathematical terms, this is written as:

$$P \geq AVC \qquad (9.2)$$

or Price must be greater than Average Variable Cost
for the operation to continue.

PRINCIPLES OF PRIVATE INVESTMENT

The simple graphical analysis described above is naive. All investment decisions have long-term consequences; except for the minor adjustments on the size of the vehicle fleet by buying and selling in the used vehicle market, investment decisions require forecasts of how profitable vehicle use will be in the months, years, and decades ahead. As noted in Chapter 7, vehicle lives differ greatly from mode to mode: The shortest lives are for motor vehicles, while aircraft appear to have indefinite economic lives. Unless a vehicle owner anticipates selling a vehicle in the used market in the future, the economic life of a vehicle will determine the planning horizon over which projections will need to be made. To see how long-term consequences of investment decisions are taken into account, it is useful to have a specific example.

In 1986, the Union Pacific Railroad purchased Overnite Transportation Co., a large trucking business, for $1.2 billion. This decision was criticized by Drew Lewis, the president of Union Pacific, who took over the job several years after this investment was made. According to Mr. Lewis, at 10 percent interest, it was costing $120 million a year for a company that was generating $60 million in profits.[2] This comparison shows that Union Pacific made a bad investment decision.

There are several ways to show that the decision was faulty. The most common way is to compute how much money Union Pacific would have had to invest, at 10 percent interest per year, to earn the $60 million per year that their investment in Overnite was earning. This amount, $600 million, is the *present discounted value* of Overnite's earnings. A present discounted value for a stream of payments is the amount of money that would be needed to be invested today, at some interest rate, to be able to withdraw that stream of payments in the future. If a present discounted value is correctly calculated, an investor should be indifferent between having an amount of money in hand today equal to the present discounted value as opposed to the guaranteed promise to pay specific amounts in the future.

Columns 2 through 4 of Table 9.1 show how to calculate the present discounted value of $60 million per year if interest rates are 10 percent per year. In order to earn $60 million in 1987, Union Pacific would have had to invest $54.54 million in 1986 at 10 percent interest. The principle and interest on that investment would have been worth $60 million one year later. In order to earn $60 million in 1988, the company would have had to invest $49.587 in 1986. Again, the principle and two years' interest at 10 percent on this amount would have enabled the company to withdraw $60 million in 1988. The formula for determining how much money needs to be invested in any year in order to be able to earn a specified number of dollars in a future year is:

$$\text{PDV}(n) = \frac{I(n)}{(1+r)^n} \tag{9.3}$$

where: $\text{PDV}(n)$ = present discounted value of the nth year's income
$I(n)$ = income n years from now
r = interest rate, expressed in decimal format
n = number of years from now.

TABLE 9.1   Present Discounted Value Calculations for Union Pacific's 1986 Purchase of Overnite Transportation

Year	$ Million Revenue	10% Discount Factor	Discounted Amount	5% Discount Factor	Discounted Amount
1987	60	1.10	54.55	1.05	57.14
1988	60	1.21	49.59	1.10	54.42
1989	60	1.33	45.08	1.16	51.83
1990	60	1.46	40.98	1.22	49.36
1991	60	1.61	37.26	1.28	47.01
1992	60	1.77	33.87	1.34	44.77
1993	60	1.95	30.79	1.41	42.64
1994	60	2.14	27.99	1.48	40.61
1995	60	2.36	25.45	1.55	38.68
1996	60	2.59	23.13	1.63	36.83
1997	60	2.85	21.03	1.71	35.08
1998	60	3.14	19.12	1.80	33.41
1999	60	3.45	17.38	1.89	31.82
2000	60	3.80	15.80	1.98	30.30
2001	60	4.18	14.36	2.08	28.86
2002	60	4.59	13.06	2.18	27.49
2003	60	5.05	11.87	2.29	26.18
2004	60	5.56	10.79	2.41	24.93
2005	60	6.12	9.81	2.53	23.74
2006	60	6.73	8.92	2.65	22.61
2007	60	7.40	8.11	2.79	21.54
2008	60	8.14	7.37	2.93	20.51
2009	60	8.95	6.70	3.07	19.53
2010	60	9.85	6.09	3.23	18.60
2011	60	10.83	5.54	3.39	17.72
2012	60	11.92	5.03	3.56	16.87
2013	60	13.11	4.58	3.73	16.07
2014	60	14.42	4.16	3.92	15.31
2015	60	15.86	3.78	4.12	14.58
2016	60	17.45	3.44	4.32	13.88
Total			594.89		1,095.36

The discount factor, $1/(1+r)^n$ is listed for each year in column 3 of Table 9.1. The discount factor for any particular year shows how much money would be necessary to invest today, at interest rate r, so that the original amount plus compound interest over the years would be equal to $1.00 in that year. Column 4 is the product of the discount factor and the annual $60 million expected earnings of Overnite. The sum of the present discounted value of each year's returns, shown as $594 million at the bottom of column 4, is the present discounted value of the earnings of Overnite at 10 percent interest carried out for 50 years. The sum at the bottom of column 6 shows that if interest rates in the economy were 5 percent per year, then the same $60 million per year for 50 years would be worth $1,095.36. The formula for these calculations is:

$$PDV = \sum_{n=1}^{50} \frac{I(n)}{(1+r)^n} \qquad (9.4)$$

which simply says that the discounted income amounts are to be added up for years 1 to 50. In the especially easy case where neither the annual incomes nor the interest rate change and where the expected returns continue indefinitely, the formula can be simplified to:

$$PDV = I/r \qquad (9.5)$$

Using this formula it is quick and easy to show the value of $60 million per year, if interest rates are 10 percent, is $600 million (Note that the difference between discounting for 50 years and discounting forever, the difference between $594.89 million and $600 million is less than 1 percent of the amount). This is the amount Union Pacific should have been able to invest in an alternative investment which gave them a 10 percent return on their investment and which would have given them an equivalent income stream from the one that Overnite promised. Since Union Pacific paid $1.2 billion for an investment that gave them returns equivalent to what they could have gotten from a $600 million investment, one can understand Drew Lewis' complaint that the railroad made a bad investment.

While the present discounted value criterion is the easiest and most reliable way to evaluate an investment opportunity, there is another commonly used method that, under most circumstances, will give the same information. The *internal rate of return* on an investment is the interest rate that equates the investment cost with the present discounted value of the annual earnings from the investment. In the case here, the internal rate of return can be calculated as $60/$1,200 = 0.05. That is, the internal rate of return is equal to the annual income from the Overnite investment divided by the amount that Union Pacific paid for the trucking company. From columns 5 and 6 of Table 9.1, it appears that 5 percent is at least close to the internal rate of return on the investment. The difference between $1.2 billion and $1.095 is again due to the fact that discounting was carried out for only 50 years rather than indefinitely. If the calculation were carried out for infinite time, when interest rates are 5 percent, the present discounted value of the expected annual earnings of Overnite will exactly equal the $1.2 billion payment for the company.

The internal rate of return on an investment can be compared with interest rates available elsewhere in the economy to compare investment opportunities. Another way of characterizing Drew Lewis' complaint about the decision made by his predecessor to buy Overnite for $1.2 billion is to say that the internal rate of return of this investment was only 5 percent while there were other investments that Union Pacific could have made that would have had higher rates of return.

Why did Union Pacific make the $1.2 billion investment in Overnite if it was such a bad idea? There are several possibilities. Perhaps the company expected interest rates to fall in the near future to an amount below 5 percent. Then the 5 percent internal rate of return would have been higher than that available elsewhere and the present discounted value of an annual $60 million income would be greater than the purchase price. Another possibility is that Union Pacific expected that income would be higher than $60 million per year. This in fact is the correct explanation. Drew Lewis, in commenting on the purchase of Overnite by his predecessor, noted, "They talked synergism with the railroad, and there is none." Apparently the previous management expected that the trucking line would help increase the income of the railroad and that the railroad would help increase the income of the trucking company. This did not happen.

If Overnite was a bad investment for Union Pacific, does that mean that the railroad should disinvest itself of the trucking company? Not necessarily. When making an investment, the amount paid is the opportunity cost and the desirability of the investment is determined by comparing opportunity cost and the present discounted value of expected future earnings. The disinvestment decision is analogous, except that opportunity costs are calculated differently. The $600 million mistake that Union Pacific apparently made (the amount that it paid above what Overnite was worth) is a sunk cost. The opportunity cost of keeping Overnite as a unit of Union Pacific is the amount a potential buyer would be willing to pay for the motor carrier. If the opportunity cost is higher than the present discounted value of Overnite's expected earnings, they should sell; if it is less, they should retain the company. Of course, any potential buyer in trying to decide how much to pay for Overnite would make the same present discounted value calculation as is shown in Table 9.1. The only reasons that other buyers would be willing to pay more than the amount shown at the bottom of column 4 are that they think they could manage the company differently so that it would earn more money than the amounts in column 2 or they are more optimistic than Union Pacific about what market interest rates will be in the future and thus will use lower discount factors when discounting future earnings.

CRITERIA FOR PRIVATE INVESTMENT AND DISINVESTMENT IN FIXED FACILITIES

Except for the terminals used by LTL operators, motor carriers tend to have low fixed facilities needs, as described in Chapter 6. When a private company makes an investment in fixed facilities, it needs to use the same principle of comparing the present discounted value of expected future earnings with the opportunity costs of the action as Drew Lewis made of the Overnite purchase. But fixed facility investment decisions need to be made with even more care than investments in more mobile types of capital, since the value of the investment will be largely sunk—especially for railroads, a sector that has been shrinking rather than expanding. Fixed facilities investments are also risky because they often are large and lumpy and are made in advance of demand. Fixed facilities investment decisions also tend to be more difficult to evaluate since investments generally affect both future costs as well as revenues, sometimes in unpredictable ways.

To illustrate the principles that a private firm goes through in making a fixed facilities investment decision, consider the drilling of the new 31-mile railway tunnel between England and France, a project known as the "chunnel." The project was privately financed and built and was thus subject to the private investment analysis rather than the tools of public project evaluation that will be described later in this chapter. The tunnel is designed to carry conventional passenger and freight trains as well as automobiles and trucks on specially designed drive-on flat cars. Prior to the building of the tunnel, all surface transportation between the two countries was by ferries.[3]

Like most investments in transportation fixed facilities, the chunnel had three effects: (1) it increased transportation capacity between Britain and France; (2) it lowered costs of operation compared to ferries; and (3) it improved service quality by providing a much faster and more reliable crossing. The project was costly, however. By the time the tunnel was opened for business the company had amassed a debt of more than $12 billion. This is money that could have been spent on other fixed facilities projects on the railroad system or on some of the other modes of transport or non-transportation projects. As an investor, how would you decide whether the chunnel was the best place to employ your money?

To answer this question, you would have to forecast the future profits from the investment. On the cost side, this requires forecasting construction costs, the costs of buying the special vehicles necessary to carry road traffic, and the costs of operations. On the demand side, it would be necessary to forecast traffic levels and the price that could be charged for services. Since the chunnel is a new service that has not been offered before, there was no direct experience that could be extrapolated to the new crossing. Investors in the project needed to make a decision based on their best forecasts of construction costs, operating costs, prices, traffic levels, and, of course, the level of interest rates that would be necessary to discount projected costs and revenues.

Like many investors in projects with no track record, the banks that put up most of the capital for the project were disappointed. First, the construction costs were far higher than originally projected. At several points the question of whether the project should be abandoned was addressed and the decision was made to continue. By the time the project was completed, the interest costs on the debt incurred during construction had increased to $3 million per day. In other words, the chunnel needed to earn $3 million more in revenue than it paid in operating costs every day in order to repay its construction loans.

The forecasts of construction costs turned out to be one of the two major errors made in the original evaluation of the project.[4] Operating costs projections were far more accurate—though there were some start up problems in the technologically sophisticated train-sets and the rail links connecting the tunnel with the city of London were not improved to the level originally anticipated. Forecasts of traffic levels were correct as well. However, what was not anticipated were the fares that chunnel users were willing to pay. Due to the excess capacity on crossings of the English Channel that was the result of the opening of the tunnel (recall that the ferries, like all transportation equipment, have long lives), fare levels plummeted. In order to retain at least some of the business for themselves, the ferries competing with the tunnel developed new advertising and marketing strategies and drastically cut fares. As a result, the operators of the channel tunnel were not able to charge as high a fare as they had originally anticipated.

The chunnel has been able to charge fares that cover the costs of operating trains through the tunnel. As described in Chapters 6 through 8, railroads have a cost structure that is tilted toward the fixed costs of vehicle and track ownership costs. The variable costs of operations are very low—certainly much lower than the costs of operating ferries. However, the inability of the tunnel operator to charge fares as high as anticipated has meant that less than $3 million per day in net revenues has been earned. Thus there are insufficient funds to pay the debt on the construction costs. As this is written, the private company that owns the tunnel has defaulted on payment on the interest on its debt. It is bankrupt.

Bankruptcy does not mean that the tunnel will cease to operate. The reason is that—as in much transportation infrastructure spending—the costs of building the tunnel are sunk. "You cannot sell a hole in the ground for much if you've closed it," was the comment of an official of the company.[5] Thus passengers will not see any effects of the bankruptcy. The losers are the original private investors who lent the company the funds to build the tunnel. They will see the value of the original investment drastically shrink. As long as revenues continue to cover operating expenses, however, the company will have a greater value as an operating concern than as an owner of abandoned property.

The dominance of transportation fixed facility investment by sunk costs has two important implications. First, transportation fixed facilities investment is generally risky. Banks are far less willing to lend funds for investment in fixed facilities, which are dominated by sunk costs, than they are to lend for investment in vehicles, whose value—assuming that they are not uniquely suited for a particular service—is little diminished if a particular operator fails. Second, since the opportunity cost of using transportation fixed facilities is generally quite low, the facilities are used for their original purpose for years beyond the point at which they earn a return high enough to justify the original investment.

The fact that investment costs are primarily sunk is what allowed U.S. railroads to operate for decades despite the fact that they did not earn a normal rate of return on their original investment. Once some of the ferries that compete with the channel tunnel wear out and are not replaced, or until demand rises sufficiently to eliminate the excess capacity on the crossing between England and France, fares should recover to a more normal level.

PUBLIC EVALUATION OF TRANSPORT INVESTMENTS

Given the riskiness of transportation projects, it is rare for funding to be purely private, as was the case for the channel tunnel. Most investment in transport infrastructure—highways and airports, for example—is done by public agencies using the criteria of public finance rather than corporate finance. In this section we shall compare the public financial and corporate financial evaluation of transport projects and show that while they often result in the same projects being funded and the same underused facilities being abandoned, they do not always do so. Where they differ, it is almost always the case that public finance justifies investment that a private firm would not undertake. Later in this chapter we will see a transportation project that is economically justified even though the operator does not anticipate making a profit.

■ Net Social Welfare

The economic, as opposed to financial, evaluation of investment is not made on the basis of profitability (or, more precisely, the net present discounted value) of an investment but rather on the basis of net social welfare. *Net social welfare* is defined as benefits minus costs. This compares with a company's profits, which are defined as revenues minus costs. One way of thinking about private investment decisions is to think of them as private benefit-cost calculations, with revenues replacing the concept of benefits. With rare exception, however, public projects do not collect payments that can be considered the same as benefits.

Public projects do, however, have demand curves, and this is the source of the benefit calculation in cost/benefit analysis. A demand curve is, as described previously, a relationship between the amount per unit that a consumer pays and the number of units that he or she purchases. A typical demand curve is shown in Figure 9.3. The usefulness of demand curves in defining the benefits of a transport project is revealed when we change the way we look at Figure 9.3. The usual way to view Figure 9.3 is to say that at price P*, consumers would willingly use Q* units of the good or service. However, we could also ask, "What is the maximum price that consumers would be willing to pay for an additional unit of the good or service if they are currently using Q* units of it?" The answer is found by finding the price that corresponds to Q*. In

FIGURE 9.3   Net Social Surplus Calculations

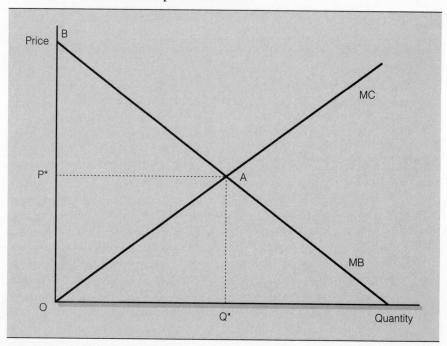

Figure 9.3, it is shown as P*, which is the marginal value that consumers place on a unit of Q if the current consumption level is Q*. Since the demand curve is downward sloping, if fewer units are available, the marginal value will be higher. The total value that consumers place on consuming Q* is the sum of the marginal values of all the units consumed. This is the area under the demand curve up to consumption level Q* in Figure 9.3.

It is traditional to divide the total benefit into two parts, one corresponding to consumer expenditure and one corresponding to consumers' surplus. In Figure 9.3, consumer expenditure is the area OP*AQ*. Consumers' surplus is the area above this box but below the demand curve. This is the area P*AB. Consumers' surplus is the additional amount that consumers would be willing to spend, over and above what they actually do spend, in order to have a good or service rather than do without any of it. Consumers' surplus is difficult to measure with accuracy. Measuring consumers' surplus requires that the entire demand curve be known. For complete accuracy in evaluating the entire length of the demand curve, you would have to offer a good or service at many different prices, including prices far above costs.[6]

The main measurement of social benefits of a project is the area under the demand curve for it, up to the level of service that it provides—i.e., the sum of consumer expenditure and consumers' surplus. This says that the benefits of transportation can be measured by the willingness to pay by those people who pay transportation bills. It is easy to be misled into thinking that the benefits of transportation facilities are larger and more widespread than they actually are. One source of inflated benefit estimates for transport projects is counting the same benefits twice. For example, a retailer who is able to receive goods more cheaply due to the construction of a new highway will be able to pass cost savings along to the customer. In this case, the general public benefits from the new road. However, consumer demand will be reflected in the demand for transportation and thus in the willingness of trucking firms to pay tolls on the new highways. To count as benefits not only the willingness of truckers to pay for a road but also the lower prices that consumers pay for the goods that they buy double-counts project benefits. To avoid double counting, public finance assumes that the total benefit of a new facility can be measured by the total willingness to pay among direct users only and ignores indirect benefits.

A direct comparison of willingness to pay with the costs of a facilities provider is a valid cost-benefit exercise only in the case in which there are no externalities. An externality is an effect that one person's consumption has on another person's well being. If there are external effects of taking a car trip, then the total benefit to the economy is something different from simply the benefit to the person making the trip. In the case of external costs (e.g., from air pollution due to burning motor fuel), the total benefit measure will have to be adjusted downward by an amount equal to what a person affected would have been willing to pay to avoid being injured. (Equivalently, and more commonly, the marginal cost measure could be adjusted upward). Thus if Jack's car trip to the movie theater cost him $1 and if the total amount that people who breathed the exhaust out of his tail pipe would have been willing to pay to have air cleaner by the amount of one car trip is $0.20, then the total social benefit due to Jack's car trip would be $0.80. The measurement of external costs and benefits of transportation is one of the most difficult parts of cost-benefit analysis of transport projects. Some techniques for measuring transport externalities are described in the final chapter of this book.

Another situation in which a social evaluation of the willingness to pay will differ from private methods is where there is a competing mode of transportation whose prices are less than its full marginal cost. For example, a competitor may be subsidized or may not be charged the full cost of pollution that it costs. In these circumstances, the true social benefit of transportation using the non-polluting or non-subsidized mode of transport will be greater than the amount that users may be willing to pay. An example of this is provided later in this chapter.

Since consumer expenditure and a company's revenue are the same thing (neglecting sales and exise taxes), a private firm's profitability calculation and a public agency's cost-benefit calculation appear to have two main differences. Cost-benefit analysis (1) takes into account externalities and (2) includes consumers' surplus. There is, however, one additional difference that has not been emphasized to this point. In cost-benefit analysis, expenditures that consumers would have been willing to pay to the owner of the fixed facility are treated as a benefit, whether or not they are actually paid. Of course, in profitability analysis, consumer expenditure is treated positively only to the extent that it becomes revenue for the company making the investment. For example, if rates are regulated so that a private company cannot collect revenues that consumers are willing to pay, a private company may be unwilling to make an investment even when potential revenues would be greater than the cost of the investment.

Net social welfare is the difference between social benefits and social costs of an investment; or more accurately, the present discounted value of social benefits less social costs. For most transport investments in the United States social costs can be considered to be well represented by the expenditures involved in making and maintaining the fixed facility, adjusted for any external costs.[7] According to the principles of economic efficiency, an investment is socially justified if net social welfare in the economy is increased. In addition to defining net social welfare as the area under the demand curve minus total costs, another useful way of describing net social welfare uses the following definition:

$$\text{Profit} = \text{Revenue} - \text{Costs.} \qquad (9.6)$$

This means that Cost = Revenue − Profit. But a company's revenue is the same as consumer expenditure, assuming that there are no externalities and that the only cost of using a facility is payments made to the facility owner. Remembering that total social benefits can be written as the sum of consumers' surplus and consumer expenditure, net social welfare can be written as:

$$\text{Net Social Welfare} = \text{Consumers' Surplus} + \text{Profit} \qquad (9.7)$$

or

$$\text{Net Social Welfare} = \text{Consumers' Surplus} + \text{Revenue} - \text{Costs.} \qquad (9.8)$$

This formula is a useful way of thinking of net social welfare, the criterion for determining whether an investment should be made, because it emphasizes that cost-benefit analysis is indifferent to the question of who gets the benefits and who bears the costs. For example, the criterion of making an investment for which net social welfare is positive would say that an investment should be made as long as consumers' surplus is greater than any loss that an investment might incur. So projects that benefit consumers should be undertaken even if they force the investor to take a loss. But by the same logic, even projects that have no consumers' surplus should be undertaken as long as they produce a profit for the investor. According to cost-benefit analysis, public investment decisions should ignore distributional effects.[8] This is the logic behind the public investment in maintaining Great Lakes navigation channels at depths sufficient for 1,000-foot ore boats, when only a few large steel producers benefit from the improvement: Even if the country as a whole takes a loss on the project, it is justified if the benefit to the steel companies is larger than the cost to the public treasury.

If those who benefit from a project do not have to pay for it, they will inflate their demands for fixed facilities. It is then the responsibility of the political system to select only those projects that are truly justified on cost-benefit principles, refusing to fund other projects. This system frequently breaks down, as illustrated in the example of the Tennessee-Tombigbee waterway described later in this chapter. It is impractical to ask those who benefit from a project to voluntarily pay an amount equal to the benefit that they receive from it. If this were possible, there would be no tendency for the political system to over-invest in sometimes questionable projects. The inability of voluntary payment systems to finance public projects is known in the economics literature as the *free rider problem*. In order to partially counteract the tendency of local or regional authorities to request funding for projects that may not meet cost-benefit standards, the federal government requires that state and local authorities partially match federal expenditures. For some highway projects, the proportion is as generous as 9 to 1: The federal government pays 90 cents of a construction dollar and the local government pays only 10 cents. Not all transportation projects have such matching requirements, however. Waterway improvements, for example, were until recently fully funded by the federal government.

INVESTMENT IN PUBLIC FREIGHT FACILITIES

A famous example of the use of cost-benefit analysis in justifying an investment in transportation fixed facilities is the Tennessee-Tombigbee waterway, a canal that was finished in 1986. The canal allowed barges to travel from the Tennessee River to the Tombigbee River and then to the Gulf of Mexico at Mobile, Alabama, without using the Mississippi River. Some people described the Tenn-Tom, the canal's nickname, as "double tracking the Mississippi." In order to justify construction of the project, the U.S. Army Corps of Engineers, the agency in charge of inland navigation, commissioned several cost-benefit analyses.

The essence of the cost-benefit analysis is shown in Table 9.2. This table presents a rough view of the cost-benefit analysis presented by the Corps of Engineers in 1977. At that time, the Corps estimated that the total construction cost of the canal would be $1.41 billion. They further estimated annual benefits of $94.69 million and annual costs of maintaining and operating the canal of $36.30 million. Each year the canal was expected to produce $58.40 million in net benefits, ignoring the initial cost of building the canal. The Corps used a discount rate of 3.25 percent to discount the net benefits over the 50-year expected life of the canal to produce a present discounted value of net benefits

TABLE 9.2   Cost-Benefit Calculation of Tennessee-Tombigbee Waterway Presented in 1977

Year	3.25% Discount Factor	Annual Benefits	Annual Operating and Maintenence Costs	Discounted Net Benefits
1986	1.00	94.69	36.30	58.40
1987	1.03	94.69	36.30	56.56
1988	1.07	94.69	36.30	54.78
1989	1.10	94.69	36.30	53.05
1990	1.14	94.69	36.30	51.38
1991	1.17	94.69	36.30	49.77
1992	1.21	94.69	36.30	48.20
1993	1.25	94.69	36.30	46.68
1994	1.29	94.69	36.30	45.21
1995	1.33	94.69	36.30	43.79
....	....	.....	.....	.....
2026	3.59	94.69	36.30	16.25
2027	3.71	94.69	36.30	15.74
2028	3.83	94.69	36.30	15.24
2029	3.96	94.69	36.30	14.76
2030	4.08	94.69	36.30	14.30
2031	4.22	94.69	36.30	13.85
2032	4.35	94.69	36.30	13.41
2033	4.50	94.69	36.30	12.99
2034	4.64	94.69	36.30	12.58
2035	4.79	94.69	36.30	12.18
Grand Total of Project Discounted Net Benefits				$1,480.30
Projected Cost of Project				$1,410.00
Benefit/Cost Ratio (Estimated)				1.04

SOURCE: Calculated from data in Carroll, Joseph L. and Srikanth Rao, "Economics of Public Investment in Inland Navigation: Unanswered Questions," *Transportation Journal* (Spring 1978), p. 39. Discount factor is the accumulated compound interest of $1.00 invested at 3.25 percent in 1986. Annual Operating and Maintenance Costs are approximated as the reported annualized charges and amortized charges on the 1,410 initial cost of the project. Note that this calculation assumes that the entire initial outlay occurred in 1986. Discounted net benefits are calculated as annual benefits less operating and maintenance costs divided by the discount factor.

of $1.48 billion. Since the present discounted value of benefits was greater than the $1.41 billion initial cost of the project, they argued that the waterway was economically justified.

Two aspects of the analysis were strongly criticized by economists. First, they argued, the interest rate used to discount the future costs and benefits of the project was far too low. If a more realistic interest rate was used—6.875

percent was suggested—the present discounted value of the net benefits would be reduced to far below the initial project cost, thus making the canal ineligible for construction. The Office of Management and Budget now recommends that 7 percent be used as a discount factor for making cost-benefit analyses.

The second criticism concerned the calculation of benefits. The $94.69 million annual projected benefits were composed of area redevelopment benefits ($15.65), recreation benefits ($4.78 million), and navigation benefits ($74.07 million). Area redevelopment benefits consisted primarily of payments to workers who were unemployed at the time of the study, but whom the drafters of the study believed would become employed due to economic development in the area of the canal project. Recreation benefits were based on estimates of the willingness to pay for recreational use of the new lakes and channels created by the Tenn-Tom project. But the great majority of the benefits that were used to justify the project were navigational benefits and the predominant navigational benefit was predicted to be a lowering of the cost of moving coal from Illinois, Kentucky, Tennessee, and Alabama to the Gulf of Mexico for further shipment to utilities in the Southeastern United States and for export.

The calculation of navigation benefits is easily illustrated on Figure 9.4, which displays the demand for shipping coal to the Gulf of Mexico from the coal producing area served by the canal.[9] Figure 9.4 shows that the effect of the canal is to reduce the cost of shipping coal, represented by a downward shift of the relevant marginal cost curve from MC(2) to MC(1). According to estimates made by the Corps of Engineers, the canal was expected to reduce shipping costs for coal shippers by about $2.00 per ton. This reduction in shipping cost was expected to increase the amount of coal shipped from the producing region to the Gulf of Mexico from about 20 million tons to about 25 million tons per year. The navigational benefit is shown as the area of ABCFE in Figure 9.4. This area is best calculated as the sum of the areas ABFE ($40 million per year) and BCD ($5 million per year).

This calculation of navigation benefits, while theoretically sound, depends critically for its accuracy on the position of the demand curve for shipments to the Gulf coast and the amount of the cost reduction that the canal would afford shippers over their next best alternative. Transport economists claimed that the demand curves were based on overly optimistic projections of the amount of coal that would be produced in the region served by the canal. In fact, for the Corps of Engineers estimates to be accurate, coal production would have had to increase by several times between the time that the cost-benefit analysis was made and the time the canal opened.

In addition, transport economists doubted that the canal would allow shippers to save $2.00 per ton. In fact, there was considerable doubt that the canal would allow shippers any cost saving over the next best alternative—moving coal on the Mississippi River—and unless there were cost savings, shippers would continue to use the Mississippi rather than the new canal. The reason for

**FIGURE 9.4 Navigation Benefits Attributed to the Tennessee-
Tombigbee Waterway**
Units on the horizontal axis represent levels of usage. Units on the vertical axis
represent the marginal cost and demand for transportation between the coal fields
in the Tenn-Tom's catchment area and the Gulf of Mexico.

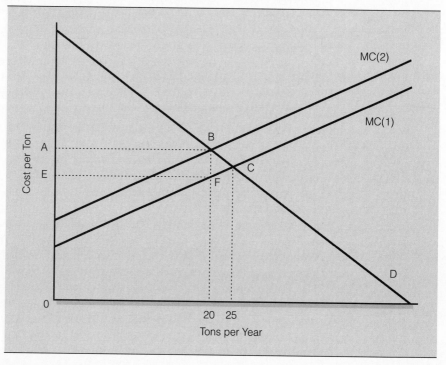

doubt was that the Mississippi has a much wider channel, thus allowing for
considerably larger barge tows. The cost of barge shipping is more closely
related to the size of the tow than to the actual distance shipped. In effect, the
Tennessee-Tombigbee waterway was engineered to be too small; a correct calculation of the costs and benefits of the canal should have been made for a
larger system that allowed for larger tow sizes.

Unfortunately, the predictions of transport economists turned out to be
entirely accurate. In its first year of operations, 500,000 tons of coal were
shipped on the canal rather than the 17 million tons that had been forecast; in
succeeding years, less than 1 million tons have been shipped on the waterway.
The reasons for the stunning shortfall in shipments are that much smaller quantities of coal were dug in the service area of the canal than had been predicted
and shippers continued to route their shipments via the Mississippi River rather
than by the new canal. The final cost of the project also increased to more than

$2 billion. In retrospect, it is clear that the canal would not have passed an accurate cost-benefit analysis and should not have been built.

Had economists' doubts about the cost-benefit analysis of the Tennessee-Tombigbee waterway been heeded, the country could have saved $2 billion. Unfortunately, the lumpy and sunk nature of transport fixed facilities investments guarantee that this sort of mistake will be made in the future as well. As illustrated by the Tennessee-Tombigbee waterway project, it is impossible to accurately forecast traffic levels that a facility will attract until it is put in place. This contrasts with most other sectors of the economy where a firm will test market its product to make sure that there are willing buyers before it makes an investment. Had it been possible to build, say, only the first 10 miles of the Tennessee-Tombigbee waterway to get an accurate gauge of what future traffic levels would be like, it would have been possible to avoid the mistake that was made. The lumpiness of transport fixed facilities investment generally prevents this, thus making fixed facilities investment riskier than they would otherwise be.

Construction costs of the waterway are now a sunk cost. The opportunity cost of continuing to operate the canal are now simply the maintenance costs of keeping the channels open and the operating costs of the locks. If the benefits to users are larger than these much smaller annual costs, the canal should be kept open. Barge operators do not pay tolls on inland waterways, so benefits cannot be measured in terms of actual revenues from using the canal. Instead, to calculate whether the canal should be kept open, an analysis like that in Figure 9.4 should be used, in which the important question is how much more current users would have to pay to move their products if the canal were to be closed. If the total saving to current users of keeping the canal open is greater than the opportunity cost of maintaining it for transportation purposes, it should be kept open.

INVESTMENT IN PUBLIC PASSENGER FACILITIES

The procedure for justifying investment in public passenger facilities using cost-benefit analysis is essentially the same as that used for freight facilities. The major difference is the identification of the source of benefits. In 1993, Metro-North Railroad, a commuter railroad that is a unit of the New York Metropolitan Transportation Authority, proposed building a new railroad crossing of the Hudson River north of New York City. Figure 9.5 shows the six different routes for the proposed river crossing that were considered by the analysis. One crossing was suitable only for a bridge crossing and another was suitable only for a tunnel, but for the remaining four crossings, analyses were made for either a bridge or tunnel at that location.

Table 9.3 shows the numeric results of the analyses. The column marked Net Present Value shows that each project is expected to lose money over the

FIGURE 9.5   Locations of Proposed New Hudson River Crossing

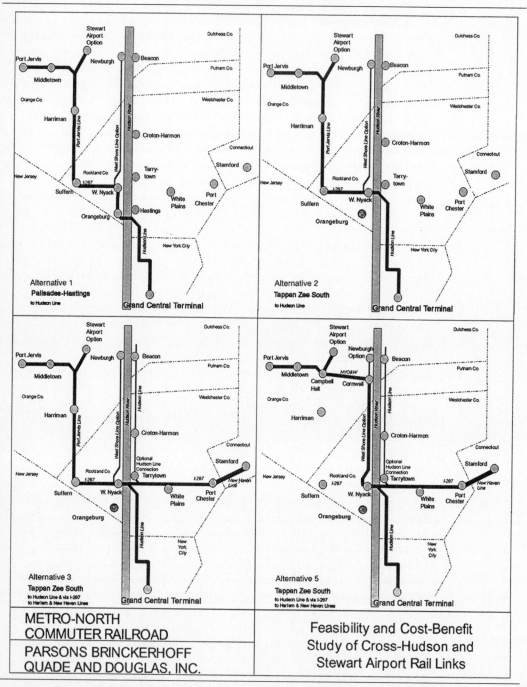

Courtesy of Metro-North Railroad and Parsons Brinckerhoff Quade and Douglas, Inc.

FIGURE 9.5 (continued)

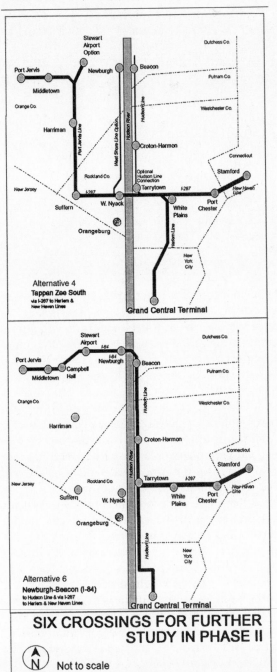

Alternative 4
Tappan Zee South
via I-287 to Harlem &
New Heven Lines

Alternative 6
Newburgh-Beacon (I-84)
to Hudson Line & via I-287
to Harlem & New Heven Lines

SIX CROSSINGS FOR FURTHER STUDY IN PHASE II

Not to scale

70-year life of the project. The project that would lose the least money—a bridge using route 2 or 3—would require $1.0 billion more in discounted costs than in projected discounted revenues over the life of the project. The project with the worst financial outlook is the tunnel in route 5.

Nonetheless, on the basis of figures in the last column, Metro-North Railroad argues that a crossing is economically justified. While crossings 4, 5, and 6 each have benefit cost ratios less than 1 and are thus not economically justified, a strong economic case can be made for building a crossing for routes 1, 2, or 3. The best option is the bridge for route 2 or 3, which has a benefit cost ratio of 1.45, meaning that each dollar of costs expended is repaid by $1.45 of benefits.

It is worthwhile to look behind the calculations to see how these numbers were made and to understand how it is possible for a project to be economically justified even when it is projected to lose money over its lifetime. The first step is to make an estimate of the total number of travelers between the region served by the new crossing and the central business district of New York City, the main destination for these travelers. For crossing 2, the current rail share of total traffic is 60 percent. The presence of a new Hudson River crossing was assumed to increase rail ridership by 0.5 percent per year and thus, assuming that the total number of trips did not increase, to increase rail share to 87 percent at the end of the 75-year lifetime of the project. This would then result in 27 percent of the traffic diverting from other modes (predominantly car-trips) to rail.

TABLE 9.3   Cost-Benefit Calculation for New Hudson River Crossing

Crossing Location	Construction Type	Net Present Value (in $ Billions)	Benefit Cost Ratio
1	Tunnel	$-1.3	1.23
2	Bridge	-1.0	1.45
2	Tunnel	-1.2	1.27
3	Bridge	-1.0	1.45
3	Tunnel	-1.2	1.27
4	Bridge	-1.5	.99
4	Tunnel	-1.7	.90
5	Bridge	-1.9	.82
5	Tunnel	-2.1	.75
6	Bridge	-1.1	.23

SOURCE: New York Metropolitan Transportation Authority, Metro-North Railroad. See text for description of methods for calculation.

The second step was to calculate the time saving that the new rail crossing would offer to passengers. The existing base of rail passengers was assumed to value the shortened travel time at $9.00 per hour. Riders who are diverted from automobiles are similarly assumed to have a value of time of $9.00. A count of such drivers was made and an additional value of $12.90 was assessed for each automobile-trip to Manhattan that would be eliminated by the presence of the new facilities. Such a charge can be rationalized on the grounds that roadway pricing is likely to be inefficient, especially in the absence of congestion tolls. The $12.90 could be understood as follows: Highway users are paying too little for use of the highways. The community as a whole values the resources (especially highway space) used by a car entering New York City at $12.90 more than the individual driver actually pays for the trip. Thus eliminating the trip through diversion to rail will save the community $12.90 per trip.

Metro-North Railroad noted that there were other benefits that were not quantified. Prominent among these were the dollar values that the community would place on improved air quality and decreased petroleum consumption due to less driving. They noted that improved access would increase land values in the New York City central business district and near new stations. They also argued that building a new railroad crossing would decrease pressure for expanding highway facilities, thus leading to further unmeasurable future benefits. (They also note that environmental considerations would favor deep bore tunnels to bridges and thus, depending on the value that the community places on environmental quality, tunnels rather than bridges would be preferred at sites 2, 3, 4, and 5 despite the lower measured benefit cost ratio).

But if the benefits of the projects are so large, why is it that the projects will make financial losses? The answer can be seen in Figure 9.6 which shows

FIGURE 9.6   Benefits of Improved Hudson River Crossing

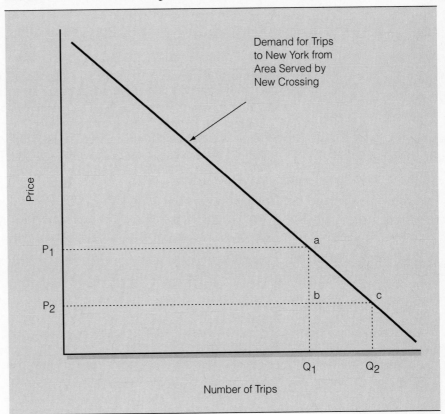

the demand for trips from the area served by the new connection to the New York City central business district. The effect of improved service focused on by the cost-benefit analysis of the project is the decreased amount of time it will take to travel in this corridor. A decrease in time is shown by a lowering of the full price of the trip in Figure 9.6 from P_1 to P_2. The total benefit of this time saving is given by the areas P_1abP_2 for existing rail ridership and abc for the ridership attracted from other modes. Were Metro-North a profit maximizing firm, it could be expected to charge for improved service an amount equal to the willingness to pay for the enhancement. That is, one would expect the railroad to be able to increase its revenues by at least P_1abP_2, and perhaps be able to capture some of the willingness to pay for the new customers, abc. In fact, however, in its calculations, the railroad has assumed that its fares would stay the same. It is the fact that the railroad does not plan to convert (at least some of) the benefit of the investment to its own revenue that creates the difference between the financial consequences of the investment and the cost-benefit analysis.

If the forecast of ridership and willingness of passengers to pay for the project is correct; if the railroad's forecast of the costs of construction and operation of the project is correct; if the forecast of the real discount rate for costs and benefits is correct; and if the railroad were willing to convert consumers' surplus to its own profit by raising fares by an amount equal to the increase in consumer benefit, then it should be possible to finance the project in private capital markets without the use of government assistance. A discounted return of $1.45 for every $1.00 invested would be quite attractive to private investors. The chief attraction of the use of private markets to raise investment funds for transport projects is that they will look at each of the assumptions with a critical eye. An investor who is putting his or her own funds at risk is less likely to be fooled by the faulty cost-benefit analysis of the Tennessee-Tombigbee project, for example. The community is then saved the expense of investing in projects whose assumptions turn out to be faulty.

As this is written, there are several private highway projects under construction in the United States and several rail projects that have been proposed. A recent evaluation by Gómex-Ibáñez and Meyer of international experiences with private transportation infrastructure investment concludes that the circumstances under which private investment in transportation infrastructure can be relied on to provide adequate amounts of capital are relatively uncommon.[10] Chief among the problems is that the public is unlikely to cede complete authority on pricing to a private company. Thus, for example, it is unlikely that, even if Metro-North were a private firm, fares could be raised to transfer all consumers' surplus generated by improved service into producers' income. Since the public is concerned about monopoly power of the operator and is unwilling to allow unplanned land use, those who lose by a project (perhaps land owners whose land is made less valuable by the project) have the ability to block new projects. Gómex-Ibáñez and Meyer conclude that private provision of transport infrastructure requires the special circumstances of projects that are not excessively profitable, have relatively little redistribution consequences, little in the way of market power concerns, and a public convinced that they will not get the project financed from the public treasury simply by waiting.

CONCLUSION

Investment decisions for transport vehicles are quite simple. Since transport vehicles are mobile pieces of equipment with a ready second-hand market, it is economically justified to invest in additional vehicle capacity whenever the price of transport services is greater than its cost. Another way of stating this principle is that transport capacity should be increased whenever the business is economically profitable and be shrunk whenever it is not economically profitable. This is the simple rule learned by all students of economics.

Investment in transportation fixed facilities is more complicated, since the investments are sunk. A forecast of expected demand for and costs of using the facilities must be made in order for sensible decisions to be made. The criteria for making investment decisions are different depending on whether the investment is to be made by a private firm or by a public body. Private companies make decisions by comparing discounted future net revenues with current construction costs. Public bodies use cost-benefit analysis.

If all investments in transportation fixed facilities followed simple financial principles, there would be far fewer problems associated with the investments and the subject of transportation economics would be far less interesting. A project would be undertaken if and only the present discounted value of net revenues were greater than the costs of the project. Projects would not operate at a loss and funding to pay off the project would be guaranteed in advance.

Transportation fixed facilities investments are rarely like that, however. Projects tend to be lumpy rather than incremental. Demand forecasts need to be made on the basis of projections of traffic levels after the facility is put in place, without being able to run a market test. Often, projects will be built in advance of demand on the expectation that the presence of the new facilities will generate the traffic to justify the project. Transportation fixed facilities projects are generally sunk-cost intensive as well. A sunk cost is one that cannot be recovered by converting the investment to its next best alternative use. The implication of sunk costs is that in general the project will still be operated, even if traffic projections turn out to be overly optimistic.

Most investments in transportation fixed facilities are not made by private firms but by governments using cost-benefit analysis as a criterion rather than using a profitability analysis. Cost-benefit analysis, by counting as benefits certain sums which users do not pay the facility owner, encourages the building of projects that will not be able to cover their own costs. Cost-benefit analyses of transportation projects treat as the primary benefits, cost and time savings to users, reduction in accidents, as well as benefits that accrue to people other than the users of the facility. Since these benefits are generally not collected from the beneficiaries, the government agency that makes the investment usually anticipates making a loss on each investment it undertakes.

NOTES

1. The determination of the profitability of investment from short-run curves requires constant returns to scale, a reasonable assumption in the case of vehicles.
2. Daniel Machalaba, "Union Pacific Changes Its Hidebound Ways under New Chairman," *The Wall Street Journal*, January 18, 1989, p. 1.
3. An analysis of the chunnel is found in John Kay, Alan Manning, and Stefan Szymanski, "The Economic Benefit of the Channel Tunnel," *Economic Policy* (1989), pp. 212–234.
4. An excerpt of the evaluation of the channel tunnel that was prepared for the British government in 1963 can be found in Denys Munby, *Transport: Selected Readings* (Baltimore: Penguin Books, 1968). The government believed that the original pro-

posal was far too hopeful about projected costs. They projected construction costs at a little more than 10 percent of the final figure.

5. John Darnton, "Channel Tunnel, in Fiscal Crisis, Stops Paying Interest on Big Debt," *The New York Times*, September 15, 1995, p. A1.

6. There are additional problems of correct measurement of consumer surplus that deal with income effects and the interdependence of markets. See, however, Robert D. Willig, "Consumer's Surplus without Apology," *American Economic Review*, Vol. 66, No. 4, September 1976, pp. 589–597.

7. This is not the case in underdeveloped countries where there is widespread unemployment and the absence of functioning markets for labor, capital, and foreign exchange. Under these circumstances, the resources used in a project must be evaluated at their shadow prices. See Hans Adler, *Economic Appraisal of Transport Projects, A Manual with Case Studies: Revised and Expanded Edition* (Baltimore: Johns Hopkins University Press, 1987).

8. The indifference of cost-benefit analysis to income distributional consequences is vulnerable on several theoretical grounds. A shorthand way of describing these concerns is to note that a blindness to income distribution consequences requires that one believe that the marginal utility of income is identical for all people.

9. Figure 9.4 should be taken as a stylistic representation of the calculation of benefits to coal shippers. For a more accurate representation, see Joseph L. Carroll, "Tennessee-Tombigbee Waterway Revisited," *Transportation Journal* (Winter 1982), pp. 5–20.

10. José Gómex-Ibáñez and John R. Meyer, *Going Private: The International Experience with Transport Privatization* (Washington, D.C.: The Brookings Institution, 1993).

10

Efficient Pricing

The previous chapter discussed economic principles for investment in transportation facilities. In this chapter, the pricing of
those facilities will be considered. The two topics—pricing and
investment—are closely related. The capacity of the facilities
created by the investment process will determine the prices that
can be charged for using the facilities; and the prices that people
are willing to pay for using the facilities are the main indicators
of when and where investments in transportation facilities
should be made. This chapter will describe the concept of economic efficiency and how it is used in the economic analysis of
transportation.

THE EFFICIENCY PRINCIPLE

The fundamental economic criterion under which a price structure is judged is called *economic efficiency*. A good structure of
prices for using a facility is one that encourages economic efficiency; price structures that lead to inefficient use of the facilities is condemned as not being based on economic principles.

Economic efficiency requires that producers make the best
use of the resources available to them. A trucking company
that has more empty return miles than necessary is obviously
guilty of inefficiency. A bus repair facility that uses five people

when four could do the same work just as well in the same amount of time is similarly responsible for inefficient use of resources. When the economy is organized inefficiently, goods and services are being sacrificed that could have been produced had land, labor, or capital been used differently. The reason that economic efficiency is such an important principle is that following the rules for efficiency allows people in an economy to maximize their standard of living given the quantity of land, labor, and capital that they have. In economic terms, saying that an economy is using its resources efficiently is the same as saying that economic welfare, or the average standard of living, is being maximized.

Equating efficiency with maximizing economic welfare broadens the concept to take in much more than simply limiting miles driven with empty vehicles. Economic efficiency also concerns which goods or services are produced and whether the production levels of those goods or services are ideal. It seems illogical at first that efficiency should deal with *what* services are offered in addition to *how* they are produced, but an example makes it clear that they are both tied together. Traffic congestion—which causes a tremendous waste of human and capital resources—is an example of an inefficiency caused by excessive demand for service on a crowded roadway. The inefficiency can be seen in the fact that, if people and vehicles were not tied up in the jam, they could be productively engaged in producing goods and services. A traffic jam and a firm that uses three workers to complete a job when only two are necessary are both causing the economy to waste resources. Both cause the average standard of living to decline. Both cause a reduction in social welfare. Therefore both are examples of economic inefficiency. One is the result of too many workers being used to produce an item; the other is the result of wrong pricing signals that guide consumers to demand services that the economy cannot provide cheaply.

Many instances of inefficiency can usually be traced to improper pricing. Prices guide choices made by consumers and by producers. Prices that are too low encourage over-consumption of some good or service. That is, a price for some good or service that is too low encourages consumers to draw too many resources into producing that good or service. Prices that are inefficiently high cause people to reorient their purchases away from those things that could be produced relatively cheaply and toward those things that the economy has more trouble producing; inefficient prices mean that the economy must spend more resources than necessary to provide some level of consumer satisfaction.[1] Private producers of transport services will also respond to prices; the prices that they see will lead them to make efficient or inefficient choices. An *efficient* or *optimal price* is one that causes producers to offer exactly the variety of services and in exactly the correct amounts to best satisfy consumer demands.

Efficiency is the basic criterion that economists have for evaluating prices. Efficiency requires that those who get to consume particular goods and services are those who are willing to pay the most for the privilege. If there is only one empty seat on a flight from New York to Denver and Smith is willing to bid $500 for the seat while Brown is willing to bid only $200 for the seat, the economy would be throwing away $300 worth of value to give it to Brown. This would be inefficiency in the same sense as idling a worker who is capable of producing $300 worth of goods in a day.

The reader will recognize that using economic efficiency to analyze prices implicitly weights the importance of individuals' preferences according to their willingness to pay, which is closely related both to ability to pay and to income. That is, one reason that Smith may be willing to pay more than Brown for the seat to Denver is that Smith is wealthier. To some it would seem unfortunate that the principle rules out wishes of those with no income as being uninteresting or less necessary to satisfy. This point is granted by defenders of the principle of economic efficiency, but they note that problems of maldistribution of income will not be solved by distorting one particular sector. This is, after all, the basic way a market system decides what will be produced and who will get it. Why should the transport sector be singled out to operate under different rules of efficiency than, say, the refrigerator industry or entertainment sector? The problem of income distribution will not be solved by distorting prices for using the highway. Problems of income distribution should be dealt with directly through taxes and laws governing payments of rent, interest, dividends, profits, and wages; to try to solve income distribution problems through introducing inefficiencies in the transport sector seems to be using the wrong tool for the job.[2]

▬ The Golden Rule for Pricing to Achieve Economic Efficiency

In order to make the most efficient use of the resources available in an economy, the price charged for any transport service should be equal to the opportunity cost of producing it. This rule is valid under all conditions; it is valid in the short run as well as the long run. All principles of transport pricing are based on it. The logic behind the rule for economic efficiency is quite simple. If the price paid for a service is greater than its opportunity cost, the economy will devote too few resources to the service; if the price paid is less than its opportunity cost, too many resources will be devoted to the service. Only when the price of a service is equal to its opportunity cost will the economy devote exactly the right amount of resources to it. Heavy trucks should be charged for the amount of damage that they do to highways not because it is fair, but because it is efficient to do so. If truckers weren't charged for their damage, they would cause an excessive amount of it—that is, the cost to community of fixing the roads would be higher than the benefit to truckers of cheap infrastructure. This is the efficiency argument. While in many circumstances it will lead to the same conclusions, it is a quite different perspective from saying that it is only just that those who damage something should be responsible for making it whole again.

Assume that the opportunity cost of producing a car-trip from Scarsdale, New York to Tenefly, New Jersey is $10.00, but the price that the driver pays for the trip is $5.00. Drivers are then being given incorrect information about the scarcity of resources: They are acting on the belief that their trip costs only $5.00, when in fact taking the trip reduces other things that the economy is capable of producing by $10.00. Some drivers will be willing to pay $10.00 for at least some of their trips, and they clearly should be encouraged to make the trip—it would be inefficient to deny them the opportunity. However, some drivers will value a trip at an amount between $5.00 and $10.00. These drivers are the source of the problem, since they would not make the trip if they had to pay the full price, but do make the trip because the price is so low. They are wasting resources because their decision to take the trip takes $10.00 of resources out of the economy so that they can enjoy a trip which they value at less than $10.00. If they were faced with the true price of the trip, they would not make it and these resources could be saved.

The opportunity cost of an individual making a single trip is called the *short-run marginal cost*. It is called *short run* because decisions on the number of trips to make are made after all decisions on the amount of fixed facilities to put in place or the number of vehicles to purchase. The most familiar form in which the rule for pricing to maximize economic efficiency is quoted is:

$$P = SRMC \tag{10.1}$$

In order to encourage economic efficiency, the price charged for an individual trip or shipment should equal the short-run marginal cost of making this trip or shipment.[3]

Equation 10.1 provides the first half of the solution to the problem of maximizing social welfare. The second half requires that summing over all people who use the service:

$$\text{Total Willingness to Pay for Service} \geq \text{Opportunity Cost of Resources} \tag{10.2}$$

The difference between the total value that all users place on a service (measured by the total willingness to pay for it on the part of all users) and the opportunity cost of the resources consumed in producing it is named social surplus, as described in the previous chapter. So another way of describing the second condition is that the social surplus of providing a service must be positive.

Note that the decision contemplated in the second efficiency condition is not one of levels but rather a yes/no decision about abandonment—should this service be provided at all? That is the reason that economic efficiency does not require that the total willingness to pay be equal to its opportunity cost, but rather that it be equal to or greater than the opportunity cost of keeping the service. Economic analysis requires that both the condition that combined willingness to pay be greater than or equal to the opportunity cost of the service and the condition that price equal short-run marginal cost hold simultaneously. Remember from Chapter 9, however, that if abandonment's have consequences over several years, the future cost and revenue consequences must be discounted. Thus in the most general form, the rule for maintenance of a service should be written as:

$$PDV(\text{willingness to pay}) \geq PDV(\text{opportunity cost}). \qquad (10.3)$$

In words, inequality 10.3 says that the present discounted value of gross benefits to all users of a service must be greater than or equal to the present discounted value of the opportunity cost of the service if a service is to be maintained. Otherwise, the principle of economic efficiency will call for elimination of the service.

Figure 10.1 illustrates the principles for efficient pricing just described. The diagram shows a normal downward sloping demand for a service and a normal marginal cost curve that slopes up beyond some point. Where these two curves intersect, at X^*, is the efficient level of activity, assuming that the inequality 10.3 is satisfied. The price that induces X^* to be chosen is P^*. Thus P^* can tentatively be taken to be the efficient price for the service.

Whether or not the inequality is satisfied cannot be definitively determined by Figure 10.1. As noted in Chapter 9, the total willingness to pay for a service

FIGURE 10.1   Efficient Pricing of a Service
Units on the horizontal axis represent levels of service. X^* and P^* are the efficient quantity and price if the fixed costs attributed to providing the service do not exceed the area ABC.

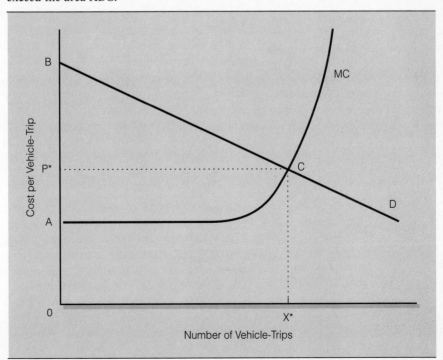

(or its total benefit) is equal to the area under the demand curve up to the level of the service provided. If pricing is optimal, this is the area OBCX* in Figure 10.1.[4] The opportunity cost of the service is composed of two parts, only one of which is shown on Figure 10.1. The area under the marginal cost curve is the variable cost of providing a service. The reason this is the case mirrors the logic of why the area under the demand curve is total willingness to pay: Marginal cost is the cost of producing one more item, so if we add the height of the marginal cost line for every unit produced, we will get the sum of all costs except the fixed costs. By definition, this corresponds to the variable costs of operation. In Figure 10.1, this is area OACX*. The cost of providing the fixed facilities cannot be shown in Figure 10.1 and must be added to OACX* to get total cost. The best that we can say is that if the partial social surplus, shown as ABC on Figure 10.1, is greater than the fixed facilities cost attributed to a service, then it should be maintained; otherwise the service should be abandoned.

EFFICIENT PRICES AND VEHICLE COSTS

The reader will recall from Chapters 5–8 that transportation costs can be divided into three categories: fixed facilities, vehicle ownership, and vehicle operating costs. The question of how fixed facilities costs influence efficient pricing will be postponed until later in this chapter since this issue is more complicated than the others and is logically separate from the others. We will begin our discussion of efficient transportation pricing with vehicle costs.

New large aircraft have an opportunity cost of about $100 per seat-day for each aircraft. This derives from the fact that an airliner could be leased to other airlines (perhaps in other countries) for approximately $100 per seat-day. In calculating prices to charge its customers, an airline must earn at least $100 per seat-day for each of its aircraft if it is to maximize its profits. But pricing based on this calculation is also efficient. If another airline is willing to pay more to lease an aircraft than an airline can make by using the plane itself, it would be inefficient not to take the offer. The airline that leases the aircraft can apparently provide services for which customers are willing to pay more and thus not to turn it over to others for their use is to deprive the economy of creating some value that it is capable of generating.[5] For example, the airline looking to lease additional capacity may be in a growing part of the country, while the airline that finds that it cannot produce as much net revenue per seat-day may be in a part of the country with stagnating economic conditions. The efficiency of basing prices on the opportunity cost of vehicle ownership derives partly from the power of markets to allocate scarce resources (in this case, transportation vehicles) to markets that are willing to pay more for their services. Another source of efficiency gains that derive from basing prices on opportunity costs derives from the discretion that fleet owners have in performing maintenance on their fleets. At high rental charges, fleet owners will speed maintenance to keep their operating fleet as large as possible, while at low daily charges, they will delay maintenance and allow their operating fleet to shrink. Opportunity cost-based pricing of vehicle services provides an incentive to the fleet owner to make the correct tradeoff between vehicle maintenance expenditures and fleet size.

▬ The Price of Using Vehicles for One-Way Trips: Back-Haul Pricing

Competitive pressures will also ensure that the cost of making a round trip is efficiently allocated between the front-haul and the back-haul of any round trip. We have dealt so far only with the question of the rental price of transport vehicle at a particular location. But the idea of transportation is to go from one place to another. That is, transportation is concerned with a series of one-way trips. In general, commodities after they make a one-way trip do not return to the original location, although the vehicle in which they traveled probably will. In the case of passengers, everyone except those who change their residence will return to their original location and most of them will use the same mode of transportation to get back. Nonetheless, there may be demand imbalances due to the timing of trips—morning and evening commuter service is an example— even in passenger transport. These demand imbalances will cause the prices of two legs in a round trip to be different from one another.

The technique used by transportation economics for analyzing the cost of one-way trips is to assume that all vehicle-trips are round trips. In fact, of course, airliners will not always return on the same route that they used on the original outbound trip. Truckers will often look for a return load in a location near the city where they delivered their load. A tramp operator may find that the best use for a ship that arrived in Norfolk from Halifax will be to sail it next to Jacksonville. To analyze these triangle trips and more complicated patterns of vehicle routings requires that the transportation system be seen as a complete network. However, network mathematics is beyond the scope of this text; in addition, the insights available from network mathematics are no different from those that are available from assuming that all vehicles make round trips rather than triangular or more complicated trips.

As noted in Chapter 5, the use of a vehicle to make both halves of a round trip is considered to be a joint product, since in a round trip making a front-haul inevitably creates a back-haul. Let us consider, for example, the round trip made by a container ship between Kaohsiung, Taiwan and Long Beach, California. Typical products hauled from Taiwan to California are computer components. A major export from California to Taiwan is scrap paper.

The economic analysis of assigning costs to each half of a joint product is shown in Figure 10.2. The horizontal axis measures the number of round trips made during a year by container ships. The two demand curves shown are for the use of a ship to carry scrap paper from California to Taiwan (the lower demand curve) and to carry computer components from Taiwan to California. Since the two demands do not conflict with each other—that is, since using a ship to carry Taiwanese imports does not limit the space available to carry U.S.

exports to Taiwan—we can sum the two demand curves vertically and generate a combined demand for ship round trips. The combined demand line shown in Figure 10.2 has a kink corresponding to the amount of paper that would be shipped from California to Taiwan if there were no charge for using the ship in that direction. This amount is shown as Q^* in Figure 10.2. If the number of ship-voyages is less than Q^*, both importers and exporters are willing to pay a positive amount for use of the ship. The combined demand curve, shown as a heavy line in Figure 10.2, is steeper than either of the directional demand curves since it represents changes in the combined willingness to pay of importers and exporters as the number of voyages is changed.

The horizontal line in Figure 10.2 represents the daily rental rate of a container ship multiplied by the number of days required by a round-trip voyage.

FIGURE 10.2   **Both Directions in a Round Trip Make a Contribution to Trip Costs**

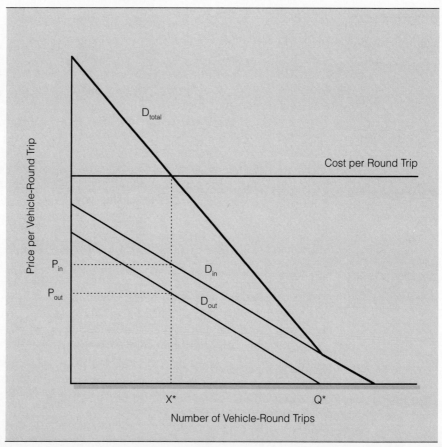

This is the opportunity cost of using the ship for a complete round trip. Its level is determined by the supply and demand for ships at either Long Beach or Kaohsiung—wherever the price for using a ship is lower. This line can be seen as a supply curve for using a ship for a trip to California, for example, instead of to Singapore or Osaka. The equilibrium number of ship voyages is seen in Figure 10.2 to be X^*, the quantity that equates supply and demand. This quantity is determined by the marginal willingness to pay of Taiwanese exporters for trips to California, an amount listed in Figure 10.2 as P_{in} and the marginal willingness to pay of California paper exporters, shown in Figure 10.2 as P_{out}. This sharing of the costs of an outbound and inbound trip exactly balances the interests of all parties. Importers into the United States are not frustrated since they are able to get all of the space they need at the going rate; exporters from the United States similarly find that they have neither too much nor too little capacity for their shipments, given the rate charged by the shipping company. The shipping company finds that its loads are balanced in both directions and that the costs of renting the ship for the voyage is exactly covered by the total payments in each direction.

If the market for shipping is competitive, the market will automatically allocate a higher proportion of the trip cost to the high-demand direction and a smaller proportion to the low-demand direction (usually called a back-haul). This is efficient since, if each direction were to be charged the same amount, there would be many more ship-voyages demanded in the high-demand direction than in the back-haul direction. Either there would be empty cargo space in the back-haul direction or there would be a shortage of capacity in the main haul direction, or both.

The analysis to this point has assumed that both the outbound and return directions will be filled to capacity. A more typical situation, however, is shown in Figure 10.3. This figure is identical to Figure 10.2 with the single modification that the demand in the back-haul direction is lower. Demand is so much lower that X^*, the maximum number of ship-voyages that the back-haul direction would use even if space in the ship were offered for free, is less than X^{**}, the equilibrium number of ship-voyages. In this situation we would observe a traffic imbalance. That is, some vehicles would return less than fully loaded. When this happens, all of the cost of using vehicles, during both the time that it is moving fully loaded as well as the time that it is returning partially empty, will be borne completely by the front-haul. The name given to this situation is *peak load pricing*. Competition among carriers for the limited amount of back-haul cargo will force down rates in that direction so far that there will be little if any additional net revenue from returning with a larger load.

Another illustration of the peak load pricing is provided by commuter rail cars which typically will make at least two round trips per day: one in the morning to carry commuters into the city center, with a return trip to the outlying rail yard; and a second round trip in the evening from the rail yard to pick up the commuters with a fully loaded return trip back to the outlying rail yard. Typically, the morning return trip to the rail yard and the evening trip into the

**FIGURE 10.3   One Direction in a Round Trip Makes No
Contribution to Trip Costs**

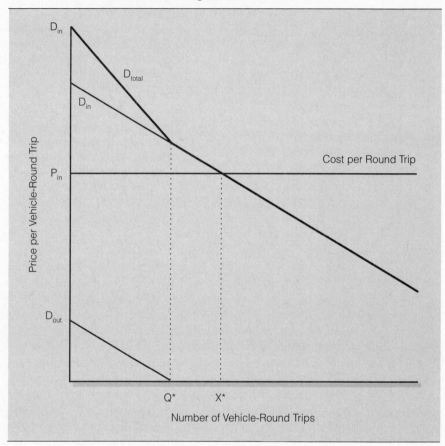

city center to pick up commuters have very light loads. The principle of back-haul pricing states that in this case, all costs of vehicle ownership should be placed on the direction used by great majority of commuters; large discounts should be given to travel in the off-peak direction. This principle is partially honored in some urban transit systems like the Washington, D.C. metro system in which passenger fares are higher during the morning and evening rush hours than during the middle of the day and the evening, though the fares would have to vary by direction as well for it to represent true peak-load pricing.

When prices are determined by competitive conditions, the high-demand direction can be inferred from the relative prices charged for transportation on each halves of a round trip. Thus in the early 1990s, the charge for shipping a container from Hong Kong to California was about $1,200 while the charge for shipping a container from California to Hong Kong was about $1,000. A correct inference from the pricing imbalance was that the strength of demand for eastbound shipments on the North Pacific is higher than the strength of westbound shipments. The fact that the price differential is not even larger is perhaps a reflection of the fact that competition is not completely free on the route, but governed partly by a legal cartel. Since the number of loaded containers shipped eastbound is higher than westbound shipments, none of the daily container rental cost of the round trip would efficiently be applied to westbound shipments. That is, the appropriate characterization of the market would be that shown in Figure 10.3. While it is possible that only $200 of the total cost of a container round trip is traceable to container rental costs (the remainder being container handling costs and weight-sensitive movement costs), a more likely reason is that the rate conference on the North Pacific is preventing exporters from the United States to the Far East from receiving the full advantage of the trade imbalance between the two areas.

EFFICIENT PRICES AND VEHICLE OPERATING COSTS

The logic of efficient pricing requires that the user of transportation pay marginal operating costs. There is no ambiguity about this requirement. If prices are set below marginal operating costs, then too much transportation will be demanded; if prices are set above marginal operating costs, then there will be wasteful under-consumption of transportation—consumers will spend their money in ways that give them less enjoyment than they could have gotten had resources been used on transportation.

Despite the simplicity of the rule that users pay operating costs, there are two subtleties that make the application of the rule more difficult than appears initially. First, while private transporters (automobile drivers, owner-operators of trucks, etc.) obviously pay their own costs, much transportation involves the shared use of transportation vehicles. The question then arises as to how the operating costs are to be shared among different users. The tools for answering this question are identical to those involved in allocating fixed facilities costs among different user classes and so will be postponed until the next chapter.

A second subtlety in the efficient allocation of operating costs to transport users arises in the case of congested facilities. In this case, operating costs rise as more users are added to the system. The result is the fundamental characteristic of efficient transport pricing: the *congestion toll.*[6]

Efficient Prices and Congestion Tolls

Figure 10.1 shows demand curves and marginal cost curves that have shapes that will be familiar to any student of the principles of economics: Demand curves slope down and marginal cost curves (beyond some point) slope up. But why do marginal cost curves slope up? The answer given by economic theory has several names but the logic is always the same: Short-run marginal costs slope up beyond some point because variable inputs begin to congest the fixed inputs. In transportation economics, it is particularly easy to show how congestion of the fixed facilities causes marginal costs to rise. Traffic congestion causes flow rates to slow, as discussed in Chapter 8. In that chapter, an example was offered in which each additional car slows traffic for all cars on the highway. The short-run average cost of using a road is the cost of a typical driver. The marginal cost of driving on a congested highway is the change in the total cost of the entire traffic flow as the number of vehicles trying to use the highway increases. The slower the traffic, then, the higher the marginal cost.

Efficient pricing requires each user of a section of highway to pay the short-run marginal cost of their use. This means that, in addition to paying for gasoline, oil, depreciation of the vehicle, and their own cost of time, individuals should also be assessed an amount corresponding to the value of time lost by other drivers from the traffic slowing caused by the presence of an additional vehicle. The implication is that when there is traffic congestion, it is efficient to charge a toll against each driver. Note that the toll is not justified by any cost incurred by the highway authority. The toll is justified simply as a device for allowing traffic to flow more smoothly. By reducing the traffic levels, a toll on a congested highway can speed traffic flow and thus allow users to complete their trips in less time.

The size of the optimal toll on a congested highway is shown in Figure 10.4. This figure shows the identical curves as Figure 10.1, but adds an average variable cost curve labeled AVC. This curve is constructed by summing together the direct operating costs, including time costs, of all of drivers, and then dividing by the number of drivers. It is an average cost curve in the sense that it divides by the number of drivers per hour that make trips on the highway segment. But in a real sense, it is the cost that a typical or average driver incurs in driving the segment of highway. It is the direct cost plus time costs of each individual driver. It is less than marginal cost because it does not include the traffic slowing effects that an additional driver imposes on others. In other words, as traffic becomes congested, average cost rises because traffic slows. But marginal cost rises faster than average cost because an additional vehicle causes further traffic slowing.

The price that a single driver sees, unless there is a toll on a highway, is simply the costs that he or she incurs. This is the same as short-run average cost for the typical driver. Where the demand curve and the short-run average cost curve intersect, at point E in Figure 10.4, determines the traffic level that the untolled highway will carry. This is shown as traffic level X′. But X′ is larger than X*, the efficient traffic level. So the lack of a toll has caused an inefficiency. This is due to the fact that drivers do not pay the marginal cost of their trip. They pay less than the marginal cost, and therefore cause the economy to devote too many of its resources, human and vehicular, to sitting in congested traffic.

If a toll were charged equal to distance CF on Figure 10.4, the amount of traffic would be reduced to X*, the optimal level. While there would be less traffic, the traffic that does remain would all complete the trip more quickly, as

FIGURE 10.4   Identifying an Efficient Congestion Toll

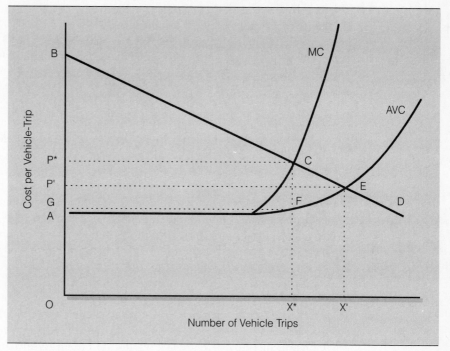

shown by the decline in average costs between point E and point F. The price that drivers would pay, including toll and their own costs, would be equal to P*, the efficient price level.[7]

One of the inefficiencies created by the failure to charge congested tolls is that there is no mechanism for allocating the scarce highway space to those who value it most highly—for example, transit buses. In fact, there is a perverse incentive: People who value their own time at the lowest level have least to lose in a traffic jam and so are most likely to crowd onto congested highways. If congestion tolls were charged, people who valued their time least would not take space on crowded highways, thus allowing a freer flow of traffic of multiple rider vehicles and those for whom the use of the highway is most important. Congestion tolls would increase the average number of riders per vehicle on crowded sections and thus increase the capacity of the highway. Congestion tolls would reduce the distortion currently in effect in public/private transport choice by allowing public transport to have more use of congested facilities.

The failure to charge congestion tolls in crowded airports creates similar inefficiencies. If all aircraft paid a congestion toll, scarce runway space would be reserved for those aircraft that were willing to pay most for it. Larger aircraft would then have first priority at the most crowded airports since private planes would be unable or unwilling to pay landing fees at the most popular times of the day. By increasing the average size of aircraft at the largest airports, congestion tolls would effectively increase the passenger-per-day capacity without building any new runways. Private planes would choose to land at off-peak times, use airports that were less crowded, or fly less frequently.[8]

Practical Problems in Implementing Congestion Tolls

Congestion tolls would be easy to apply for aircraft. Since all aircraft must receive permission to land from controllers, it would be simple to announce a schedule of landing fees for each airport. Airport administrators would adjust their landing fees throughout the day to equate the number of flights wishing to land in each period with the capacity of the airport. In those times of the day when there was excess capacity, landing fees would be determined simply by the opportunity cost of handing one more aircraft on an uncongested runway. In congested airports, landing fees would be highest at the beginning and end of the day when demand is highest. Each airport would have a different fee schedule. Before deciding on a flight plan, private pilots could inspect the fee schedules of airports serving their destination to determine the best airport and the best time to fly to minimize their costs. Scheduled aircraft would buy the necessary landing rights when they set up their schedules, and would try to arrange their schedules in a way that minimized the landing fees that they had to pay.

Congestion tolls for highways would be far more difficult to administer than airport tolls. A mechanism would need to be developed to allow drivers to know what the congestion tolls would be at different times of the day on different routes that they might contemplate and then to charge drivers tolls on the routes that they have selected. Such a mechanism would undoubtedly require the development of sophisticated electronic devices, both to identify and record the presence of a vehicle as well as to provide drivers with necessary pricing information. Traditional toll booths are inadequate for congestion pricing since each section of a highway needs to have a different price and have prices that vary with the traffic level. It would be grossly inefficient to have drivers stop every few miles, pitching 53 cents into the first bin, 22 cents into the next, $1.55 into the third, and so on; moreover, these amounts would necessarily change hour by hour depending on congestion levels. Toll booths themselves create congestion and are costly to staff and maintain.

As this is written, the technology exists for vehicles bearing an electronic tag to be identified when they pass single-file through a reserved lane at a toll plaza. What will be needed for true congestion pricing is for such tags to be read simultaneously as cars proceed at normal highway speeds, driving in clumps several vehicles abreast, as they normally do on urban expressways. The price of tags will also have to decline from their approximately $100 per tag price today to a price below $5.00. When this occurs, toll plazas can be eliminated and vehicles can be charged for their presence in traffic jams wherever they occur.

Current highway finance does not use the principle of congestion pricing. In fact, the tradition of highway finance is the opposite. Bridges and tunnels have often used tolls to pay off construction costs—tolls that are removed when the bridge is paid off. This was the means of finance for the Mackinac Bridge, which is described in Chapter 12. In this method of finance, as traffic increases, the tolls are reduced, in contradiction to the principle of efficient pricing. The main sources of revenues that highway authorities collect from drivers—license fees and fuel taxes—also do not vary according to route or time of day, and thus do not follow efficiency principles.

The country of Singapore has used a crude form of congestion pricing with some success. Cars entering the city center during business hours require a special pass that costs about $5.00 per day.[9] There is, however, no attempt in the Singapore system to optimize toll levels or to vary them by time of day or route. Prices that vary rapidly and widely with the time of day and location is the essence of congestion tolls. Any system of efficient tolls will undoubtedly be complex with widely disparate charges on different routes and in different directions at different times of the day.

The use of sophisticated electronic devices necessary to deal with the complexity of the structures of optimal congestion tolls causes some concern about individual liberties. In principle, a meter in a vehicle could provide an electronic record of exactly where and when the vehicle was driven. The ability to monitor citizen movements runs counter to the movement toward increasing amounts of individual liberty in the world today. In response to this concern, road pricing could take the form of bulk pre-payment, under which an individual purchases a $50 driving card, from which congestion tolls are automatically debited as toll points are passed; under this scheme, there would be no record of where or when a vehicle had been driven.

Congestion pricing will also encounter opposition on income distribution grounds. No one likes to pay for something that was formerly free; the claim will undoubtedly be made that road pricing falls hardest on those least able to pay. But this is an easy argument to counter. It will be simple to give every licensed driver a certificate entitling him or her to use $100 worth of roadway during a month. These certificates could then be bought or sold; a person who did not have an urgent need to use the most crowded highways could sell the certificate to others. The most needy people could immediately sell their certificates, giving them an extra $100 of income during a month; the only thing that they would give up is the right to use the busiest traffic lanes at the busiest periods.

It is critical that any road pricing scheme include some compensation scheme like that outlined above. Without such a scheme, everyone who uses the highways will be worse off: drivers who still use a tolled roadway pay more for that right than they had previously (i.e., their average variable cost plus congestion toll will be higher than their average variable cost before the imposition of road pricing); drivers who decide that the toll is too high are obviously worse off because they now choose an alternative that they considered less desirable before the toll was introduced; and those who had used the less congested routes before the toll was introduced are worse off because some traffic will be shifted to their routes by the tolls.[10] It could be rightly argued that the revenue collected by congestion tolls can be used by governments to reduce other tax burdens or to provide services that would not otherwise be provided, but cynical taxpayers may not believe this argument. For the system to be politically feasible, the compensation scheme will probably have to be in the form of direct transfers to drivers.

Road pricing schemes appear to increase the cost of moving within metropolitan areas: Everyone who drives in the congested parts of a city will find that the cost of a trip rises after congestion tolls are imposed. One possible consequence is to accelerate de-urbanization trends. But it is not clear that this will be the logical result. Congestion pricing will certainly lead to a more rational location of economic activity. By removing from crowded highways users who do not care about the location of their purchases or entertainment, road pricing will increase access for those for whom urban locations are important. Commuting times to downtown locations will be reduced and bus service on highways will be made more attractive.

Congestion tolls are more than an interesting intellectual exercise proposed by economists. We are beginning to see the first discussions of congestion tax proposals in news magazines and op-ed pages of local newspapers and the first attempts at implementation. By the beginning of the twenty-first century we should have considerable information on the best way to implement such schemes. The reason that road pricing schemes are inevitable is that traffic congestion is an increasingly serious problem, and in many situations, increasing road capacity is not a realistic alternative. In fact, where roads are congested for only a few hours a day, increasing road capacity is likely to be a highly inefficient alternative. Problems of air pollution and lost time in traffic jams will require rationalization programs which, if not called congestion tolls, will be at least a close cousin to them. There is no other practical solution to solving traffic problems.

EFFICIENT PRICING AND FIXED FACILITIES COSTS

The reader will notice that the logical justification for efficiency tolls is that they make traffic flow more smoothly. But the common perception of highway tolls is that they are used to pay for fixed facilities. What is the logical relationship between efficient congestion tolls and fixed facilities costs?

Efficient pricing requires that people who use the highway pay an amount equal to the marginal cost of using the highway. It is unimportant what happens to the money collected from drivers. The highway authority would optimally collect toll revenue equal to the area of the box P*CFG in Figure 10.4 from drivers who choose to use the road. This may be more or less than the fixed cost of maintaining the highway. Efficiency requires that the highway authority collect the funds despite the fact that drivers impose congestion costs not on the highway authority but on other drivers.

If there is no connection between tolls and the maintenance or expansion of fixed facilities, tolls whose revenue is simply discarded will make all transportation users worse off, as noted previously. Efficiency considerations require that tolls be calculated without consideration for fixed facilities costs, but in fact it is the level of capacity that determines the level of tolls. If capacity is large relative to traffic levels, there will be little congestion and thus congestion tolls will be low; similarly if traffic levels exceed capacity, congestion tolls will be high.

Fixed facilities costs enter the calculation of efficiency tolls only through the decision to invest or disinvest. The reader will recall from Chapter 9 that, in the absence of any prior beliefs about whether traffic levels will rise or fall, efficiency requires that capacity be increased whenever:

$$P > ATC. \tag{10.4}$$

The parallel rule is that capacity should be shrunk whenever:

$$P < ATC. \tag{10.5}$$

If toll collections are larger than the opportunity cost of expanding the highway, the case in favor of expanding fixed facilities is settled, as discussed in Chapter 9. The reason is that through their toll payments drivers have demonstrated that their willingness to pay for an improvement is at least as high as the cost of providing the improvement. A new highway would have larger capacity and thus higher speeds, and so lower congestion tolls. If the new highway eliminates congestion, the marginal and average costs of using the highway will be the same, and thus there will be no opportunity to impose a toll to increase economic efficiency. But if the expanded highway is also congested, there will still be an opportunity to impose an efficiency toll—although a smaller one—to reduce traffic levels and increase the speed of traffic.

If facilities are not lumpy, none of the construction costs are sunk, and there is perfect foresight about traffic levels, there can be a perfect match between facilities size and traffic levels. Such a situation is pictured in Figure 10.5. The curves marked SMC and SAC are the same as in Figure 10.4, and correspond to a particular size of fixed facilities. The line marked LAC is long-run average cost, a curve that is well defined as long as facilities are infinitely variable in size and no costs are sunk. LAC is shown as a horizontal line to indicate that there is no cost penalty to building facilities large or small; i.e., there are no economies or diseconomies of scale.

The efficient level of capacity to provide is given by the intersection of LAC and the demand curve. Since the facility is built to be exactly the right size, SRMC also intersects the demand curve at the same point. The optimum congestion toll is BC, which exactly corresponds to the average fixed cost. The area of the box CEGB is the fixed cost while OBGX* is variable cost. Assuming that the driver pays his or her own variable cost, the efficiency toll exactly covers the fixed cost of the facility. By financing construction through congestion tolls— tolls whose level is not computed by any consideration of infrastructure costs—

FIGURE 10.5   Under Some Conditions, Optimal Tolls to Peak Period Users Will Finance the Entire Facility

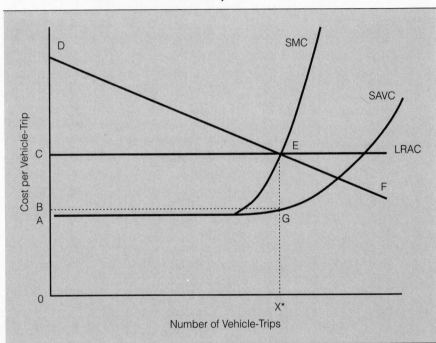

a means is presented to install the efficient level of capacity. This is the connection between tolls and highway finance.[11]

The reader will note that using congestion tolls to pay for infrastructure cuts off the source of rebates to consumers necessary to make drivers better off (on average) after the imposition of a toll. The problem is that infrastructure financing, as described in Chapter 6, has been generally invisible to drivers. While a comprehensive plan for congestion toll financing of transportation facilities could be introduced as part of a package of fuel tax reductions, it is likely that the direct rebate portion of the program would have to be larger and more explicit than a simple reduction in gas taxes if the plan is to prove politically feasible.

CONCLUSION

Once fixed facilities are in place, the next considerations are how intensively to use them and what price to charge for their use. These questions can be jointly answered by the principle of economic efficiency. If efficiency conditions are met, the social value of transportation facilities is maximized.

To achieve economic efficiency, two conditions are required. First, the prices charged should lead to the use of resources that maximizes the social value of the facilities; and second, in order for a service to be provided, the total benefit from the service must be greater than the short-run opportunity cost of making it available to consumers. The first condition ensures that members of the economy are getting the full benefit of the facilities—that no one who is willing to pay his or her own way is deprived from the opportunity of doing so, and that only those people who value the facility most highly are permitted to use it. The second condition ensures that those facilities that are valued most highly are retained while those that not valued as highly as their opportunity cost are abandoned, to the benefit of the economy as a whole.

One area where the principle of efficient pricing has been applied is to the pricing of back-hauls. In the usual case where vehicles must be returned after a trip, the principle of efficiency determines how much of the total cost of the round trip should be allocated to each direction. If traffic flows are balanced, this principle calls for allocating costs according to the level of demand in each direction. In the more typical case of traffic flows in which some vehicles return empty, the entire cost of the round trip should be assessed to the high-demand direction.

The most powerful application of economic efficiency criteria is in setting tolls for congested highways or other pieces of transportation infrastructure. As noted in Chapter 8, the marginal cost of using fixed facilities is constant until they begin to be congested. For example, traffic flows are not slowed until a critical number of vehicles per mile begins to use the highway; since the marginal cost of using a stretch of highway must include user costs as well as costs to the facility owner, as traffic congestion increases, so does marginal cost. The efficient price to charge for using a highway, or any fixed facility, is that that makes the full price to the user equal to the marginal cost of using the highway. Prices that are intended to optimize use of fixed facilities are often called congestion tolls to emphasize the main cost of using roads, tracks, and other transport facilities.

The efficient toll is determined by the difference between the average and marginal cost of using a facility. The reason is that the average user pays (in the form of direct outlays and time) the average cost of using the facility, while the cost of each usage is marginal cost. A congestion toll is then necessary to make sure that a driver pays the efficient amount.

Congestion tolls are efficient, but unless the proceeds of the toll are rebated back to the traveling public, they will make all transport users worse off. When properly rebated, they can lead to the situation where everyone is better off with the toll than without it.

The classic way in which congestion tolls can be returned to drivers is by using them to finance the fixed facilities. In the case of constant returns to scale (in which fixed facilities can be incrementally expanded and contracted without a cost penalty), efficient congestion tolls will exactly pay for the costs of the fixed facility. This is sometimes seen as a just payment since what the users of the facility pay goes to pay for the costs of the facility. However, the height of the toll is not determined by the level of the fixed costs of the facility. Efficient tolls are determined by the costs of driving and are justified as a means for inducing drivers to make efficient decisions.

In the typical case where transport facilities are placed in service ahead of demand, congestion will be low in the early years and high in later years; and given the lumpiness of facilities, there may be many occasions in which a facility is built with the anticipation that it will never be congested. In these circumstances, if the authority is to retrieve the costs of fixed facilities, alternative mechanisms need to be used to recover the costs of fixed facilities. Techniques for doing this will be the subject of the next chapter.

NOTES

1. The essential problem of welfare economics is the reconciliation of different tastes and incomes of different user groups. The usual shortcut is to describe the economy as if it consisted of single producers and single consumers, since under these conditions these problems disappear.

2. The uncoupling of income distribution questions from those of economic efficiency, while appealing to the economic practitioner, is logically more difficult than appears on the surface. The reason is that it is incomes that determine the weighting of tastes that will be responded to by a competitive economy. Thus what is produced, and thus the allocation of resources, is not independent of the distribution of income.

3. The classic statement of the virtues of marginal cost pricing is William Vickrey, "Some Implications of Marginal Cost Pricing for Public Utilities," *American Economic Review, Supplement,* Vol. 45 (1955), No. 2, pp. 605–620.

4. The identification of the total benefit of a service as the area under the demand curve up to the amount of consumption is correct only if there are no important income effects. If a change in the price in a transport market causes more widespread changes throughout the economy, the classic approximation loses its validity. Under these circumstances, the *partial equilibrium* models like those shown in this textbook must be replaced with a *general equilibrium* framework. General equilibrium models, however, in almost all circumstances, make simplifying assumptions that make them not useful for the sort of measurements that are the done here.

5. This statement is correct if all markets are competitive. Once the problem of monopoly motivations is introduced, the efficiency implications of marginal changes in operations are greatly complicated.

6. The basic reference on congestion tolls is A. A. Walters, "The Theory and Measurement of Private and Social Cost of Highway Congestion," *Econometrica,* Vol. 29 (1961), pp. 676–699.

7. A classic calculation of optimal congestion tolls on an urban expressway system is found in Theodore E. Keeler, and Kenneth A. Small, "Optimal Peak-Load Pricing,

Investment, and Service Levels on Urban Expressways," *Journal of Political Economy*, Vol. 85, No. 1 (1977), pp. 1–25.

8. This point is made in Steven A. Morrison, and Clifford Winston, "Enhancing the Performance of the Deregulated Air Transportation System," *Brookings Papers on Economic Activity*, Special Issue, 1989, pp. 61–112.

9. See B.W. Ang, "Restraining Automobile Ownership and Usage and Transportation Energy Demand: The Case of Singapore," *Journal of Energy and Development*, Vol. 17, No. 2, Spring 1992, pp. 263–278; Rex S. Toh, "Experimental Measures to Curb Road Congestion in Singapore: Pricing and Quotas," *Logistics and Transportation Review*, Vol. 28, No. 3, September 1992, pp. 289–317; and Peter Smith, "Controlling Traffic Congestion by Regulating Car Ownership: Singapore's Recent Experience," *Journal of Transport Economics and Policy*, Vol. 26, No. 1, January 1992, pp. 89–95.

10. This point is made in Martin Wohl, and Chris Hendrickson, *Transportation Investment and Pricing Principles: An Introduction for Engineers, Planners, and Economists* (New York: Wiley, 1984). Note that this conclusion is true only for homogeneous traffic. If traffic is non-homogeneous, it is possible that drivers who value their time higher will be better off as may be some drivers who now choose this route because it is now less crowded.

11. A plea for congestion tolls to be the primary tool for infrastructure finance is found in Clifford Winston, "Efficient Transportation Infrastructure Policy," *Journal of Economic Perspectives*, Vol. 5, No. 1 (Winter 1991), pp. 113–127.

11

Paying for Use of Transport Facilities

Efficient transportation prices are based on vehicle costs, not on the costs of providing infrastructure. As described in the previous chapter, in long-run competitive equilibrium with constant returns to scale, the appropriate level of fixed facilities can be installed so that congestion tolls exactly cover the costs of fixed facilities. There is, then, no inherent contradiction between pricing criteria that purposely ignore the costs of fixed facilities on the one hand and the financial viability of the transportation system on the other.

The efficient pricing rule does not assume that fixed facilities are somehow unproductive or unimportant. Quite to the contrary, efficient pricing rules attempt to make the most use out of available fixed facilities. Under ideal conditions, efficient pricing will allow exactly the right level of fixed facilities to be financed; the payments made to discourage over-use of the facilities will exactly compensate fixed facilities owners for their expenses.

But while under ideal conditions there is no problem with paying for fixed facilities using congestion tolls, conditions are not always ideal. There are at least three reasons that the problem of paying for fixed facilities are common: First, as noted in Part I of this book, transportation infrastructure is often very long-lived. In many instances, investments made on transportation fixed facilities represent permanent changes in the landscape. These expenditures are sunk in every sense of the word and economic criteria are quite clear that sunk costs are irrelevant for determining prices. In addition, the longer-lived are facilities, the more likely it is that inflation will drive a wedge between original construction costs and their current value. Due in large part to inflation, the original cost of the current highway system is a tiny fraction of what would be needed to rebuild it today.

Given the uncertainty of investment returns, the financial markets are not usually willing to accept the pattern of returns that are typical in very long-lived investments. For example, if a bridge is erected with an expected 75-year life, and if it is not expected to be congested for 25 years, efficiency pricing principles would say that no tolls should be charged for the first third of its life. That is, the operator should receive no return on investment for a quarter of a century. In order to encourage investment, it may be necessary to accept a certain amount of inefficiency in the short run in the form of prices above marginal costs.

Second, one of the fundamental characteristics of transportation infrastructure investments is their lumpy nature. As noted in previous chapters, this leads to the installation of transport infrastructure that is larger than traffic conditions require when facilities are first opened. This is especially true of rural interstate highways which, were they not designed to be part of a standard system of four-lane limited access highways, could more efficiently be designed as two-lane highways. Whenever a system is overbuilt relative to the traffic it will carry, congestion tolls cannot be levied and there will be no efficient mechanism to cover the costs of the facilities.

Third, as recalled from Chapter 9, there may be an economic justification for infrastructure projects that will not be able to recover costs from their tolls. If a decision has been made to not recover the benefits of fixed facilities improvements through higher prices charged to users, it may be the case that there is an economic justification for fixed facilities projects that will not be financially viable. A railroad line, for example, might be built in place of a highway where the economic justification for the line is the reduction in pollution that traffic shifts from a parallel highway might cause. Such a line might not be able to cover its costs, but might be optimal from a global perspective. In addition, transportation infrastructure in many nations has been installed to serve a variety of non-economic purposes, most notably regional development and military defense. Whenever infrastructure is installed for non-economic reasons, there can be little surprise that prices based on strictly economic criteria will not lead to financial viability.

For these reasons, while it is possible that efficient prices will cover the cost of transport infrastructure, it is reasonable to expect that in the majority of cases efficient prices will not cover the costs of capital. If a government stands ready to absorb the losses associated with the failure to cover the fixed costs of maintaining fixed facilities, it may be possible to achieve efficient pricing even in the case of uncongested facilities. However, in the case of privately financed infrastructure improvements, a deviation from strict efficiency criteria will be necessary because financial markets will not allow a builder to borrow without a reasonable expectation that the funds be paid back—whether or not it is economically efficient to do so. Whatever the reason that efficient prices are insufficient to cover the financial costs of infrastructure obligations, the techniques for handling the problem are all the same and are the subject of this chapter.

FAMILIAR TOOLS FOR ALLOCATING FIXED COSTS AMONG MULTIPLE USER GROUPS

The problems of pricing fixed facilities is usually thought of as the problem of cost allocation. For example, what percentage of the $90 billion annual expenditure of state and federal highway authorities calculated in Chapter 6 should be paid by trucks as opposed to passenger vehicles? It is a problem of intense interest to the trucking industry and motorists as well as railroads. The problem of cost allocation arises because in almost all cases transportation fixed facilities are used by multiple classes of users. Roads are used by trucks as well as by private cars. Railroad tracks are used by freight and passenger trains. Freight trains carry commodities of many different shippers; airports serve general aviation as well as commercial passenger flights and freight. How much of a contribution should each user group make to cover the costs of the facilities? There are two traditional answers to this question, each of which will be described next.

The Fully-Allocated Cost Standard

It is only common sense to distribute the costs of providing the fixed facilities among those that use them. Or is it? The logic behind the so called *fully-allocated cost* method is based on simplicity and basic equity. An example of a fully allocated cost approach to highway use fees would be to divide the total annual expenditure, $90 billion, by the number of vehicles on the road. Neglecting motorcycles and bicycles, there were about 200 million vehicles registered in the United States in 1995. Dividing the two figures yields $450 per vehicle. This is a form of fully-allocated cost because it accounts for the complete cost of the fixed facility by dividing it by some measure of usage. Defenders of fully-allocated cost approaches point out that equal shares for all corresponds to basic equity and that fully-allocated cost methods give a definite answer to the question.

Unfortunately, different people using the fully-allocated cost method may not come up with the same answer; it is not as definite or obviously fair as at first appears. For example, one person might decide that dividing expenses by vehicles is the obvious and fair way to divide costs, but another might believe that dividing by axles is more appropriate. After all, trucks are larger and thus should pay more. Large trucks usually have five axles instead of two for a passenger car. Thus each large truck should be given a share two and one-half times that of a passenger car. A third person might note that large trucks have eighteen wheels compared to a passenger car's four. Perhaps, then, each large truck should have a share four and one-half times larger than a passenger car. Another person applying the fully-allocated cost principle might note that the gross vehicle weight for large trucks is 80,000 lbs. compared to approximately 4,000 lbs. for a passenger car. This person would use the principle to charge trucks 20 times more than a passenger car. But there are more possibilities: Trucks travel more than twice as many miles per year as passenger cars. If the cost allocation were made on the basis of vehicle-miles, axle-miles, wheel-miles, or gross vehicle weight-miles, the answers would be different still. Which is the fair allocation? Which is the right one? The principle of fully-allocated costing gives us no guidance.

But there are more serious problems than the ambiguity of choosing the fair index of vehicle comparison. These common sense-based or equity-based pricing principles tend to lead users of fixed facilities to make decisions that make the economy worse off. For example, if heavy trucks were to be taxed as lightly as the first proposal above calls for, it would give an incentive to expand the use of heavy trucks at the expense of lighter trucks and other modes of transportation. This would lead to faster deterioration of highways and eventually higher costs to the economy. When fully-allocated cost principles are applied to single facilities, the irrationalities of using the principle are even more obvious. For example, if the principle were applied to the Tennessee-Tombigbee waterway described in Chapter 9, the pleasure craft and occasional coal barge that use the facility would each be asked to divide the annual expenses of creating and maintaining the facility. But this would amount to thousands of dollars per boat. As the high fees drove away users, the remaining boats would be asked to pay higher and higher fees until eventually no user would be able to afford to pay to transit the canal. On the other side, crowded facilities like the San Francisco Bay Bridge would have a low per-vehicle charge, which would attract even more vehicles to an already overcrowded facility. The mathematical logic of dividing a fixed amount by an index of use inevitably will lead to the further crowding of overcrowded facilities and the penalizing of users of facilities with excess capacity. A facility that was overpriced on the first day it opened (leading to few users) would find itself in a spiral of fewer users, higher cost per user, and fewer users yet; one that was underpriced on opening day would find itself in a spiral in the opposite direction leading to over usage.

The major criticism of fully-allocated cost methods for pricing fixed facilities is that they do not lead to the best pattern of usage of existing facilities.

In other words, fully-allocated cost methods violate the principles of economic efficiency.

Peak-Load Pricing

One of the earliest applications of economic analysis to transportation was a demonstration of the efficiency benefits of using peak-load pricing models rather than fully-distributed cost models. The classic economic solution to the problem of allocating the costs of a facility among different user classes has been based on the joint costing exercise described in Chapter 10 for pricing back-hauls. In the context of fixed facilities pricing, the joint costing exercise is one of determining time-of-day prices, or peak-load prices due to the rule of thumb solution suggested by the model.

Efficiency considerations call for congestion tolls to vary throughout the day depending on traffic levels. If a transportation facility is not congested, there will be no efficiency toll. Price will equal marginal cost in the region before it begins to rise. This is the situation shown in Figure 11.1. The optimum

FIGURE 11.1   When Congestion Tolls Will Not Yield Any Revenue

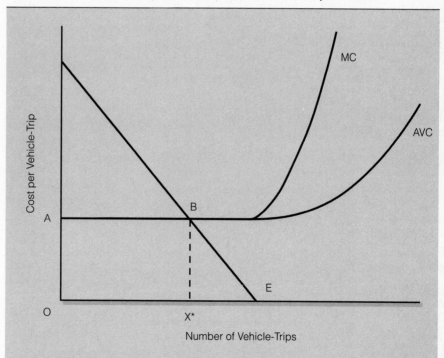

price is OA, the efficient service level is X*. The variable cost, the area under the short-run marginal cost curve, is OABX*. But the total expenditure by users of the facility is also OABX*. When facilities are not congested, optimal prices cover variable costs only, not the fixed costs. As traffic builds, congestion tolls should increase as well.

The classic demonstration of peak-load pricing assumes that traffic does not fluctuate smoothly throughout the day, but rather can be characterized by two different levels of demand. This situation is shown in Figure 11.2, which shows the demand curve, DEF, in the high-demand period. The demand curve in the low-demand period is suppressed as not necessary for the analysis, as discussed above. If the facility is congested only during peak periods, only users during those periods should be charged a congestion toll, in this case, BC. The only factor determining the size of the facility is the demand of this group and

FIGURE 11.2   Peak Loads Pay All Facilities Costs

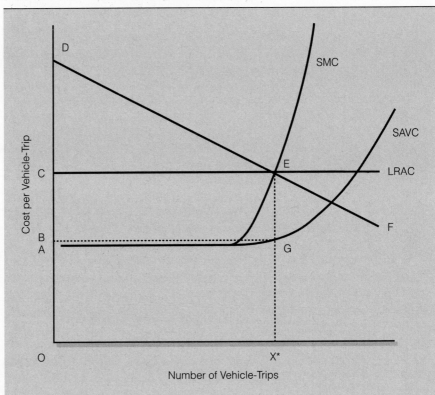

only their tolls are necessary to finance the fixed costs of the facility. Charges to users during off-peak periods are unnecessary and inefficient.

The principle that only users whose demand helps to determine the size of the facility should be charged to pay the fixed costs of the facility—the fundamental result of the peak-load pricing model—is one of the oldest in transportation economics.[1] It must be used carefully, however, since any scheme that allocates current capital costs to current users tends to lock in old technologies and to reward investors for mistakes. If mistakes are charged to current users, the community will be deprived of some opportunities to use a facility during the period when the investment is being recovered; furthermore, the guarantee that capital costs can be recovered may tempt investors to be less cautious than they should be in evaluating the prospects of a project.

The peak-load pricing model's rule of thumb under which peak users pay capital costs and off-peak users pay nothing toward fixed facilities is in fact correct only under very limited circumstances. The peak-load pricing model should be understood to say that in the circumstance where capacity is not lumpy but can be provided with constant returns to scale, where off-peak and on-peak users do not congest one another, where off-peak users do not use facilities to capacity, in long-run equilibrium with no externalities, it will be found that optimal congestion tolls levied on peak users only will return net revenues that exactly equal capital costs.

SUBSIDY-FREE PRICING RULES

The peak-load pricing model shows that it is possible to use efficiency standards to determine cost responsibilities of different users in a transportation network. Unfortunately, the principle of economic efficiency does not give guidance on how these costs should be allocated if, for example, a facility is always uncongested. The reason is simply that if the facilities are in place but uncongested, the decision by a user to take one more trip has no cost consequences to the facility owner or to other users of the facility. As long as the total willingness to pay from all user classes is greater than the total opportunity cost of maintaining the facilities, it is efficient to maintain the facility in place. Since the marginal cost of using the facility is zero, so should be the price charged for using it. Of course, a zero price retrieves zero revenue. Are you sure, says the economist, that you need to retrieve the costs of the facilities from the users?

This is an unhelpful answer for those who need to finance facilities. When coal shippers claim that they are being charged too much for using railroad tracks and that more of the burden should be placed onto shippers of other commodities, the statement that no one is responsible for the costs of the tracks does not help to resolve the dispute. To provide some guidance we need to introduce one more criterion for guiding prices: that no user class subsidize any other user class. The subsidy-free pricing rules have similar language to the criteria of economic efficiency, but are in fact based on non-efficiency-based considerations.

Subsidy-Free Prices Defined

The concept of *subsidy-free prices* starts with the principle that the users of transport facilities as a whole must cover all of the costs of the facilities that they use. If they do not, they are being subsidized by someone else. Thus all costs of roads must be covered by road users and all opportunity costs of railroads must be covered by railroad users in order for the prices charged to the users to be characterized as subsidy-free.[2]

But even if users as a whole pay the entire opportunity costs of a system, it is possible that some of the users pay too much of the opportunity cost (the subsidizing group) and another group pays too little (the subsidized group). A price structure is said to be subsidy-free if no user group or combination of user groups could make themselves better off by cutting off the remaining users of the system, using it only for their own transportation.[3] If one group could lower its overall transportation costs by eliminating another group, we say that the first group is cross-subsidizing the second group. In other words, to describe a price structure as subsidy-free, no matter how users are grouped, each group must pay at least the additional cost that their presence causes to the network. The additional cost of maintaining a service (or group of services) is called incremental cost, as described in Chapter 5. This contrasts with the concept of marginal cost which measures the additional cost of increasing the level of one transport service. Marginal cost includes only the variable costs of transport operations. Incremental cost involves fixed facilities costs as well. In this sense, incremental costs more closely resemble the total cost of providing a service or group of services than marginal cost.

The principle of pricing to prevent cross-subsidization of one group of users by another is a powerful mechanism for allocating the fixed costs of transportation facilities. The concept of subsidy-free pricing is closely related to the concept of efficient pricing extended to multiple user groups. The reader will recall from the previous chapter that the principle of efficiency has two parts: first that price equal marginal cost; and second that total willingness to pay (what actually is paid plus consumers' surplus) be greater than total opportunity cost (including fixed costs). We noted that private competitive firms will not always provide efficient levels of service since the they do not correctly evaluate the second condition. Competitive firms calculate whether revenue is greater than or equal to opportunity cost; efficiency requires that they compare cost with total willingness to pay.

The criterion of subsidy-free prices is an extension to the case of multiple users and multiple services of the principle that revenues must be greater than or equal to costs. This extension is critical in the case of transportation since shared facilities is the norm in transport enterprises. Prices are subsidy-free if it is impossible to find some group of users that do not pay in revenue an amount equal to their incremental costs.

If the transport company is pricing its services to maximize profits, prices charged by private companies will pass the subsidy-free test. If they did not, it would be possible to suspend service to some group of customers and thereby increase profits—which contradicts the assumption of profit maximization. The problem of implementing subsidy-free pricing standards is critical in the case of facilities provided by governments—primarily fixed facilities. Governments do not naturally maximize profits when deciding on a fee schedule for use of transport facilities and thus there is no guarantee that the subsidy-free principle will be satisfied.

The subsidy-free pricing principle that every possible combination of users be charged at least the incremental cost of serving them is an inequality condition. It says that incremental revenue must be greater than the incremental cost of serving any group of customers. Since the condition is an inequality, it is not surprising that subsidy-free principles do not give absolutely firm numbers of dollars that each customer should pay toward the maintenance of the fixed facilities that they use. Nonetheless, the limits placed on pricing by the subsidy-free principle often set quite narrow limits on permissible prices, as shown by the example later in this chapter.

Incentives to Invest and Disinvest under Subsidy-Free Pricing Rules

The criterion that a network price structure be subsidy-free requires a calculation of the cost saving and revenue losses from abandoning for transportation uses a portion of transportation infrastructure. In essence, the subsidy-free pricing criterion requires that user groups pay an amount at least as great as the costs of the facilities used to support them. This counteracts one of the problems of government provided fixed facilities: namely, a tendency to overly-optimistically evaluate investment and abandonments. Potential users, if they believe that they will not have to pay for them, will clamor for the government to build them. Of more concern, however, is the fact that without comparisons between revenues and cost, there may be a tendency by governments to maintain in operation facilities that would fail the efficiency test that total willingness to pay be greater than or equal to the total opportunity cost of maintaining the facility in operation. In this way, subsidy-free pricing standards can aid efficient decision making, even if the rules themselves are not directly derived from efficiency considerations.

As noted previously, private owners of fixed facilities do not make completely efficient abandonment decisions. A formal analysis is presented in Figure 11.3; the efficient decision on whether or not to abandon a facility would be whether the sum of consumer surplus and operator's revenues, BDEG, is greater or less than the opportunity cost of maintaining the facility in operation. The operator, however, would simply calculate whether his or her own revenue,

FIGURE 11.3   Private Operators Tend to Abandon Facilities Too Soon

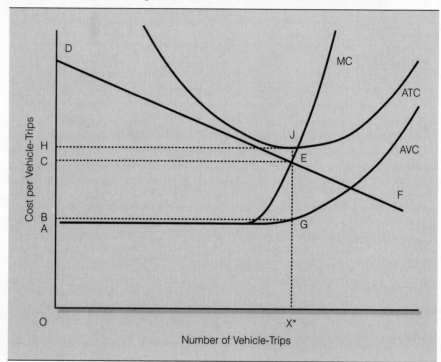

BCEG, is greater or less than the opportunity cost of the operation. Thus, with declining demand, the private operator is likely to abandon a facility too soon. For example, if it is unable to capture consumers' surplus of its customers, a railroad may wish to abandon a little used line sooner than the economic efficiency criterion would call for; in this case, a direct subsidy may be justified.

Private operators' abandonment decisions are influenced by financial costs rather than opportunity costs which, among other things, differ by sunk costs. The reason is that a private operator has obligations quoted in original dollars. If the operator fails to pay an obligation, the facility can be seized by creditors, but lenders who repossess the facilities will be able to sell them for no more than their original cost less sunk costs. There are thus dual valuations of each fixed facility: one based on true opportunity costs, which have sunk costs removed; and one based on depreciated original cost, which include sunk costs. Calculations of efficient prices for abandonable facilities should be based on true opportunity costs. Of course, private operators may not be willing to accept a valuation of their facilities at opportunity cost rather than original cost. As explained in the previous chapter, the sunkness of transportation investment makes lenders reluctant to offer funds for fixed facilities development.

While private operators are more likely to abandon facilities too soon, at least the financial requirements of making revenue and cost calculations for each facility do provide a framework for abandonment decisions to be made. Railroads, for example, routinely calculate whether they should maintain a line segment in operation. This is possible since they collect revenue data by segment. By contrast, governments that do not get revenues from particular facilities cannot easily make any sort of cost-benefit calculation and thus are likely to abandon facilities too late. Waterways, once built, are rarely abandoned. Subsidy-free pricing rules impose a discipline on investment and disinvestment that mimics the (somewhat too harsh) criteria used in private industry.

An Example of Subsidy-Free Pricing to Allocate Fixed Facilities Costs

The major use of subsidy-free pricing rules is that they provide guidance on who should pay for fixed facilities. It is easiest to describe how subsidy-free pricing constraints allocate fixed costs among different groups by using an example. Figure 11.4 shows a hypothetical network containing four cities. Rice moves

FIGURE 11.4   Structure of a Hypothetical Transportation Network

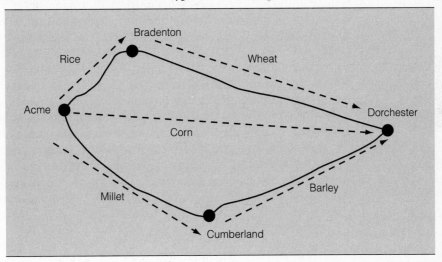

Movement	Commodity	Distance	Variable Cost of Movement	Fixed Cost of Maintaining Fixed Facilities on Route
Acme to Bradenton	Rice	3	3	3
Bradenton to Dorchester	Wheat	12	12	12
Acme to Dorchester	Corn	15 (via Bradenton)	15 (via Bradenton)	
Acme to Cumberland	Millet	10	10	10
Cumberland to Dorchester	Barley	10	10	10

from Acme to Bradenton; wheat from Bradenton to Dorchester; corn from Acme to Dorchester; millet from Acme to Cumberland; and barley from Cumberland to Dorchester. Each traffic flow is assumed to be equal to one unit of traffic. The figure shows two routes from Acme to Dorchester, one through Bradenton, and one through Cumberland. The route through Bradenton is shorter than the one through Cumberland, so it is less expensive in terms of the variable costs of movement. On the assumption that fixed facilities costs are invariant with traffic levels, there are no additional fixed facilities costs associated with the movement of corn, since it would use facilities that are already in place to serve other commodities. That is why the fixed facilities costs for corn movement are absent in the table at the bottom of Figure 11.4.

In order for the concept of cross-subsidization to be meaningful, the transport operator must minimize the total cost—fixed plus variable—of transportation. In the particularly simple map shown in Figure 11.4, it is easy to show that cost minimization requires that all links be used.[4]

The subsidy-free pricing criterion for allocating fixed costs gets its power from the reengineering of the system to take into account the presence of different users. When cutting off a user does not change the minimum cost network, the rules for subsidy-free pricing give no guidance on how the cost of fixed facilities should be allocated. However, if eliminating a user group allows some of the facilities to be abandoned, the foregone cost saving of not abandoning facilities is the cost responsibility of that user group.

From Figure 11.4 it can easily be seen that barley must be assessed the fixed costs of the route from Cumberland to Dorchester. That is because barley is the only user of this route, and thus eliminating barley from the system would allow the savings of the fixed cost of the route. By the same argument, millet should be assessed the cost of maintaining the route from Acme to Cumberland.

But what about the northern routes? This is more complicated since these routes are shared between corn, rice, and wheat. The subsidy-free criterion says that each user and user group must pay for the costs incurred in serving it. If wheat were eliminated from the system, it would be economical to abandon the route from Bradenton to Dorchester. This is because corn could be rerouted on the southern route, at a variable cost of 20 or 5 more than it costs to use the northern route, while the fixed facilities cost saving would be 12. In other words, a cost of 7 (the difference between the fixed cost saving of 12 and increased variable cost of 5) is incurred to serve wheat. Thus, at a minimum, wheat should pay at least 7 of the fixed costs of the system. Rice, on the other hand, has no minimum cost allocation since if rice were removed from the system, it would still be economical to maintain the link between Acme and Bradenton to serve corn.

If corn were removed from the system, it would then be economical to abandon the route from Bradenton to Dorchester, routing wheat through Cumberland. The reason is that the increase in the cost of shipping wheat the longer distance (23 instead of 12) is less than the reduction in the fixed cost from abandoning the Bradenton-Dorchester route (12). Thus the cost to the system of carrying corn is 1 in addition to the variable costs. The minimum cost allocation to corn is thus 1. It is of course also true that the users of the Bradenton-Dorchester route, wheat and corn, must together pay a minimum of the 12 fixed route costs. Similarly, rice and corn together must contribute at least 3 to the fixed costs of the system if we are to avoid a cross-subsidy from other users to them. And, finally, corn cannot be asked to pay a contribution toward fixed costs of more than 15, the cost of a standalone network designed solely for it, wheat cannot be charged more than 12 and rice more than 3 for the same reason.

The requirement that prices charged be non-cross-subsidizing greatly reduces the amount of uncertainty about how fixed costs should be distributed among the users. It is not the case that the fixed costs of the system can be arbitrarily allocated to users. In the example here, 28 of the 35 units of fixed cost of the system can be allocated, and even the remaining 8 units of cost can be broken down into the joint responsibility of two or three users rather than the entire group.

Adapting the Rule to Disequilibrium Positions

The economic theory of subsidy-free pricing was originally developed for a world in which there is no distinction between the long and short run or between fixed and sunk costs.[5] The appealing justice of the rule also derives from a world in which there is instantaneous adaptation of traffic and infrastructure to new prices. But in the world of lags and imperfect foresight, there may be reasons to deviate somewhat from the price structure dictated by the combination of efficiency and subsidy-free pricing rules.

One reason to be hesitant about the strict application of the rules derives from the fact that efficient and subsidy-free prices are inherently more variable over time than are alternatives. If there are costs of adaptation to expected prices, it may be efficient not to impose apparently efficient prices. An example of this phenomenon is provided by Small, Winston, and Evans, who calculate that the interstate highway system is underengineered for large trucks.[6] They argue that large trucks are causing the road surface of the current system to deteriorate more rapidly than is optimal. Thus short-run marginal cost pricing would call for raising tolls on such vehicles. However, they argue, had the system been correctly constructed, each traffic lane would have been made several inches thicker. Under an optimally-constructed system, the damage caused by trucks would be less than it is today. An efficient pricing and investment plan would call for raising truck charges today to limit the use of the fragile highway system while simultaneously rebuilding it to optimal specifications. When it is rebuilt, charges on large trucks would be lowered. But this pattern of raising prices today in the full knowledge that they will be lowered later may encourage an adaptation to higher prices that will then need to be undone in the future when prices are reduced. A case can be made for keeping charges on heavy trucks inefficiently low today in order to avoid the adaptation of trucking services to a system that will not be a long-run equilibrium.

There is another argument in favor of not taking the relentlessly forward-looking perspective that efficient and subsidy-free pricing rules require. We should be realistic in recognizing that current facilities use will affect future investments. Governments do take current usage levels of roadways as an indication of where and what kind of investments should be made. Under these conditions, it may appropriate that current charges to different types of users should reflect the effect that their usage levels will have on future investment decisions.

As described in Chapter 6, highways and bridges are engineered differently depending on expected traffic volumes of different classes of vehicles. Thus highways that are anticipated to be used by heavy trucks must be made thicker, wider, and with lower grades. Bridges used by heavy trucks must be made stronger. Navigable waterways that are expected to be used by deep-draft ocean-going vessels are made deeper and wider than if usage is expected solely by motorized barges and pleasure craft. It is reasonable to extend the principle of subsidy-free pricing to retrieving the costs of different engineering if current usage levels affect future investment. Thus payments by heavy trucks should at a minimum recoup the extra costs of all extra investments made to accommodate the expected usage by trucks. Similarly, ocean-going vessels should pay at least for channel deepening beyond what is appropriate for traffic by smaller boats. If a mode will require some new investment (in the form of renewal or expansion of fixed facilities), if the facilities can be designed differently depending on the traffic mix, and if current traffic levels are used as an indication of future investment needs, then it is clearly appropriate that every class of traffic pay the incremental costs not only of current facilities but also of investments made to accommodate them.

There is a danger in using this rule retrospectively: that is, charging prices to different classes of vehicles to reflect engineering decisions made in the past. The reason for this is that previous engineering decisions might have been faulty, based on previous technologies, or based on demand considerations that are no longer relevant. For example, the investment in the Tennessee-Tombigbee waterway was clearly a mistake, as described in Chapter 9. It would be inappropriate (and impossible) to try to recoup the cost of the investment from the few coal barges that use the waterway merely because the canal was engineered primarily to haul coal. Similarly, it would be inappropriate to charge the great majority of railroad track costs to Amtrak passengers simply because railroad tracks were originally engineered primarily to handle passenger trains.[7]

By contrast, since roadways are still being built and rebuilt to accommodate future expected traffic levels, it is appropriate to apply the principle to allocating road construction costs to the different kinds of traffic that use the system. In particular, heavy trucks should pay not simply the cost of damage they do to current highways but also an amount to cover the expected extra costs of (re)constructing highways to accommodate them as opposed to lighter trucks, buses, or passenger cars. Application of the principle would cause heavy trucks to be used at a level that correctly reflects the cost to the economy of using them; appropriate use levels will then give correct signals to highway planners concerning the location and types of highways that are most efficient to build. According to a calculation by Small, Winston, and Evans, appropriate highway building would require much thicker pavements to accommodate heavy trucks and thus trucks should pay through license fees for added construction costs to accommodate them; but they would be charged less on a per-mile basis to account for damage that they do to the road surface.

ALLOCATING VEHICLE COSTS TO PASSENGER-MILES AND TON-MILES

The efficient and subsidy-free pricing rules used to allocate fixed facilities costs among different user classes are, in fact, quite general. They can be used whenever there is heterogeneous capital stocks and some portion of non-traceable costs. Just as the fact that transport fixed facilities are generally used by more than one class of user introduces the conceptual problem of allocating cost responsibility of those users for use of the facilities, in the same manner, transport vehicles that carry many passengers or the freight of many different shippers brings up the problem of cost responsibility of the multiple users for the costs of owning and operating the vehicle. The problem of non-traceable costs, as noted in Chapter 5, occurs whenever marginal cost is less than average cost at normal operating ranges.

Transport vehicle operations appear at first glance to have substantial problems of cost allocation. Consider a flight from Cleveland to Tampa that has 100 seats, only 50 of which are filled 10 minutes before flight time. What would be the marginal cost of carrying one more passenger? The answer appears to be virtually nil: perhaps a small amount of extra fuel; perhaps a little extra time of baggage handlers or flight attendants; if a meal is served, perhaps one extra meal would be consumed; existing passengers might be delayed by having one more passenger on board. If each passenger is charged marginal cost, as called for by principles of economic efficiency, none of the passengers will pay more than a few dollars for their tickets. Where, then, will the revenue come from to operate the flight?

This problem is identical to that of retrieving the cost of uncongested transportation fixed facilities. Indeed, the source of the problem is the same: the lumpiness of transportation facilities. Just as the fact that roads and railroads can only be built using discrete multiples of lanes or tracks, so airplane sizes are not infinitely variable. If they were, the size of the aircraft could be adjusted for each flight so that there were never any empty seats, in which case the marginal cost of handling one more passenger would no longer be nil but rather the difference in cost of operating an aircraft efficiently designed to carry 50 passengers and one designed to carry 51 passengers.

Since the problem of defining marginal cost in the case of passengers in an aircraft is formally identical to that of tracing user cost responsibility in the case of fixed facilities or of attributing costs to two halves of a round trip, it is not surprising that the same basic mechanisms are available: congestion tolls and subsidy-free pricing rules. Congestion tolls are actually far more useful for identifying the opportunity costs of individual passengers than it would seem at first, since the marginal costs of serving passengers are more like those of normal transportation economics than is generally appreciated.

It sometimes seems that marginal airline passenger costs are minimal until the capacity of the flight is reached. At that point the marginal cost curve rises to a level equal to the total flight costs of flying an airplane with one passenger on it. It then drops down to the same minimal level. It would appear, then, that only the one hundredth (and two hundredth, and three hundredth) passengers who use an airline service covered by 100-passenger planes have any significant marginal costs associated with them; the flight should be (virtually) free to all except the unfortunate last passenger whose presence requires using another airplane. It would seem that economic efficiency would require instituting a game of chance under which, when one asks for a reservation one has a 99 in 100 chance of getting a seat at $10.00 and a 1 in 100 chance of having to pay a bill for $10,000.00.

The problem with this perspective is that it fails to take into account the full costs of taking a flight. Just as the analysis of the costs of highway congestion required taking into account the user cost of highway transport, so the analysis of seat pricing requires an understanding of the costs that passengers impose on one another. Just as the marginal costs of using highways begins to rise as traffic slows, so too the marginal cost incurred by passengers begins to rise well before load factors approach 100 percent. The reasons are twofold: First, more crowded flights are less comfortable and are slower due to lengthened times of loading and unloading aircraft; and second, as expected load factors rise, the more likely it is that passengers will not be able to find a seat on their preferred flight, but will have to wait for another, less preferred time. This second, called *stochastic delay*, is the factor that economic analysis has focused on.[8]

A scheduled service must first announce times for service and then wait to see what the passenger loads are that appear. The airline makes a forecast about what the load factor will be at each time of the day. The more flights it offers within any short period, the lower the projected load factor is likely to be, and thus the more likely it will be that on any particular day the flight will be full, requiring passengers to postpone travel to a less preferred time. An airline knows that it is virtually impossible to operate every flight with a 100 percent load factor and would not wish to do so since it will in the process give frus-

FIGURE 11.5   Cost Curves for Multiple Flights

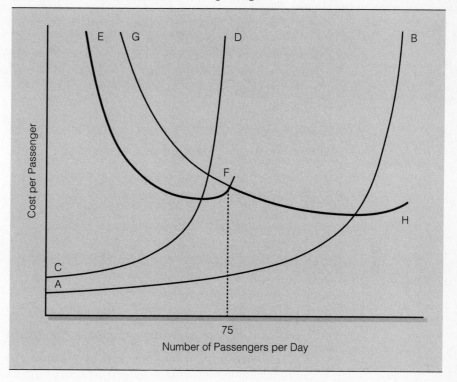

trated passengers to its competitors. Instead, it will have a target load factor for each flight that is something less than 100 percent.

Figure 11.5 shows a more realistic marginal cost curve for an airline company trying to schedule its flights. The actual number of passengers on each flight is not predictable with certainty at the time that the flights are scheduled. Instead, airlines work with a relationship between costs and expected passenger loads. The marginal cost curve at scheduling time will rise well before expected load factors reach 100 percent, reflecting the lower service quality inherent in more crowded flights as well as the expected stochastic delay associated with high predicted load factors. Figure 11.5 contains two pairs of cost curves, one assuming that a single flight is operated and a second assuming that two flights are operated during a given time period. Lines AB and CD are marginal cost curves while AF and GH are average cost curves. Lines CD and EF refer to the costs of making a single flight while AB and GH are the costs for providing two flights.

The marginal cost of operating two flights with relatively low load factors is shown as less than the marginal cost of operating a single flight, reflecting the increased probability that the flights will closely match passengers' preferred travel times. The dark envelope underneath the two average cost curves shows the minimum cost way of providing service to different numbers of passengers. At fewer than an average of 75 passengers per day in this time period, the cheapest way to provide service is with one flight; at more than 75 passengers, it is efficient to offer two flights in order to decrease stochastic and schedule delay to the passengers and to offer them a higher quality of service. The relevant marginal cost curve of the efficient flight offering would be a discontinuous line following the MC curve for a single flight up to 75 passengers and then following the MC curve for two flights.

The marginal costs in Figure 11.5 are full prices and thus include the traveler's own costs. Actual prices charged will be lower by the amount of those costs. In essence, efficient airline fares are congestion tolls imposed on passengers. Just as efficient congestion tolls are determined as the amount by which the costs seen by individuals must be increased so that marginal willingness to pay is equal to the marginal cost of all users in the system, so too here, the price charged for a seat will reflect the full cost of service, which will include an amount for the delay that one passenger's presence imposes on others.

As in the case of infrastructure pricing, the optimum toll will not necessarily cover the opportunity cost of the flight. For example, imagine there are 10 passengers per day who are willing to pay up to an average of $500 for a flight at 8 a.m., there are few other passengers who are willing to fly at that hour, and the only aircraft available for the flight has 100 seats. The benefit that those passengers receive from the flight may justify it on economic efficiency grounds despite the fact that congestion toll is nil for these passengers. This problem is recognizable as identical to that of retrieving the cost of fixed facilities that are justified for construction but which, due to the lumpiness of transport facilities, will never be congested. The solution to this problem is to introduce the extra criterion that prices be subsidy-free. That is, the entire system must be self-financing and it must be impossible to break the system up in such a way that any subset of users could be provided service at lower cost by breaking away from the group as a whole. If the 10 passengers per day provide no net revenue to the system but cause the system to incur costs, they would enjoy a cross-subsidy from other users. A subsidy-free pricing system would require that the passengers as a group pay the opportunity cost of their flight, despite the fact that it would raise prices above the opportunity cost of serving individual passengers.

The discussion on attributing vehicle costs to individual passengers is also relevant for analyzing prices of other modes of transportation, where more than one customer is served by a vehicle. LTL motor carriers provide another example. As in the case of airlines, the problem for motor carriers is predicting the amount of equipment that will need to be made available to serve an expected traffic load. No carrier will aim for a 100 percent load factor since that will cause either excessive delays to customers or too many loads to be lost to other carriers. The optimum load factor is determined by the equation of the marginal cost curve and the demand curve; the efficient price to charge for a shipment will be the difference between the user cost and the overall marginal cost at the optimum load factor.

ALLOCATING RESIDUAL FIXED COSTS

The subsidy-free criterion is not so much a pricing condition as a revenue rule. The distinction arises when a user pays more than one price for the services he or she receives. Drivers must pay a license fee each year regardless of the number of miles they drive. In effect, then, the first mile that one drives each year is extremely expensive—$50 per mile, or whatever the license fee is—and then succeeding miles are considerably cheaper. This is known in the literature as a *two-part tariff*. Such schemes are efficient mechanisms for retrieving the fixed costs of facilities if the initial lump sum charge is not so high that it eliminates potential users.[9] Drivers can still drive the efficient number of miles if the price they are charged for the marginal mile is equal to marginal cost while fixed costs are recovered by fees that are levied independent of mileage charges.

Freight carriers cannot charge similar license fees to their customers. They will nonetheless charge rates that decline with the amount of freight offered. This is sometimes done through rebates at the end of the year or negotiating other forms of volume discounts. Rates that decline with the quantity of service purchased have similar properties to licensing fees. As long as the lowest rate charged is equal to marginal cost and the non-constant price level does not drive away potential customers, the efficient level of service will be chosen; the higher rates for the first units of service purchased can be used to cover the fixed costs of the facilities.

All pricing schemes under which more than one price is charged for the same service are characterized by economists as discriminatory. It does not matter that the same individual is being charged different prices for the different units of the same service. Classic price discrimination charges different prices to different people for the same service; what is discriminatory is that different prices are charged for different units of service, not that different prices are charged to different people. If there is a single class of users, the only possible form of discrimination is to charge different prices to the same customers for different levels of service.

As shown previously, subsidy-free pricing rules will not provide a unique, definitive allocation of fixed costs to different user groups. They will simply put limits on maximum and minimum amounts that should be raised from different groups. In general, subsidy-free pricing rules will not allocate specific amounts to individual users, but rather to groups of users. In the grain shipments example above, most of the fixed costs of operating the system were allocated among the five user groups, but the pricing rule was unable to definitively split part of the bill between the corn and wheat.

Several rules have been suggested for dealing with the problem of non-unique fixed cost allocations.[10] One such suggestion, offered by Fanara and Grimm, is that costs be allocated on the basis of the stand-alone costs of the different user classes.[11] A stand-alone cost is the cost of a network designed to serve only the user groups whose cost allocation is to be calculated. Since corn has a stand-alone cost of 30 (15 fixed + 15 variable), while wheat has a stand-alone cost of 24 (12 fixed + 12 variable), the Fanara and Grimm proposal would share the costs allocated jointly to these two traffics on a 5/9 – 4/9 basis with the traffic. Other rules would share costs on the basis of marginal costs or net benefits from the service. All such schemes are, however, inherently arbitrary.

One way of eliminating the arbitrariness of the residual fixed cost allocation is to accept some inefficiency and to use a second best pricing scheme. The term *second best* refers to the fact that it is the second choice under the circumstance that the best (that is, efficient or welfare maximizing) pricing pattern cannot be used. Such a scheme may be necessary if it is impossible to retrieve fixed costs using two-part tariffs. Second best cost allocation, also called *Ramsey pricing*, recovers fixed costs by marking up the variable costs of different user groups by different amounts determined by the elasticities of demand.[12] Under Ramsey pricing all user groups pay something toward the fixed costs of the system, but those who have the lowest elasticity of demand are given the highest markups over marginal cost. That is, those groups with fewest alternatives will have prices raised over marginal cost by the largest amount. The logic behind the argument is that raising prices above marginal costs creates an inefficiency and the higher the elasticity of demand, the greater the reduction in purchases and so the greater will be the inefficiency created by raising price above marginal cost. In order to minimize the combined inefficiency, prices are raised most in those situations in which the efficiency loss is lowest.

Mathematically, Ramsey prices are expressed as:[13]

$$(P_i - C_i)/P_i = (\lambda/e_i) \tag{11.1}$$

where:

P_i is the price per unit of transportation charged to user group i
C_i is the marginal cost of transportation by user group i
e_i is the elasticity of demand by user group i.

λ is a constant for all user groups. The value of λ is determined by the requirement that the revenue target be reached.

Ramsey pricing does provide a tool for making a definitive allocation of residual fixed costs among different user groups. It does so, however, at the cost of introducing an inefficiency that is not created if fixed costs are recovered by license fees, block pricing, or other first best non-uniform pricing schemes. Ramsey pricing should only be applied to the residual allocations after the subsidy-free cost allocation has been determined.

Ramsey pricing will not necessarily assign the largest percentage of the allocable cost to the group with the highest markup. Since Ramsey pricing retrieves costs by marking up marginal costs, with equal demand elasticities and equal traffic levels, the higher the marginal cost, the higher will be cost allocation. For example, in the previous numerical illustration, wheat and corn traffic were supposed to raise between them an amount equal to 5 above the subsidy-free minimum allocation to wheat of 7. Since the variable cost of wheat traffic is 12 and corn traffic is 15, if the elasticity of demand for transportation is the same for both grains, the Ramsey rule would charge wheat an additional 2.22 and corn 2.78. In order for the two traffic classes to make equal supplementary contributions, wheat traffic would have to have a substantially lower elasticity of demand.

CONCLUSION

The advice of transport economists has been solicited more on the topic of the allocation of fixed facilities costs than on any other subject. The reason is that fixed facilities costs are, for many modes, a large part of the total, and fixed facilities are often provided by governments. Economists are unanimous in repudiating the traditional technique of fully allocated costing. Under this procedure, costs are divided among users by dividing by some arbitrary usage indicator—tons, ton-miles, equivalent axle-miles, etc. Fully-allocated cost methods lead to inefficient use of facilities. They encourage further overcrowding of already congested facilities and discourage use of lightly-used routes. The traditional defense that they are based on equity considerations also can be disputed since what is equitable to one user may not appear so to another.

The first advice that the transport economist gives on the subject of cost allocation is to directly employ efficiency principles. In particular this means that congestion tolls be used as the fundamental method for financing fixed facilities costs. Using congestion tolls in facilities finance has the further advantage of giving an element of fiscal discipline in decisions of where investments should be made. But there are many circumstances in which efficiency considerations will call for building facilities which are not expected to be self-supporting. And economic efficiency criteria are based on opportunity costs, not financial costs. If a transport authority has a financial obligation that it must cover, efficiency principles will not always be helpful in giving guidance about how it should be done.

When efficiency principles are inadequate to produce useful cost allocations, transport economists have added the supplementary criteria that prices be subsidy-free: that the revenue paid by any combination of users must be at least as large as the incremental cost of providing services to those users. Unless revenues are at least as large as incremental costs, those users are being subsidized either by other users or by the taxpayer. The subsidy-free pricing principle is a powerful tool for determining which users or user groups should pay for particular fixed facilities in the transportation system. The costs of facilities that would be abandoned if a user group did not demand their services should be paid by that user group.

The principle of subsidy-free prices will not, in general, give strict dollar fixed cost responsibilities for each user. Instead, the rule will produce a series of inequalities that may provide narrow limits on the minimum and maximum amount of revenue that is to be raised from each user group of users. Since a user is likely to be a member of many different combinations of user groups, each of which will have minimum and maximum cost allocations, the subsidy-free pricing principle greatly reduces the degree of arbitrariness in the allocation of fixed costs beyond congestion tolls.

In almost every case, however, a degree of uncertainty will remain as to exactly which users should be assessed the responsibility for the fixed costs of the system. A principle that has been frequently recommended for assigning these costs is the Ramsey principle of second best pricing. Under the Ramsey principle, a fixed facilities owner is encouraged to engage in a degree of monopoly price discrimination by raising prices charged to user groups with inelastic demands more than prices charged to groups with higher demand elasticities. The degree to which monopoly pricing should be encouraged under the Ramsey principle is limited by the amount of fixed facilities costs that are to be recovered. Ramsey prices are an inefficient way of retrieving fixed costs and are justified only when nonlinear pricing schemes cannot be used; but they do have the advantage that they give an unequivocal answer to the question of who should bear the burden of the cost of providing fixed facilities.

NOTES

1. The first development of this principle is found in J. Dupuit, "On the Measurement of the Utility of Public Works," *Annales des Ponts et Chaussees, 2nd Series*, Vol. 8 (1844), reprinted in Denys Munby, *Transport: Selected Readings* (Baltimore: Penguin Books, 1968). The idea has since been rediscovered numerous times. See Richard W. Ault, Robert B. Ekelund Jr., "The Problem of Unnecessary Originality in Economics," *Southern Economic Journal*, Vol. 53, No. 3, January 1987, pp. 650–661. A modern survey can be found in Sanford V. Berg, and John Tschirhart, *Natural Monopoly Regulation: Principles and Practice* (Cambridge: Cambridge University Press, 1988). A classic application of peak-load pricing to highways is found in Herbert Mohring, "The Peak-load Problem with Increasing Returns and Pricing Constraints," *American Economic Review*, Vol. 60, No. 4 (September

1970), pp. 693–705. See also A. A. Walters, "The Allocation of Joint Costs with Demands as Probability Distributions," *American Economic Review*, Vol. 50 (1960), pp. 419–432.

2. The discussion in this chapter assumes that the costs to be covered by revenues of users are internal rather than external. The problem of subsidies that arise due to external costs will be treated in Chapter 14.

3. The original development of the idea was in terms of defecting from the network and setting up another one using identical technology. See Gerald R. Faulhaber, "Cross-Subsidization: Pricing in Public Enterprises," *American Economic Review*, Vol. 65 (1975), pp. 966–977. Given the dominance of sunk costs in transportation, this is not a useful way of thinking about transportation fixed facilities. Rather, standalone costs should be thought of in terms of forcing burdening groups outside the network.

4. It turns out that the problem of choosing a network to minimize costs is not mathematically easy. For an easy summary of the computational complexity of this problem, see Marshall W. Bern, and Ronald L. Graham, "The Shortest-Network Problem," *Scientific American* (January 1989), pp. 84–89. The example presented in this chapter is so small, however, that it can be solved simply by trying all possible ways to set up the network and choosing the one with the lowest costs.

5. The theory of subsidy-free pricing is closely related to the idea of contestable markets. See William Baumol, John C. Panzar, and Robert D. Willig, *Contestable Markets and the Theory of Industry Structure* (New York: Harcourt Brace Jovanovich, 1982). In this construction, there is no distinction between long- and short-run cost, thus blending the output and investment decisions. In the case of transportation fixed facilities decisions, this assumption is clearly inappropriate.

6. Kenneth A. Small, Clifford Winston, and Carol A. Evans, *Road Work: A New Highway Pricing and Investment Policy* (Washington, D.C.: The Brookings Institution, 1989).

7. There is no economic justification for basing prices on long-run marginal costs, despite the fact that the analysis in this chapter seems to suggest that long-run considerations may play a role in optimal pricing. See the exchange between John W. Jordan, "Capacity Costs, Heterogeneous Users, and Peak-Load Pricing (Heterogeneous Users and the Peak-Load Pricing Model)," *Quarterly Journal of Economics,* Vol. 100, No. 4, November 1985, pp. 1335–1337 and William Vickrey, "The Fallacy of Using Long-Run Cost for Peak-Load Pricing (Heterogeneous Users and the Peak-load Pricing Model)," *Quarterly Journal of Economics,* Vol. 100, No. 4, November 1985, pp. 1331–1334.

8. This terminology is due to G. W. Douglas, and J.C. Miller III, "Quality Competition in the Airline Market" *American Economic Review* Vol. 64, No. 4 (September 1974), pp. 657–669.

9. See, for example, Willig, Robert D., "Pareto Superior Nonlinear Outlay Schedules," *Bell Journal of Economics*, Vol. 9 (1978), pp. 56–59. On the general question of non-linear pricing schemes, see S. J. Brown, and D.S. Sibley, *The Theory of Public Utility Pricing* (Cambridge: Cambridge University Press, 1986).

10. For other possibilities, see Susan S. Hamlen, William H. Hamlen, and John T. Tschirhart, "The Use of Core Theory in Evaluating Joint Cost Allocation Schemes," *The Accounting Review*, Vol. 52, No. 3 (July 1977), pp. 616–627.

11. Philip Fanara Jr. and Curtis M. Grimm, "Stand-Alone Cost: Use and Abuse in Determining Maximum U.S. Railroad Rates," *Transportation Research-A*, Vol. 19A, No. 4 (1985), pp. 297–303.

12. The name *Ramsey pricing* was developed by William J. Baumol, and David F. Bradford in "Optimal Departures from Marginal Cost Pricing," *American Economic Review*, Vol. 60 (1970), pp. 265–283. Some recent theoretical contributions to the theory of Ramsey pricing in transportation are Richard Arnott, Marvin Kraus, "The Ramsey Problem for Congestible Facilities," *Journal of Public Economics,* Vol. 50, No. 3, March 1993, pp. 371–396; Kenneth E. Train, *Optimal Regulation: The Economic Theory of Natural Monopoly"* (Cambridge, Mass. and London: MIT Press, 1991); Tae Hoon Oum and Michael W. Tretheway, "Ramsey Pricing in the Presence of Externality Costs," *Journal of Transport Economics and Policy,* Vol. 22, No. 3, September 1988, pp. 307–317. A few of the recent discussions of practical application of Ramsey theory to transportation are Bruce W. Allen, "Ramsey Pricing in the Transportation Industries," *International Journal of Transport Economics,* Vol. 13, No. 3, October 1986, pp. 293–330; Henry McFarland, "Ramsey Pricing of Inputs with Downstream Monopoly Power and Regulation: Implications for Railroad Rate Setting," *Journal of Transport Economics and* Policy, Vol. 20, No. 1, January 1986, pp. 81–90; Sylvester Damus, "Ramsey Pricing by U.S. Railroads: Can It Exist?" *Journal of Transport Economics and Policy,* Vol. 18, No. 1, January 1984, pp. 51–62; and Steven A. Morrison, "The Structure of Landing Fees at Uncongested Airports: An Application of Ramsey Pricing," *Journal of Transport Economics and Policy*, Vol. 16, No. 2, May 1982, pp. 151–159.

13. In the typical transportation case where prices of different modes affect the demands of others, the Ramsey formula is far more complicated. See Ronald Braeutigam, "Optimal Pricing with Intermodal Competition," *American Economic Review*, Vol. 698 (1979), pp. 38–49.

IV

GOVERNMENT REGULATION OF TRANSPORTATION

12

Market Power in Transportation

The traditional focus of government regulation has been market power. The earliest experiences in regulation were almost exclusively in transportation. As transportation has been extensively deregulated, the transport industries are again being used to provide lessons on the general effects that regulation has on an industry.

Throughout the history of transport regulation, the perception of the extent of market power has been a matter of controversy among passengers, shippers, carriers, and land owners. To understand the regulation of market power in transportation, it is important to fix our perspective so that we can agree on how market power should be recognized. To gain this perspective, we will use a specific example of market power.

A PURE FIXED FACILITIES MONOPOLY

Toll bridges are not modes of transport, but rather fixed facilities that are used by other modes of transport. But toll bridges do sell their services to vehicle operators and it is possible for the toll bridge to have market power even if the vehicles using the bridge do not. Toll bridges are an especially simple example of how fixed facilities can lead to market power since, unlike railroads or air-lines, they are not integrated into vehicle operations.

The analysis of unregulated monopoly behavior in American industry has been hampered by the fact that there are virtually no cases of pure monopoly other than those granted by patents or licenses. Similarly, there are no examples of unregulated transportation operators that are monopolies and there are no unregulated monopoly toll bridges. This example will therefore be based on a hypothetical derivation of how one toll bridge would operate if it were per-mitted to operate without any controls placed on it by government authorities. The example discussed is that of the Mackinac Bridge in northern Michigan. This bridge is the only surface transportation connection between the Upper and Lower peninsulas of Michigan. For travelers or shippers between the two peninsulas, the only alternatives to using the bridge are to fly or to drive an extra 500 miles or more around Lake Michigan via Chicago. With no practical alternatives to using the bridge, the Mackinac Bridge Authority has a monop-oly on travel and freight transportation between the peninsulas. Moreover, the monopoly is absolutely secure since there are no other practical sites to build another bridge. It would be a classic example of a monopoly but for the fact that the bridge is owned by the state of Michigan's Mackinac Bridge Authority rather than by a private firm. State ownership means that profit maximizing tendencies are restrained. Currently the bridge authority charges $1.50 per passenger car (plus $1.00 for each additional axle; more for heavy trucks). This fare was established following the advice of the state legislature which lent the funds to build the bridge. The original charge for passenger cars was $3.75. As is typical of bridge finance, when the bonds used to finance the bridge were paid off, the fare dropped to reflect the fact that amortization payments were no longer needed.

The bridge cost approximately $150 million to build in 1956 and is among the longest suspension bridges in the world. There is virtually no traffic con-gestion at any time of the year and thus no hope of retrieving the costs of the bridge through optimal congestion tolls. The bridge needs constant maintenance due to brutal winter weather; vehicles cause little in the way of depreciation or traffic control costs. In short, the opportunity cost of crossing the bridge is nil. The bridge is used by residents of the sparsely populated Eastern Upper Peninsula as their main connection with the rest of the United States. The main economic activity in the Eastern Upper Peninsula is tourism, with a limited amount of industry based on forest products. The main freight across the bridge consists of supplies for residents crossing to the north and some forest products southbound. Most passenger traffic consists of local residents or tourists in private automobiles. There is essentially no bus traffic.

▬ Classic Simple Monopoly Pricing

It is an interesting and instructive intellectual exercise to imagine how a private firm that followed the strict principles of profit maximization would operate the

FIGURE 12.1   Simple Monopoly Pricing

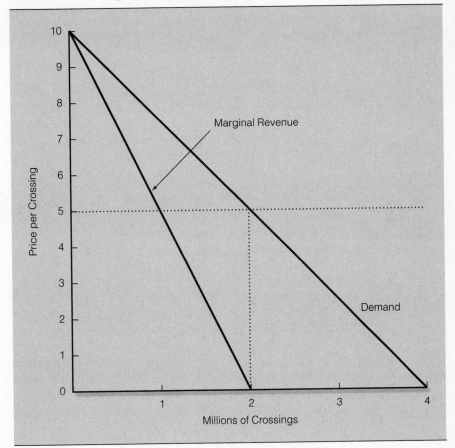

bridge differently. Figure 12.1 shows a hypothetical demand curve for crossings of the Mackinac Bridge. If this were the true demand curve, the classic analysis of monopoly behavior says that a private firm would raise the fare to $5.00, thus reducing the number of crossings to 2 million. At this point, revenue to the bridge owner is maximized (as is profit, since all costs are assumed to be fixed). This is shown by the marginal revenue curve—constructed as the addition to revenue from allowing one more bridge crossing, after making adjustments for the necessary reduction in price to induce one more bridge crossing—having a value of 0 when 2 million crossings are made. Total revenue that the profit maximizing fare would generate is $10 million. If the fares were lowered below $5.00, the increase in crossings would not compensate for the price reduction necessary to generate the increase in business; for fares higher than $5.00, the price increases would not compensate for the fall in the number of crossings.

The efficient price, in contrast to the profit maximizing price, is equal to opportunity cost of a crossing, which is essentially 0. Thus the efficient number of crossings would be 4 million. The total benefit from the bridge would be given by the area under the demand curve computed as $10 \times 4/2 = \$20$ million/year. The bridge owner, using monopoly pricing, is able to capture only $10 million of this amount. Two areas of consumer benefit would remain uncaptured by a monopolist: the area below the demand curve but above the $5.00 price line, which remains as consumers' surplus to users; and the area under the demand curve to the right of the 5 million crossings line, which is the deadweight loss of monopoly pricing. Deadweight losses are pure inefficiencies; they represent value of services that are not provided (at zero cost) because potential users are unwilling to pay the fare. Each of these areas is $5 million. A rational firm would try to find ways to capture both of these benefit areas as profit to itself. The way that the bridge operator can capture these areas is to change its pricing mechanism from a single price per crossing to a more complex price structure.

Market Segmentation Pricing

Charging different prices for the same product is price discrimination. For most industrial products, price discrimination is impractical due to the problems of resale. An aluminum monopoly could not sell a standard grade of the product at two different prices to two different customer classes since those who purchase at a low price could resell the commodity to those charged a higher price by the manufacturer. In order for price discrimination to be successful, a seller must control its market. At a minimum, it must be able to evaluate the demands of its buyers and be able to distinguish units of sale that can command a high price and those for which it can expect only a low price; it must also be able to prevent units that are sold at a low price from being substituted for units that should command a high price. Transportation companies are in an especially good position to engage in price discrimination. It is generally possible to find a characteristic of customers that indicates their level of demand and, since the service is not storable, it cannot be resold: Production (bridge crossings) is instantaneously consumed by those crossing the bridge.

One can speculate on what sort of indicators a monopoly such as the fictitious Mackinac Bridge Corporation might use to discriminate among its customers. One possible characteristic might be whether the customer lived locally or was a tourist from more distant parts of the state or from out of state. Local residents are likely to use the bridge more frequently, but are also likely to be much more price sensitive in their use of the bridge. For tourists, the bridge toll is a small part of the total cost of their vacation; it is unlikely that they would be greatly affected in their decision to take a vacation in the Upper Peninsula

FIGURE 12.2   Market Segmentation Price Discrimination

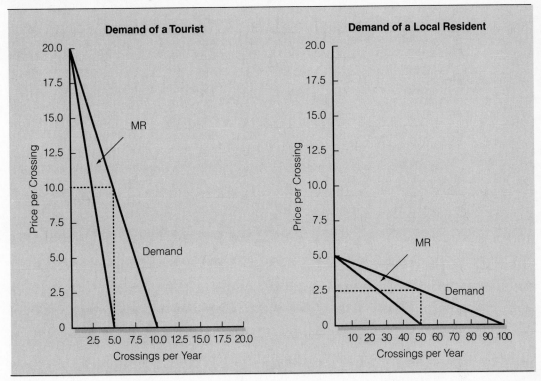

if bridge tolls were $10.00. Local residents are, by contrast, likely to take far fewer shopping or recreation trips across the bridge if tolls were $10.00 rather than $1.50. Figure 12.2 shows a pair of demand curves that are consistent with this logic. The left panel shows the demand curve for bridge crossings by a typical tourist while the right panel shows the demand curve by a local resident.[1] For reasons described above, the tourist demand is shown as steeper than the demand by a typical local resident, while the local resident's demand curve extends much farther to the right. The profit maximizing price to local residents, $2.50, is much lower than the profit maximizing price to charge to tourists: $10.00. The likely form that such price discrimination would take is to set the tourist price as the standard price and then allow local residents to cross at a discount from the standard price by showing a pass that certifies local residency.

There are other indicators that the Mackinac Bridge Corporation could use to segment its market: It could charge higher prices on weekends, when the bridge is more likely to be used by tourists, and lower prices during the week.

Alternatively, it could offer lower prices at inconvenient times in the expectation that those who were willing to postpone their usage until those times are people who have higher price sensitivities. It could also provide bridge crossings cheaply one particular day of each week which would be announced in advance in local newspapers; the market would then segment itself by the cost that users are willing to undertake to get the information necessary to know when cheap fares are offered. The Bridge Corporation could also distribute coupons in local newspapers offering substantial discounts on crossings in the knowledge that only those who are price sensitive will take the time to look for and clip the coupons.

All of these market segmentation techniques, referred to in the economics literature as *third degree price discrimination*, are designed to help the Bridge Corporation to capture some of the total willingness to pay for bridge crossings that is either wasted as deadweight loss or retained by users as consumers' surplus when a single monopoly price is charged. It is likely, however, that a private, profit-maximizing Bridge Corporation would not be satisfied with these measures and would likely look for other techniques to capture more of the total benefit of the bridge. Even with third degree price discrimination, there is still a deadweight loss and consumers still retain some surplus.

Two-Part Tariffs

A rational monopoly will look for ways to increase the amount of total benefit that it is able to capture. To do this it will need to change the technique of charging for its services. Referring back to Figure 12.2, it is easy to calculate that the maximum total benefit that the typical tourist could get from the bridge is $100. The maximum total benefit that a typical local resident could get from the bridge is $250. The goal of the Bridge Corporation would be get that amount from each person. If it could do this, it could capture all consumers' surplus as well as eliminate the inefficiency created by monopoly pricing. But this is easy to do. Simply offer to local residents an annual sticker that allowed for unlimited free bridge crossings and charge a lump sum amount equal to $250 for the right. Tourists would be offered annual subscriptions for $100.

Offering annual subscriptions for bridge crossings is an efficient way of converting social benefit into revenue from users to the Bridge Corporation. It has the equivalent effect to what is known as *first degree price discrimination*, under which a consumer is charged the maximum price that he or she would pay for each unit of consumption.

Unlike the case of simple market segmentation pricing, if the Bridge Corporation can sell an annual pass, local residents will pay a much higher fee for their pass than tourists. In order to make the scheme administratively feasible, the Bridge Corporation would probably have to offer two different unlimited crossing passes: perhaps an annual pass for $250 per year and a weekly pass for $25 per week. In order to make the passes attractive, the Bridge Corporation might have to raise the price of a crossing to a price so high that few users would choose *not* to buy the pass. The Bridge Corporation might also offer the passes at lower prices to senior citizens or to the poor in order to further segment the market. Such a combination of first and third degree price discrimination is usually necessary for profit maximization. A private Mackinac Bridge Corporation would probably experiment with a number of different combinations of prices for crossings and passes targeted at different groups until it found the combination that provided it with the most revenue.

Promotions and Tie-Ins

An aggressive Bridge Corporation is unlikely to passively accept the demand curves which were the basis for pricing in the previous section. It would attempt to manipulate the demand curves as well. Such a program would start with an advertising campaign in areas where tourists live in the hope of encouraging them to take a trip across the bridge. But since the bridge's business is dependent on the attractiveness of the area to which tourists go, it is logical that the Bridge Corporation would take an active role in making sure that the areas on either end of the bridge were developed in a way that maximized the number of bridge crossings. One possibility would be to try to make sure that shopping and services were available at only one side of the bridge. Those needing furniture, for example, might have to cross the bridge in one direction while those who needed to buy an automobile would have to cross the bridge in the other direction.

A more likely possibility is that the Bridge Corporation would take an active role in developing land in the area, encouraging land owners to create resorts that are attractive to tourists who live on the other side of the bridge. The Bridge Corporation could probably buy large parcels of land and develop them in a way that was attractive to people who would take the bridge as opposed to flying into the area, for example.

Alternatively, the Bridge Corporation could work with local residents to develop land in a way that generated the greatest demand for bridge crossings. A development corporation would probably be set up to give advice and market analysis to potential developers. As an added inducement, the Bridge Corporation would probably enter into tie-in promotions under which resorts could offer tourists a package that included a pass to cross the bridge; the Bridge Corporation would probably insist that this tie-in be offered to all customers of the resort rather than being optional. In fact, offering such a tie-in would probably allow the Bridge Corporation to further raise the price of a bridge pass. Resort owners who did not come to an agreement with the Bridge Corporation on a joint promotion program would find themselves at a disadvantage, since their customers would have to pay an increased toll whereas their competitors' customers would not have to. The Bridge Corporation could then use this fact as a bargaining tool when it had discussions with each of the land owners on the price that they would pay to join with the Bridge Corporation in creating a package deal for their customers.

Promotional tie-ins between land owners and the bridge, while apparently quite attractive, are in fact quite dangerous to land owners. A clever Bridge Corporation could use the tie-ins to capture all land rents in the area to which access requires use of the bridge: A resort owner who appeared to be doing well would be charged a high fee for the tie-in promotion while a resort that appeared to be only marginal could be charged a low fee. The development office would probably spend a good part of its time trying to evaluate the maximum fee that could be charged to each land owner before it caused him or her to shut the operation. The Bridge Corporation could also refuse to deal with a resort owner, thus forcing them out of business if they thought that the resort was not bringing enough traffic to the bridge.

The ability to control access to one's land and property gives tremendous economic power to those who control economic access. *Economic power* is a name given to the discretion that the Bridge Corporation has over setting business conditions that have an important influence on the lives of the land owners and residents in the area. If the Bridge Corporation is successful in its attempts to maximize its profits, virtually all implicit rents on land for which the bridge provides access can be transferred to the bridge corporation. That is, all benefits of the bridge would be transferred to the monopoly.

It is also the case that following the promotion and tie-in campaigns, total benefits of the bridge may also have increased. Compared with the period before the bridge was turned over to private owners, crossings may have increased due to the lower marginal toll, and there may in addition be greater economic development in the area due to the Bridge Corporation's energetic promotion. Yet the survival of local businesses would be dependent on a favorable annual negotiation with the Bridge Corporation. The wish to control this private discretion, if history is any guide, would cause area residents and land owners to take actions to protect themselves from the Bridge Corporation.

Economist's Advice

At this point—indeed, well before this point—an attempt would have begun to try to rein in the economic power of the Bridge Corporation. It is unlikely that landowners and local residents would be willing to have their welfare decided by a private corporation over which they have no control. The ability to price discriminate and thus transfer benefits of the bridge to the Bridge Corporation would be taken as evidence of naked monopoly power that needs to be restrained. If it were technically feasible, local residents would probably try to organize a company to build a second bridge to provide competition that would allow them to escape from the their vulnerability to decisions made by the

Bridge Corporation. Since it appears technologically infeasible, a ferry service would probably be organized and improved air service implemented.

Land owners and local residents would also probably try to use regulation, public ownership, or other means to limit the ability of the Bridge Corporation to price discriminate. When the possibility of government intervention was contemplated, expert economic advice would probably be called in to comment on whether or not local residents' complaints were justified. What would the economist say?

Using the strict efficiency standpoint of economic analysis, the economist would determine whether the optimal number of bridge crossings were made. The economist would note that the replacement of individual fares by passes allowing unlimited crossings made the marginal price of crossing the bridge zero, thus encouraging the efficient use of the resource. Indeed, there is an efficiency gain compared with the period where cars were charged per crossing since more cars cross the bridge with the pass system. The economist would further note that in order to prevent bridge users from being cross-subsidized by others, the Bridge Corporation must use at least some price discrimination to cover its fixed costs if it is to charge the efficient price. The bridge is technically a *natural monopoly* since average cost slopes down throughout the entire extent of the market, making provision of service by one provider the cheapest way to satisfy demand.

The introduction of ferry service to compete with the bridge would probably be criticized by the economist because, with excess capacity on the bridge, it is wasteful to carry some passengers using expensive ferries when these passengers could cross at virtually no additional cost to society if they were to use the bridge. The community could provide its transportation needs more cheaply by relying solely on the bridge rather than introducing a second mode of transportation. The economist, in short, would come down entirely on the side of the Bridge Corporation, perhaps noting in addition that the Corporation had worked hard to increase economic development and that bridge crossings had increased since the bridge was privatized, indicating that the piece of capital was getting more use and thus a greater benefit than ever. To be sure, the people around the bridge may be poorer due to having to buy expensive annual passes or having to enter into partnership with the bridge to offer passes to customers, but the transfer of rents to the Bridge Corporation, the economist might note, is simply a matter of income redistribution, on the desirability of which economic analysis has no special insight.

■ The Valuation of Facilities

This advice will undoubtedly not satisfy those who worry about the economic power of the Bridge Corporation. The reason is that residents are concerned about the exercise of economic power or private discretion, while the economist's advice is based simply on efficiency effects. The Bridge Corporation in a real sense would have the ability to dictate which of the businesses in the area survived and which did not. This is surely economic power and is bound to be resented even if it is used wisely. Americans have traditionally been suspicious of such concentrations of economic power in private hands and have looked toward the government to protect themselves against its misuse.

It is important to recognize that while the Bridge Corporation will be accused of being a monopoly, the charge against it is not really economic inefficiency, but rather the possession of the power to dictate to area residents who lives and who dies. Thus the economist, in using a strict efficiency analysis of what is optimal, may be missing the heart of the complaint. But this is typical of regulatory proceedings in which the concern is about the exercise of power but the discussion is in terms of the public interest, which can be thought of as questions of economic efficiency.

The opponents of the Bridge Corporation will counter the economist's arguments saying that, while of course the Bridge Corporation is entitled to cover its costs, this does not justify the degree and extent of price discrimination that it is undertaking. At this point, the discussion would probably turn to the minimum amount of revenue that the Bridge Corporation is entitled to. The argument will be that one cannot complain about market power unless the bridge is making a monopoly profit—that is, revenues so far in excess of costs that it must clearly be evidence of monopoly behavior. But how much revenue is too much? The answer given in Chapter 11 is that subsidy-free pricing requires that at least as much revenue be raised from users as the annual opportunity cost of maintaining the bridge for transportation purposes. This includes maintenance and depreciation costs as well as an annual payment necessary to induce bridge owners to keep it used for transportation instead of in its next best alternative use.

But all expenses in bridge building are sunk: There is no non-transportation use for a bridge. Thus, argues the anti-bridge group, the revenue which the private firm is economically justified in raising is simply the annual maintenance and depreciation with no return for invested capital. The economist must agree that this is correct. On the one hand total transfer to the Bridge Corporation of profits to be made by property owners and, on the other hand, total confiscation of property by refusing the Bridge Corporation any rate of return on its investment are both consistent with economic efficiency as long as the price charged for a bridge crossing is zero at the margin.

If the anti-bridge group is successful in arguing that the economic power of the Bridge Corporation needs to be restrained by having the government set limits on the revenues it can earn, the standard that will probably be used is the famous *fair return on fair value*. A fair return is usually taken to be approximately equal to a market return on capital. But what is a fair value of the bridge? Following are some possible ways of valuing the bridge.

Opportunity Cost

The opportunity cost of the bridge, as noted previously, is its value in the next best alternative use. Thus the minimum revenue that is required by the Bridge Corporation is simply an amount above maintenance and depreciation expenditures that just induces the company to stay in operation rather than to sell the bridge for scrap. To set the value of the bridge at opportunity cost is to confiscate its value.

The argument against setting the value of the bridge at its opportunity cost and confiscating for the community its commercial value is that it would scare off future investment. If the community is confident that this investment is unique and that there will never be a need for any kind of future investment, there is no efficiency penalty from preventing the Bridge Corporation from earning a return on its investment. It is a rare circumstance, however, where a region wishes to be known as a place where investors need to fear the loss of their capital if they choose to invest there. In order to keep the option of future investments open, a regulator will surely allow the bridge owner to earn a return on a positive value of the bridge.

Market Value

The market value of a bridge is the present discounted value of profits that a bridge owner could earn from the asset. Thus the valuation of a bridge is dependent on how much revenue the bridge owner can earn. The logic of fair return on fair value is circular when fair value is calculated as market value. Valuing the bridge at the present discounted value of the maximum monopoly profits means that the bridge owner who charges monopoly prices will only earn a market return on the value of the asset. In fact, no matter what pricing policy is decided on for the bridge, the market value of the bridge will adjust to guarantee that a market return on market value is always earned. The capitalization of monopoly profits in the value of an asset is the reason that governments looking to maximize the relief that they can give their taxpayers by getting as high a price as possible for privatized assets will sell the facilities to a party that will hold them as a monopoly rather than sell them to operators who would compete against one another. In the case of the Bridge Corporation, if the value of the bridge is determined by its earning capacity as a monopoly operation, and if the company is allowed to earn a normal rate of return on those assets, regulation will provide no relief to those complaining about the high prices charged by the bridge.

Depreciated Original Cost

This is the value of the bridge on accounting books. It is easy to calculate. In times of inflation, this method tends to place a low value on assets that were built many years earlier when labor, equipment, and materials costs were much lower than they are today. Moreover, since depreciation schedules used by accountants tend to be arbitrary, it is unlikely to represent true economic depreciation of even the undervalued resources used to build it. The use of depreci-ated original cost of assets as a valuation technique prevents the owner of the bridge from benefiting from the capital gains that would naturally accrue to someone holding a similar asset that could be bought or sold on the open market. The use of depreciated original cost in inflationary times is highly ben-eficial to consumers. (Indeed, with the bonds used to finance bridge construc-tion retired as previously noted, the bridge structure is currently carried on the books of the Bridge Authority at a value of zero).

Depreciated Replacement Cost

In order to prevent the obvious undervaluation of assets that depreciated orig-inal cost entails, one could value the bridge at the cost of replacing it at today's prices. If there has been little change in technology, there would be little diffi-culty in making this calculation: Simply make a list of all the types of labor, material, and land values used and, instead of valuing them at 1956 prices, value them at today's prices. This technique quickly becomes impractical, how-ever, in the case where there has been a change in technology. If new materials or methods for bridge building have been developed (or if a better site for the bridge had been discovered) since 1956, the task will be far more complex. Economic values are always based on satisfying demand at the least cost way—i.e., with best current technology. In the case where there has been dramatic technological progress, calculating the replacement cost of the bridge will prob-ably require a complete re-engineering of the project. The cost of a bridge with optimum technology would be calculated and then depreciation schedules applied in recognition of the age of the current structure. Despite its technical difficulties, depreciated replacement cost is the economist's favorite technique for valuing resources that would be replaced if they did not exist since it comes closest to the concept of opportunity cost. It is probably the value that an eco-nomic expert would recommend for determining the minimum amount of rev-enue that a Bridge Corporation should receive from its customers.

Distributing Fixed Costs

But determining an amount of revenue that the Bridge Corporation would be allowed to earn is only the first part of the problem. The second part is how to distribute the revenue requirement between local residents and tourists. If the Bridge Corporation is allowed to raise its revenue only by tolls rather than passes and if the tolls must be uniform within each class of customers, then the powerful Ramsey rules can be used to determine an allocation of revenue. The customer class with the higher elasticity of demand will be charged the lower price. But as noted in the previous chapter there is in transportation rarely a need to limit pricing alternatives in this way, and thus it is unnecessary to accept the inefficiencies implicit in Ramsey pricing. Most transportation firms are able to track their customers' purchases well enough that they can charge the equivalent of two-part tariffs. With two-part tariffs, it is possible to achieve an efficient use of the facility while maintaining its financial integrity.

Assuming that the Bridge Corporation does use passes or other types of two-part tariffs, there is little advice that the economist can give as to how the prices of the passes should be set. Since there would be no saving of fixed facilities costs from eliminating either class of customers, the subsidy-free pricing rules will not help to make the allocation. If the Bridge Corporation could cover all of the revenue requirement from selling passes to tourists without having to retrieve any of it from local residents, it would be efficient to do so, just as would be the reverse case if it is feasible (assuming that the price of a pass is set sufficiently low that no potential user balks at buying one). Someone will need to pay for the bridge, but economic criteria cannot tell who it should be.

This is a situation familiar to regulators who see themselves as setting rules based on fairness, resolving disputes among three parties: the Bridge Corporation, local residents, and tourists. Regulatory statutes invariably direct regulators to look for a solution that is fair to all parties. In the example here, a broad range of values for the bridge and of allocations of revenues between local residents and tourists were consistent with rules of economic efficiency and subsidy-free pricing and thus there is broad latitude that a regulator would have to set prices on the basis of equity criteria. (In more complex networks, economic criteria are likely to impose narrower bounds for prices, and there is thus a danger that regulation will introduce a variety of inefficiencies.)

RECOGNIZING AND CONTROLLING MARKET POWER

It is natural that small firms and individuals will see market power where larger firms see none. As noted above, what those who worry about market power are concerned with is the exercise of discretion or the transfer of rents. If a firm does have market power in this sense, how can one tell whether it is using that power to harm the economy; or alternatively, how can we recognize a price structure that is justified under the criteria of efficiency and subsidy-free pricing?

It is economically efficient to ensure that prices paid for transportation are equal to their opportunity cost. In particular, this means that when deciding on whether to make another shipment or take another trip, the user must be faced with a price equal to marginal cost. But subsidy-free pricing may also require that additional sums be levied on users to pay for fixed facilities. The next part of this chapter will describe how these principles are applied to different modes of transportation and the extent to which competitive forces can be relied on to generate efficient and subsidy-free price structures without the need for government regulation.

Fully Integrated Operators: Railroads

In the period during which railroads were subject to very restrictive regulation, observers thought it contradictory that shippers would complain about the monopoly power of railroads at the same time that they were not making even a normal rate of return on their invested capital. But this misses the point. The railroad mode is the only one that is fully integrated. Individual operators own vehicles, own fixed facilities, and provide service. This integration gives railroads considerable discretion in pricing their services—more than any other mode of transportation. But it was exactly this discretion that was at the heart of the arguments for public control of the Mackinac Bridge Corporation at the beginning of this chapter. This is likely the reason that railroads are the sole domestic mode of transportation that are still subject to meaningful economic regulation.

The first step in analyzing railroad market power is to measure costs that are attributable to individual users. As with any transportation service, the efficient price to charge to a railroad customer is the opportunity cost of providing the service. Market power will lead to pricing above the efficient level. The opportunity cost in turn is calculated as the sum of the opportunity cost of owning fixed facilities, the opportunity cost of owning vehicles, and the opportunity cost of handling freight and passengers in moving vehicles. When the sum of payments for opportunity costs fail to cover the full costs of operations, the second criterion of subsidy-free prices needs to be invoked. The implications for these two pricing criteria for railroad rates are described below.

Allocating Train Costs

The attribution of train costs to individual cars in the train is done in a way that is formally identical to the assignment of airline flight costs to individual passengers described in Chapter 11. As with airline costs, user costs must be included in the calculation. The opportunity cost of moving one additional car on a train is the difference in the full costs of operating the system with and without the car. For example, if an extra car is included in a train, the extra fuel of pulling it will be part of the opportunity cost of the movement; so will be the time taken to couple and uncouple the car from the train. Potentially far more important, however, are the extra transit time that including one more car in a train will impose on other shippers. This is equivalent to a congestion cost and must be attributed to individual cars. The longer the train, the higher will be the congestion costs imposed by each additional car. These marginal congestion costs should be charged to the shipper that has caused delays in the dispatch of others' freight.

In parallel with the airline case, as additional cars are added to a train, congestion costs will rise until it is less expensive to operate two shorter trains rather than one long one. Efficient train operation requires that the cost minimizing number of trains per day be run, with the number of cars determined by the requirement that price be equal to the opportunity cost of adding additional cars. As in the case of airlines, there is no guarantee that the sum of congestion costs will be equal to the total opportunity cost of running a train. It is, in fact, far more likely that the sum of efficient prices will be greater or (in general) less than the sum of efficient payments from each user. When this occurs, the principle of subsidy-free pricing must be invoked. Subsidy-free pricing requires that the elimination of any group of users from the system cannot reduce the costs that remaining users are required to pay. This, in turn, says that the users of each train must pay at least the opportunity cost of running the train. This is one of many restrictions that the subsidy-free pricing principle will place on charges. As noted above, the efficient way to raise the additional sums that may be required is to tax each of the users with a lump sum tax, though it is unlikely that the subsidy-free principles will give a definitive statement on exactly how much of the train cost each shipper should pay. That is, it may be possible to determine that as a group users of a particular train should pay $1,000 in addition to the congestion tolls that are due for using the train, but it may be impossible to tell how that $1,000 should be broken down among the users. Any allocation appears to be as economically justified as any other, as long as it does not cause any user to decide not to use the train.

Allocating Track Costs

Railroad tracks are used by a variety of commodities being moved between many different points. In most of the world, railroad tracks are shared by freight and passenger trains. The problem of track costing is to attribute the cost of track ownership to individual tickets or to individual shipments that use the track. Few of these costs can be attributed directly to depreciation caused by particular shipments or passengers to the tracks. Rather, the familiar techniques of congestion pricing and subsidy-free pricing must be used to approach the problem.

Most American railroad tracks are not used to capacity, in the sense that it would be possible to operate more trains per day over each track. Nonetheless, in most instances, the use of tracks by more than one train at a time has a tendency to reduce operating speeds. This is especially noticeable in a single track system used by trains in both directions. Such operations require that one train wait at a siding to allow the train approaching it to pass. The more crowded the track, the more frequently the trains will have to wait on sidings and thus average trip times will be slower. But this logic parallels that used to justify congestion tolls for private passenger cars. The diagrams of the marginal cost of a train operation would look identical to those presented for automobiles. When there is a choice between one track and two, the diagrams will look like those in Chapter 11 drawn for an airline choosing between one flight or two flights per day in a time slot. Where passenger and freight trains share a track, the congestion tolls to freight trains must include the cost penalty of slowing passenger trains as well as other freight trains. Efficient congestion pricing would encourage freight trains to use congested tracks at times of the day when delays to passenger trains were less, or to use routes without passenger trains.

As in all cases of congestion tolls with lumpy facilities, there is no guarantee that the total revenue collected from congestion tolls will equal the opportunity cost of maintaining the facility for transportation purposes. Congestion tolls for a particular link of railroad might amount to more or less than the annual payments for labor and equipment to keep the line in good operating condition plus a payment to offset the alternative use of the land. The lighter the traffic on a line, the lower will be the congestion tolls and the less likely it will be that a link's opportunity costs will be covered. As with each of the other modes discussed in this chapter, to assure that the opportunity costs of fixed facilities are paid by users, the subsidy-free criterion must be imposed.

The principle that prices should not be cross-subsidizing says that every user and group of users must pay revenues that are in total (1) at least as large as the opportunity cost of serving them and (2) no larger than the minimum cost of operating a network that served only that user or group of individuals. Chapter 11 presented an extended example to show that cost allocations that are subsidy-free are not obvious. They depend on exactly how operations would be changed if particular users or groups of users were to be removed from the system. In some cases, removing users would allow substantial savings in the fixed costs of a system by permitting extensive abandonment. The users whose presence causes the maintenance of those facilities should, under the principles of subsidy-free pricing, pay for the opportunity costs of owning those facilities. In other cases, removing a group of users would have little effect on the efficient operation of the system. These users would then have, at best, a small responsibility for the costs of the system beyond those covered by congestion tolls.

Subsidy-free pricing principles can help allocate track costs between passenger and freight trains. Tracks designed for passenger trains are generally constructed for much faster operation. They are banked higher on curves and are maintained to provide a smoother ride. If a link is used only by freight trains, there is a considerable saving in the opportunity costs of fixed facilities by reducing the permissible track maintenance standard. The principle of subsidy-free pricing says that passenger trains should make a revenue contribution at least as great as the increase in cost to bring track standards to passenger train levels.

The practical difficulty in implementing subsidy-free pricing standards for railroad rates should not be underestimated. The rule requires that separate opportunity cost calculations be made for a railroad system containing every possible combination of users. The power of the rule in allocating costs comes from the limits placed on contributions by the thousands of different inequalities generated by combining users in different ways. But each of these calculations depends on a hypothetical engineering of the system: that is, projecting what the most efficient way to organize a railroad would be if it contained only this or that customer group. Such hypothetical calculations can be costly and of questionable reliability.

Railroad Shippers Are Price Sensitive

If railroad cost finding were easier, it would be possible to give much more useful advice on how rail rates should be structured. While railroads undoubtedly have economic power over at least some of their users, and while the principles covering efficient pricing are clear (though incomplete in the sense that subsidy-free cost allocations are rarely unique), it is by no means sure that it is possible to judge whether or not railroads are exercising their economic power. To do so would require that an outside observer be able to perform the necessary cost studies to see whether railroads are pricing excessively high above their own costs.

Unfortunately, the results of railroad cost analysis can have life-or-death consequences to shippers and carriers; thus transport economists who propose cost standards for railroad pricing are likely to be challenged precisely in those places in which they are least confident. The reason is found in the type of freight carried by railroads. For the most part, railroad freight consists of *commodity products*, that is, products that are good substitutes for products of other sellers. For example, newsprint, an important railroad commodity, is a product that is sold by many producers and has a price that is determined not by any one seller but by supply and demand conditions at each locality. A single seller of a commodity product cannot ask for higher prices to compensate it for higher railroad rates; sellers of commodity products are price takers. The only way that newsprint makers will be able to pass along some of a railroad rate increase is if all sellers have to pay the same rate increase. The fact that the price that sellers can get for their products depends on the rates charged to their competitors leads to an intense concern about the structure of rates; for newsprint makers, it is far more important that their rates be low relative to their competitors than that the rates for newsprint shipment as a whole be low. (This is a very different situation from motor carriers where a few cents' change in a freight rate will not make a production location uneconomic.)

A price increase to a single shipper of newsprint not charged to other sellers will come directly out of the profits of the company. Price-cost margins on commodity products are typically small and transportation costs are a large portion of the selling price. As a result railroad customers are extremely sensitive to the rates that are charged. Under railroad regulation, shippers could appeal individual railroad rates to regulatory authorities. The regulatory agency might then turn to economic analysis to give some guidance on what the structure of rates should be. Unfortunately, the complexity of railroad costing rarely allows concrete answers to be given. It is far easier to describe the principles of efficient railroad pricing than to settle on a particular set of numbers as accurately reflecting true railroad costs. It is small wonder that regulatory authorities relied on gross rules of thumb like fully allocated cost measures and the evaluation of rate reasonableness by making comparisons with similar shipments. Unfortunately, as shall be described in the next chapter, this method of railroad regulation proved disastrous both to carriers and their customers.

Fully Unintegrated Commercial Vehicle Operators (Truckload Motor Carriers, Charter Planes and Buses, Charter Barge Operators, and Tramp Tankers)

To describe the problem of market power that fixed facilities ownership gives to transportation companies, it was most useful to develop a hypothetical example. By contrast, the opposite case in which the lack of ownership of fixed facilities means that operators have no market power is easily described using real examples.

Since the price that private transporters pay is identical with the costs they incur, their pricing must be efficient as long as their costs are correctly charged. As discussed above, the most prominent source of inefficiency for private vehicle transportation is the failure to correctly charge for the use of scarce road and runway space. The transport services considered in this section are closely related to private vehicles: Fixed facilities costs are minor and do not have any network economies of operations. They differ from private transportation only in that they sell their services to others. These modes are susceptible to exactly the same type of inefficiencies that private vehicle operators are: Unless fixed facilities are correctly charged for, the prices charged by unintegrated operators are likely to be inefficient.

Transport operators who neither own nor lease any fixed facilities are free to move their vehicles to wherever they can find a load. The vehicles that they use are standard equipment with a ready second-hand market. A truckload operator who carries a load of lumber from Oregon to California has no practical limitation in the type of load or in geographic location of other loads that he or she can carry. A shipper who finds that Schneider provides a better price for hauling motors from Milwaukee to Peoria than that offered by J.B. Hunt can easily switch from one carrier to another. The carrier who loses a load can simply move equipment to another location without any penalty other than a few more empty miles.

Industries in which entry into particular submarkets is easy and which involve no sunk costs are characterized as *contestable*. The word contestable is used in place of the word competitive to emphasize that particular traffic lanes may have only a few carriers, and thus may look to be oligopolistic or non-competitive, but the carriers on those lanes may still be limited in their ability to price above cost by the fear of loss of traffic to other carriers. The concept of contestability is most useful when markets are not clearly delimited; contestability theory tells us that in these cases, the structure of particular submarkets is less important than entry and exit conditions for determining the price structure that an unregulated market would set. According to contestability theory, prices charged when entry and exit is free and instantaneous and scale and scope economies are unimportant will be equal to opportunity cost. That is, fully unintegrated commercial vehicle operators will be like private vehicle operators in that there is no difference between prices and opportunity costs. The same tools that are available for ensuring efficient service offerings in private transportation are also available to ensure efficiency when transporters are fully unintegrated. In particular, congestion tolls can be used to ensure optimal use of fixed facilities.

While it seems clear that market power should not be a problem in fully unintegrated modes, several have been subjected to economic regulation in years past. The standard arguments have pointed to ruinously low prices charged for services. The implication is that a price war, which was presumed to be the reason for the low prices, would force firms out of the market one by one until a single firm or a tight knit oligopoly resulted. This argument now seems quaint, but it is nonetheless useful to analyze the source of the periodically very low prices charged in this sector of the transport market.

Importance of Supply/Demand Balance in Vehicle Markets

Pricing for unintegrated commercial operators is dominated by the opportunity cost of using vehicles in any particular submarket. As discussed in Chapter 10, the opportunity cost of using a vehicle in any traffic lane will depend on directional supply/demand balances. When there is an imbalance of inbound traffic, providing a pool of equipment that needs to be returned to pick up another load, the opportunity cost of using a vehicle on that run will be extremely low. The price that one would expect for such a back-haul is little more than the loading and unloading expenses plus the extra fuel and insurance required to run full rather than empty; this pricing imbalance is efficient since it exactly corresponds to the opportunity costs of moving vehicles in each direction. On the other hand, the price that one would expect for a haul where no back-haul is anticipated is the opportunity cost of tying up the vehicle and driver both on the outbound direction as well as the return. According to the principle of back-haul pricing outlined in Chapter 10, if traffic flows are balanced, the total cost of the round trip will be shared between the two directions according to the height of demand in each direction; the prices charged will be those that cause the quantity demanded for trips to be equal in both directions.

The opportunity cost of a vehicle-day is in turn determined by the overall demand for services in submarkets served by the mode of transport. This means that in periods of recession when there is less demand for service, the opportunity cost of tying up a truck, bus, or barge for one day will be lower. Logically, then, the prices charged in recessions will be lower than in periods of high economic activity. Similarly, tanker rates between Venezuela and New York vary with shipping conditions throughout the world. For example, when the Suez

Canal was closed, oil tankers from the Persian Gulf had to travel down the length of Africa to reach Europe or North America. Since this took longer, there was an effective decrease in the availability of tanker space, thus driving up the opportunity cost of using tankers. When the Suez Canal opened again, the opportunity cost of tanker-days was lowered throughout the world, even for tankers that never used the canal. By the same logic, lower speed limits increase the opportunity cost of using truck days. Premature retirement of a class of aircraft has similarly increased the opportunity cost of using aircraft and raised the charter rates for all air service. Gluts of barge capacity due to overbuilding have also periodically depressed rates that waterway operators are able to get for their services.

Unstable Prices

The prices charged by fully unintegrated commercial vehicle operators tend to be unstable. This is due to the long life of vehicles and the dominance of prices by the opportunity cost of owning vehicles. During periods of capacity surplus, the low prices can lead to financial distress. The price charged for making a run should equal the sum of the opportunity costs of all capital and labor used by the transporter. However, while this guarantees that a transporter will earn the opportunity cost per day for his or her vehicle, there is no guarantee that this will be greater than the financial obligation per day on the vehicle. For example, an owner-operator may have a mortgage on his or her tractor and trailer that requires a payment to the bank of $50 per day. But the market for trucks may be glutted due to a recession or harvest failure, thus placing the opportunity cost of using the vehicle at only $25 per day. The owner-operator will then make a financial loss on the truck; unless there is a savings account which can be drawn down, competitive pressures may force him or her into bankruptcy or foreclosure on the rig. Of course, a bank that repossesses the rig will not be able to sell it for more than the present discounted value of the net revenues that it can expect to earn, so the bank may take a larger financial loss than the operator whose vehicle was repossessed. The bank will likely be willing to renegotiate the terms of the loan rather than take the loss associated with writing down the value of the rig.

The owner of the equipment bears the financial risk associated with the instability of prices in the market for services of unintegrated commercial vehicle operators. An individual who drives for a company that owns vehicles will not be affected directly by the financial distress of his or her employer. (Of course, if a trucking company finds that it cannot find profitable places to use its trucks, it is likely also to find that it cannot find profitable opportunities for all its drivers; so a driver will be at least indirectly affected by the financial difficulties of the employer.) If the market for truckload or charter services suddenly turns up, the direct beneficiaries will be vehicle owners and not their employees. As discussed in Chapter 10, the opportunity cost of owning a vehicle is frequently greater than the financial cost. These are the times when it is most profitable to invest in new equipment.

There is nothing in economic theory that guarantees that firms will make a profit at all times. In periods of excess capacity, it is efficient that firms make an economic loss. Observing that there are firms that cannot make a profit in a competitive environment does not suggest that there is a problem with market power. This point was not understood in the arguments surrounding trucking regulation in 1935 when the financial distress of trucking companies throughout the nation (a direct result of excess capacity generated by the Great Depression) was used to argue that competition was financially ruinous and would inevitably lead to an industry in which the remaining handful of firms that survived after the price war would be able to exercise monopoly power over their customers. While it is not inherently illogical to argue that less-than-truckload carriers have a potential problem with market power (for reasons explained later in this chapter), it is surely the case that there is no logical justification for concern about market power among carriers who do not own any of the fixed facilities that they use.

▬ Partially Integrated Vehicle Operators (LTL Motor Carriers, Scheduled Airlines, Buses, Container Liners)

There should be no concern about market power among fully unintegrated modes of transportation. There is a justified worry about market power with the fully integrated mode—railroads—although, as described above, the inability to make the cost studies necessary to evaluate whether a railroad is exercising market power makes the economist's advice far less useful than it might be. The important public policy questions cover the middle ground, evaluating whether partially integrated modes of transport should have public oversight.

The previous section discussed vehicle operators who do not own any of the fixed facilities that they used. This allows them to enter and leave individual traffic lanes freely and to move vehicles around to match demands that may arise, if only briefly. Partially integrated vehicle operators differ from this group of carriers in that they own some of their own fixed facilities. LTL motor carriers own freight terminals at which different loads are sorted, broken down, and consolidated. Scheduled airlines and buses similarly have a long-term investment in gates and passenger terminals. They do not however, own all of their fixed facilities. In particular, airlines do not own runways or the air traffic control system and motor carriers do not own the highways that they use. These carriers, then, are a hybrid operation between railroads, who own all of the facilities that they use, and truckload carriers, who own no fixed facilities.

The ownership of fixed facilities provides these partially integrated carriers with a geographic base of operations. The immobility of fixed facilities also ties these carriers to the geographic area where they are based. The geographic ties fundamentally alter the economics of carrier operations from those of unintegrated suppliers. Integrated carriers are faced with the classic problems of fixed facilities financing and operations: sunkness of investment, lumpiness of optimal facilities size, heterogeneity of users, and the problem of pricing services to get efficient use of the facilities.

The lumpiness of facilities size guarantees that facilities devoted to a single market will be underused much of the time. Except in the rare instance such as an air shuttle service, where traffic is so large that fixed facilities can be devoted to a single corridor, it will be more efficient to have facilities used by more than one market. This, combined with the lumpiness of vehicle sizes, is the basis of network economies. As demonstrated in Chapter5, a carrier with a network of operations is likely to be able to carry another passenger at lower cost than a carrier that depends solely on point-to-point service. In general, an operator with a larger network can achieve better load factors than one with a smaller network, though congestion at hub points tends to limit the efficient size of networks. Operators with larger networks are also able to provide more frequent service between any two points it serves and consumers are willing to pay a premium for more frequent service.

During the deregulation debates of the 1970s, scheduled air carriers were sometimes considered to be contestable in the same sense as truckload motor carriers or charter buses. Airplanes were characterized as nothing more than marginal costs with wings. Deregulation, it was argued, would lead to marginal cost pricing since any attempt to raise prices in any intercity pair above the efficient price level would invite hit and run entry to take advantage of the profitable price-cost margins. But this forecast was wrong. Hit and run entry does not occur in partially integrated transportation industries. One reason is the requirement that a new carrier obtain fixed facilities—gates and support staff in the case of airlines—in order to serve a new city. Some of the costs of opening new gates will invariably be sunk, thus contradicting the assumption of contestable markets theory.[2] The lumpiness of the fixed facilities also means that it will be efficient to introduce service only if a carrier can serve multiple markets. Moreover, the markets served will have to be rational given the size and location of other points served in the network. This was demonstrated in Chapter 5. In short, given the network economies of these carriers, entry will occur only if the new routes are a good fit in the existing pattern of service.

Moreover, in the airline industry there is a great deal of consumer inertia. Airlines find that new routes must be advertised and that promotional fares must be given to build up volume. These promotional fares and advertising expenses are decidedly sunk. As a result, airlines have some leeway at raising prices above marginal cost on different routes without inviting entry. In short, the scheduled airline industry is unquestionably not contestable. Several empirical studies of airline pricing have confirmed this fact.[3]

Where numbers are small and entry impeded, it is clearly possible for tacit collusion to occur. An extreme case of tacit airline collusion is provided by the air shuttles between New York and Washington. Air shuttle service is provided by only two companies. In 1990, these companies were Pan American and Trump Air. Trump Air had no other routes and Pan American operated its shuttle outside of its normal route structure. Entry is foreclosed to new firms by gate and landing slot limits in the two cities at either end of the route. The service provided by each company was identical, with one firm providing service on the hour and the other on the half hour; there was essentially no difference in amenities provided by the two companies.

It is no surprise that the fares charged for service were also identical. Through July 1990, both companies charged $119 during the week and $89 on weekends. A large increase in oil prices in August 1990 caused both companies to increase fares by $10 on both weekday and weekend flights. The changes were not only the same amount, but also were made on the same day within hours of one another. There were no charges that the companies colluded with one another in setting fares. There was no need to conspire. With blockaded entry and identical cost structures (brought about by the identical type of service, operated independently of the rest of the airline route network), no guessing was needed about the prices that the other company was charging, and with only two companies in the market, it is unnecessary to overtly collude about prices. One company merely needs to announce a price change and then let the other follow or make a counteroffer in the form of a different price change. Such price leadership, while producing the same result as overt collusion, is legal under U.S. antitrust laws.

The New York-Washington shuttle is unusual in that its operations are unintegrated with the rest of the air travel network. In general, airline cooperation is inhibited by the fact that each carrier is strong in different parts of the nation and on different routes. This means that their demand and cost conditions, unlike those of the air shuttle service, are not identical. With different demand elasticities and different costs on each route, different airlines would find that different price structures were profit maximizing. In contrast, the air shuttle service has no similar disagreements based on cost or demand structures. The ability of firms to tacitly collude with one another depends critically on the number of firms, the homogeneity of their interests, the quality of information, and the ability to exclude new entrants. The larger the number of firms, the more disparate their cost and demand structures, the poorer the information that firms have about the prices that their competitors charge and the easier it is to enter an industry, the more likely it is that firms will compete vigorously with one another.[4]

Cooperation in price setting on the shuttle route is helped by its starkly simple price structure. More complex structures, as are typical among airlines, make it more difficult for airlines to communicate their intentions through newspaper announcements and to make their intentions clear when they do or do not match each other's price changes. However, the use of computer reservation systems make price changes by one company instantly apparent to competitors. Unlike most sellers of industrial products, airline companies do not have to guess about the prices that their competitors are charging. This differs from motor carriers where essential elements of pricing are now secret from one another.

Pricing of Scheduled Services

Partially integrated transport services often operate on a regular schedule. Scheduled service economizes on transactions costs of using for-hire transportation. Chapter 11 developed principles for pricing scheduled service and demonstrated that the opportunity costs of using different services can vary widely from departure to departure for reasons that are not apparent to customers. The reason traces back to the opportunity cost of using vehicles and the subsidy-free pricing criterion that users of a departure pay, in aggregate, an amount that is expected to cover the opportunity costs of the movement.

Airlines. All scheduled transportation services provide service to multiple types of users. The important distinction between these groups is the expected cost of stochastic delay that these groups have. For example, business travelers often schedule their time tightly and will pay a great deal to get a seat on their preferred flight, while vacation travelers usually are far more relaxed as to preferred flight times. The rise in marginal costs as load factors rise is thus due primarily to business travelers. It is they, with higher values of time and more unpredictable schedules, who cause average load factors to be reduced in order to guarantee that space will be available on flights that they prefer.

If all travelers were able to plan ahead and had as weak preferences on optimal departure times as vacation travelers, it would be possible to operate without scheduled transport service; all flights could be run as charters, announced well in advance and designed to have 100 percent load factors. Obviously, the cost of operating such a system would be far less than the scheduled networks that we have today. In fact, the argument in favor of network operations—that optimal frequency of service, optimal vehicle size, and average load factors are higher if service is offered as a network—is irrelevant in an all-charter operation. Without hubbing, there would be less need for gates and runways, fewer landings, and so on. All passengers could be carried in the largest, most efficient aircraft.

Scheduled networks, with their additional costs of operations, are designed to serve travelers who are keeping tight or unpredictable schedules. It is thus appropriate that travelers with these characteristics, primarily business travelers, pay higher fares than vacation travelers. If both groups of customers paid the same fares, vacation travelers would find that they could get better, cheaper service on charter flights and would leave the scheduled system. But business travelers benefit from having vacation travelers carried in the scheduled system as long as they make some contribution to the costs of operating the system and do not decrease the likelihood that a seat will be available on their preferred departure. The key to making the system work is to ensure that the two groups of travelers are separated for pricing purposes and that neither group cross-subsidize the other. It is also efficient to guarantee that vacation travelers on a flight do not increase load factors sufficiently to cause a business traveler to be denied a seat on the preferred departure since this will eliminate the advantage that a system of scheduled service has to business travelers.

Airlines undertake some of the most ambitious market segmentation of any industry. As with all transportation services, airlines charge different prices for different classes of service; this practice has often been considered discriminatory because the price differential between first class and economy travel appears to be higher than the passenger service cost difference. Airlines also segment the market by the willingness to purchase tickets in advance. Often there are several different fare levels depending on how far in advance a traveler is willing to purchase a ticket, with the lowest fares charged to those who are able to purchase their tickets farthest in advance. A closely related market segmentation device is the willingness of passengers to forego the right to alter travel plans after they are made. Consumers who are willing to forego this right by agreeing to purchase a non-refundable ticket are given much lower fares than those who reserve the right to change travel plans after they purchase their tickets. Markets are also segmented by the willingness to fly through a hub, with higher prices charged to those who insist on a direct flight. A classic market segmentation criterion is the willingness to stay over Saturday night, with much lower fares charged to those who are willing to do so.

The market segmentation based on these criteria is made more complicated by airlines' yield management programs which flexibly limit the number of seats on each flight that are available for each discount group. By monitoring the rate at which seats in every fare grade fill up, airline companies can update on a daily basis the number of seats assigned to each fare level. Thus an airline can tell if there is a conference in New Orleans between December 27 and December 31 since seats on flights over that period will fill at a higher rate than their historical records would have anticipated. The airline can then reduce the number of discount tickets on those flights, encouraging casual travelers to fly at a different time and simultaneously guaranteeing that it will get as much revenue as possible from flights during that period. This practice encourages the efficient use of the nation's aircraft stock by decreasing the stochastic delay associated with particular flights.

The airline price structure is one of the most complex of all price structures used in American industry. A large part of the complexity can be explained by the differing opportunity cost of apparently similar flights and by serving both time-sensitive and non-time-sensitive passengers with the same scheduled air system. However, since the industry cannot be considered contestable, there is no guarantee that the prices charged for services will necessarily be true opportunity costs. There is ample opportunity to use market power to enhance a system's net revenues.

Less-than-Truckload Carriers. Less-than-truckload motor carriers have a scheduled service that is similar to that used in the airlines. The schedule is very simple: For shipments in the same region, delivery is promised overnight. For more distant shippers, second-day or third-day arrival is guaranteed. For large companies on heavily traveled routes, this rudimentary scheduling does not require them to operate in a manner that would be different from how cost-minimization would dictate. In less densely settled regions, however, smaller companies may have difficulty in finding sufficient loads to fill a truck a day in all the traffic lanes that it serves. This gives a clear cost advantage in rural areas to firms that offer service to more destinations, since they are more likely to be able to collect the one-truckload per day minimum necessary to meet their schedule. Competitive pressures of network economics are thus likely to lead to a small number of large trucking firms serving rural areas. To the extent that geographic coverage is important to shippers, the small number of firms that can fit into rural markets will allow a small number of carriers in the national market as well.

Less-than-truckload costs are dominated by the costs of owning and operating vehicles. The problem, as with the airlines, is to allocate the costs of owing and operating vehicles to the multiple shippers of the different loads carried in each truck. Unlike the airline industry, there is no simple distinguishing characteristic between the equivalent of business and vacation travelers. (In a very rough sense, all of an LTL carrier's business is the equivalent of business travelers, with the equivalent of vacation travelers handled by the truckload industry.) The LTL industry uses a system of negotiated discounts from a list price system based heavily on the handling characteristics of freight. Those firms with the largest amount of freight to ship are likely to get the largest discounts.

Network economies are also causing a rapid increase in concentration among less-than-truckload (LTL) motor carriers. The industry appears to be quickly dividing into a group of three carriers with nationwide coverage and a series of regional carriers that are large enough to exploit network economies.[5] Part of the rapid increase in concentration is the result of deregulation in 1980 which removed the protection that small carriers had enjoyed. These uneconomically small carriers have been placed under severe economic pressure by carriers that are able to offer a broader service area, more sophisticated freight services, and lower fares. As this is written, it is unclear how far network economies will drive LTL concentration. Whatever the reason, however, an LTL motor carrier industry that became highly concentrated might be able to eliminate rate discounting, and this is worrisome.

The degree of market power that a collusive LTL group would have might still be small: A shipper can hold freight until it collected a truckload (which would be priced at opportunity cost), or turn to freight forwarders and brokers or develop its own private trucking fleet if a collusive LTL group tried to raise prices far above costs. In addition, firms that ship in less-than-truckload lots and are willing to pay the price premium for that service are unlikely to find themselves financially pressed by a collusive LTL group. That is, unlike the railroad industry which has the power to transfer all profits from a captive shipper, it is implausible to imagine that there are shippers who could be considered captive to a collusive LTL group. In the absence of captive shippers, it is unlikely that there will be public pressure to control market power of LTL carriers, despite the fact that a tightly concentrated industry would undoubtedly possess some.

Simple Monopoly Restriction in Scheduled Service

If price variation among different users is not necessarily an indication of market power but could be simply the result of pricing at opportunity costs, what sorts of observations would be evidence of the exercise of market power? To answer this, one needs to understand how monopoly power would be exercised in the case of partially integrated transport operators. The simplest behavioral response is to reduce service frequency. Operators of scheduled services must make two decisions simultaneously: the number of flights to offer in a time period and the price to charge for those services. The combination of flight frequency and price then determines the load factor. Low load factors are a measure of quality since they imply a higher likelihood of getting on one's preferred flight (as well as less delay from fellow passengers in embarking and debarking). Higher flight frequency is also a higher quality service since the delay time to the next departure is lower. Where, then, should we look for evidence of monopoly behavior: in higher prices, higher load factors, or less frequent service?

The standard monopoly model described in the previous chapter does not show how a monopolist would make these interrelated decisions. The analysis of how optimally to reduce service quality is quite complex.[6] Decreasing the number of flights will clearly raise the full cost to travelers of service on an intercity link. How these costs will be apportioned between higher average waiting times (due to fewer flights), higher fares, and lower load factors cannot be determined without knowing more about the particular market that one is interested in. As long as demand is inelastic, fewer flights will increase load factor on each flight, but monopoly tendencies are to reduce load factor within a flight. One would presume that prices would rise when traffic is restricted, but demand seen by airline companies in a system with fewer flights is lower than in a system with more flights, thus restricting the ability of the monopolist to raise fares. In the large numbers case it is clear that a monopolist will raise load factor and fares, but reduce frequency; in the case of a small number of flights, it is uncertain.

Other Monopoly Responses

The policies of limiting flights and limiting the number of passengers per flight, a combination of which a monopoly airline would choose to support higher fares, are based on the assumption that an airline can charge only a single price. It is the equivalent in the case of the hypothetical Mackinac Bridge

Corporation of charging a single toll on the bridge. Just as in the case of the toll bridge, these policies are inefficient; from the perspective of an airline monopoly, it also allows too much of the total benefit of air transport to be retained by consumers. Just as in the case of the toll bridge monopolist, it is predictable that the main response would be not to raise prices but to manipulate demand, segment markets, and discriminate in fares both to particular individuals as well as among individuals.

Scheduled airlines have brand names and work hard to advertise and promote their names. Since airlines were deregulated in 1978, the proportion of revenue dollars that have gone to advertising have increased. Advertising has the effect of moving company demand curves to the right, supporting higher prices, and increasing revenues for every price level. Advertising, to the extent that it increases brand loyalty, will also make company demand more inelastic; demands that are more inelastic are able to support higher markups over costs.

Another way that airlines have tried to increase brand loyalty is through the use of frequent flier programs. Under these schemes, airlines keep track of the travel of individual customers and reward them with free tickets after they have traveled a specified number of miles. These programs increase the advantages of large scale networks by encouraging passengers to use the same airline in many different markets; airlines that fly only limited networks find that they must link up with larger carriers to offer their customers frequent flier benefits. The demand penalty of operating small networks caused by frequent flier programs is a significant barrier to entry into the scheduled airline industry.

Frequent flier programs are effective in part because they exploit different incentives to the payer and the decision maker in a transaction. In the case of business travelers, frequent flier rewards are made to the passenger rather than to his or her employer despite the fact that the employer pays for the ticket. While the employer (the principal in this transaction) has an incentive to choose the airline with the lowest fare, the principal's agent (the passenger) has an incentive to choose the airline that gives the highest frequent flier rewards. The program thus distorts airline decisions away from choosing the cost minimizing carrier to the detriment of business travel accounts. The unwillingness of business travelers to fly on new, small airlines but rather to select larger, more established airlines with generous frequent flier programs disadvantages new entrants into the industry.

Airline companies also try to manipulate demand by influencing travel agents; variable commission rate schedules encourage travel agents that book flights primarily through one airline to direct as much traffic as they can to that carrier in order to get the highest commission. In addition, computer reservation systems, owned by airline companies themselves, have been used to give preferential listings to the owner's flights.

Finally, it should be recognized that the same market segmentation that is used to efficiently separate business from casual travelers can also be used to price discriminate among them. While the subsidy-free pricing criterion requires that business travelers pay higher fares than others, it is also reasonable to assume that they have lower elasticities of demand and thus can support higher fares. This is classic price discrimination as would be practiced by any firm with market power. There have been no estimates of the extent to which market segmentation pricing reflects the fact that scheduled service is primarily useful to the business traveler and are thus consistent with economic efficiency. However, it must be assumed that part of the fare difference is a reflection of market power that results from the partially integrated structure of the airline industry.

CONCLUSION

The economic perspective on market power is rooted in the concept of efficiency, which requires that prices paid for transportation be equal to the full marginal cost of providing service, with both user and carrier costs included in the marginal cost calculation. By raising prices above marginal cost, a transport operator with market power forces some customers off the system, thus generating an inefficiency. Of course, there are some cases in which an operator must raise revenues in excess of what would be generated by marginal cost pricing in order to cover the full costs of providing a service. If additional revenues were not raised, the service offerings would not be subsidy-free.

The public distrust of market power is not based on the same analysis as the economist's. Using an extended example of a toll bridge, this chapter described some of the techniques that have been used by transport operators to increase their profits beyond those that they could get by simple monopoly pricing. These techniques involve market segmentation, moving to nonlinear prices, manipulating demand, and trying to promote tie-ins between the operator and the transport user. From the perspective of economic efficiency, these techniques are benign since they enable the operator to get increase services from their facilities. However, there is a clear redistribution of wealth involved in these actions, from the customer to the transport operator. The economist is supposed to be an impartial observer, not passing judgment on such matters, but public policy toward transportation has always been driven by attempts by customers to prevent what they consider to be an unwarranted reduction in their wealth.

The extent to which transport operators can engage in market segmentation and similar actions depends primarily on the extent to which they are integrated with their fixed facilities. Fixed facilities create a geographic base of operations for the operator and tie customers in that area to firms operating the facilities. In the extreme case, the transport operator can control access and can thus capture all of the customer's consumer surplus.

The mode that is most completely integrated with its fixed facilities is rail. This has given railroads the power to capture for itself the advantages of different locations. However, more than other modes, railroads must price above marginal cost in order to retrieve the costs of operating trains and maintaining tracks. The subsidy-free pricing rules necessary to do this are so complex that the effort of making the calculations necessary to see whether particular prices are above costs is not generally justified by the efficiency gains that might flow from reducing market power.

At the opposite extreme from railroads are fully unintegrated commercial operators. These include truckload motor carriers, charter airplanes and buses, charter barge operators, and tramp tankers. Since they are unintegrated with their fixed facilities, they are not geographically bound in their operations. This allows them to be analyzed with models of contestable markets in which competitive conditions and the threat of entry from other unintegrated carriers forces prices to be equal to opportunity costs. There is, however, no requirement that prices be equal to financial costs of operation. It is predictable in these markets that prices for round trips will be higher in the high demand direction than in the low demand direction despite the fact that the financial costs of moving in each direction may be nearly the same.

Prices charged in unintegrated markets are likely to be unstable. In periods where there is a capacity glut, unintegrated carriers may not earn enough to cover the financial obligation of their equipment leases. In times of equipment shortage, the opportunity cost of using equipment may be far higher than the amount they actually pay to the equipment owner.

Between the fully integrated railroads and the unintegrated truckload operators are carriers who are partially integrated, owning some of their fixed facilities but depending on government agencies to provide most of their fixed facilities. The most prominent examples of these carriers are scheduled airlines and less-than-truckload motor carriers.

Partially integrated carriers like less-than-truckload motor carriers and scheduled airlines cannot be considered to be contestable. Network economies and the effect of lumpy facilities and vehicle sizes hinder the sort of free entry and exit that would allow markets to anonymously police the price structure of these modes of transport. Scheduled airlines and similar modes need to decide on both the frequency and the price of service. This joint decision will be efficient if the price charged to each passenger makes the expected full price paid by each passenger equal to the marginal cost of carrying a passenger and if the number of flights is determined by the condition that social welfare is maximized. The efficient airline fare is the congestion toll for the optimal number of flights. This may or may not cover all flight costs. The private firms that provide airline service will enforce the subsidy-free criterion that all flights and all groups of flights must at least cover their opportunity costs. Enforcing this condition may require that some fares be above marginal costs.

Scheduled airline service is of primary benefit to business people and others who need to make travel plans on short notice. In order to prevent other users from subsidizing these passenger, fares for traveling at short notice must be much higher than fares to passengers who are flexible in their travel plans and can reserve well ahead. The extremely complex price structures adopted by airlines are at least partially justified by the principle of subsidy-free pricing. Whether they are fully justified is difficult to determine given the variety of ways in which market power can be exercised in these industries.

NOTES

1. Note that locals might be willing to pay a great deal more than tourists for the first trip or two. This implies a nonlinear demand, the complications of which are unnecessary for the purposes of the exposition here.
2. R.V. Butler and J.H. Huston, "How Contestable Are Airline Markets?" *Atlantic Economic Journal*, Vol. 17, No. 2 (June 1989), pp. 27–35.
3. Among the studies that have demonstrated the deviation of airline markets from perfect contestability are: Severin Borenstein, "Hubs and High Fares: Dominance and Market Power in the U.S. Airline Industry," *Rand Journal of Economics*, Vol. 20, No. 3, Autumn 1989, pp. 344–365; Severin Borenstein, "The Dominant-Firm Advantage in Multiproduct Industries: Evidence from the U.S. Airlines," *Quarterly Journal of Economics*, Vol. 106, No. 4 (November 1991), pp. 1237–1266; Diana Strassmann, "Potential Competition in the Deregulated Airlines," *Review of Economics and Statistics*, Vol. 72, No. 4, November 1990, pp. 696–702; Jan K. Bruecker, Nichola J. Dyer, and Pablo T. Spiller, "Fare Determination in Airline Hub and Spoke Networks," *Rand Journal of Economics*, Vol. 23, No. 4, Autumn 1992, pp. 309–333.
4. For an elaboration of this list of factors, see F.M. Scherer and David Ross, *Industrial Market Structure and Economic Performance, Third Edition* (Boston: Houghton Mifflin Co., 1990). For an overall evaluation of the state of inter-airline competition, see Tae Hoon Oum, Anming Zhang, and Yimin Zhang, "Inter-Firm Rivalry and Firm-Specific Price Elasticities in Degregulated Airline Markets," *Journal of Transport Economics and Policy* (May 1993), pp. 171–192.
5. See Robert W. Kling, "Deregulation and Structural Change in the LTL Motor Freight Industry," *Transportation Journal* (Spring 1990), pp. 47–53.
6. Randall W. Bennett and Kenneth D. Boyer, "Inverse Price/Quality Tradeoffs in the Regulated Airline Industry," *Journal of Transport Economics and Policy* (January 1990), pp. 35–47.

13

Regulation of Market Power in Transportation

The actions of the mythical Mackinac Bridge Corporation in the previous chapter find parallels in the history of American transportation. In one sense, railroads at the turn of the century had even more economic power than the fictitious profit maximizing Mackinac Bridge Corporation described in the previous chapter. Since railroads are integrated into vehicle ownership and operation in addition to owning the fixed facilities, they had an even stronger control over access than that allowed merely by ownership of a fixed facility. It would be as if all people who wished to use the Mackinac Bridge were required to use buses or trucks owned by the Mackinac Bridge Corporation.

At the end of the nineteenth century, there was a popular call for economic regulation of the railroad industry to control its economic power. The authority to regulate railroads was granted to the Interstate Commerce Commission (ICC) through laws passed between 1887 and 1920. Regulation was extended to the newly developed trucking industry in 1935 and the airline industry in 1938. In 1940, the ICC was granted the power to control domestic water transportation. The process reversed beginning in the late 1970s and by 1995, transportation regulation as practiced for most of the twentieth century had virtually disappeared.

The history of transportation regulation and the analysis of the effects that deregulation had on the industry provide important lessons that are useful for understanding the control of market power in transportation. The story of transport regulation makes clear how difficult it is to recognize and control market power in this industry. Regulation of transportation did quiet complaints about the abuse of market power, but at the expense of serious efficiency costs. Some suggestions for alternative mechanisms for controlling market power in transportation are contained in the final pages of this chapter.

WHAT DID REGULATION CONTROL?

While there are some differences among the regulations that governed different modes of transportation, the written laws in most respects were very similar.[1] One reason was that regulation of other modes were copied from the original limits placed on railroads. In essence, other modes were regulated as if they were railroads.

Route Structure

Railroads in North America were privately financed, though often with the support of business interests in locations served by the railroad. At the end of the nineteenth century, a town without a railroad was sentenced to die since it was uneconomic to do business there. Every community felt that it was vital to be served by at least one railroad. But it was also important to have as many railroads as possible serving your town. The best way to guarantee low rates and good service has always been to have alternatives not in control of a single transport operator. For this reason, localities in the nineteenth century were willing to offer generous economic incentives for new railroads to route their tracks through or near their area. The hope was that with more than one railroad bidding for business, they would be in a better position to bargain for low rates and to receive the economic development advantages that such low rates provide.

The result of this subsidized railroad construction was overbuilding on a massive scale. The nation has since the late nineteenth century had many more railroad lines than were required to economically carry all freight and passengers that they handled. But given the cost structure of the railroad industry described in Chapters 6–8, overbuilding meant that each railroad had less traffic to support their fixed facilities than would be the result in a normal competitive industry. The result of the overbuilding was to put even more pressure on railroads to find revenues above direct costs to cover the costs of carrying excess capacity. This made railroads vulnerable in bargaining with large shippers.[2]

When the power of the Interstate Commerce Commission to oversee business decisions of railroads was finally confirmed in the Transportation Act of

1920, one of the first decisions of the ICC was to require that railroad companies apply for a *certificate of convenience and necessity* before any new lines could be built. To obtain a certificate, the new line needed to show that existing carriers were not providing adequate service—a burden of proof that was not possible to bear except in the case of a few lines in underserved areas. Essentially, the regulators froze the railroad map in the form it took at the end of the First World War. This served economic efficiency (since the country was already overbuilt), prevented localities from wasteful bidding against one another for new lines, and guaranteed existing carriers that they would be protected from new competition.

In return for preventing railroads from being subject to new entry, the regulatory authorities insisted that a railroad must get permission to abandon lines and to merge with other carriers. Mergers and abandonments would be a logical step toward the exercise of monopoly power that entry restrictions appeared to allow. However, at the time that the railroad map was frozen, some carriers were financially strong and others weak. This was the result of the fact that not all railroad networks were equally as well placed; some served areas with little traffic and some had circuitous routings. But this meant that regulatory policies that provided a reasonable rate of return on investment for strong railroads would be ruinous for weak lines; alternatively, regulations to ensure the financial viability of a weak line would make strong carriers unusually profitable. Considerable regulatory energy was spent on trying to solve the so-called *weak-road/strong-road* problem. For example, as recently as 1968, the Interstate Commerce Commission required that the Pennsylvania and the New York Central (two apparently strong railroads) absorb the New Haven (a weak railroad) as a condition for their merger.

Born of the concern about equalizing opportunities for different railroads, the ICC action had the unintended consequence of preventing the sort of concentration of traffic in a limited number of routes that would have been natural had the railroad system been operated as a single company. For example, the Union Pacific's lines extended from Omaha to the West, but there were six railroad connecting Omaha to Chicago. The concern of the ICC was to ensure the survival of all six railroads. For that reason, it held up the purchase of one of the carriers by the Union Pacific for fear that the other lines would not receive traffic from the big Western carrier when it had its own line. The effect of regulation was to keep in business all six lines when business conditions would probably have supported at most two or three of them. The inflated costs associated with maintaining an overly extensive track network then made American railroads more vulnerable over time. However, the limitations on line abandonments and route rationalizations were supported by communities that would otherwise have lost service and guaranteed railroad access to a larger part of the country than would have been possible without the rules. The practice of inflating costs to guarantee services to a broader part of the population than a competitive market would have served is typical of regulatory behavior.[3]

The Interstate Commerce Commission was happy with the results of route certification when the Motor Carrier Act of 1935 gave it the power to control trucking. Just as for the railroad industry, trucking regulation set up a route structure for each company and subjected them to a regulatory process that was essentially the same as that covering railroads. There is no economic reason that trucking firms should have a fixed network. They have no fixed facilities other than the terminals that they use to collect, break, and distribute less-than-truckload commodities. One of the advantages that trucking firms have over railroads is that they are not bound to a route. If they lose a customer in one traffic lane, they can easily switch their equipment to a different lane. By requiring all motor carriers to have a route certificate (granted by a simple showing that the company had carried goods on this route before 1935) for all connections that they might wish to serve, regulation forced trucking companies to look and act like railroads. It also prevented trucking companies from achieving the advantages of traffic density that an efficient hub-and-spoke system provides. The licensing procedure also effectively protected small local trucking companies from competition from larger firms with a broader national coverage.

When airlines were brought under regulatory control, the same system of freezing networks was used. As is the case in trucking, airlines are not fixed facilities intensive. While they require terminals and repair facilities, the placement of these facilities do not by themselves define a route structure. Without regulation, there is every reason to believe that airlines would have developed a hub-and-spoke system. But the process of route certification prevented this. Regulation imposed on airlines a route map. As in the case of trucking, the original route map was granted based on the demonstration that the carrier had flown those routes prior to regulation. If an airline had a major presence at Atlanta, for example, but could not show that it had flown from there to Orlando prior to regulation, it was forbidden from flying the route. Passengers wishing to fly from other points on the airline's route map would have had to switch carriers in Atlanta to continue the journey to Orlando.

The problem of weak and strong route systems that plagued railroad regulation was also a problem with airlines. However, since airline traffic was growing, the regulators were able to correct some of the problem by awarding lucrative new routes to weak carriers. The result, however, meant that strong airlines (like United Airlines) were forbidden to fly new routes, while weak carriers (like National) were given lucrative new opportunities. This disparity in how regulators treated weak and strong carriers was at the heart of the disunity of the airline industry in the 1970s that permitted deregulation.

The Regulated Rate Structure

The second main focus of regulatory energy was on prices charged for services. Particularly in the case of freight transportation, there were two different procedures—one for rate levels and one for rate structures. Rate level regulation took the form of a request from the industry for a percentage increase in freight rates—for example, a 3 percent increase in all rates. This general rate increase was supported by evidence on the increase in costs or the average profitability of a typical firm in the industry. Since the railroad industry at least from the 1950s did not earn a normal rate of return on its invested capital, the Interstate Commerce Commission was quite generous in its approval of general rate increases. By contrast, general rate increases requested by the trucking industry were not as liberally granted because the trucking industry was highly profitable up to the time when it was deregulated.

It is important to note that the practice of general rate increases involved collective rate making. That is, regulation permitted and encouraged firms in each mode of transport to get together to prepare rate requests. The ICC then played a passive role in approving or denying requests prepared by the industry as a whole.

While general rate increases were the most visible part of rate regulation, they were not the most important part. Like the practice of the fictional toll Bridge Corporation of the previous chapter, the regulated rate structure consisted of a set of high list prices under which almost no traffic moved, combined with a regulatory-approved set of rate reductions for each commodity and locality. Virtually all traffic moved under these reduced rates. The rate reductions were negotiated between shipper and carrier and were then passed on to the industry rate bureau. If a rate proposed for one shipper was sufficiently low that it threatened the profitability of traffic moved by another carrier, the rate could be disapproved by the rate bureau. If approved by the rate bureau, it was passed on to the Interstate Commerce Commission for approval or disapproval. If it was rejected by the rate bureau, a carrier who wanted to put the rate into effect had to bear the expense of publishing the rate itself and defending it before the regulatory commission.

The rate structure that developed was very complex. Since effective rates were applicable for specific commodities in specific sizes between very finely defined end points, published rates numbered in the billions and there was little indexing. Given vast number of rate changes that required action, the Commission had little choice but to approve most of them. The Interstate Commerce Commission, even if it were inclined to closely supervise rate setting, did not have the practical ability to do so.

Price regulation of passenger service was on paper very similar to freight rate regulation. For example, rate bureaus of airline companies proposed rate changes to the Civil Aeronautics Board, which then accepted or modified them. Unlike freight transportation, however, most traffic was carried at listed prices rather than at discounts tailored to individual customers. Thus, unlike railroads and motor carriers, the essential element of airline fare regulation was the general rate increase rather than a discussion of the structure of rates. For most of the period of airline regulation the rate structure was based on the system of first class railroad passenger rates adopted when the industry was first competing for traffic against railroads. Only late in the period of regulation did regulatory discussions center on the now familiar discounts offered to particular segments of the traveling public.

Regulation of Operations

Regulation established for each carrier a system of fixed networks with limited coverage. In order for customers to travel to or make a shipment to a point off the route system of the originating carrier, a connection was necessary to a second carrier and sometimes additional carriers. One way of exercising market power would be for a carrier to leverage a strong position when making a traffic interchange—perhaps by insisting on a high rate division or interchanging only a small quantity of traffic. In order to prevent this from occurring, and to ensure that the transportation map would be operated as a unified system, regulatory agencies were required to make rules governing the interchange of freight, baggage, and equipment. An important part of these rules was the prices that carriers could charge for services that they provided to one another. In particular, the ICC had the power to control the division of rates between originating, terminating, and bridge carriers.

The rules governing carrier operations were most stringent in the case of interrailroad interchange of equipment. An interconnected system means that one railroad's cars will find themselves on another railroad's tracks. In essence, interconnection means that your own capital investment can be used by a competitor to earn income. Under these circumstances, it would seem irrational to invest in cars and locomotives if you can use those of another railroad rather than purchase your own. To encourage railroads to invest in equipment, the owner must be compensated whenever another company uses its equipment.

While the intent of the ICC rules on the prices and terms under which railroads would rent equipment to one another was to eliminate costly haggling between railroads and to prevent discrimination against those shippers who chose to interline their shipments, the result of the uniform rates selected by the ICC were exactly what would be predicted by economic analysis—car shortages and car surpluses. The analysis is contained in Figure 13.1. If the price for using a car were set below the equilibrium price, perhaps at the $5.00 per day level indicated by the lower line in Figure 13.1, the number of car-days demanded by users would be 1,500, higher than the 500 vehicle-days willingly offered by the car-owning companies. On the opposite side, if the price for using a car were set above the equilibrium level, for example at the $15.00 per day level shown in Figure 13.1, the number of cars offered by owners for rent would be 1,000 greater than those for which there were willing users, implying a surplus.[4]

The ICC regulation of car-hire rates has caused both shortages and surpluses in the past since demand for using some types of railroad cars is highly erratic and thus the equilibrium price—the opportunity cost to the car

FIGURE 13.1   Shortages and Surpluses Due to Car Rental Fee Regulation

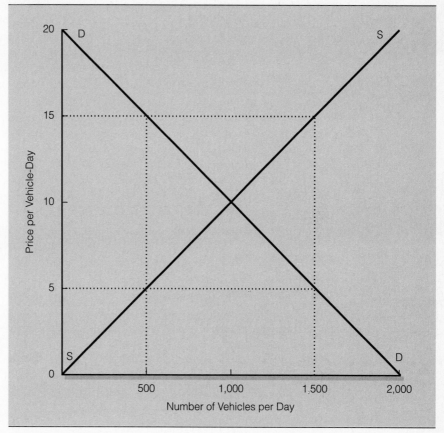

owner—is erratic too. Grain shipments in particular are highly variable. Railroads invested heavily in grain cars in the late 1970s but found that the cars that they purchased sat idle much of the time, since less grain was actually shipped than was predicted. The opportunity cost of holding a covered hopper car in the early 1970s was thus quite low. However, during peak periods, grain shippers are willing to pay surcharges for use of railroad cars. Under traditional ICC equipment interchange rules, the rent that railroads were allowed to charge each other and charge their customers for use of equipment was fixed at the same level regardless of the opportunity cost of equipment. The failure of prices to respond to changes in market conditions tended to exaggerate peak demands by underpricing car services; since railroads could not charge a low price for use of cars when their opportunity cost was low, shippers had no incentive to shift some of their demand for grain shipping to periods when there were plenty of cars.

Another way in which setting a common price for using equipment distorts decisions on using railway equipment was that the price was fixed regardless of whether in a particular city there was a surplus of railroad cars. If the price charged for using cars were allowed to vary between locations, the price that railroads could get for using a car in a city with many cars relative to demand would be low, giving them an incentive to shift cars to markets in which demand is higher relative to supply. This rapid change in equipment hiring rates to correspond to market conditions is common in the move-it-yourself business. U-Haul Corporation routinely places surcharges on equipment moving into areas with an equipment surplus and provides discounts for equipment moves into areas with equipment shortages. Since a single price gives no incentives to shift railroad cars to offset local surpluses and shortages, regulators had to supplement its price regulation with car service orders. One such order directed railroads to return cars after they are unloaded in the direction of the owning railroad, regardless of whether the car was in high demand at the location where it was unloaded or in a nearby location. Regulators also periodically issued orders to railroads to shift a specified number of cars to a location in order to relieve acute car shortages.

▬ Other Aspects of Transportation Industries Covered by Regulation

The most economically important aspects of transportation regulation were investment, pricing, and operations rules. But transport regulation was more far-reaching. For example, to prevent railroads from favoring their own commodities over those of others, railroads were forbidden to carry their own goods for sale. This forced railroads to divest ownership in mines. To ensure that the Panama Canal would provide competition in transcontinental service, railroads were forbidden to have a financial interest in shipping lines providing service through the Panama Canal and were required to get specific permission to buy carriers outside the railroad sector.

Regulation also provided for the development of uniform systems of accounts. The ICC was a record keeper of equipment liens and leases and determined how railroads and motor carriers could present their profit statements. For this reason, until 1983 railroad accounting was different from that for any other industry. The ICC also had rules on interlocking directors and the issuance of railroad securities.

Regulatory commissions were also charged with ensuring carrier safety. Under this charge, transport regulators issued rules governing the maintenance of equipment and right of way. It controlled the number of hours that drivers were permitted to be behind the wheel and how hazardous materials were to be handled. Under deregulation, many of these functions have been dispersed to other agencies without any responsibility for economic affairs of carriers.

Traditional regulatory rules also contained extensive labor protection. For example, when railroad lines were abandoned or merged, it was the Interstate Commerce Commission that determined what could be done with the redundant labor. Similar rules were used in the trucking industry. Labor protection rules were credited with facilitating the organization of trucking labor by the teamster's union.[5] The ICC enforced rules on the extent to which drivers could be asked to load and unload their own trucks as well as conditions under which owner-operators could lease their services to major carriers.

CRITERIA FOR REGULATORY DECISIONS

Under the Interstate Commerce Act and the laws that have amended it, the regulatory authority was directed to "promote safety, honesty, and efficiency; to avoid 'undue' concentration of economic power; to encourage energy conservation; to promote the national defense; to encourage fair wages and working conditions; and to encourage sound economic conditions in transportation and among carriers." The regulatory agency was also directed to "further the 'public interest' and the 'public convenience and necessity.'"[6] When the agency made its rate decisions, prices were required to be "just, reasonable, and non-discriminatory."

The reader will notice that the promotion of economic efficiency is not prominently listed among the criteria that the regulatory agency was empowered to use in making regulatory decisions. Economists have assumed that regulation was designed to be a substitute for a competitive market in the case of market failure; since the economic analysis of market failure, as noted in Chapter 12, is based on the failure of a market system to achieve an efficient result, it seems only logical to assume that the regulatory substitute would focus on efficient pricing. The initial complaint about railroads that led to regulation was monopoly power. Monopolies do lead to inefficient use of resources. Thus it seemed plausible that the control of monopoly should focus on how to correct for the inefficiencies of monopolies.

This logic seriously misunderstands the purpose of transport regulation, however. Railroads, which provided the model for transport regulation, were never monopolies; they have always had rivals and they have never, as a group, earned monopoly profits. The rate of return on invested capital earned by railroads was never as high at that earned in the American trucking industry, and even at the best of times, a significant proportion of the U.S. railroad system was at or near bankruptcy. Why, then, was the language of monopoly power used in discussions of transport regulation?

Railroads, like the fictitious Mackinac Bridge Corporation of the previous chapter, had wide discretion in determining the rates that it charged individual customers and this latitude had profound effects on the economic health of the communities it served. Moreover, the excess capacity in the railroad system forced carriers to search for ways to raise the maximum revenue possible to cover their fixed costs. While they did not earn monopoly profits (due to overbuilding caused by rivalry among railroads and communities), they did exercise economic power and this power was thought of in terms of monopoly.

This confusion about how a financially ailing carrier can have monopoly power has been at the heart of the controversy about railroad policy and continues to influence the debate today. A shipper who sees a competitor able to enter a new market because of a low rate granted by a railroad while at the same time being denied a similar rate so that he can achieve the same delivered price is not making the same complaint as someone who argues that a company has purposely slowed production to keep prices and profits higher than a competitive market would allow. The shipper is arguing about arbitrary use of discretion, not about market power. Railroad regulation was geared to dealing with the first complaint, while using the language of monopoly power.

Railroad regulators were far more interested in the *structure* of rates than in the *level* of rates.[7] During the long period of railroad decline under regulation, the Interstate Commerce Commission was quite free in its granting of general rate increases. Its time was spent on controlling which shippers would be granted rate reductions off of list prices and which shippers could be denied them. The concern that the regulators showed with the structure of freight rates was as attempt to give to individual shippers and communities the sense that they had a say in the decisions that affected their lives. Economists are probably the only ones who see the fundamental problem of monopoly as that of efficiency losses. The common perception is that monopolies are unfair and rob the person who has to deal with a monopoly of the power to control their own environment.

Regulatory agencies are quasi-judicial bodies, and like all courts are geared to make decisions based on justice and fairness. While the concept of a *just rate* is foreign to modern economics, the concept can have meaning in legal proceedings. One element of fairness that regulatory agencies have tended to use is that no one should be deprived of service without due process. Thus abandonment of a service required regulatory hearings at which interested parties could explain why it was that they wished service to be maintained. Among the considerations given at the hearing, the financial viability of the service received only limited attention. Thus under economic regulation, considerable excess trackage was maintained and extensive railroad passenger service was offered long after it was economically profitable. An inevitable aspect of regulation was, therefore, the maintenance of uneconomic services. In fact, the preservation of such services was often given as an indication that the regulator was making a difference and thus was successful.

Railroads were also covered by rules limiting so-called *long-haul-short-haul discrimination*. Under this rule, railroads were forbidden to charge less for going beyond a city than for going to it. This was seen as a matter of simple fairness, since carrying passengers or freight farther cannot cost less than an identical run of shorter distance. The result of this fairness-based rule was that railroad rates were strongly distance-based. The reader will recall from Chapters 6–8, however, that railroad costs are only weakly related to distance. The great majority of railroad costs are associated with fixed facilities and vehicle ownership costs. Actual movement costs are less than 20 percent of the total. While it is true that an *identical* haul that goes beyond some point cannot cost less than one that stops there, movements are rarely identical. The long-haul-short-haul rules ruled out the possibility of charging congestion tolls, for example, where appropriate, or for requiring that different types of service cover their incremental costs. Since railroad costs are so weakly related to distance, forcing them to adopt a distance-based rate schedule introduced inefficient and cross-subsidizing prices.

Also in the interests of equity, railroad regulators were careful to make sure that each locality's rate allowed it to compete with others shipping the same or similar commodities. Thus the rates on California produce were allowed larger rate discounts than Florida produce so that both could compete in the major northeastern markets. Rates from the Midwest to all East Coast ports were identical so that no port would be advantaged relative to any other. Occasionally, lower rates were allowed on more circuitous (and thus higher cost) routes to compensate for the slowness of service.

Noticeably absent from the regulatory overview of railroad rates was a comparison of rates with calculations that economists would recognize as even rough proxies for opportunity costs of shipment. Of course, without cost comparisons, there is no hope that the rate structure will be efficient or subsidy-free. Indeed, there was little incentive to make a serious attempt to discover the costs of individual shipments since these calculations were of no use in pricing or setting service standards.

The Interstate Commerce Commission, the railroad regulator, believed that it was incapable of calculating the cost of making a movement. Thus when judging the reasonableness of a proposed rate, the main factors considered were the rates charged for similar movements. Within the limits of other fairness-based concerns, the ICC tried to make sure that no rate was seriously out of line with others in similar situations. The absurdity of the result of this consideration was exposed in the *yak fat case*, in which an exasperated shipper proposed a particularly low rate for shipping yak fat between two communities, despite the fact that no such commodity was actually shipped. The boilerplate complaints to the Interstate Commerce Commission about the dire consequences of allowing such a ruinously low rate, and how it would burden other shippers of other commodities, along with the regulatory agency's sober refusal of the rate, was gleefully exposed to the general public as an example of bureaucratic stupidity. This charge was unjust to the regulatory process. The decision was the natural result of an attempt to preserve an equitable rate structure in the absence of any information about costs.

Trucking regulation used the identical equity-based standards to evaluate requests for rate changes and permission to offer new services. In evaluating rates, the regulatory agency tried to ensure that large shippers could not use their bargaining power to get lower rates than small shippers, and similarly, that rural areas—with their necessarily sparser route network—were not disadvantaged relative to urban areas. The protection of small shippers and rural areas was an essential part of equity-based transportation regulation.

The same concern over rural service was also at the base of the arguments in favor of airline regulation. The Civil Aeronautics Board considered it an achievement that in the 1960s and '70s jet service was provided to small communities throughout the nation. This was done partly by subsidizing service to small airports, partly by requiring that airlines take rural routes when granted the more lucrative densely traveled routes and partly by enforcing a strongly distance-based fare structure.

Since airlines were initially in competition with railroads for passengers, the industry chose as its list price schedule the first class fare structure of railroads. With its superior service, this practice allowed the airline industry to get the maximum revenue from passengers while being able to take traffic away from its competitors. When the industry was regulated, this fare structure was maintained. As noted previously, the railroad price structure was, in turn, based on the law limiting long-haul-short-haul price discrimination. This effectively built a distance-based rate structure in which travelers who went a little farther paid a little more. When the newly regulated airline industry adopted this rate structure, it also embraced a rate scheme that charged customers primarily by distance traveled. While airline costs are determined a little more by operating expenses than are railroads, their costs were not nearly as distance-based as the fare structure that they adopted. This was especially true as jets replaced the propeller aircraft in their fleets. Under airline regulation, longer routes had higher prices relative to costs than shorter routes. Short routes, however, are typically to smaller towns in rural areas. Thus the distance-based fare structure served as a convenient cross-subsidization scheme to guarantee service to lightly populated areas.

Transportation regulation cannot be understood without attempting to analyze concepts of fairness used by the regulatory commissions. Regulators tried to create a transportation system in which everyone—carriers, customers, and the wider community—were treated fairly. But regulators and legislators had other, broader, social goals as well. For example, the Hoch-Smith Resolution of 1925 called on the Interstate Commerce Commission to help agriculture by setting rates on farm products at the lowest possible level. In 1952, the number of agricultural commodities exempt from trucking regulation was broadened in an attempt to provide farm interests with lower rates. In 1973, the Interstate Commerce Commission tried to encourage recycling by forbidding rate discrimination against recyclable commodities. In 1976, Congress went further by compelling the ICC to set rates on recyclables at the minimum profitable level.

Regulation was also seen as improving transportation safety. By providing financial stability to the airline and trucking industries, it was hoped that airlines and motor carriers would have the resources and the financial incentive to maintain their fleets in good operating condition. Licensing requirements were seen as a way to eliminate the fly-by-night operator who was considered to be most likely to create safety problems.

Perhaps more fundamentally, regulation was seen as furthering the goals of stability in transportation. It eliminated the rate wars that were common among railroads in the nineteenth century and the ruinously low trucking rates seen during the Great Depression. Regulation encouraged coordination among carriers and between modes of transportation. It appears to assure dependable service at reasonable rates while simultaneously encouraging fairness for all involved. Essentially, regulation was seen as making the transportation industry into an invisible neutral helper—much like water supply, sewage services, and power systems. In short, the goal of regulators was to convert the transportation system into a public utility.

ADVANTAGES TO REGULATED MODES

In retrospect, regulation did prevent rate wars among railroads and it did eliminate consumer complaints about the economic power of railroads. In this sense, it was a clear success. It eliminated complaints by removing from railroads sole discretion in determining how the burden of costs would be shared among its customers.[8] Once it is understood that the goal of regulation was not to protect consumers, but to assure a stable, neutral transportation system with equity for all involved, it is less mysterious that the system could have ended up as benefiting parties who were not originally intended to be beneficiaries of the system.

The Trucking Industry

Trucking companies in particular found that regulation provided it with two great advantages: (1) the route certification process effectively protected the industry from new competition and (2) the rate regulation process could be used to control competition among carriers on any route. The reason that regulation could be used in this way was that the rates negotiated between a carrier and shipper were routinely passed to a rate bureau of motor carriers for endorsement before being sent to the Interstate Commerce Commission for final approval. While it was nominally possible for individual carriers to independently publish their own rate for a movement and defend it before the regulatory agency, independent actions were uncommon.

The sort of collusion that regulation of transportation actively encouraged would have been illegal in the rest of American industry—a violation of Section 1 of the Sherman Act. But when it was permitted as part of economic regulation, the trucking industry had an advantage that illegal conspirators do not have. The regulator hired inspectors who could stop trucks on the highway and ask to inspect their papers. One of the elements that could be checked for was whether or not a good was being carried at the tariffed rate. The first break in trucking deregulation occurred when the deregulation-oriented commissioners appointed by the Carter administration chose to eliminate policing functions.

The ability to set rates collectively and the protection that the route licensing requirements provided for the industry afforded an ideal environment for trucking companies to make profits.[9] Operating margins throughout the period of regulation were so high and consistent that trucking companies were considered to be very low risk. President Tom Donohue of the American Trucking Associations, speaking more than a decade after trucking regulation, described regulated trucking as such an easy business that you could "send a second son into it."[10] Motor carriers took this opportunity to invest by borrowing heavily, using as collateral their route certificates—which became very valuable as demand for trucking services increased far faster than new certificates were awarded. This financial leverage, combined with lack of any capacity controls under regulation, left the industry vulnerable when deregulation appeared.

The structure of regulation also benefited the Teamsters Union, which was able to use the traffic interchange rules of regulation to extend union organization to those carriers that connected with a teamsters-organized firm. The licensing requirements then provided the Union with protection against entry from non-union carriers. So successful was the union of trucking employees in negotiating with its employers that trucking wages rose to historic highs relative to comparable manufacturing jobs during the period of deregulation.[11]

The Airline Industry

The trucking industry and its organized labor were undoubtedly the primary beneficiaries of transportation regulation. The airline industry, by contrast, benefited less. Unlike the trucking industry, the airlines had a perennial weak-line–strong-line problem that left some carriers unusually profitable and others in financial difficulty after a general rate increase. As noted previously, the Civil Aeronautics Board tried to solve this problem by distributing lucrative new routes to the weak carriers, in disregard for considerations of which airline could make the most efficient use of the new link. But the Board, like all regulatory agencies, saw its basic charge as guaranteeing stability and equity, not efficiency.

The airline industry, unlike other industries, saw an outbreak of quality competition on some of the higher priced routes, which had the effect of dissipating profits. In order to control such profit dissipation, the regulatory agency tried to limit food service on some flights to a "sandwich" and then had to define "sandwich" when their size started to get too large. It is also possible that deregulation caused there to be excess flight frequency on some of the long distance links which, due to the distance-based fare structure adopted by the industry, had higher profitability than shorter hops.

Regulation was good to the airline pilots and, to a lesser extent, to other parts of airline labor. Because they worked for employers who did not face any competition from non-union companies, airline pilot wages and working conditions became some of the best in all of American industry.

Unmasking the Beneficiaries of Regulation

Regulation is sometimes seen as a program for consumer protection, rather than a system to guarantee fairness to all parties, including producers. It is likely that the political support for regulation came from this belief. It was, then, a revelation to the public and the Congress that represents them that, in the few intrastate markets where regulated and unregulated carriers competed against one another, the unregulated carriers had far lower fares.[12] In retrospect, the comparison was probably not exactly a fair one: The dense intrastate market between San Francisco and Los Angeles, for example, offers the opportunity for high load factors and thus low prices, and it is precisely these profitable routes that the regulatory system depended on to cross-subsidize lightly used and rural routes. But clearly as well, regulation did not put an emphasis on efficient production and regulators did allow costs to rise. With higher costs, the regulated industry was hard pressed to produce as cheaply as unregulated carriers in those few cases where they competed against one another.

When airline and trucking regulation were unmasked as not protecting the average consumer, political support for it began to crumble. It was attacked on both the left and the right as representing a conspiracy of the industry, and regulators were accused of being *captured* by the industry—a charge that is surely unfair.[13] Regulators were trying to be fair to all parties, including the regulated industry. Airline regulation began to unravel when United Airlines, the largest airline and one that had been denied new routes in favor of weaker carriers, broke ranks with others in the industry and backed deregulation. The trucking industry presented a united front against deregulation; the break came when the Teamsters Union was found to be attempting to bribe a senator to defeat the deregulation bill.

The essential features of both the Airline Deregulation Act of 1978 and the Motor Carrier Deregulation Act of 1980 were the blanket granting of route certificates on a showing of financial ability to operate and a good safety record and the withdrawal of the requirement that carriers get government approval to change prices. No longer was there any need for prices to be similar for large and small shippers or for rural and urban areas. Rates no longer needed to be just, reasonable, and nondiscriminatory. Route rationalization was permitted and encouraged.

The Railroad Industry

It is important to recognize that, while the regulatory agencies were attempting to be fair to all, the railroad industry got few of the benefits that the other modes did. The industry was repeatedly granted permission to raise the rate level, but was denied the opportunity to tailor its rate structure to the new competition that it was experiencing with the motor carrier industry. The industry lost its most profitable traffic to motor carriers and was denied the opportunity to raise rates on the remainder. The regulators forced the industry to maintain passenger service long after it was profitable and prevented the route consolidation and line abandonments that economic efficiency required.

The result was an industry that was remarkably unprofitable. Academic studies claimed that not only were returns on average investment below the opportunity cost of capital, but the *net marginal return* on new investment was negative.[14] With investment so unprofitable, little effort was put into maintaining and modernizing the railroad system. Locomotives broke down and were not repaired; tracks deteriorated and were not put back in good condition. Most of the major carriers east of the Mississippi River were forced into bankruptcy.

Why is it that the same regulatory system that provided the trucking industry with such generous rates of return was sufficiently tough to force large segments of the railroad industry into bankruptcy? There is no reason to suspect that regulators were pro-truck and anti-railroad. Rather, the problem was the regulation itself. In trying to maintain a stable and equitable system, regulation proved incapable of adapting to changed market circumstances after the Second World War. Regulation tried to maintain the stability and equity of the system by freezing the railroad map and rate structure in a previous decade. Attempts to change were met by hostility by those who would be hurt. Regulation in essence provided everyone the right to challenge anything that would alter the status quo.

Railroad deregulation was triggered by the recognition that the financial condition of the railroad industry was causing service levels to be unsatisfactory for large parts of the shipping public. Congress was also forced to pay mounting subsidies to continue service on bankrupt lines. The railroad deregulation bill was explicitly seen as a way to solve the financial problem of the railroads by encouraging consolidation, abandonment, and increases in rates. Congress hoped that the railroad industry would become more profitable by scrapping the system of rate structure regulation that had been in place for 60 years. Believing that there was little market power for railroads left to exploit, Congress directed the Interstate Commerce Commission (which eagerly undertook the task) to encourage the negotiation of secret rates between shippers and carriers. Under the Staggers Act of 1980, the Commission made a graceful exit from the classic form of rate regulation.

THE CURRENT STATE OF TRANSPORT REGULATION

Transport deregulation did not occur in one instant, but was phased in over a period of 10 years or more. In all three of the main regulated industries—railroads, airlines, and motor carriers—the regulatory agency led Congress in weakening or eliminating its own rules. (Indeed, it was crucial for deregulation that the regulators lead, since Congress could then be seen as not harming the interests of any constituents, but rather maintaining a new, deregulated, status quo.)

Today, little is left of the elaborate regulatory structure that used to govern the transportation industries. The Civil Aeronautics Board was disbanded and the Department of Transportation (DOT) is now given the responsibility of overseeing airline operations. The Department of Transportation grants licenses to operate airlines, but the only factors that an applicant needs to show are fitness to serve and a commitment to safety; and when a license is granted, there is no limitation on the routes that may be served. In domestic service, airlines are free to price their services as they see fit, without any need for approval from either rate bureaus or the regulatory authorities.

The only substantial role in the airline industry played by the Department of Transportation is in international relations. Permission to carry passengers internationally is governed by bilateral treaties between the countries connected by the flight. Thus the United States must abide by agreements drafted, in most cases, years ago during the period of domestic airline regulation. Foreign countries have been less willing to move in the direction of complete deregulation of services. Part of the reason is that the United States was the first major nation to decontrol domestic airline operations. The U.S. airlines thus have more experience dealing in a deregulated environment and have adapted labor rules and other practices to take advantage of an environment in which being the low-cost carrier is a major advantage. The Department of Transportation has pushed other nations to deregulate international air links; while recognizing the efficiency advantages of deregulation, foreign countries have been suspicious of U.S. motives, knowing that deregulation puts U.S. carriers in an advantageous position.

Motor carrier deregulation has been as complete as it was for airlines. A carrier applying for operating authority need only show proof of safety, fitness, and insurance. The federal government has now preempted state regulation, so the elimination of entry requirements into the industry (other than safety and insurance considerations) is now extended to local trucking as well.

Rates charged for trucking services are not filed, but are negotiated (confidentially) between shippers and carriers. Under the ICC Termination Act of 1995, tariff filing requirements exist only for household goods movers, intercity buses, water carriers sailing to Alaska, Hawaii, and U.S. territories, and those proposing through rates involving two or more carriers. While the 1995 Act represented an apparently sweeping change, the elimination of formal regulatory oversight over trucking operations in that bill has little practical effect. Since the Motor Carrier Act of 1980, the ICC received no complaints that existing tariff schedules are unreasonable; of the one million proposed rate changes published in 1993, only 20 were protested.

The sole traditional regulated mode of transport that continues to have substantial regulatory oversight is the railroad industry. But since railroads were subject to by far the most severe regulation prior to 1976, railroad deregulation has been more extensive than in any other mode. The primary mechanism by which rail deregulation was implemented was by granting the regulatory agency the authority to make exemptions in specific cases to the existing regulations. The regulators used the authority widely. They exempted from regulation all traffic moving in boxcars or in piggyback service; in addition, they exempted a long list of individual commodities such as motor vehicles, fresh fruits and vegetables, and lumber. For exempt commodities and shipments, rates are subject to negotiation between the railroad and individual shippers.

Railroad regulation is now governed by the ICC Termination Act of 1995 and the new Surface Transportation Board established by the Act. Since the board is very new, many of the regulations that Congress has asked it to administer have yet to be interpreted. Notable among these are standards for reasonableness of rates—standards that Congress directed the board to develop in the next year. Some of the language of previous regulatory statutes is retained in the new law, however. For example, the ICC Termination Act of 1995 requires that before the board makes a determination of whether a rate is *just and reasonable*, as required by regulatory statues, it must first determine that the railroad is *market dominant*. If the proposed rate is less than 180 percent of the government calculated variable cost of movement, the presumption is that the railroad is not market dominant. When a rate on some traffic is set at greater than 180 percent of government calculated variable cost of a movement, a full inquiry can be initiated to discover whether the railroad is market dominant and thus should be required to show that the rate is not unreasonable.

The elimination of tariff filing requirements for railroads, under a decision of the Surface Transportation Board in the summer of 1996, will make meaningful regulation of railroad rates in the future almost impossible. Rather than publish rate schedules, railroads must now merely be prepared to respond within 10 days to a request for rate information from a customer or potential customer. Information about changes in existing rates need to be given only to current and previous customers.

While the full dimensions of rate regulation under the ICC Termination Act of 1995 are yet to be developed, other decisions of the board make it appear that the board will be quite friendly to railroad interests and skeptical of the desirability of inter-railroad competition. In early 1997, the Surface Transportation Board decided that a shipper who has only one railroad serving it cannot use the threat intra-modal competition as a bargaining lever with its carrier. Under this decision, for example, a power plant that is served by railroad A may not enter into a contract to receive coal from a mine served by railroad B unless railroad A agrees—even if the coal is cheaper, less polluting, or of higher quality than the power company could get from mines served by railroad A. The logic is that railroad customers could use the threat of switching sources of supply to a different location as a way of reducing the rates that they had to pay for services to on-line sources of supply. This fear of intra-modal competition is in the tradition of transportation regulation throughout the twentieth century, though the overtly pro-railroad nature of the distrust is new. The decision gives railroads far more power over their customers than is typical of supplier/customer relationships in other industries and has been seen by some observers as likely to spark a push for re-regulation of railroads. At a minimum, the decision will return us to the nineteenth century situation in which producers were reluctant to choose locations not served by at least two railroads.

The Surface Transportation Board continues to hear complaints about unreasonable practices such as refusing to use private cars. It continues to have jurisdiction over rail car supply and interchange, but has ceased to attempt to defeat the law of supply and demand in car supply by setting a uniform price for using cars that does not vary by time or location; questions of car supply are now delegated to an industry committee that is immunized from antitrust prosecution. The board will only intervene in inter-carrier disputes or when it believes that an inefficiency has been created. The board also retains the right to order a railroad to allow another to operate over its lines in the case of emergency.

Unlike other modes, there is no suggestion that the decision to invest or disinvest in railroad lines be deregulated. Unlike the withdrawal of an airline or trucking company from a market, the abandonment of a railroad line is a permanent elimination of the service of a mode of transport to an area of the country. New construction still requires permission, as does abandonment of an existing line. However, the Surface Transportation Board is much more sensitive to the financial burdens placed on carriers by forcing the retention of an unwanted line; regulators have thus been quite liberal in their permission to cease service. Continuing its traditional role as a preserver of services, however, the board has encouraged the takeover of lines to be abandoned by other units that might be able to operate them more economically.

Perhaps the most striking change in the new regulatory statute is the language used in the preamble giving direction to regulators as to what elements to take into account in making decisions. In previous laws governing railroads, the language of consumer protection was most prominent, but under the new law, regulators are directed to give predominant concerns to questions of economic efficiency. In the language of the ICC Termination Act of 1995:

> In regulating the railroad industry, it is the policy of the United States Government—(1) to allow, to the maximum extent possible, competition and the demand for services to establish reasonable rates for transportation by rail; (2) to minimize the need for Federal regulatory control over the rail transportation system and to require fair and expeditious regulatory decisions when regulation is required; (3) to promote a safe and efficient rail transportation system by allowing rail carriers to earn adequate revenues, as determined by the Board; (4) to ensure the development and continuation of a sound rail transportation system with effective competition among rail carriers and with other modes, to meet the needs of the public and the national defense; (5) to foster sound economic conditions in transportation and to ensure effective competition and coordination between rail carriers and other modes; (6) to maintain reasonable rates where there is an absence of effective competition and where rail rates provide revenues which exceed the

amount necessary to maintain the rail system and to attract capital; (7) to reduce regulatory barriers to entry into and exit from the industry; (8) to operate transportation facilities and equipment without detriment to the public health and safety; (9) to encourage honest and efficient management of railroads; (10) to require rail carriers, to the maximum extent practicable, to rely on individual rate increases, and to limit the use of increases of general applicability; (11) to encourage fair wages and safe and suitable working conditions in the railroad industry; (12) to prohibit predatory pricing and practices, to avoid undue concentrations of market power, and to prohibit unlawful discrimination; (13) to ensure the availability of accurate cost information in regulatory proceedings, while minimizing the burden on rail carriers of developing and maintaining the capability of providing such information; (14) to encourage and promote energy conservation; and (15) to provide for the expeditious handling and resolution of all proceedings.[15]

Regulators are still directed to take into account some non-economic goals (e.g., energy conservation), and there is still a direction to control market power, but these themes are much muted in the new law.

THE EFFECTS OF DEREGULATION

Economists have treated transportation deregulation as a great natural experiment. The effects of deregulation have been studied to try to understand the fundamental effects that regulation has on industry in general. There are two reasons to hesitate about accepting documented changes between the regulated and deregulated environments as representing the effect of government regulation generally. First, transportation regulation was in many ways unique. For example, in no other area of government intervention was the focus so completely on the structure of prices rather than their level. Second, all the transportation industries were adapting to new technologies, opportunities, and cost conditions both before and after deregulation.[16] For example, in the years before deregulation there were annual improvements in the cost and safety of airline services, and this pattern continued after deregulation. It would seem incorrect to attribute the continuation of the trend to the deregulatory event. Studies of the effect of deregulation must control for other influences of the changing times.

Railroad Deregulation

Railroad deregulation generated less controversy than could have been expected, perhaps in part because it brought about an immediate improvement in the financial condition of American railroads which allowed an improvement in railroad service quality; track maintenance improved following deregulation, speeds increased and locomotive shortages disappeared. Safety improved as hazardous chemical spills caused by derailments were reduced. For many shippers, the level of service provided under regulation was intolerably poor and higher rates were an acceptable price to pay to achieve a more acceptable quality of service.

Railroad deregulation has been the subject of numerous analyses.[17] Without exception, they have found that railroad deregulation generated efficiency improvements, though the magnitude of the savings is subject to disagreement. It is indisputable as well that railroad deregulation increased the financial health of the industry. But what is perhaps most striking about the studies of deregulation is the range of factors that railroad deregulation did not affect. For example, despite the predictions that railroad deregulation would lead to a large and rapid shift of traffic from trucks to railroads, this did not occur. As noted in Chapter 3, the percentage split of freight traffic between railroads and trucks is essentially the same as it was in the 1970s under regulation. In the past several years, there have been some documented shifts of traffic from trucks to trains—most notably transcontinental movements of manufactured goods—and it can be argued that these shifts would not have been possible under regulation. But railroads have continued to lose market share to trucks in the shorter-haul markets where there is a great deal more traffic than in long-haul markets. Apparently, the market shifts brought about by deregulation did not solely advantage either railroads or trucks.

Another aspect of the railroad business that was not affected by deregulation was labor relations. The ability of rail labor to prevent the erosion of wages of workers is in contrast to the airline and trucking industries where workers' wages were among the first elements affected by deregulation. Labor was not as successful, however, in retaining employment levels. Following deregulation, railroad employment fell by half.

The decline in railroad employment following deregulation is only one part of the large shift in railroad operations that followed deregulation. As described in Chapter 8, the number of miles of railroad track declined and the number of train-miles fell as well. At the same time, the level of railroad traffic continued to climb. Following deregulation, there was a consolidation of traffic on fewer lines with fewer but much longer trains. As a result of this stunning increase in productivity, railroad costs per ton-mile declined markedly after deregulation.

Before and after descriptions of employment and mileage in the railroad industry do not touch on the improved service quality that followed railroad deregulation. It seems odd that a service that provides fewer trains with more cars attached to them can be considered to have improved service, but that is the case. The reason is that quality has many aspects and service frequency is only one of them. It has long been argued, for example, that the predictability of delivery was more important to railroad customers than average transit time. Following the financial improvements in the railroad industry, investment funds could be secured to repair tracks and locomotives and to buy new rolling stock. This allowed higher speed service with more reliable connections.

Railroad service in some corridors is now sufficiently fast, reliable, and inexpensive that some trucking companies are contracting to have trucks carried by the railroads with whom they compete.

It is difficult to imagine that a regulated railroad industry would have been able to achieve comparable improvements in service quality. One reason is that regulation interfered with the setting of service quality. When it limits prices but not the type of service that the prices buy, regulation of firms with market power effectively encourages a reduction in service quality to the monopoly level or the minimum permissible by the regulator. Deregulation has allowed the sale of services with different qualities at different prices, thus allowing those who wish to pay for higher quality to be able to get the premium service that they need.

▬ Motor Carrier Deregulation

Deregulation of trucking had as its first expression the realignment of the maddeningly irrational route and commodity structures imposed on carriers.[18] With deregulation, the trucking industry began to develop an efficient hub-and-spoke system for collecting, transporting, and delivering freight for a wide enough group of shippers to assure a consistently high load factor. It was also immediately apparent to industry members that the ability to freely develop a route structure would give overwhelming advantages to firms with the largest route structures. With mergers ruled out by problems of unfunded pension liabilities, the for-hire industry embarked on a program of terminal building. The capacity expansion occurred in the early 1980s, at precisely the period when a severe recession reduced the amount of freight being moved. The logical consequence of the resulting over-capacity was financial pressure on the for-hire industry. Unfortunately, the financial leverage that the industry had taken on during the period of regulation left it vulnerable when competition and over-capacity appeared. A majority of the top 20 trucking firms prior to deregulation slid into bankruptcy in the years following deregulation and stopped service.

Not all of the members of the trucking industry felt the financial pressures of over-capacity and competition equally. Non-union regional carriers expanded rapidly at the expense of the high cost unionized firms. In addition, a group of three carriers with national route structures (Roadway, Yellow, and CNF Transportation) took advantage of the network economies of a large system described in Chapter 5 and expanded at the expense of the failing companies, often by buying the facilities of bankrupt carriers. The Big 3 of the trucking industry also developed their own regional non-union carriers to compete for traffic.

Network economies are especially important for collection and distribution of traffic, and this is the main function of the less-than-truckload (LTL) sector of the industry. In this sector, deregulation produced a rapid increase in concentration. It is now clear that regulation maintained a competitive structure of the industry by protecting inefficiently small carriers. How far the increase in concentration in the LTL sector will continue is not clear.

Deregulation also had the effect of producing specialization of trucking firms. While under regulation, less-than-truckload and truckload services were performed by the same firm; increasingly we now find different sets of firms performing these functions. There has been a rise of specialized truckload carriers who have very little investment in terminal buildings, but use data processing to optimally dispatch vehicles and match front- and back-hauls. As described in Chapter 8, by keeping load factors high, these so called *advanced truckload firms* have been able to operate with costs that approach those of railroads.

Along with stockholders in trucking companies, the major losers under trucking deregulation were unionized truck drivers. The pressure on the Teamsters Union to offer carriers lower wage rates and more flexible working conditions comes from the expansion of non-union carriers, especially in the truckload market. Competition from non-union carriers allowed entry into the market because deregulation led to the layoff of as much as one-third of the teamsters union membership. Deregulation has reduced wages and time paid for but not worked, and has forced more flexible work rules.

Unlike the railroad industry, in which deregulation has clearly led to large improvements in productivity, the real effects of trucking deregulation have been surprisingly modest. While the decrease in drivers' wages that followed deregulation have clearly lowered trucking costs, there has not been a similar major effect due to system rationalization following deregulation. By one estimate, deregulation caused an increase in productivity in the for-hire industry by increasing the usage of trucks between 4 and 13 percent per year, though in all cases the effect of deregulation is statistically insignificant. However, there is reason to believe that this figure is too high: The increased mileage per truck occurred at the same time that the interstate highway was being completed and is similar to productivity improvements that occurred in exempt sectors of the trucking industry. It appears, then, that the major effects of trucking regulation were in the form of income transfers rather than efficiency losses.

While the effect of deregulation on trucking productivity may have been modest, it can be argued that the effect on the economy has been much larger. It is possible that non-cost based rates caused an inefficient switch of economic activity to rural areas (though the feared loss of service to lightly populated areas that was put forward as a justification for regulation does not appear to have occurred). Similarly, if rates increase more rapidly than costs as distance increases, production will be held too close to consumption areas. Unfortunately, as noted in Chapter 2, location theory and economic geography have not progressed to a point where they can be used to make even the roughest magnitudes of the size of location distortions that may have been generated by regulated rates. Perhaps one of the most important consequence of trucking regulation is thus unmeasurable.

Another unmeasurable but perhaps extraordinarily important consequence of price regulation was its discouragement of service innovation. To prevent costly quality competition and to support price regulation generally, the ICC forbade service offerings with performance guarantees and financial penalties in the event that a carrier did not deliver a shipment when promised. However, without performance guarantees, just-in-time inventory methods are impossible. Thus economic regulation was incompatible with one of the most important innovations in modern manufacturing.

A potentially measurable consequence of economic regulation, but one that has not yet been attempted, was the transactions costs imposed on shippers by the remarkably complex rate structures and route systems used under regulation. The limitation on commodities and routes meant that a shipper could not depend on any particular carrier to be able to handle all of its freight. As a result, a shipper might have several carriers calling at its loading docks during the day, each picking up freight for a different destination. Shipping to a new destination similarly might require a search by the shipper's traffic department to identify which carriers had authority to handle freight to that location. Deregulation has meant that each shipper can deal with many fewer carriers, each of which may be able to serve all of its shipping needs; deregulation has also brought a movement to far simpler rate structures. The combination of these two factors has meant that shippers are able to operate with much smaller traffic departments. Since these transactions costs will appear only in the finances of shippers, a study of the transportation industries before and after regulation will not reveal any of these savings.

The relative rates of LTL and truckload shipments will also determine the extent to which a shipper will ship more frequently and in smaller lot sizes or hold shipments until it is economical to ship an entire truckload. The reduction in the relative costs of LTL service following deregulation has apparently led to a shift toward greater use of LTL service. This reorganization of inventory methods to make better use of smaller shipments—part of just-in-time inventory systems—must have led to economic efficiencies in the economy as a whole. Again, however, these savings will show up in the books of the shippers in the form of a lower sum of inventory and transportation costs. In the transportation sector as a whole, the costs show up as an increase in average revenue per ton-mile as shippers reduce their use of low cost truckload service in favor of the more expensive partial-lot shipments.

A final aspect of trucking use that was affected by price deregulation was the decision to use private versus for-hire trucking. Economic controls encouraged shippers to develop their own trucking fleets to bypass the relatively high-priced regulated industry. But regulation also imposed higher costs on private shippers by limiting their ability to pick up back-hauls and to share capacity with other shippers. The combination of these two factors apparently offset one another. There was no perceptible shift following deregulation to for-hire trucking. The for-hire truck share of combined rail and truck ton-miles remained at about 17 percent throughout the 1970s and '80s, while private fleets appear to have gained a percentage point or two to about 24 percent of combined ton-miles at the expense of railroads over the same period. The stable market shares hide a movement toward increased specialization in the use of trucking fleets. Private fleets generally expanded following trucking deregulation with the new trucks devoted to truckload shipments of a firm's own shipping needs with LTL shipments increasingly turned over to the for-hire industry. Shippers also moved out of the general purpose trucking business.

As noted earlier, transportation regulation never had as its sole purpose the promotion of economic efficiency. Far more important have been the promotion of a safe, stable, and predictable system of transportation which does not give undue preferences to one shipper or another. These criteria of justness, reasonableness, and nondiscrimination have often incorrectly been ignored by those who have attempted to measure the effects of regulation. The Interstate Commerce Commission's interpretation of its mandate that rates be just, reasonable, and nondiscriminatory included, among others, the provision that small shippers be afforded the same rates as large shippers even when the cost of serving them was higher. While there have been no systematic studies of the change in the rate structure following deregulation—with rates now secret, it is hard to imagine how one could carry out such a study—it is reasonable to assume that much or all of this *equalizing discrimination* has disappeared. In its place has come a system dominated by volume discounts to large shippers.

Airline Deregulation

Economists were active in advocacy for airline deregulation, and it was natural that they also were eager to evaluate the results of the experiment.[19] Yet the pure effect of deregulation has been hard to distill among the other factors that affected the industry. One reason is seen in Figure 13.2, which shows trends in air traffic and average fares before and after deregulation. While there has been a sharp increase in traffic and a significant decrease in fares following deregulation (which for airlines can be assumed to have taken place between 1976 and 1980), both of these apparent effects were extrapolations of long established trends. It appears that there may have been an acceleration of the increase in airline traffic, and this has been attributed to the introduction of differential pricing to attract price-sensitive passengers.

The decline in average fare levels following deregulation was not the result of reductions in the standard fares, as it had been prior to 1976. Rather, the changes were brought about by changing the structure of fares, and particularly by varying the availability of discounts. Whereas most traffic prior to deregulation was at posted fares, after deregulation there was a shift to variable discounts as the primary form of pricing. Today, about 90 percent of passenger-miles are flown on discounted tickets.

There was also a strong movement away from the old linear distance-based fare scheme toward one that also reflects the importance of traffic density. Fare structures now contain what would have been considered long-haul-short-haul discrimination and discrimination against small communities. The new fare structure undoubtedly better reflects the costs of serving different airports. Several studies have demonstrated, however, that the concentration of sales in individual intercity pairs also affects the fares on those routes.

Economic analysis had not anticipated that the main effect of deregulation would be seen in changes in fare structure rather than fare levels. Deregulation has apparently increased rather than decreased the importance of systematic price discrimination and product differentiation in the industry, even as it has moved rates closer to costs. In 1994, promotion and sales expenses stood at 15 percent of industry revenues.

FIGURE 13.2   Trends in U.S. Airline Fares and Traffic

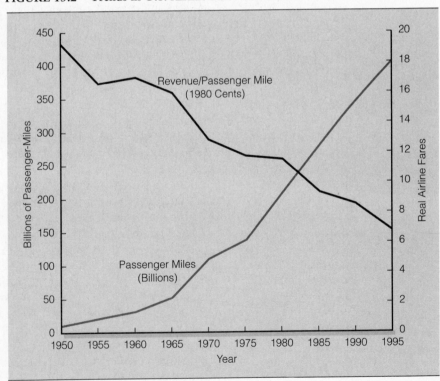

SOURCE: *Transportation in America*, 14th edition

A striking effect of deregulation has been the restructuring of airline networks as hubs and spokes. Combined with an adaptation of the aircraft stock to service such a system, this change should have the effect of increasing load factors, thereby increasing productivity and lowering costs. In 1996, industry load factors averaged approximately 70 percent, far higher than the 60 percent load factors that were common in the mid 1970s, prior to deregulation.

Since the birth of the industry, changes in productivity have been associated with changes in the size and utilization of aircraft. One of the most important factors reducing airline productivity under regulation was claimed to be the buying of aircraft that were larger than appropriate for the routes served in order to compete on the basis of service quality. Quality is multidimensional and notoriously difficult to measure, and thus has been ignored in most standard economic analyses. In the airline industry, however, the analysis of service quality played a central role in the deregulation effort, where excessive service quality was offered as an explanation for why airline profits were not excessive before deregulation despite higher prices in corridors where regulated and unregulated airlines competed against one another. Quality attributes have variously been identified as load factor, size of aircraft, food preparation, baggage handling, and flight frequency.

Whether service quality dropped after deregulation depends on which aspect one considers. Flight frequency generally did not fall following deregulation. Load factors have risen, in part due to the greater use of smaller aircraft to serve thin markets. Some studies suggest that non-capacity aspects of air service (amenities, comfort, on-time service) declined in quality following 1978. Any movements in the average level of service quality are overwhelmed by changes in the structure of service quality between city pairs. There has been a marked increase in flight frequency between large hubs and a decrease in number of seats flown to smaller airports. Some smaller cities have lost air service completely, and those that retain it are served by companies using smaller aircraft.

Shortly after deregulation, there was entry by new non-union airlines. These airlines had lower costs and fares as a result of higher load factors, less restrictive work rules, and lower wage rates. By the late 1980s, however, these airlines had almost all disappeared, either through their own mismanagement or through predatory behavior on the part of incumbent carriers. In the 1990s, partly due to the availability of fleets of inexpensive used aircraft, non-union entrants were again beginning to challenge the dominance of the major airlines. In the mid-1990s, several crashes of possibly undermaintained older aircraft flown by new airlines again cast doubt on the ability of new carriers using old equipment to successfully challenge the dominant firms.

Like the trucking industry, the airline industry has seen a large increase in concentration, though in this sector, the reduction in firms was achieved through mergers rather than bankruptcies. The mergers have left many airports as *fortress hubs* in which the dominant carrier is able to protect its market share despite charging higher fares at that airport than it does at airports where it has a smaller market share. In some cases, it costs a customer less to fly through a hub than to get off the plane at the hub. This appears to be irrational to passengers and clearly a sign of market power. Economic observers have been more willing to attribute it to subsidy-free pricing rules. [20]

Unlike motor carriers, there is no segment of the airline industry that has been consistently profitable. Aggregate losses of the industry in the early 1990s reached a total of $10 billion, with each of the traditional major carriers making losses. The industry throughout the deregulated era has been subject to numerous bankruptcies. These financial losses have continued to feed the merger movement that is generating higher concentration throughout the industry. By the mid-1990s, the financial decline in the industry had stopped, with a stable and modestly profitable equilibrium apparently achieved.

Deregulation has been especially hard on unionized labor. Deregulation permitted non-union carriers to enter markets traditionally flown only by unionized airlines. Non-union airlines eliminated craft distinctions and enjoyed wage rates that are 25–30 percent below union pay scales. This combination allowed them to charge lower prices. Despite the fact that the new carriers did not divert substantial amounts of traffic from the major carriers, the new airlines were the major cause of the concession bargaining in the industry. The new union contracts increase pilot hours per month, permit employees to cross craft lines, allow limited use of part-time workers, and reduce cockpit crew requirements. The contracts also contain lower wage increases than were traditional and permit a two-tier wage structure with much lower wage-tenure profiles for new workers.

DEREGULATION'S LESSONS ABOUT THE CONTROL OF MARKET POWER IN TRANSPORTATION

In all modes, deregulation led to an immediate restructuring of networks and an increase in concentration. It appears that regulation had the effect of protecting inefficiently small carriers and imposing route networks that were not operationally well balanced. Regulation gave favorable access to rural areas and small shippers at the expense of more densely populated sections of the country and larger firms. Deregulation also had as its immediate effect the alteration of the structure of prices; the change in the average level of rates charged is of secondary magnitude. Given the intensity of effort expended by regulators on the structure of rates and services, and the limited oversight given to their level, it should come as no surprise that structural effects were the main effects of deregulation.

These two changes occurred following deregulation in all modes of transportation. In other aspects, deregulation treated modes differently, though often it is the railroad industry that was different and the airline and motor carrier sectors whose experiences were alike. For example, rail labor appears to have benefited by deregulation, while airline and trucking labor have been hard hit. Airline and trucking profits have declined since deregulation, while the net income of railroads has soared.

Regulation can correctly be criticized for ignoring efficiency questions in the quest for stability and equity, and eventually it was the high costs of the regulated transport system that helped cause the collapse of the institution as the unfavorable price comparison between comparable regulated and unregulated airline and motor carrier services were publicized. Regulatory-imposed inefficiencies similarly led to the service problems and financial difficulties that eventually led to railroad deregulation.

It is also hard to argue against the proposition that interested parties manipulated the regulatory process for their own advantage. This appears to be most clear in the case of motor carriers and the truck drivers that they employed. But such manipulation is not inevitable in the system, as illustrated by the fact that railroads were harmed by regulation despite their best efforts to use the system to their advantage. Regulation also appears to have been unnecessary for railroad labor to win unusually favorable wages and working conditions (though the inherent barriers to entry into a sunk-cost intensive declining industry can perhaps be used to explain the why deregulation did not leave rail labor vulnerable).

Other effects of transport regulation are somewhat more speculative since it is difficult to separate regulatory effects from changes in technology and pressures for change that has affected all of American industry since 1980. For example, deregulation appears to have improved service quality in many instances, or at least to have offered customers the option to purchase a higher quality service than was offered under regulation. There is reason to believe that deregulation would have had this effect: The equity-based standards applied by regulators were suspicious of special services being offered to individual customers that were not available to others, and the delegation of decisions on operations to industry groups tended to give the veto power to carriers who were slow to adapt. Deregulation, by eliminating the concern that each customer be treated equally, has encouraged the development of a menu of services.

Perhaps the most important lesson of the period of regulation is the difficulty in undertaking the task that the regulatory commissions took on. Opportunity costs in transportation are highly variable and sensitive to exact times and locations. In order to efficiently regulate individual prices when costs are so variable, it would be necessary to constantly alter the prices that carriers can charge, with different prices being charged depending on the season, direction of travel, and the time and route of travel. This is administratively impossible. The Interstate Commerce Commission recognized the unfeasibility of this task and so delegated much of its rate making authority to the very carriers whose rates it was charged with controlling. To make the process of control a bit more practicable (as well as to encourage the sort of fairness that it aimed for), all transportation regulatory commissions tried to find rules to make pricing manageable—for example, the distance rules of airline regulation or the uniform rate rules of railroad car rentals. But by trying to develop regularities to gain some administrative order on transportation regulation, the regulatory commissions necessarily imposed prices that deviated from costs. Inevitable market distortions and inefficiencies followed.

ALTERNATIVE MECHANISMS FOR CONTROLLING MARKET POWER IN TRANSPORTATION

Regulation to control market power in transportation is now recognized as a failure—or, at least regulation of the form practiced in the mid to late twentieth century is now seen as having led to unacceptable inefficiencies.[21] But the problem of market power in transportation, while much attenuated relative to earlier in the twentieth century, has not disappeared. In the railroad industry, coal shippers and to a lesser extent agricultural and chemical interests continue to complain about railroad abuses of market power. Consumers complain about the high prices that they must pay for tickets to fly from airline hubs. Business men and women complain of the high prices that they must pay to fly at short notice. Given the increasing concentration in all modes of transportation—even though they are probably the result of the network economies described in Chapter 5—one can anticipate that these voices will be making a continuing plea for public oversight over carriers who have the power to arbitrarily make decisions that strongly affect the lives of communities, industries, and individuals.

It is easy to sympathize with these efforts. For example, coal shippers are captive to railroads in the sense that the railroad that connects to the mine mouth is in the position to capture the profits of the mine by appropriately pricing railroad transport. But how would one recognize that a railroad was abusing its market power? According to the definition of subsidy-free prices, for coal shippers to show that they are cross-subsidizing some other group of shippers, they must be able to show that a railroad network that stripped away some other group of shippers could be operated more profitably than the current one. This is the stand-alone test for cross-subsidization.[22] Unfortunately, this is impossible for coal shippers to show since, with rates secret, they do not know the revenue contributions of other shippers on the system. We are left in the position of saying that railroads have a group of costs that can be allocated subject to efficiency and subsidy-free criteria, and that it is therefore not impossible that the allocation that railroads wish to retrieve from coal shippers is justified. But it just as easily may be unjustifiably large as well. The information is simply not available to make that judgment.

Similarly, it is easy to understand the anger of passengers who feel that the airline that provides the only acceptable service has sized up their demand and decided that they can afford to pay more. All market segmentation devices are designed to get as much net revenue as possible from the customers. But the suggestion that we return to the more uniform prices of the regulated era should certainly be resisted. As noted in the discussion of the hypothetical toll bridge monopolist in the previous chapter, market segmentation that attempts to convert as much of the consumer willingness to pay into company revenue has the desirable effect of reducing the inefficiency of monopoly pricing. By allowing those travelers in the right tail of the demand curve to travel at lower fares, price discrimination increases the efficiency with which airline equipment is used. A uniform fare would surely reduce the amount of air travel.

It is also likely that airlines who charged a single fare to all passengers in an airplane would not cover the costs of many flights. In order to give airlines an incentive to schedule the efficient number of flights, it is necessary to guarantee that flights do not cross-subsidize one another; thus fares of passengers on each flight should be charged, as a group, the opportunity cost of operating a flight. As described in Chapter 12, for flights that an airline expects to be uncrowded, subsidy-free pricing conditions will require that fares charged be above the marginal costs of carrying a passenger. Since airlines cannot in general sell annual passes to take particular flights, the Ramsey pricing second best rule will call for charging higher prices on a flight to those with the lower elasticities of demand. Many market segmentation criteria are proxies for demand elasticities for particular flights; the classic example is the requirement that passengers stay at their destination over Saturday night in order to get a discounted ticket—a condition that is widely assumed to separate business travelers (whose demand elasticity is presumed to be low) from those with higher elasticities of demand.

Recall, in addition, from Chapter 12 that a scheduled airline service is more costly to operate than one based on charter services with their high load factors. To induce occasional travelers to use the same system as business travelers, it is necessary to offer them fares that are not so high that they would turn to charter service. That is, lower fares for non-business travelers are necessary to prevent them from cross-subsidizing travelers who benefit from scheduled service. Thus it is not at all clear that high ticket prices charged to those who value the assurance that a seat will be available at short notice on their preferred flight in fact cross-subsidize vacation travelers with their much lower priced tickets. It could be quite the opposite—that even with their high ticket prices, travelers with short planning horizons are cross-subsidized by those with low ticket prices; this would occur if splitting the air travel industry into two halves with occasional travel offered by charter service would allow the low priced ticket to be even less expensive.

Some of the market segmentation devices used in the airline industry may thus be consistent with economic efficiency and subsidy-free pricing. As noted previously, this is particularly likely for market segmentation tools designed to charge higher prices to travelers who value the ability to make last minute travel plans. It is also a reason to charge travelers who fly through hubs lower prices than those who fly direct since travel through hubs can achieve the same likelihood of being able to get a seat on your preferred flight with higher average load factors. It is not as clear that the rule requiring a stay over Saturday night is consistent with efficient and/or subsidy-free pricing principles. This requirement may simply be a mechanism for identifying a group that has less elastic demand. On the other hand, the groups with low demand elasticities tend to be business travelers; public policy has generally approved of schemes that charge higher prices to business users, if it allows lower prices to be charged to the general consuming public.

Much, if not most, of the complex airline fair structure can at least partially be justified by principles of efficient pricing and/or subsidy-free pricing. It is virtually impossible to impose a regulated fare structure that would satisfy the two principles since it is infeasible for an outsider to be able to estimate the opportunity cost of a particular traveler on a particular flight. The remarkably complex airline price structure is justified by an equally complex structure of opportunity costs. A regulator who tried to guarantee efficient and subsidy-free pricing would have to accept a complex and volatile fare structure. It is inconceivable that a regulator would be able to oversee the adjustments that an airline makes each night in the number of seats on each flight that are devoted to each fare class; but these adjustments, which are necessary to encourage efficient use of airline seats, can also be use to enhance monopoly positions. Efficient airline regulation is, in short, like efficient railroad regulation, technically infeasible; a fare system that could be practically overseen by a regulator would have to be much simpler than the current one and thus inherently less efficient.

While direct price regulation in transportation appears to have fatal flaws, there are alternative mechanisms for controlling market power. For example, if shipper complaints about railroad abuse of economic power continue to be heard, consideration should be given to disintegrating railroad operations from their fixed facilities. It is, after all, the fixed facilities that are the basis of railroad monopoly power. Disintegration of track ownership and train operation is not an untried option. Some European countries currently divide track ownership and operations as a way of more accurately calculating costs and thus the need for subsidies to different classes of service. A current proposal in the European Union calls for opening a series of open-access freight corridors on rail lines among major cities. The separation of electricity generation from transmission and distribution line ownership is currently used in Britain as a device for deregulating that sector.

If railroad tracks were commonly owned by all operators or by the federal government and any shipper or train operator could use any tracks—as is the case now with highways—the problem of railroad economic power as well as the necessity of funding fixed facilities through rent transfers would disappear. A partial move in this direction could be achieved by directing railroads to permit the use of their tracks by other operators who are willing to pay an appropriate rental fee.[23] One must assume, however, that even with full disintegration of track ownership and operations, train operators would retain classification yards and would thus at best become partially integrated carriers like airlines or LTL motor carriers. Nonetheless, disintegration of tracks and operations might reduce the economic power of railroads sufficiently to eliminate the political call for economic regulation.

Similarly, while efficient regulatory oversight of the airline price structure appears to be impractical, there are public policy tools that can be used to discourage monopoly pricing. These tools are all designed to encourage competition among airline companies. Most important is the maintenance of adequate numbers of independent airlines to inhibit tacit monopoly pricing.

In order to simplify tacit cooperation among themselves, airlines will typically separate changes in rate levels from rate structures. Rate level changes are announced in the national media and are quoted in simple percentage or dollar terms. If other airlines match these price increases, the rate level change will stick. Otherwise, it will be rolled back to a level that other airlines are willing to go along with.

Separating rate level changes, which are easy to communicate to one's competitors, from rate structure changes, which are difficult to communicate, increases the likelihood of cooperation among airlines. This tends to focus competitive attention towards alteration in rate structures. Making rate structure changes is as easy as lowering the posted fare in the computerized reservation system. But every airline is immediately aware of the fare change, and a response from those who feel threatened is certain. For example, if Reno Air attempts to increase its traffic out of Minneapolis, a Northwest hub, by lowering its fares out of those city, Northwest is likely to match the fare decrease, and perhaps even overshoot the fare decrease to indicate to Reno that its action has been recognized and disapproved of. The fare code that Northwest might attach to the fare could be interpretable as a fighting, strategic action designed to make its competitor back off.[24] The ability of computerized reservation systems to provide instantaneous information on your competitor's rate structure and the ability to respond quickly in nonverbal form helps the industry to control fare cutting. The practice is currently under review by antitrust authorities as allowing airlines to take predatory actions against new entrants—in effect scaring them away by threatening to engage in prolonged economic warfare if they try to enter an established market.

One of the best ways to control the ability of airlines to use their market power is to ease entry barriers and to try to limit the ability of airlines to collude with one another using some of the tacit, nonverbal means that they have been using. One technique is to try to control information that companies have about their competitors' pricing or to try to prevent the sort of instantaneous retaliation that helps incumbent carriers police their price structure. If airlines were able to successfully challenge each other's price structure, the importance of price level changes would decline. If existing airlines could not immediately introduce fighting fares into the computer system whenever a new competitor appeared and eliminate them when the competitor disappeared, entry would be more common.

Another tool that airlines have used to control entry into the cities in which they are dominant is to control the availability of gates or landing slots. For example, with US Air controlling most traffic to and from Pittsburgh airport, it is in a strong position to influence the airport authority's decisions on expansion and the assignment of gates. Dependent as they are on revenues from the incumbent carrier, airport authorities are far too willing to accede to requests from existing carriers to adopt policies that make entry difficult for new carriers. Several important airports also have federally-mandated limitations on landing slots. It could be a public policy objective to distribute these slots in a way that increased, rather than limited competition. (It should be noted, however, that there is a conflict between wishing to minimize tax burdens by getting as high a price for the use of public property like airline slots and wishing to encourage competition, which necessarily reduces the value that potential users will be willing to pay.)

As in the case of railroads, there has been dismay among economists about the lenient treatment given to mergers within the airline industry. If re-regulation is to be avoided, structural competition must be maintained, and this requires adequate numbers of independent companies. To maintain or increase the number of independent carriers, it may be necessary to act to control aspects of behavior that enhance network economies.

Important among these may be the limitation or elimination of frequent flier programs and controlling the nature of travel agent reimbursements. If these fail to maintain a sufficiently large number of carriers, federal authorities could act to open up domestic markets to carriers based outside the country. The hope of those who propose this alternative is that by integrating U.S. airlines with the rest of the world, a larger number of carriers could be supported in equilibrium; this appears to be an unlikely solution, however, since, as demonstrated in Chapter 5, network economies are local and depend on the geographical position of travel origins and destinations; it seems implausible that the international traffic can be used to maintain a carrier whose domestic route network is not sufficiently dense.

Market power in trucking derives from network economies. There is some concern that a concentrated LTL industry will be able to coordinate pricing policies in the same way that the New York-Washington air shuttle participants have been able to do. To date, such monopoly pricing has not been possible for LTL carriers; their main problems have stemmed from extensive overcapacity as individual carriers have rushed to increase the geographic extent of their networks by building new terminals and acquiring new equipment. If the equilibrium structure of the LTL industry is as concentrated as it now appears that it will be, however, there will be ample opportunity for the industry to coordinate its pricing.

Even an industry with very high concentration may not cause public concern about market power, however. As long as there is an unconcentrated truckload sector, an active market in freight forwarding and brokerage, and the ability to do private trucking, the ability of an oligopoly trucking industry to limit the profitability of their customers would seem to be small. An example of this phenomenon is provided by the small package delivery business which is overwhelmingly dominated by a single carrier, UPS. There are few complaints about the firm's market power, however, since users believe that they are protected by arbitrary actions by the availability of parcel post and air express services. If the need should arise to try to control market power by a future concentrated LTL sector, it is now clear that rate regulation and entry limitation should be avoided. Rather those factors that lead to network economies—notably, the ownership of fixed facilities—should be examined to see if it is possible to increase the number of attractive alternatives available to shippers without resorting to price regulation.

CONCLUSION

Economic regulation has all but disappeared from American transportation. Nonetheless, the transport industries developed under regulation and the issue of the control of market power continue to be discussed. It is thus important to understand transportation regulation and what effects it had on the industries.

Regulation as practiced on American railroads tried to guarantee railroads a normal rate of return on a fair value of their assets while controlling the price structure to equalize advantages and disadvantages of shippers. Most of the regulatory effort was directed toward rate structure regulation, rather than rate level regulation. In order to support a rate structure in which railroads were not allowed to disadvantage vulnerable shippers, the Interstate Commerce Commission had to control a large segment of railroad operations. Chief among the operating decisions that were controlled by the government was the decision to abandon service. In the interests of equity and stability, regulation forced the industry to operate a much more extensive system of routes than it would have wished to use. This put more pressure on the industry to look for revenues from shippers in a position to pay more. In the process of protecting these shippers and communities, the ICC enforced an extremely inefficient price structure which hastened traffic loss to trucks and accelerated the financial distress of the industry.

Railroads do have economic power over their customers in the sense that they have discretion in setting rates and that rate decisions made by railroads have important economic consequences. The main dispute currently concerns the rates that are charged to coal shippers. Optimal rail rates are determined primarily by the condition that rates be subsidy-free. Unfortunately, it is impossible for those outside the railroad industry to determine whether or not coal shippers are cross-subsidizing other shippers or being cross-subsidized by them.

The fact that the railroad industry was severely disadvantaged by economic regulation shows that regulators were not *captive* to the industry. They attempted to be fair to all interested parties—consumers, labor, and carriers—and tried to ensure stability of firms in the transport sector. The motor carrier industry took advantage of the willingness of regulators to curb competition in the name of equity and stability and prospered under regulation. The entry controls that were given as a payment for the loss of freedom to set their own price structure provided a huge advantage to regulated carriers. In fact, the administrative unworkability of direct price regulation in the motor carrier industry allowed the industry to use the regulatory apparatus to eliminate competition among members of the industry, with government regulators providing, at best, nominal oversight.

Deregulation had the effects of dismantling the government-sanctioned collective ratemaking in the trucking industry and allowing free entry. Due to its partially integrated structure, the less-than-truckload industry is not properly characterized as perfectly competitive. Market power is not yet a problem among LTL motor carriers, but the partially integrated structure of the industry suggests that problems may appear in the future. The industry is rapidly concentrating into a triopoly of firms with national coverage with a fringe of regional carriers. As this is written, it is not clear how far the network economies associated with terminals and the size of trucks will increase industry concentration. However, even an industry that is tightly concentrated would be limited in its power to exercise economic power due to the ability of firms to turn to the truckload industry, private carriage, and intermediaries if rates got too high.

Currently, truckload carriers in essence subcontract much of their marketing services to freight brokers. Brokers are especially useful in finding backhauls for a trucker who has hauled a load in one direction. However, brokers are becoming increasing influential in the less-than-truckload market as well, finding what are essentially LTL loads for carriers who specialize in truckload shipments. This has blurred the distinction between the two industries and further eroded the power of the LTL industry to raise prices above what a competitive market would allow.

Airlines also have some economic power, though it is not as serious as the economic power of railroads since airlines cannot through their pricing make life-or-death decisions about the health of particular localities or industries. Monopoly behavior in the airline industry will be expressed as some combination of higher fares and less frequent service than would be observed under competitive conditions.

Airline market power is best controlled through increased competition among carriers. Airlines have been successful at limiting entry into the industry through a variety of predatory and apparently benign policies: frequent flier programs, directed price cutting, advertising, price discrimination, control of gates at airports, rebates to travel agents, and preferential listing of flights on reservations computers. A policy of curbing market power of airlines will have to deal with these practices. The history of transport regulation shows that direct attempts to control market power by limiting the prices charged for services will be extremely unwise.

NOTES

1. An encyclopedic description of transportation regulation as practiced in the stable period prior to deregulation is found in Locklin, D. Philip, *Economics of Transportation*, various editions from 1935 through 1972 (Homewood, IL: Richard D. Irwin).
2. For example, the Standard Oil Company was famous for its ability to negotiate large rebates on shipments of its own oil as well as shipments that its competitors made. The Standard Oil monopoly at the turn of the century that was broken up in the first major application of the Sherman Act was, in part, created by manipulation of railroad rates in a way that prevented competitors of Standard Oil from being able to deliver oil at a reasonable cost. (221 U.S. 1 (1911).
3. See, for example, George Hilton, "The Basic Behavior of Regulatory Commissions," *American Economic Review*, May 1972, pp. 47–54.
4. The reader will note that the question of car shortages has been analyzed within the model of perfect competition, while railroads constitute an oligopoly. The reason is that the simplicity and definitiveness of result in the competitive model cannot be replicated when the mode of analysis is switched to oligopolies, and the results of the competitive analysis appear to be a good approximation to reality. On the question of regulated car supply, see John Richard Felton, *The Economics of Freight Car Supply* (Lincoln: The University of Nebraska Press, 1978).
5. See Charles R. Perry, Craig M. Waring, and Peter N. Glick, *Deregulation and the Decline of the Unionized Trucking Industry* (Philadelphia: Industrial Research Unit, The Wharton School, University of Pennsylvania, 1986).
6. Interstate Commerce Commission, "Study of Interstate Commerce Commission Regulatory Responsibilities Pursuant to Section 210(a) of the Trucking Industry Regulatory Reform Act of 1994" (October 25, 1994), pp. 4–5.
7. Kenneth D. Boyer, "Equalizing Discrimination and Cartel Pricing in Transport Rate Regulation," *Journal of Political Economy* (April 1981), pp. 270–86.
8. On the other hand, the reduction in complaints about railroad power should not be seen as a triumph of regulation: the major reason for decreasing concern about railroad economic power is that most shippers now use trucks or have the option of using trucks. A. Scheffer Lang, in his paper "The Great Economic Leveling-Out of the Intercity Freight Transportation Market," K.D. Boyer and W.G. Shepherd, eds., *Economic Regulation: Essays in Honor of James R. Nelson* (East Lansing: MSU Public Utilities Institute, 1981), refers to the rise of motor carriers as "leveling the landscape," thus reducing the need for an outside arbitrator to control railroad incentives to try to take advantage of customers with an especially lucrative place in the landscape.

9. This perspective is articulated, among many others, in Thomas Gale Moore, "The Beneficiaries of Trucking Regulation," *Journal of Law and Economics,* Vol. 21, No. 2, October 1978, pp. 327–343.

10. Quoted at meeting of The Surface Freight Transportation Committee of the Transportation Research Board, Washington D.C., June 30, 1993.

11. Nancy L. Rose, "Labor Rent Sharing and Regulation: Evidence from the Trucking Industry," *Journal of Political Economy,* Vol. 95, No. 6, December 1987, pp. 1146–1178 and Nancy L. Rose, "The Incidence of Regulatory Rents in the Motor Carrier Industry," *Rand Journal of Economics,* Vol. 16, No. 3, Autumn 1985, pp. 299–318.

12. Among the most widely quoted of the intrastate studies is W. A. Jordan, *Airline Regulation in America: Effects and Imperfections* (Baltimore: Johns Hopkins University Press, 1970).

13. The charge of capture is made by leftist historian, Gabrial Kolko in *Railroads and Regulation, 1877–1916* (Princeton: Princeton University Press, 1965). On the right, the charge was made by George J Stigler, "The Theory of Economic Regulation," *Bell Journal of Economics,* Vol. 2 (Spring 1971), pp. 3–21 and developed by Sam Peltzman, "Toward a General Theory of Regulation," *Journal of Law and Economics,* Vol. 19 (August 1976), pp. 211–240. The Stigler-Peltzman theory has become known as "Positive Political Theory" and is described in Roger G. Noll, "Economic Perspectives on the Politics of Regulation," Chapter 22 in R. Schmallensee and R. Willig, eds., *The Handbook of Industrial Organization,* Vol. II, (Amsterdam: North Holland, 1989), pp. 1253–1287.

14. Keeler, Theodore E., *Railroads, Freight, and Public Policy* (Washington: The Brookings Institution, 1983).

15. ICC Termination Act of 1995, Section 10101.

16. The difficulties in separating the true effects of deregulation from simply those that occurred after deregulation are emphasized in Clifford Winston, "Economic Deregulation: Days of Reckoning for Microeconomists," *Journal of Economic Literature,* Vol. 31, No. 3, September 1993, pp. 1263–1289.

17. Among the more recent studies, see Wesley W. Wilson, "Market Specific Effects of Rail Deregulation," *Journal of Industrial Economics,* Vol. 42, No. 1; March 1994, pp. 1–22; Mark L. Burton, "Railroad Deregulation, Carrier Behavior, and Shipper Response: A Disaggregated Analysis," *Journal of Regulatory Economics,* Vol. 5 No. 4, December 1993, pp. 417–434; Ann F. Friedlaender, et al., "Rail Costs and Capital Adjustments in a Quasi regulated Environment," *Journal of Transport Economics and Policy,* Vol. 27 No. 2, May 1993, pp. 131–152; C. C. Barnekov and A. N. Kleit, "The Efficiency Effects of Railroad Deregulation in the United States," *International Journal of Transport Economics,* Vol. 17, No. 1, February 1990, pp. 21–36; James M. MacDonald, "Railroad Deregulation, Innovation, and Competition: Effects of the Staggers Act on Grain Transportation," *Journal of Law and Economics,* Vol. 32, No. 1, April 1989, pp. 63–95; Kenneth D. Boyer, "The Costs of Price Regulation: Lessons from Railroad Deregulation," *Rand Journal of Economics,* Vol. 18, No. 3, Autumn 1987, pp. 408–416; Henry McFarland, "The Effects of United States Railroad Deregulation on Shippers, Labor, and Capital," *Journal of Regulatory Economics,* Vol. 1 No. 3, September 1989, pp. 259–270; and Henry McFarland, "Did Railroad Deregulation Lead to Monopoly Pricing? An Application of q," *Journal of Business,* Vol. 60, No.3, July 1987, pp. 385–400.

18. This section is based on Kenneth D. Boyer, "Deregulation of the Trucking Sector: Specialization, Concentration, Entry, and Financial Distress," *Southern Economic Journal,* Vol. 59, No. 3, January 1993, pp. 481–495. Other recent studies of trucking deregulation are: John S. Ying, Theodore E. Keeler, "Pricing in a Deregulated Environment: The Motor Carrier Experience," *Rand Journal of Economics,* Vol. 22 No. 2, Summer 1991, pp. 264–273; Clifford Winston, et al., *The Economic Effects of Surface Freight Deregulation* (Washington, D.C.: Brookings Institution, 1990); Curtis M. Grimm, Thomas M. Corsi, and Judith L. Jarrell, "U.S. Motor Carrier Cost Structure under Deregulation," *Logistics and Transportation Review,* Vol. 25 No. 3, September 1989, pp. 231–249; Janet M. Thomas, and Scott J. Callan, "Constant Returns to Scale in the Post Deregulatory Period; the Case of Specialized Motor Carriers," *Logistics and Transportation Review,* Vol. 25 No. 3, September 1989, pp. 271–288; B. Starr McMullen, and Linda R. Stanley, "The Impact of Deregulation on the Production Structure of the Motor Carrier Industry," *Economic Inquiry,* Vol. 26, No. 2, April 1988, pp. 299–316; Theodore E. Keeler, "Deregulation and Scale Economies in the U.S. Trucking Industry: An Econometric Extension of the Survivor Principle," *Journal of Law and Economics,* Part 1, Vol. 32, No. 2 (October 1989), pp. 229–253; Katherine Schipper, Rex Thompson, and Roman L. Weil, "Disentangling Interrelated Effects of Regulatory Changes on Shareholder Wealth: The Case of Motor Carrier Deregulation," *The Journal of Law & Economics,* 30:67–100 (April 1987); and John S. Ying, "The Inefficiency of Regulating a Competitive Industry: Productivity Gains in Trucking Following Reform," *Review of Economics and Statistics,* Vol. 72, No. 2, May 1990, pp. 191–201.

19. The best-known evaluation of airline deregulation is the one done by those most closely involved in implementing it. See Elizabeth E. Bailey, David R. Graham, and Daniel P. Kaplan, *Deregulating the Airlines* (Cambridge: MIT Press, 1985). Other recent studies include: Martin Gaynor, and John M. Trapani, III, "Quantity, Quality and the Welfare Effects of U.S. Airline Deregulation," *Applied Economics,* Vol. 26, No. 5, May 1994, pp. 543–550; J. P. Keeler and John P. Formby, "Cost Economies and Consolidation in the U.S. Airline Industry," *International Journal of Transport Economics,* Vol. 21, No. 1, February 1994, pp. 21–45; Kenneth Button, ed., *Airline Deregulation: International Experiences* (New York: New York University Press; distributed by Columbia University Press, 1991); Michael D. Whinston, and Scott C. Collins, "Entry and Competitive Structure in Deregulated Airline Markets: An Event Study Analysis of People Express," *Rand Journal of Economics,* Vol. 23 No. 4, Winter 1992, pp. 445–462; William N. Evans, and Ioannis Kessides, "Structure, Conduct, and Performance in the Deregulated Airline Industry," *Southern Economic Journal,* Vol. 59, No. 3, January 1993, pp. 450–467; John R. Meyer, and John S. Strong, "From Closed Set to Open Set Deregulation: An Assessment of the U.S. Airline Industry," *Logistics and Transportation Review,* Vol. 28, No. 1, March 1992, pp. 1–21; George W. Mechling, Jr., "Deregulation and the Capacity, Productivity and Technical Efficiency of Equipment of Former Trunk Airlines," *Journal of Transport Economics and Policy,* Vol. 25, No. 1, January 1991, pp. 51–61; Severin Borenstein, "The Evolution of U.S. Airline Competition," *Journal of Economic Perspectives,* Vol. 6 No. 2, Spring 1992, pp. 45–73; John P. Formby, Paul D. Thistle, and James P. Keeler, "Costs under Regulation and Deregulation: The Case of U.S. Passenger Airlines," *Economic Record,* Vol. 66 No. 195, December 1990, pp. 308–321; Richard V. Butler, and John H. Huston,

"Airline Service to Non-hub Airports Ten Years after Deregultion," *Logistics and Transportation Review,* Vol. 26, No. 1, March 1990, pp. 3–16; Lee J. Van Scyoc, "Effects of Airline Deregulation on Profitability," *Logistics and Transportation Review,* Vol. 25, No. 1, March 1989, pp. 39–51; David Card, "The Impact of Deregulation on the Employment and Wages of Airline Mechanics," *Industrial and Labor Relations Review,* Vol. 39, No. 4, July 1986, pp. 527–538.

20. Andrew N. Kleit, and Stewart G. Maynes, "Airline Networks as Joint Goods: Implications for Competition Policy," *Journal of Regulatory Economics,* Vol. 4 No. 2, June 1992, pp. 175–186; Lisa F. Saunders, and Shepherd, William G., "Airlines: Setting Constraints on Hub Dominance," *Logistics and Transportation Review,* Vol. 29, No. 3, September 1993, pp. 201–220; Margaret A. Peteraf, "Intra-industry Structure and the Response toward Rivals," *Managerial and Decision Economics,* Vol. 14 No. 6, Nov.–Dec. 1993, pp. 519–528; and Samuel H. Baker, and James B. Pratt, "Experience as a Barrier to Contestability in Airline Markets," *Review of Economics and Statistics,* Vol. 71, No. 2, May 1989, pp. 352–356.

21. While this opinion is widely shared it is not universal. See, for example, Paul Stephen Dempsey, *The Social and Economic Consequences of Deregulation: The Transportation Industry in Transition* (Westport, Conn. and London: Greenwood Press, Quorum Books, 1989) and Frederick C. Thayer, Jr., "The Other Side: A Brief Sermon on the History and Necessity of Economic Regulation" in E. Scott Maynes, ed.; ACCI Research Committee, ed., *The Frontier of Research in the Consumer Interest: Proceedings of the International Conference on Research in the Consumer Interest* (Columbia, Mo.: American Council on Consumer Interests, 1988), pp. 462–466.

22. Two mistakes are sometimes made in application of the stand-alone test. First, the standard is sometimes stated as requiring that current coal rates be able to fund an entirely new railroad rather than eliminating users from the existing system. This is critical since current railroad track costs are sunk whereas new track costs are not sunk. Second, the criterion must allow coal shippers to create a coalition that includes them and any other group of shippers that they nominate; the criterion does not require that a stand-alone system be devoted solely to coal shippers. For a thorough analysis of the problem of determining reasonable rates for shipping coal, see Ann F. Friedlaender, "Coal Rates and Revenue Adequacy in a Quasi Regulated Rail Industry," *Rand Journal of Economics,* Vol. 23, No. 3, Autumn 1992, pp. 376–394.

23. See William B. Tye, "Pricing Market Access for Regulated Firms," *Logistics and Transportation Review,* Vol. 29 No. 1, March 1993, pp. 39–67 For a contrary opinion, see Andrew N. Kleit, "The Unclogged Bottleneck: Why Competitive Access Should Not Be an Antitrust Concern," *Logistics and Transportation Review,* Vol. 26, No. 3, September 1990, pp. 229–247.

24. Asr Q. Nomani, "Fare Game: Airlines May Be Using Price-Data Network to Lessen Competition," *The Wall Street Journal,* p. A1 (June 28, 1990). For a less critical view, see Andrew N. Kleit, "Computer Reservations Systems: Competition Misunderstood," *Antitrust Bulletin,* Vol. 37, No. 4, Winter 1992, pp. 833–861.

14

Regulation of the Social Costs of Transportation

The classic rationale for government regulation was based on market power. This led to the regulation of prices and entry for railroads, airlines, and trucking companies, and, to a lesser extent, water and pipeline transport. The experiences with the traditional form of transport regulation were described in Chapter 13.

But there are other sources of market failure identified by economic analysis in addition to market power. Whenever there is a market failure, there is at least the potential that government regulation can improve economic efficiency. As the economic regulation of transportation recedes, there has been an increasing interest in these alternative motivations for transportation regulation. This chapter will lay out the basic analysis of these social cost justifications for the regulation of transportation. As is the case with economic regulation, there is a partial mismatch between the economist's approach to the problem and the more equity-based policy prescriptions that are used by political decision makers and the general public.

THE ECONOMIC ANALYSIS OF SOCIAL REGULATION

As described in Chapter 10, the efficient economic policy is one that maximizes net benefits to all citizens in the economy.

When one takes into account the fact that most policies have long-term effects, this rule can be written as

$$\text{Maximize W} = \sum_{t=0}^{\infty} \frac{(B(t) - C(t))}{(1+r)^t} \qquad (14.1)$$

where r = discount rate

$B(t)$ = measure of the dollar benefits in year t
$C(t)$ = measure of the collar costs incurred in year t

Chapter 10 described how each of these three elements is typically determined. The discount rate is market-based: Those who save and invest make a statement through their actions about how they value the future relative to the present; the market rate of interest can be seen as the result of an impersonal negotiation between lenders and borrowers about the rate charged by lenders to borrowers for use of their money for a period of time. The benefit of a project is measured as the total willingness to pay, an amount that is typically measured as the area under the demand curve for services of a project, up to the level of services provided. Costs are ideally the opportunity costs of the resources consumed, but are typically measured by expenditures paid to build and operate a facility.

The movement to justify new regulations based on the social costs of regulation criticizes each of the procedures used to define efficient economic policy. For example, the use of market rates of interest to discount future costs and benefits leads to justifying a more present-oriented policy than many people would like. If a typical market interest rate of 3 percent is used, discounting current benefits over 100 years yields a discount factor of 5 percent: that is, a dollar of benefit today will justify $20 of costs being imposed on people 100 years in the future. At 200 years, the discount factor is 0.2 percent: In other words, a $1 benefit received today offsets $500 of costs imposed on people 200 years from now. Thus even if the effects of a policy are catastrophic for future generations, their wishes can efficiently be ignored under cost-benefit analyses using market rates of interest to discount the future consequences of current actions. Those who argue that we should be stewards of the earth, giving to our children a livable world, are in effect arguing that the discount rate for future effects of current policies is too high. They would perhaps prefer to use a discount rate of 1 percent, or even—in the extreme case— 0 percent. (In the latter case, the welfare of great-grandchildren 100 years in the future is given equal weight to your own).

Arguments that the discount rate used to compare current benefits with future costs is too high often are used to claim that the current rate of depletion of motor fuels is excessive or non-sustainable.[1] If the discount rate were lower, there would be an incentive to postpone the consumption of oil to a later date. The way that this would be done would be by raising the price of fuel today, reducing its consumption and thus leaving more in the ground for future generations. Thus arguments that an inappropriately high discount rate is being used are often part of the support for higher fuel prices.

The opposing opinion notes that the rate of time discounting has a strong influence of social class with the poor having extraordinarily high rates of time discount while the wealthy tend to have much lower rates. The use of market rates of interest to discount the future is a compromise between those who have much higher and those who have lower rates of time discount. In this view, using a lower discount rate in evaluating policies is simply an attempt by wealthier groups in society to impose their own tastes on the entire population.[2] The act of protecting the environment using arguments of land stewardship, for example, is then seen as evidence of an elitist or undemocratic approach to policy making. Environmentalists in reply point to the environmental destruction in poor nations like Haiti and Nepal, to note that in the long run, the effect of ignoring the future in economic policy (which high rates of time discounting does) is to guarantee that the earth will be made uninhabitable for all.

The measurement of the second element in Equation 14.1, the benefits of a policy, is also subject to criticism. Since modern economics sees the benefit of a good or service as the reflection of an individual's own subjective values, the measurement of the benefit of a policy is the total willingness to pay. As explained in Chapter 10, this is approximated as the area under a demand curve. For example, in calculating the gross benefit that the economy derives from an individual's driving decisions during a year, the ideal measurement would find the maximum amount that person would have been willing to pay for the amount of driving that they did, rather than forgo driving completely. There is in economic efficiency calculations no benefit to mobility generally or to the social interaction that transportation permits other than the willingness of individuals to pay for the activity of transportation.

The idea that the willingness of individuals to pay is the only valid measurement of the benefits of consumption is not universally accepted. Environmentalists would reject the notion that the value of a tree or a wild animal is measured only by the willingness of people to spend money to prevent their destruction. Much of the discussion about transportation policy that uses the concept of the *social cost* of transportation in fact is based on a rejection of the idea that willingness of individuals to pay, as expressed through their market conduct, is the only valid yardstick by which to evaluate economic policy. A wide variety of criticisms of cost benefit have a foundation in concepts of equity, the health of the community, or more broadly defined aspects of good social policy. To the extent that the goal of transportation policy is to encourage equity or equal access, or enhance mobility for its own sake, the policy argument rejects the willingness to pay criterion as the sole measure of benefits.

For example, in 1995, the New York City Metropolitan Transit Authority voted to raise fares on subways and buses that operated within the city limits by 25 cents and on commuter trains that carried suburban residents into the city by an average of 9 percent. The subway and bus increase was 20 percent of the existing fare. Moreover, city transit riders paid 63 percent of the operating costs of the their system while suburb-to-city railroad riders paid only about 50 percent of the operating costs of commuter rail systems. Some city transit riders sued to prevent the fare increase, arguing that since 60 percent of New York City transit riders were nonwhite, while 80 percent of commuter rail users were white, the higher percentage increase on subway and buses together with their already higher operating cost coverage percentages represented discrimination against black and Hispanic riders in violation of the 1964 Civil Rights Act.[3] This same tactic has been used to try to prevent fare increases in Philadelphia, Los Angeles, and other cities.

An argument that transit fare policy should try to promote racial equality is contrary to the economic criteria of efficiency and subsidy-free pricing. Such analyses, while arguably valid, must be understood outside the framework used in this textbook. (Economic analysis will still be useful, however, to achieve non-economic goals at minimum cost.) The essence of a non-economic argument is one expressed in non-maximizing terms; for example, that transport policy should be geared to guaranteeing a minimum degree of mobility to all citizens or that transport policy should try to offset inequalities created elsewhere in the economy. If as a society we wish to promote certain values—for example, self reliance—and if the promotion of these values requires that we guarantee a basic level of mobility to all, we have left the realm of efficiency-based policy making. In fact most political leaders would argue that we as a country cannot turn our backs on the less fortunate in society. It is only the economist who has the luxury of acting as if only efficiency should matter in political decision making.

Some moral philosophers would argue that in fact public policy should be based on a very different accounting system than the one used by economists. One such line of reasoning notes that there is general agreement in society about a basic package of human rights that all citizens should possess.[4] Two such fundamental rights would be freedom and well being. For example, people generally refrain from causing others to run off the road, not because it would be inefficient to have more accidents, but because they see other drivers as having a basic right to life and safety. To injure another driver deprives him of his right of well being. Thus traffic safety is something that public policy should encourage, whether or not there is a market failure associated with the care taken in driving. It is possible to extend this line of argument into other areas to give a prescription for good transportation policy that is quite at variance with economic cost-benefit analysis.

The power of the cost-benefit criterion is illustrated by the fact that even non-economic approaches to decision making appear to have to use economic language. Thus the *rights-based* calculus described in the previous paragraph has been presented as a *moral cost-benefit analysis,* when in fact it does not make a balance between costs and benefits using a common currency—the hallmark of the economist's technique. Alternatives to economic cost-benefit analysis have, in fact, not yet been developed to a usable state. It is the economist's benefit-cost analysis that forms the basis of the discussion of transportation policy and it is this discussion that will be followed in this chapter.

The Measurement of Full Costs of Transportation

The overwhelming majority of current arguments for transportation regulation are based on the claim that without government intervention, the market price of transportation will be too low. That is, the free market price does not account for the full cost of transportation.[5] In the discussion below, we will review the possible sources of transportation underpricing. It is worthwhile describing the consequences of not charging users the full cost of the transportation that they undertake. The basic analysis is contained in Figure 14.1. The upward sloping line marked Private Cost of Transportation shows the marginal cost of transportation seen by the individual user. The equilibrium price of transportation set by the market, in the absence of government intervention, is P_2 and transportation will be consumed up to level Q_2. But if the individual user does not have to pay all of the costs of transportation, this level will be inefficient. In Figure 14.1, the Marginal Social Cost of Transportation is shown as lying above the marginal private cost to account for the existence of costs not charged to the individual user. If users were to pay the full costs of transportation, they would find that the price of transport rose to P_1. As a consequence of the higher costs of transportation, the quantity demanded would fall to Q_1.

According to economic analysis, the problem with underpricing services (in this case by $P_1 - P_2$) is that too much is consumed. It would be better if the use of transportation were restrained to Q_1. To see this, note that at Q_2, the willingness to pay for unit Q_2 of transportation is only at the level marked b, while the cost to the economy of consuming that unit is at the level marked c. So the economy is forced to accommodate the production of that unit, despite the fact that its benefit is less than its cost. Only when transportation is reduced to level Q_1 is there a balance between the amount that people are willing to pay for (that is, their benefit from) transportation, and the cost of producing it. At price P_1 and quantity level Q_1, it is impossible to improve the use of resources by giving more or less to transportation. This is the efficient price and quantity, and it will not be achieved without government intervention.

The solution to the problem of underpricing is, most naturally, to raise the price seen by users of transportation. It is important to recognize the logic of this argument: Unless they face the full consequences of their actions, individuals will act to draw too many resources into transportation relative to other things. While it is often expressed in terms of fairness or justness (it is unfair for railroad users to subsidize drivers, for example), the justification has nothing to do with being evenhanded. It may seem equitable if people only get what they pay for, but the efficiency argument that underlies cost-benefit analysis is quite different: Unless people pay full costs, they will not make cost-minimizing deci-

FIGURE 14.1   **Excessive Transportation When Full Cost Is Not Charged**

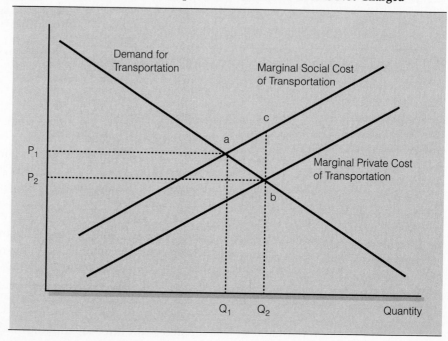

sions about what to ask for, thus causing the economy to produce fewer or less satisfying goods and services than there is a capacity to create.

While taxes or fees on certain types of transportation have been justified by arguments that the free market underprices transport, a variety of other interventions have also been rationalized with the same arguments. For example, subsidies to commuter railroads have been claimed to be necessary to offset the underpricing of automobile transportation. Safety regulations have been claimed to be needed because accident victims do not pay the full cost of the medical care that they receive. Similarly, catalytic converters have been required on automobiles using the argument that automotive pollution imposes an external cost on non-drivers. As described below, economists have tended to be critical of such standards-based or *command and control* regulations that bypass market mechanisms on the grounds that they might not be the most efficient way to overcome the market failure represented by underpricing.

Sources of Transportation Underpricing

The most common argument about how transportation can be underpriced is that transportation produces negative externalities. An externality produces a reduction in the well-being of someone other than the transporter and the purchaser of his services. (In the case of drivers, of course, these are the same people.) Air pollution is a familiar example of such an externality, but there are many others. Drunk drivers injure not only themselves, but others as well. To the extent that the damage that they cause to others is not fully compensated, their behavior represents a negative externality. Transporters of hazardous materials can impose losses on others. If the transporter is fully insured (e.g., there are no limits on liability) and if the insurance claims exactly compensate victims for their losses, then there is no externality; in the more typical case (for example, where drivers are delayed because of an accident and are not in a position to claim compensation for their loss of time, or where monetary compensation does not fully compensate for death or injury), decisions made by hazardous materials transporters can have negative external effects. Noise pollution by airplanes represents an external cost as does the chance of a major oil spill in the transportation of petroleum.

A second class of factors can also lead to the underpricing of transport modes and the resulting inefficiencies in the marketplace. When inputs are priced too low, then the services produced by those inputs will also be priced too low. The prime example of an input that may be priced too low is petroleum. As noted previously, the central concern of those who believe that petroleum prices are too low is that the world is running out of petroleum and that current prices do not properly reflect future scarcity. The opposing view says that market interest rates determine the rate at which fossil fuels are exploited. When interest rates are high, there is an incentive to move consumption toward the present. Low interest rates provide an incentive to leave discovered reserves in the ground until later. In this view, were it true that we were running out of fossil fuels, then entrepreneurs would come forward to speculate by hoarding reserves until they were more expensive sometime in the future. The fact that this does not occur confirms them in their view that petroleum prices do correctly reflect scarcity. Those who worry about the non-sustainability of current usage rates make two replies: first (noted above) that market interest rates do not correctly balance the interests of current and future generations and thus market decisions on the rate at which to deplete oil is not optimal; and second, that market forces are not as rational as sometimes believed. Entrepreneurs only partly understand the true scarcity of fossil fuels and many of those who decide on the rate at which to pump oil may be working with motives other than profit maximization (e.g., maximizing current revenue to placate an unhappy populace in developing nations).

The complaint that the automobile is leading to the paving-over of the country can also be seen as an argument that the price of a critical input to transportation (land for roads and parking) is too low. According to this view, we are rapidly converting farmland to transportation purposes in contradiction to what is in the best interest of the country. In short, the true value of farmland is higher than its market value. This argument generally notes the irreversibility of the decision to convert land from agricultural uses and doubts the rationality of markets to properly weigh the risk of loss of land that will be needed in the future to feed a rapidly increasing world population. Those who dismiss this idea argue that the only true value of a resource is the amount that people are willing to pay for it and there is no reason to believe that there is an inherent value of land higher than the market value. If the markets were misreading the scarcity value of farmland, entrepreneurs would come forward to hoard land, expecting to make a profit when its true scarcity is revealed in the future. The fact that such factors are not present, in this view, refutes the claim of farmland being undervalued. As in the previous example, the argument depends critically on the assumption that markets optimally process all available information.

Measuring Nonmarket Values

Some of the most important regulations affecting transportation are designed to affect environmental quality. According to the standard tenets of cost-benefit analysis, the correct measurement of the cost of environmental degradation is the total amount that all members of the economy would be willing to pay to avoid dirtying the land, air, and water. In the case of farmland, it is possible to put a market price tag on the land used by transportation (although reasonable people will argue about whether the efficient price should be somewhat higher than the market price).[6] But how should one deal with elements that have no market value; for example, the value of a human life or the preservation of a species? It is tempting to say that the value of the Alaskan wilderness is priceless, or to argue that putting a dollar price on an individual's life devalues our own humanity. This argument is vulnerable, however, on the grounds that decisions that we make as individuals and that our government makes in our name are not made to save lives or preserve the environment no matter what the cost. We do make tradeoffs and the placing of dollar values merely makes it possible to make more rational calculations. Moreover, as a practical matter, whenever something is declared to be valued in a system different from everything else, it is ignored in standard cost-benefit calculations. In cost-benefit terms, if you refuse to place a price tag on something, it is not then considered to be priceless, but rather to be worthless. If economic factors are to be used in making transportation policy, it makes sense to put dollar values on everything that the policy affects.

There are many indirect means that have been used to place a price tag on things that are not exchanged in the marketplace. One mechanism that has been used for making valuations of health, safety, and environmental considerations is based on averting behavior: If it is possible to offset an annoyance by taking preventative action (taking eye drops when it is smoggy, for example), the cost of taking such actions can be used to place a value on the problem. A second approach to evaluating environmental quality is to measure how much people increase spending on complementary goods or services when environmental quality is better. For example, if a more distant lake is less polluted than a nearer one, the amount that people are willing to spend to travel to the cleaner lake and avoid the more polluted lake is an indirect measure of the demand for environmental quality. A third approach is to directly measure the effect that the characteristics of a location or a job have on the price of land or the wage that is paid for work. If noise diminishes the enjoyment that one gets from living near an airport, then fewer people should be willing to live in such locations and that will have a direct effect on the price of houses in the area. Similarly, jobs that are less safe should have higher wages, all things being equal, than those jobs that have less of a safety concern. By comparing the increase in pay with the increased probability of death, economists have calculated a value of a statistical life of approximately $2 million.

It should be emphasized that the widely quoted $2 million price tag on a human life is not intended to mean that anyone with $2 million available should have the right to kill another person. Rather, it means that, through the tradeoffs that they themselves make, individuals appear to be willing to accept an increased statistical probability of death at the rate of, for example, $1,000 per year to increase the probability of their death by 0.0005.

Recently there has been a movement toward surveys as a means for placing values on factors that have no market equivalents. For example, if we really want to know how much the country is willing to pay to preserve a caribou herd in Alaska that might be threatened by oil drilling, why not ask people? This simple and direct method is not the economist's first preference since the respondent does not have to make any financial commitment to back up his or his answer. It is costless to put a very high price tag on a theoretical situation. On the other hand, defenders of such *contingent valuation* methods note that the figures generated by these surveys appear to be quite reasonable. Perhaps it is a lucky coincidence, but the amounts that people report that they are willing to pay to defend environmental quality in areas that they do not normally go to are very roughly in line with what is or could be spent.[7]

APPLICATIONS OF THE SOCIAL COST ARGUMENT IN TRANSPORTATION

The focus of arguments in favor of regulation that have their basis in the social costs of transportation are almost exclusively used to advocate greater controls on the use of motor vehicles.[8] While there are some arguments that do not fall into the two social costs of environmental and safety regulation (for example, the effect that cars have on the structure of urban centers), most of the practical discussions of social cost-based regulation focuses on these two.[9] We will first consider regulations intended to curb pollution caused by transportation.

▬ Pollution

With the exception of trains powered by electric locomotives, all transportation gets its energy from mobile sources. The major concern is with the internal combustion engines that power cars and trucks. For these vehicles, the Environmental Protection Agency (EPA) has set limits on the number of grams of hydrocarbons, carbon monoxide, nitrogen oxides, and particulates that engines can emit per mile of driving. Table 14.1 shows the limits that the EPA has placed on new vehicle emissions in the four primary categories of emissions that are of concern. The table shows that the EPA has required that engines produce successively smaller and smaller amounts of pollutants per mile. Further tightening of the emissions standards are planned for the future.

Carbon monoxide is a health concern in its own right. Excess carbon monoxide endangers those with weak hearts as well as fetuses, those with sickle cell anemia, and young children. There is also some evidence that carbon monoxide contributes to the formation of ground-level ozone. Over 90 percent of carbon monoxide in cities comes from motor vehicles.

Nitrogen oxides (NO_x) have a variety of health and environmental concerns associated with it. NO_x together with sulfur oxides (SO_x) are the primary source of acid rain that has killed forests and aquatic life and reduced crop yields in several parts of the country. In addition, direct exposure to nitrogen dioxide leads to increased susceptibility to respiratory infection. It causes coughs, runny noses, and sore throats and makes people with asthma more sen-

TABLE 14.1   EPA Emission Standards for New Vehicles

Year	Hydrocarbons (HC)	Carbon Monoxide (CO)	Nitrogen Oxides (NO_x)	Particulates
		Automobiles		
1980	0.41	7.0	2.0	—
1985	0.41	3.4	1.0	0.6
1990	0.41	3.4	1.0	0.2
1991	0.41	3.4	1.0	0.2
1992	0.41	3.4	1.0	0.2
1993	0.41	3.4	1.0	0.2
1994	0.25	3.4	0.4	0.08
1995	0.25	3.4	0.4	0.08

Automobile emissions limits are in grams per mile; heavy-duty diesel truck standards are in grams per brake horsepower hour.
SOURCE: U.S. Department of Transportation, *Transportation Statistics*, 1996

sitive to urban dust and pollen. It contributes to breathing difficulties among those whose lungs are already impaired.

Nitrogen oxides also react with hydrocarbon emissions in the presence of sunlight to form ground-level ozone. Ozone in turn is a major contributor to smog. Smog is unpleasant, contributes to health problems especially among the elderly and weak, and reduces visibility (which property value studies have shown to be a desirable property of air quality). The chemical reaction that produces ozone is complex, with most of the harmful product being produced far from the vehicle that originally emitted the nitrogen oxides or hydrocarbons that lead to ozone formation. Local wind conditions can apparently completely dissipate the problem. It is possible to avoid serious exposure to ozone on those days when levels are especially high by staying indoors.

Increasing attention is being directed to fine particulate matter generated by motor vehicles, and especially diesel powered trucks. Current evidence suggests that particles produced in a diesel engine are carcinogenic. There is much scientific uncertainty about this, however. Part of the confusion is traced to the question of whether diesel particles, which are often sulfur based, have different health effects from normal dust particles which are the same size. If it is dust in general that is the cause of increased cancer deaths, then the most efficient solution to the health problem is to control dust blown from fields and roads—a far larger source of dust—rather than dealing with diesel emissions. Current research seems to indicate that diesel particles are far more toxic than general dust particles of the same size; this belief has led to the dramatic tightening of particulate emissions standards shown in Table 14.1. While diesel motors on heavy trucks produce fine particles directly, all motor vehicles contribute to the particulate problem through their emission of other gases. Fine particles are

TABLE 14.1   (Continued)

	Heavy-Duty Diesel Trucks			
Year	Hydrocarbons (HC)	Carbon Monoxide (CO)	Nitrogen Oxides (NO_x)	Particulates
1980	1.5	25.0	—	—
1985	1.3	15.5	10.7	—
1990	1.3	15.5	6.00	0.60
1991	1.3	15.5	5.00	0.25
1992	1.3	15.5	5.00	0.25
1993	1.3	15.5	5.00	0.25
1994	1.3	15.5	5.00	0.10
1995	1.3	15.5	5.00	0.10

produced indirectly through reactions among volatile organic compounds (VOC), sulfur oxides, and oxides of nitrogen.

An emissions gas that is not listed in Table 14.1 is also of increasing concern among environmentalists. Carbon dioxide, the primary byproduct of burning motor fuel, is a major greenhouse gas. There appears to be increasing (though apparently not yet conclusive) evidence that the burning of all types of fuels has increased the concentration of carbon dioxide in the atmosphere which then traps more sunshine and raises the surface temperature of the earth. The result of this global warming is unknown but is predicted to include increasingly violent storms, more extremely hot days, rising ocean levels, and the conversion of much currently productive farmland to deserts. The effects are predicted to be most severe in the less industrialized tropical regions.

It is important to recognize that the global warming problem, if it is important, cannot be attacked by tuning the motors of cars and trucks. The problem

FIGURE 14.2   U.S. Fuel Usage by Automobiles, 1960–1994

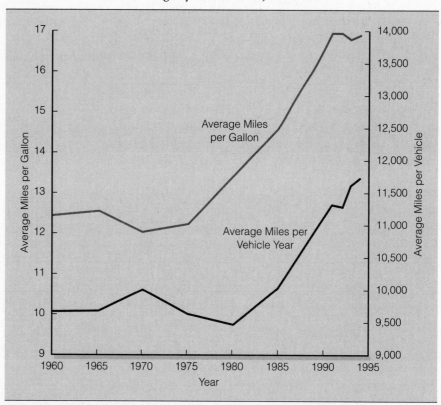

SOURCE: U.S. Department of Transportation, Bureau of Transportation Statistics. *National Transportation Statistics,* 1996 edition

FIGURE 14.3   1994 Fuel Consumption by Mode of Transport

1994 Fuel Consumption by Mode of Transport

- Other 1%
- Water Transport 6%
- Commercial Airlines 7%
- Railroad Locomotives 2%
- Combination Trucks 11%
- Single Unit Trucks 28%
- Passenger Car 45%

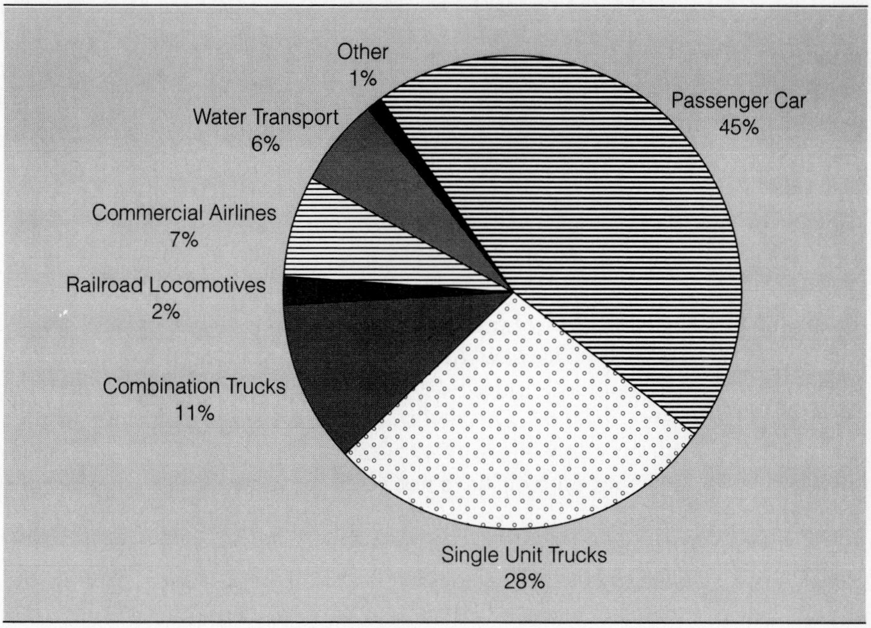

SOURCE: *Transportation in America,* 14th edition

results from the fact that vehicles have motors and that fuel is burned in them, creating carbon dioxide. Global warming can be slowed only by burning less fuel. This can be used as one rationalization for the fuel economy standards that are set by the National Highway Traffic Safety Administration.[10] But there is no guarantee that improved fuel economy will in fact lead to lowered fuel consumption. Figure 14.2 shows that over the past decades, fuel usage increased at the same time that the average miles per gallon in the automobile fleet were increasing as well. In fact, annual fuel usage per vehicle has been quite constant at approximately 700 gallons per car since 1980. Part of the explanation may be that improved fuel economy reduces the cost per mile of driving, thus causing drivers to increase the number of miles that they drive per year. The fact that automotive fuel economy improvements have not led to a reduction in fuel usage greatly complicates the problem of dealing with global warming if it is as serious a problem as some contend it is. Figure 14.3 shows that automotive use accounts for the overwhelming majority of transport fuel consumption. Thus if global warming compels a reduction in fuel usage, it almost inevitably will require drastic changes in driving behavior either through highly intrusive controls on individuals' driving decisions or greatly increasing the price of fuels, presumably through fuel taxes amounting at a minimum to several dollars per gallon. As discussed in Chapter 4, the first reaction to higher fuel prices is to choose more fuel efficient vehicles rather than to reduce driving or switch to public transportation. If reduced fuel usage required an actual reduction in the number of miles driven, given the inelasticity of demand for automobile transportation outlined in Chapter 4, the real price of driving might have to rise many fold as part of the effort to control global warming. In other words, if global warming turns out to be a serious problem, the required changes in the transportation system would be far larger than any of the other more modest controls suggested as a solution to other social costs.

Emissions standards and fuel economy guidelines are not the only tools used to control transportation-based pollution. The EPA has banned the use of lead additives from motor fuels in an attempt to reduce the amount of lead in the air and has required the sale of reformulated gasoline. Congress and some state governments have tried to induce the development of electric vehicles. The EPA monitors air in several urban areas and places limits on economic activity where existing controls have not been found sufficient to deliver improved air quality.

Measuring the Environmental Cost of Transportation

The difficulties with determining the effect of driving on the environment through the mechanism of global warming is generally recognized. The costs may be enormous, though primarily in the future, and thus subject to normal discounting. While a majority of atmospheric scientists believe that global warming is taking place through the mechanism of increased greenhouse gases, there are other reputable scientists who believe that the earth's ecosystem is more accommodating of increased carbon dioxide levels than is generally believed and will be able to adjust to the consequences of higher levels of fuel consumption. A key factor in evaluating whether fuel consumption will have serious effects on global warming turns on the chemistry of the interaction between atmospheric water vapor and carbon dioxide. There is simply no certainty or consensus about global warming.

There is almost equal uncertainty about the economic consequences of other tailpipe emissions, however. The reason is that there is a multistage process by which driving causes economic damage, as described in Equation 14.2.

$$\text{Environmental Cost of Transportation} = A \bullet B \bullet C \bullet D \bullet E \bullet F \qquad (14.2)$$

where:

A = the amount of a kind of driving
B = the amount of tailpipe emissions generated per unit of driving
C = the concentration of pollutants created per unit of tailpipe emissions
D = the level of exposure per unit of concentration of pollutants
E = the consequences of the level of exposure to pollutants
F = the cost per unit of consequence of pollution

The amount of tailpipe emissions created by driving varies greatly depending on the type of vehicle used, how its engine is tuned, its fuel type, where it is driven, as well as how and how much it is driven. Diesel trucks can be tuned to emit more particulates and less nitrogen oxide, or vice versa. In general, all vehicles emit more pollutants as they age. Cold engines generally emit more pollutants than hot ones. One of the difficulties in measuring the contribution of transportation to the level of atmospheric pollution is that, as mobile sources, it is impractical to continuously monitor the actual amounts of emissions coming from exhaust pipes. There have been improvements in monitoring technology that allow measurement of tailpipe emissions at single locations as cars pass by a roadside laser beam. But fundamentally, decisions on pollution control have been and will continue to be educated estimates based on knowledge of the fleet composition and estimates of how often each vehicle will be driven under different conditions.

The next element of Equation 14.2 is the effect that tailpipe emissions have on air quality. As noted previously, some of the gases emitted by vehicles chemically interact with one another and with sunlight. Some gases dissipate quickly, others linger near the ground. In some cases, evidence of the environmental problems caused by driving may be hundreds or thousands of miles away from the car that created the gas. There is some uncertainty about the extent to which tailpipe gases or their chemical products linger close to the roadway, are moved by winds into neighboring states or regions, or rise into the upper atmosphere where the products of the gases may be precipitated in the form of acid rain.

Whether tailpipe gases and particles are moved quickly away from the roadway is important for calculating exposure, the next element in Equation 14.2. If the particles and gases linger in urban areas, more people will be exposed to their effects. If they blow onto rural areas, then the effects of automotive pollution will be measured more by their effects on crop yield and loss of enjoyment of outdoor recreation opportunities and less by their effects on human health. Some EPA estimates of exposure to carbon monoxide, for example, have been criticized as being inflated because the stations where the level of the gas was measured were initially in downtown areas where concentrations could be expected to be higher than in suburban areas.

There is a lack of knowledge as well on the next element of Equation 14.2, the consequences of exposure to pollutants. There seems to be little doubt that those with respiratory problems as well as the old and chronically ill are at higher risk than other parts of the population. But how toxic are the particles emitted from diesel engines? Are fine particles really a carcinogenic? How many premature deaths can we expect from exposure to a given concentration of particles? The medical knowledge assumed in this part of the economic cost calculation is far beyond that which is in fact available.

The final element of the economic cost calculation, F in Equation 14.2, is the one that economists have expertise in: placing an economic value on the consequences measured in the previous step. Given the level of uncertainty at this point, whether a statistical death should be valued at $2 million or $4 million is relatively unimportant. The value of medical care to treat conditions caused by pollution could similarly be estimated with some precision, as could the value of diminished crop yields or diminished recreational enjoyment of vacation areas, but the usefulness of these estimates again depends on the reliability of emissions and exposure estimates.

An example of the difficulty in measuring the economic cost of the environmental consequences of transportation is provided by a recent calculation by the Transportation Research Board (TRB). Recognizing that the environmental consequences vary depending on the nature of the movement, the TRB chose to make the calculation for a single hypothetical truck haul: a container from Los Angeles to Chicago. Focusing first on particles, the study first accepted the EPA estimate of 1.43 grams of particulate emissions per mile of truck travel. It then used EPA estimates that, for example, in Los Angeles, the average concentration of particles in the air is 49 micrograms per cubic meter. Then, by assuming that the concentration of particles is proportional to the emission of particles, the study estimates the increase in the number of micrograms of particles per cubic meter of air breathed by the average citizen of each county traversed by the truck trip. The authors then multiply this exposure by the population of each county and apply a cost coefficient of $19.62 per person year per microgram of particles per cubic meter (derived from the projected increased mortality due to higher concentrations of particles multiplied by the value of a statistical life). This figure is then added to similar calculations of the effects of nitrogen oxide, carbon monoxide, and other gases. Finally, a calculation of $0.035 per gallon of fuel consumed is added to take into account the possibility that the fuel burned in the trip will accelerate global warming.

All of the estimates used in the calculation were taken from other sources and are subject to the validity of those calculations. For example, as noted previously, the EPA has been criticized for making inflated estimates of the exposure to pollutants. However, these are the best estimates that are available. Assuming that they approximate the true effects of pollution, the TRB estimated that the external pollution costs of making the truck trip from Los Angeles to Chicago is $63.65, or about 2.5 percent of the total cost borne by the carrier to make the trip. In short, the calculation does not appear to indicate that including the costs of pollution will have a substantial effect on the overall costs of transportation. It is important to recognize, however, that this conclusion is only as good as the numbers used to make the calculation. For example, if diesel particles are assumed to be far more toxic than fugitive dust from roads and fields, then the external pollution cost of the trip rises from $63 to $315. The calculation is similarly sensitive to a wide range of other assumptions. It should be noted as well that this haul is primarily through rural areas and thus the exposure to diesel exhaust is lower than it would be were the trip made in a more urban part of the country. It should also be recognized that the calculation ignores such issues as the effects of exhaust on crop yields or the willingness to pay for the improved views that come from cleaner air.

A calculation of the costs of vehicle-based air pollution for the Los Angeles air shed was recently produced by Small and Kazimi.[11] They note that there is considerable latitude for error, especially due to the unknown chemistry of the reactions through which volatile organic compounds and oxides of nitrogen and sulfur produce fine particles which, when inhaled, are possibly carcinogenic. They assume that volatile organic compounds and nitrogen oxides directly contribute to morbidity and that they indirectly, through interaction with oxides of sulfur, contribute to mortality and morbidity through their effect on the creation of inhalable particles. PM10 (particulate matter smaller than 10 microns) is directly created in motor vehicles (particularly diesel motors) and is assumed to directly affect mortality and morbidity. Putting price tags on the value of a life and diminished health yields the measurements of the external pollution cost of automobile travel in the neighborhood of 3 cents per mile. Most of the problem comes from NO_x and VOC. Heavy diesel trucks have pollution costs of about 50 cents per mile, with the main costs attributable to NO_x and PM10.

Evaluating the Regulation of Transportation-Based Pollution

The primary attempts to control automotive-based pollution have been based on setting emissions standards for new vehicles, as shown in Table 14.1. While there is a technical and political logic behind the decision not to require that existing vehicles be retrofitted to limit emissions, the practice has distorted the marketplace by reducing the market for new cars and lengthening the lives of old vehicles. In some cases, the effect of the policy of making new vehicles cleaner but more expensive may be to actually worsen emissions by inducing older and more polluting vehicles to stay on the road for more years than they otherwise would. Older vehicles are more polluting not only because they use technologies that do not meet current standards, but also because emissions normally get worse as a car or truck ages.

Figure 14.4 shows that several decades of controlling pollution by mandating technology used in new vehicles has had mixed success. The one clear triumph of EPA policy was to reduce lead emissions to essentially zero. This success, however, was due to banning the sale of leaded gasoline rather than requiring controls on new vehicle emissions. From Figure 14.4, it appears that the EPA has had some success in controlling the emission of volatile organic compounds. At least since 1980 the trend in nitrogen oxide and carbon monoxide emissions has been in the desired direction, though actual levels of these pollutants are still above levels recorded several decades ago. Particulate emissions continue to rise.

Given the increase in the amount of driving over the period in Figure 14.4, the fact that emissions have not risen substantially can perhaps be seen as a suc-

FIGURE 14.4   Total U.S. Emissions from Highway Sources

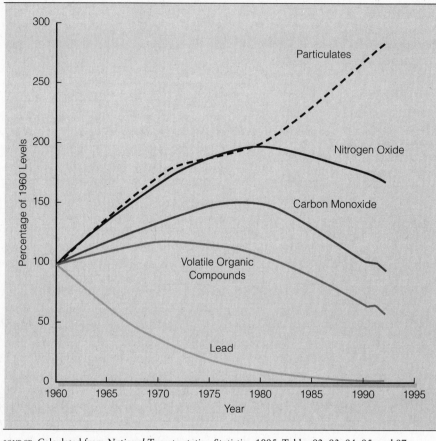

SOURCE: Calculated from *National Transportation Statistics,* 1995, Tables 92, 93, 94, 95, and 97

cess of the program. But the fact is that in several dimensions, the air today is not cleaner than it was decades ago, despite expensive pollution controls required on new vehicles. This contrasts with emissions limitations on stationary sources in which there has been a clear improvement in air quality as a result of EPA rules.

The failure of costly pollution controls to make air dramatically cleaner is at the heart of the unanimously negative benefit-cost evaluation that these programs have received.[12] Economic support for EPA programs also is weakened by the scarcity of research showing a dose-response relationship between exposure and mortality or the onset of health problems. The reader is reminded of the multi-part calculation necessary to calculate the cost of air pollution, a reduction in which would be counted as a benefit in economic assessments of pollution control programs. Given the difficulties inherent in making accurate benefit cost calculations in this area, the traditional congressional reluctance to use these findings in making environmental policy can be understood. However, this should not be used as a justification for maintaining ineffective programs or for avoiding a search for techniques that would achieve the same goals with lower cost.

Since vehicle pollution sources are by definition mobile, the most effective tools used for controlling pollution from stationary sources are unavailable. The most promising tools for stationary sources like power stations and industrial plants involve the definition of property rights in pollution and the trading of these rights among interested parties. This allows pollution to have a market price placed on it, allowing pollution control expenditures to be treated as simply another business cost. By reducing the quantity of emissions allowed but not mandating how it is to be done, Congress has succeeded in reducing sulfur dioxides emissions (a major source of acid rain) from power plants at a relatively low cost to the consumer. Defining property rights as a technique for reducing pollution depends critically on continuous monitoring of sources. In the case of mobile sources, it is generally conceded that it is impractical to continuously monitor tailpipe emissions from each vehicle and then require drivers to purchase the right to pollute the amount that they have been shown to have emitted.

Programs that require vehicle inspection before a vehicle may be registered for the year have some promise since they attack the problem of older super-polluting vehicles. However, old vehicles, even if they are perfectly tuned, are still more polluting than new ones. In order for inspection programs to have a major effect on emissions, it would be necessary to require that old vehicles meet the same emissions standards as new ones, thus effectively accelerating the retirement of vehicles from the fleet. There is little political will to reduce the value of vehicles held by the less wealthy parts of the population, people who tend to drive the most polluting vehicles, however. In some areas, programs have been established to purchase very old super-polluting vehicles. These programs provide a subsidy to the poor to give up their cars, but at the same time reduce the pool of vehicles available for the most indigent parts of the population.

Economists have seen as a puzzle the fact that there is such strong political support for environmental programs that do not meet cost-benefit tests. A strong possibility may be that the population does not use a cost-benefit type of framework when supporting policies, but rather makes decisions based on rights and morality, as described previously. Another explanation may be that the benefit/cost ratios do not accurately assess the willingness to pay for clean air.

The public may also not understand the true effects of the programs. By forcing behavior modification on manufacturers rather than consumers, it has appeared that firms, rather than consumers, pay the bill for environmental cleanup. This is, of course, a false belief. Raising the costs of producing automobiles will surely raise the price charged for those cars. It remains to be seen whether the political support for clean air remains after the next round of requirements is imposed: mandatory car pooling at large firms, for example. The public has supported mass transit programs on the assumption that *you* will use them, thus eliminating traffic jams on roads that *I* use. Chapter 4 described some of the reasons that these programs have not generally been successful. A genuine attack on automotive emissions—especially if it turns out that global warming is a serious problem—will demand that the use of motor fuel be attacked. As noted in Chapter 4, the price elasticity of demand for motor fuel is significantly different from zero despite the fact that the price elasticity of demand for driving is insignificantly small. This is due to the adaptation of the motor vehicle stock to the price of fuel. But given the inelasticity of demand of driving, if any actual reduction in the amount of driving is required to delay global warming, it will be extremely painful, highly unpopular, and will greatly increase the price paid for using motor vehicles.

Accidents/Safety

The chance that a person will die in a traffic accident in any year is 0.0001567. Another way of looking at the relationship is to say that over a period of 70 years, the chances are about 1 in 100 that an individual will die in a fatal traffic accident in one of those years.[13] Motor vehicle crashes are the leading cause of death for those between the ages of 6 and 28. Male fatality rates are three times as high as female rates. Motorcycles are 20 times as dangerous as automobiles and accounted for 2,304 of the 40,676 people killed in traffic accidents in 1994. In the same year 802 bicyclists and 5,472 pedestrians were killed.

There are some other well known correlates of traffic accidents. The best known are seat belt usage and alcohol consumption. But there is also a strong correlation between traffic safety and the level of education; the level of income has a strong negative relationship with the level of traffic accidents.[14]

Statistical Accidents versus Preventable Accidents

The analysis of traffic safety must begin with the factors that cause accidents. Many of us feel safer when we are behind the wheel because we believe that we can affect the likelihood of an accident through our own behavior. This gives us a sense of being in control of our fate, unlike the situation when we fly in an airplane—where the passengers have no way of affecting the likelihood that they will be in a crash. But not all of our safety on the highway is under our control. We know, for example, that there are traffic conditions that are inherently dangerous—driving at dusk on an undivided highway with fast traffic and a light glaze of ice, for example. Some people avoid driving on Saturday nights or New Year's Eve to minimize the likelihood of being hit by a drunk driver. To some extent we can avoid such dangerous situations, but it is impossible to take all risk out of driving.[15]

When thinking about highway safety, it is important to separate the incentives from driving safely from the incentive to drive at all. The price of travel may affect both, but to begin with, let us assume that the probability of an accident is determined solely by external conditions and not by anything that we can do. We are making such an assumption, for example, when we say that driving is more dangerous than flying—the statistical probability of dying in a car trip of 1,000 miles is much higher than a plane trip of the same distance. Is there any reason to think that the decision *to* drive (rather than *how to* drive) is an inherently inefficient one? Do we drive too much because we do not take into account the effects on safety of everyone on the road, only ourselves? That is, is there a market failure arising from traffic safety considerations that needs to be corrected by regulation?

At first, it would seem that there is such an inherent market failure. Excluding the case of vehicles running off the road, accidents will involve two cars. Thus if either car were not there, there would have been no accident. It seems, therefore, that in deciding to drive, we inevitably endanger others and the price that we pay for driving should reflect the increased risk in which we place other drivers. This would say that driving is underpriced and, to the extent that the elasticity of demand with respect to price is substantial (see Chapter 4), there may be too much transportation, or at least too much driving.[16] Efficiency considerations would then call for a reduction in the amount of driving, perhaps through charging drivers for the full cost of their decision to drive.

Determinants of Statistical Accidents. The fallacy of this argument can be seen in the relationship between accident rates and traffic levels that it implies. If I drive one mile, statistically there is approximately a 1 in 100 million chance that I will run into another car and have a fatal accident. It appears, then, that my decision to drive one mile increases the probability by 1 in 100 million that every other driver in the system will have an accident since each of them now has an additional car that they can run into or that can run into them. This implies that the accident rate will rise exponentially with increases in traffic levels. But, in fact, we do not observe this relationship. Figure 14.5 shows that accident levels and fatalities from road accidents have stayed approximately level over the last 30 or more years while traffic counts have more than doubled. As a result, the accident rate per mile driven has plunged over the same period. This is shown in Figure 14.6 which shows that driving a mile is only half as dangerous as it was 30 years ago, despite the fact that the amount of traffic carried by the highway system has increased substantially.

We should not be too quick to draw conclusions from these figures. If there were no other influences, one would have to conclude from the data in Figures 14.5 and 14.6 that increased traffic levels have made driving safer, not more dangerous, as would be required by the logic outlined in the previous paragraph. While it is implausible that increased traffic volumes have been the cause of reduced death rates, it is not totally illogical that increased traffic

FIGURE 14.5   Trends in U.S. Travel and Accident Levels

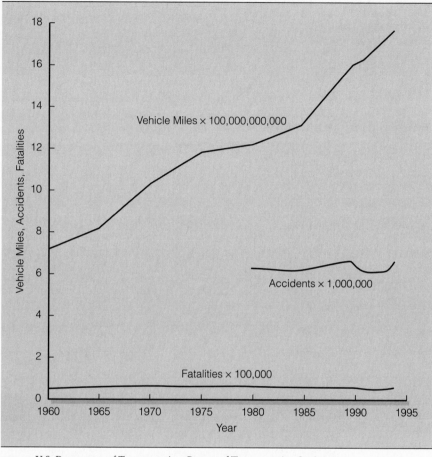

SOURCE: U.S. Department of Transportation, Bureau of Transportation Statistics

could lead to safer roads: highway safety is at least partly determined by the speed of traffic and more traffic, as noted in Chapter 8, is associated with slower speeds. It has been difficult to find any simple relationship between traffic levels and accident rates in cross-section data, in part because times at which road travel is more dangerous—at night, for example—are also times when traffic tends to be lighter. It appears that the variance of speeds on a highway is a more important determinant of accident rates than speed itself.[17]

If it were true that increased traffic made driving safer, not more dangerous, economic logic would require that all drivers not be taxed for safety but be paid

FIGURE 14.6   Accident Trends in the United States, 1960–1995

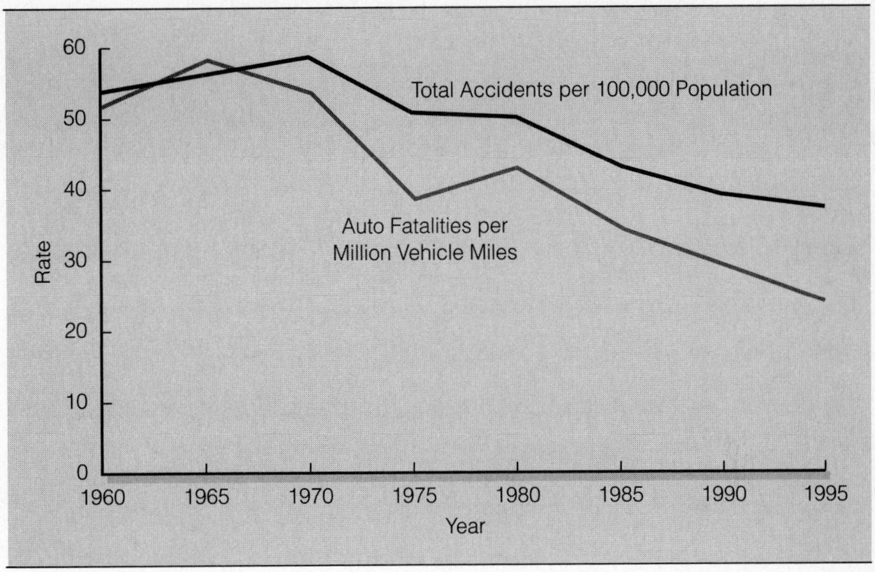

SOURCE: U.S. Department of Transportation, *National Transportation Statistics, 1995*, Table 26. Data for 1996 projected.

a subsidy to put their vehicles on the road so that the likelihood of others having an accident could be reduced. But even if there is no clear and important positive relationship between accident rates and traffic levels, there still may be a case for making a charge against some types of traffic to take into account an accident externality. Implicitly, the argument above has been based on self-insurance. We all pay the costs of statistical accidents either in the form of insurance premiums to cover expected reimbursable loses, or implicit payments for losses that we cannot expect insurance to pay for. Unless our decisions to drive increases the overall accident rate (thus endangering others), when we get behind the wheel of an automobile we accept the risks inherent in driving. This self-insurance argument is vulnerable, however, in several circumstances: First, as noted previously, we may not make a correct calculation about the probability of having an accident. If a government authority can correct our miscalculation, regulatory intervention may be justified by arguments of efficiency.[18] Second, there may be some costs of accidents that those involved in accidents are not charged for. Examples of such *cold-blooded costs* are police time, the cost of emergency rescue crews, and the costs of medical rehabilitation to the extent that an individual is insured out of a pool that includes non-drivers.[19] Closely related to these cold-blooded costs are pain and suffering imposed on those around one. If a driver, in making a decision to drive and thus expose him- or herself to the possibility of a statistical accident, does not take into account the effect that the accident will have on co-workers, friends, and family, a driver will implicitly undermeasure the full costs of driving. Finally, the self-insurance argument against general limitation on driving by making a charge against drivers for accidents that they are likely to cause fails when there is non-homogeneous traffic. For example, when cars and bicycles or heavy trucks and cars share the roadway, an accident between the heavier vehicle and the lighter one will cause more damage to the lighter one. Under these circumstances, drivers of the heavier vehicle will not bear an expected accident cost equal to the probability of having an accident multiplied by the cost of the average accident. Since their probability of injury is less, an argument can be made that efficiency requires trucks to pay a per-mile fee to make them recognize the costs of the accidents which their presence might impose on others.[20]

The Regulation of Vehicle Safety

It would be foolish to conclude from Figures 14.5 and 14.6 that there is an important negative relationship between traffic levels and accident rates since there are many other factors other than traffic levels that have made driving safer over the previous three or four decades. Increased traffic safety reflects a general trend toward reduced danger that has taken place in all parts of modern life. Figure 14.6 shows that there has been an almost parallel reduction in the total accident rate per 100,000 population over the period when highways have gotten safer.

The increase in overall safety that we have experienced can be traced to several causes. There may be some economic factors at work. For example, there have been technological improvements that have permitted all sorts of devices to be made safer than they could have been a generation or two ago. Air bags and anti-lock breaks are two examples of such improvements. Technological improvements lower the price of being safe, thus inducing consumers to choose a higher level of safety. In addition, there has been a modest increase in the average wealth of consumers and it is quite clear that wealthier people put a higher premium on safety when making purchasing decisions.[21] There may also be a change in tastes in society, reducing the social acceptability of making unsafe choices.

Perhaps in response to changes in tastes, two other factors have had a profound influence on vehicle safety: First, there has been a general change in the law making manufacturers increasingly liable for injuries that result from use of their products, and second, there has been increasing regulation of product safety.[22] No product has been more affected by these changes than motor vehicles.

Vehicle characteristics are regulated by the National Highway Traffic Safety Administration (NHTSA). Among the elements of automobile design that this agency has specified to auto makers are: padded interiors, head restraints, collapsible steering columns, windshield safety glass, seat belts, air bags, and side-door strength. The agency also has the power to require a recall vehicles if it finds that there is a specific defect in vehicle design that leads to an increased likelihood of death or injury. These findings are based on reports from accidents. When the agency finds a cluster of accidents associated with a particular type of vehicle, it will investigate whether these accidents can be traced to some element of vehicle design; if it finds such a feature, it can require a recall to fix the defect, even if the vehicle was certified as meeting safety standards when it was produced.

Both recalls and vehicle design standards have been controversial. The essence of the argument made by auto makers and other critics of NHTSA is that excessive levels of safety are built into vehicles. Figure 14.7 below describes the essential elements of this argument.[23] The diagram shows an upward sloping gray line representing the cost of building a safer car. Safer cars require sturdier bodies, better breaks, and various appliances to protect passengers, all of

FIGURE 14.7   Excessive Safety Levels due to Regulation

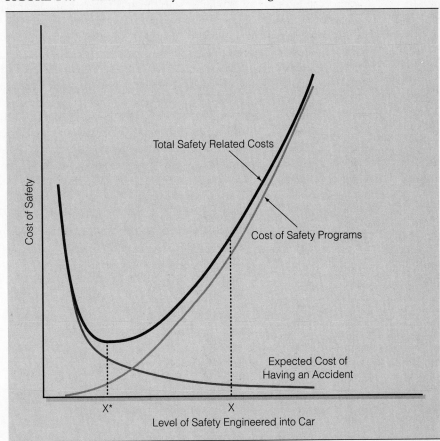

which are costly. The more of these items built in a car, the more expensive is the car. On the other hand, with safer cars, there will be fewer injuries and death due to accidents, thus the expected costs arising from accidents will be lower. This is represented in the downward sloping black line in Figure 14.7 which is drawn in the recognition that it is impossible to eliminate all accident costs by building safer cars, but the safer are cars, the lower should be the consequences and thus the costs of accidents. The sum of these two curves is shown in the u-shaped line in Figure 14.7. It slopes down at first because safety costs of unsafe cars are dominated by the costs of having accidents. It slopes up at high safety levels because at these safety levels, costs are dominated by the automobile production costs. The optimum level of safety is shown as X*. At this level, the cost to consumers of buying a safer car will exactly offset the expected cost of reduced accident costs.

Critics of NHTSA believe that the agency has mandated safety equipment that corresponds to point X in Figure 14.7. At this point, consumers are worse off because they are spending more for accident protection and avoidance than they would save by having fewer and less severe accidents. It is thus an inefficiency. As evidence, these critics point to the fact that consumers often do not use the safety appliances that are built into automobiles, or are willing to endanger their safety by buying cheaper but lighter, rather than the safer but more costly, heavy cars. On the assumption that the willingness to pay for safety is a measure of the reduction in the cost of accidents involving safer cars, consumer disinterest in safety is a measure of the inefficiency of the regulations.[24]

The NHTSA rejects this line of argument, claiming that it is based on an unrealistic view of the ability of consumers to evaluate the safety of an automobile, to predict the likelihood of an accident, and to recognize the consequences of accidents that they are likely to get into. This view is reinforced by research that shows that consumers are generally unwilling to pay for additional safety equipment if they are told that it is not part of a standard safety package, but are also unwilling to be compensated by the same amount for not having the equipment installed if they are told that it is part of the standard package.[25] If consumers were fully rational on safety issues, the argument goes, they should have identical willingness to pay as their willingness to be compensated. The fact that their apparent demand for safety can be manipulated simply by changing the list of standard equipment is evidence that they are incompetent to make such safety decisions on their own.

One hallmark of the economic approach to policy analysis is the assumption that people know their own mind—they have stable tastes and make choices to maximize their own well being. NHTSA, far from accepting consumer tastes for safety as given and seeing any attempt to regulate behavior as a limitation on personal freedom, tries to change dangerous behavior. Its mandate from Congress is to reduce deaths, injuries, and economic losses resulting from motor vehicle crashes. Current research shows that the most effective way to do this is not to require further changes in vehicle design, but to change community attitudes toward drinking and driving, the use of child car seats, motorcy-cle helmets, and seat belts.[26] Through cooperative programs with the states, NHTSA claims success in changing the behavior that leads to unsafe traffic con-ditions. The agency's estimates of their success is shown in Table 14.2. According to the agency, by far the largest saver of lives in traffic accidents is the use of seat belts. Thus they argue in favor of state laws to require seat belt usage and encourage public service campaigns to try to make the failure to use seat belts socially unacceptable. They also mandated the installation of either motorized seat belts or air bags in all new vehicles.

TABLE 14.2   NHTSA Estimates of Lives Saved and Injuries Prevented

Year	Children under Age 5 Saved by Child Restraints			Occupants Age 5 and Over Safety Belts		Air Bags Alone	Motor-cycle Helmets	Age 21 Drinking Laws
	Children in Child Seats	Children Using Adult Belts	Total	Lives Saved	Moderate to Critial Injuries Prevented	Lives Saved	Lives Saved	Lives Saved
1975								412
1976								436
1977								474
1978								509
1979								575
1980								595
1981								633
1982	68	7	75	678	15,600			578
1983	95	10	105	809	18,600			609
1984	111	15	126	1,197	19,100		813	709
1985	135	18	153	2,435	51,200		788	701
1986	132	34	166	4,094	81,200		807	840
1987	172	41	213	5,171	114,700	1	667	1,071
1988	209	39	248	5,983	149,900	4	605	1,148
1989	197	41	238	6,353	154,900	7	530	1,093
1990	193	29	222	6,596	193,200	46	602	1,033
1991	217	30	247	7,022	196,400	92	531	941
1992	232	36	268	7,403	154,800	141	559	795
1993	247	39	286	8,372	160,900	245	572	816
1994	250	58	308	9,175	211,000	374	518	848
Total	2,258	397	2,655	65,288	1,521,500	910	6,992	14,816

SOURCE: National Highway Traffic Safety Commission

The Analysis of Driver Behavior

Traffic safety laws are often taken by those with a libertarian perspective as an intrusion on personal freedoms. Thus the argument that consumer decision making skills in this area are sufficiently incompetent as to warrant government intervention is one that those opposed to government intervention have attacked with great energy. The best known attempt to dismiss the idea that individuals are incapable of making their own safety decisions (and thus need safety regulation) is by Sam Peltzman of the University of Chicago.[27] His argument can be summarized in Figure 14.8. According to Peltzman, the degree of care with which people drive is determined at least in part by the safety of the vehicle in which they are driving. There is a cost to driving safely: This is shown as an upward sloping straight line in Figure 14.8 It results from the fact that careful driving is slower and perhaps less enjoyable than reckless driving. Since a driver's time is valuable, and since people sometimes like taking chances, it is costly in terms of foregone opportunities. On the other hand, driving safely reduces the likelihood of an accident and thus lowers the cost of having a crash. This is shown in the two downward sloping lines in Figure 14.8. The gray line is for an unsafe car. If government regulation makes an accident less likely or the probability of injury less likely, the cost of having a crash will shift down from the gray line to the dashed line. That lowers the total safety-related costs, as shown in the decline from the upper u-shaped curve to the lower curve of the same shape in Figure 14.8. But from the driver's perspective, the minimum cost level of care to take in driving has also declined from X* to X**. Essentially, the driver compensates for the lowered likelihood of being killed or injured in an accident by taking more risks on the road. But Peltzman notes that unsafe driving endangers not only the driver, but others that the driver may run into; notably pedestrians, motorcyclists, and bicyclists. Thus government regulations that make automobile occupants safer are inherently inefficient and self-defeating because, by distorting the driver's internal decisions to take risks, the entire community is put at higher peril from dangerous driving.

Peltzman tests this theory of offsetting behavior by analyzing the rate of accident and injury to drivers and pedestrians, motorcyclists, and bicyclists in the years 1947 to 1965 and finds that while regulations do appear to have made drivers safer, this decrease in the likelihood of death and injury is completely offset by an increase over the same period in traffic fatalities to non-automobile occupants, an effect he attributes to drivers compensating to offset the effects of safety devices. Similarly he argues that those states in which automobile safety regulations are most stringent also had the highest rates of traffic accidents involving pedestrians, motorcyclists, and bicyclists. Peltzman concludes that driver risk-taking behavior is far more sophisticated than NHTSA regulators believe, and thus he rejects the need for traffic safety regulation based on consumer irrationality.

The Peltzman result was immediately challenged by those who support safety device regulation. The initial challenge attempted to show that there

FIGURE 14.8   The Effect of Safer Cars on Driving Care

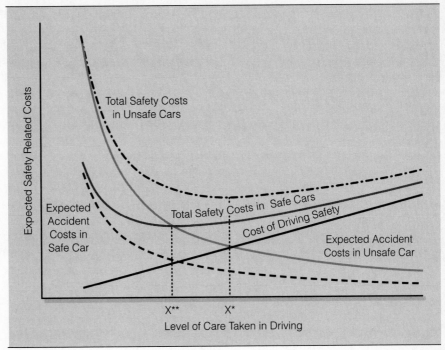

was *no* accommodation of driving habits to automobile safety at all rather than attempting to invalidate Peltzman's claim of a full offset of occupant safety by increased danger to others.[28] This view was unpersuasive and the view is now widely accepted that, when a safety measure has disappointing results, it is likely due to drivers adjusting their risk exposure to the safer environment.[29] But a full offset also seems implausible. The bulk of research published since Peltzman's article supports the idea that automobile safety regulation has made occupants safer, but that this has been accompanied by some increase in danger to non-occupants.[30] There is wide disagreement about the relative importance of the two effects, however. Whether the effect on non-occupants is measured as large or small depends on such factors as the time period from which the data are drawn and whether motorcyclists (whose death rate rose following the introduction of automobile safety regulations) are considered to be in the same class as drivers or bicyclists. The inconclusiveness of the research has permitted the debate on the efficiency of automobile safety regulation to continue.

Economic Deregulation and Safety

One of the chief concerns about economic regulation was the possibility that it could lead to a decline in safety standards. The unstable financial condition of trucking and airline industries that followed deregulation reinforced the public concern for safety of their operations. The argument is deceptively simple: When an operator is faced with financial distress, it will try to save money wherever it can. Among the places it will look are equipment maintenance and operator hours. Especially in the case of motor carrier owner-operators, lower prices for trucking services brought about by deregulation are claimed to encourage drivers to work longer hours than is optimal from the perspective of safe operations. The greater the financial stress, the worse should be their safety record, according to this argument.

While there have been some spectacular crashes that some have attributed to deregulation, overall safety statistics have not born out this fear. Studies of both the airline and motor carrier industries show that, by most measures, safety has increased rather than decreased following deregulation.[31] It is true that firms which are financially weaker or less well known are likely to have poorer equipment maintenance. This is due to the shorter time horizon over which such firms plan. Companies that expect to be around for a longer period of time will invest in equipment maintenance in order to maintain the good reputation of the company.[32] However, equipment maintenance is not a major determinant of transportation safety. The influence of financial distress through faulty equipment maintenance, while apparently present, has only a small effect on overall safety.[33]

By far the largest determinant of traffic safety is the experience and alertness of the operator. This is particularly a problem with motor carriers. The federal and state governments attempt to control driver qualifications through licensing and to control alertness through rules on the number of hours per day that a driver can be behind the wheel. In general, drivers wish to spend more hours on the road than federal law allows. As a result, federal laws are routinely violated; two traditional means by which they have been violated are by obtaining drivers licenses from multiple states and by falsifying driving logs. Falsifying logs is especially dangerous, but difficult to prevent since drivers wish to drive longer than permitted. In fact, the schedules that employed drivers are given often can only be met if the driver speeds or spends longer than is legally allowed at the wheel. This is because in a contestable market, the price that a company receives is determined by the opportunity cost of making the haul. If most drivers are willing to spend 16 hours behind the wheel, a company that hires on the assumption that its drivers will spend only the legal number of hours driving will have costs higher than the market price. Given the external cost that traffic accidents impose on others, the inability of commercial operators who drive legal hours to survive in the marketplace is a clear case of market failure.[34] Regulation is required if the number of driver hours is to be limited to what the public considers to be a safe level, but the required regulations are on working conditions, not on prices charged for services or entry to a particular traffic corridor.

The dangerous tendency of drivers to spend too many hours behind the wheel has been a part of the trucking industry throughout its history. Drivers have been spending too many hours per day on the road ever since the industry was created, and the tendency to drive too long appears to be the same regardless of the financial condition of the industry. It is, after all, not clear that longer hours should be associated with lower rather than higher compensation rates. According to economic theory, both responses to financial distress—more hours or fewer hours—are logically consistent. If drivers are paid less per mile, would they work fewer hours because extra miles are not worth as much, or would they work more to get their income back toward the previous level? Both effects are at work and either can dominate.

It would clearly enhance traffic safety if a mechanism could be found to prevent overly tired operators from using their vehicles. The place to look for this mechanism is in more foolproof logs rather than stabilizing the financial condition of transport companies. However, if a system were found to enforce driving hours, it would raise the costs of commercial vehicle operators and, with it, the prices that they charge to their customers.

It appears that economic deregulation did not adversely affect trucking safety. It is more difficult to measure airline safety effects because airline crashes are infrequent and catastrophic. A cluster of accidents in any year may be the result of random chance or may be the result of policy changes. As shown in Figure 14.9, 1985 was a particularly deadly year for airline travel. But there is no reason to think that this was the result of deregulation. To avoid the problem of the instability of the fatalities data series, some researchers prefer to analyze airline safety by analyzing the annual number of airline accidents. Figure 14.9 shows that following airline deregulation, there has been an approximately level number of accidents. But this has occurred at the same time that there has been a surge in airline travel and an increase in the number of new airlines operating. Thus on a per mile or a per flight basis, airline travel has continued to get safer following deregulation.

Since it is difficult to infer whether airline deregulation has had a measurable effect on airline safety, some researchers have tried to investigate changes in safety-related expenditures or procedures that followed deregulation.[35] One researcher has noted that deregulation does appear to have reduced the amount of safety-related expenditures. The reason that this reduction did not lead to an increase in accidents, according to this study, is that safety expenditures were more efficiently targeted toward meaningful maintenance items rather than on safety procedures that had little effect on safety but were required by government inspectors.[36]

Regulation does seem to have made railroad operations safer, but the mechanism for improving safety is primarily indirect. While deregulation did provide the industry the cash flow to fund deferred maintenance projects, this

FIGURE 14.9   **Fatality and Accident Rates for U.S. Commercial Airlines
1960–1993**

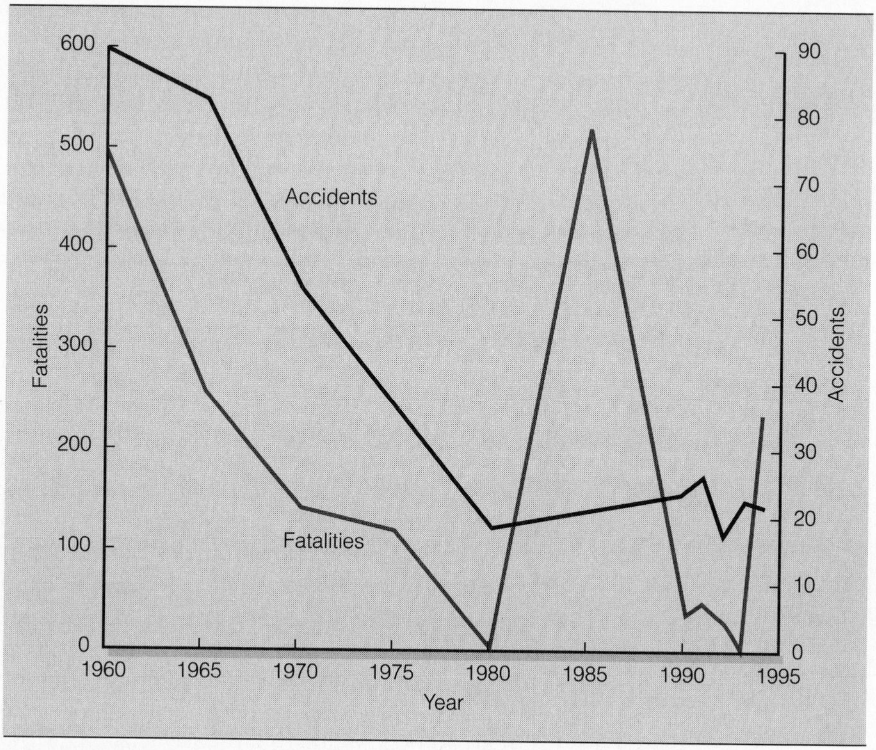

Source: U.S. Department of Transportation, Bureau of Transportation Statistics

was not the main way in which deregulation made railroads safer.[37]
Deregulation allowed railroads to abandon tracks and to consolidate traffic on
fewer lines. Following deregulation, railroads have operated many fewer but
much longer and heavier trains. But railroad accidents are strongly influenced
by the number of trains that are operated. This is because the two main forms
of railroad accidents—motor vehicle crashes at grade crossings and employee
injuries—depend on the number of trains. Fewer trains has meant fewer opportunities to hit vehicles stuck on grade crossings and are fewer train personnel to
be killed or injured when a train derails or strikes a truck at a grade crossing.

CONCLUSION

Current calls for transportation regulation are almost all based on the idea that
there are social costs of transportation—particularly automotive transporta-

tion—that are not paid by the user of transportation services. The underpricing of transportation relative to its full cost leads to an excessive amount of (primarily automotive) transportation relative to the efficient level. By raising prices to full cost, the economy as a whole can gain from the more efficient decisions made by transport users.

Some of the social cost arguments directly reject the efficiency criterion for making decisions. For example, if equity is important or if a view of the world is adopted in which all citizens have certain basic rights that are affected by transportation, then the strict efficiency analysis used by the economist will not be satisfactory. Using efficiency analysis, however, there are still several ways in which market decisions could be incorrect. For example, if one believed that the interest rate for discounting future costs of current driving decisions were too high, one must reject the market decisions on how much to drive. Or if individuals are less than perfect in their evaluations of what is best for them, it is, in principle, possible to improve their welfare by making decisions that they would make if they were fully competent to make decisions on their behalf.

Assuming that the cost-benefit framework of economic analysis is used to make decisions on transport policy, the main challenge is to measure the extent to which market prices for transportation are below the full cost. While there are often market-based proxy figures that can be used to approximate the willingness to pay for the changes brought about by transportation, in some cases there are none. Economic analysis has developed a series of tools, for example, based on averting behavior, characteristics valuation, or contingent valuation, for estimating these costs where there are important undervaluations of inputs or external costs ignored by the market.

Transportation-based pollution is the clearest example of a social cost ignored by the market. The measurement of the costs of carbon monoxide, nitrogen oxide, and particles emission has been hampered primarily by the lack of good medical data on the effects of these emissions and on a lack of understanding of how the gases behave after they leave the tailpipe. The standard methods of valuing air quality also tend to put a relatively low price on environmental degradation. As a result, cost-benefit analyses of regulations to control automotive pollution have been universally negative. Nonetheless, environmental programs have been politically quite popular. Whether this means that cost-benefit analyses do not capture the essence of the public demand for a clean environment or whether the public is fooled by the true costs and effects of environmental programs is at this point unknown.

Overshadowing all of the cost of pollution calculations, however, is the question of global warming, which may be the natural result of burning fuel. Global warming, if it is real and has the dire consequences predicted for it, will require a fundamental shift in driving behavior since it cannot be dealt with by marginal changes like changing the tuning of motor vehicle engines.

While it at first appears that the analysis of accidents can be understood as a market failure due to externalities, this is not the case. Given the apparent insensitivity of accident rates to traffic levels, the only safety externality problems occur when cars and trucks or cars and bicycles mix on the same roadway. When a driver does not measure the costs of an accident as the probability of an accident multiplied by the average cost of an accident, he or she will not engage in the efficient amount of transportation.

There may be an externality associated with the care of driving, however. This argument has been used to argue that the effects of safety regulation are perverse. Claiming that safety regulations make drivers excessively safe, motorists are seen as taking unwarranted risks in driving, thus endangering non-drivers on the road. There is considerable controversy about this theory, with federal safety regulators arguing that it assumes a rationality among drivers that is not realistic.

There is less controversy about the safety effects that followed deregulation in the transportation industries. Railroads are much safer than they were when regulated, and there does not seem to be any slippage in the safety of either airlines or motor carriers.

NOTES

1. An example of the discussion of the sustainability of current transport policies is found in David Banister and Kenneth Button, eds., *Transport, the Environment and Sustainable Development,* (New York: Chapman and Hall, Spon, 1993).

2. The argument that increased safety regulation can be seen as an attempt by wealthier groups to impose their values on others is made in W. Kip Viscusi, *Risk by Choice: Regulating Health and Safety in the Workplace* (Cambridge: Harvard University Press, 1983).

3. See Pérez-Peña, "New York Fare Increase Blocked as U.S. Judge Sees Possible Bias," *New York Times*, Nov. 9, 1995, p. A1, and Pérez-Peña, "Court Clears Way for Fare to Rise Sunday," *New York Times*, Nov. 10, 1995, p. A14.

4. The discussion in this paragraph is based on Alan Gewirth, "Two Types of Cost-Benefit Analysis" in Donald Scherer, ed., *Upstream/Downstream: Issues in Environmental Ethics,* (Philadelphia: Temple University Press, 1990), pp. 205–232.

5. A prominent example of this work is found in James J. MacKenzie, Roger C. Dower and Donald D.T. Chen, *The Going Rate: What It Really Costs to Drive* (World Resources Institute, June 1992).

6. For an extended introduction to the topics in this section, see Maureen L. Cropper, and Wallace E. Oates, "Environmental Economics: A Survey," *Journal of Economic Literature*, Vol. 30, No. 2 (June 1992), pp. 675–740.

7. A discussion of the pros and cons of contingent valuation is found in the symposium on the subject in the *Journal of Economic Perspectives*, Vol. 8, No. 4 (Fall 1994), pp. 3–64.

8. A list of studies on the social cost of transportation can be found in "Environmental Externalities and Social Costs of Transportation Systems–Measurement, Mitigation and Costing: An Annotated Bibliography," U.S. Department of Transportation, Federal Railroad Administration, Office of Policy, August 1993.

9. Among the other costs of driving not considered are noise pollution, the cost of parking spaces, and military expenditures necessary to maintain the flow of oil to fuel automobiles. For a discussion of these issues, see James J. MacKenzie, Roger C. Dower, and Donald D.T. Chen, *The Going Rate: What It Really Costs to Drive*, (World Resources Institute, June 1992). For a response to studies that aim to limit automobile usage, see Charles A. Lave, "Future Growth of Auto Travel in the U.S.: A Non-problem," in Jefferson W. Tester, David O. Wood, and Nancy A. Ferrari, eds., *Energy and the Environment in the 21st Century* (Cambridge: MIT Press 1991). A journalistic response can be found in Beshers, Eric, *External Costs of Automobile Travel and Appropriate Policy Responses*, Washington: Highway Users Federation, 1994).

10. A general discussion of fuel economy standards is found in Transportation Research Board, *Automotive Fuel Economy: How Far Should We Go?* (Washington: National Academy Press, 1992).

11. K. A. Small, and C. Kazimi, "On the Costs of Air Pollution from Motor Vehicles," *Journal of Transport Economics and Policy*, Vol. 39, No. 1 (January 1995), pp. 7–32.

12. Among the evaluations, see Robert W. Crandall, Howard K. Gruenspecht, Theodore E. Keeler, and Lester B. Lave, *Regulating the Automobile* (Washington: The Brookings Institution, 1986); and Alan J. Krupnick and Paul R. Portney, "Controlling Urban Air Pollution: A Benefit-Cost Assessment," *Science*, Vol. 252, 1991.

13. All statistics in this paragraph come from National Highway Traffic Safety Administration, *Traffic Safety Facts: 1994*.

14. Theodore E. Keeler, "Highway Safety, Economic Behavior, and Driving Environment," *American Economic Review*, Vol. 84, No. 3 (June 1994), pp. 684–693.

15. A general discussion of the tradeoff between safety and mobility can be found in Frank A. Haight, "Problems in Estimating Comparative Costs of Safety and Mobility," *Journal of Transport Economics and Policy*, Vol. 28, No. 1 January 1994), pp. 7–30.

16. A classic reference on the analysis of safety externalities in transportation is William Vickrey, "Automobile Accidents, Tort Law, Externalities, and Insurance: An Economist's Critique," *Law and Contemporary Problems*, Vol. 33, No. 3 (Summer 1968), pp. 464–487.

17. This argument is made in Charles A. Lave, "Speeding, Coordination, and the 55 MPH Limit," *American Economic Review*, Vol. 75, No. 5 (December 1985), pp. 1159–1164; see also Patrick S. McCarthy, "Accident Involvement and Highway Safety," *Logistics and Transportation Review*, Vol. 25, No. 2 (June 1989), pp. 129–138.

18. This argument has been made in support of mandatory seat belt usage in Richard J. Arnould, and Henry Grabowski, "Auto Safety Regulation: An Analysis of Market Failure," *Bell Journal of Economics*, Vol. 12, No. 1 (Spring 1981), pp. 27–48.

19. The term *cold blooded* comes from Jan Owen Jansson, "Accident Externality Charges," *Journal of Transport Economics and Policy*, Vol. 28, No. 1 (January 1994), pp., 31–43.

20. For recent estimates, see Ulf Persson, and Knut Odergaard, "External Cost Estimates of Road Traffic Accidents," *Journal of Transport Economics and Policy*, Vol. 29, No. 3 (September 1995), pp. 291–304.

21. An accessible discussion of these arguments is found in W. Kip Viscusi, John M., Vernon, and Joseph E. Harrington, Jr., *The Economics of Regulation and Antitrust: Second Edition* (Cambridge: MIT Press, 1995), Chapter 22.

22. On the effects that changes in liability laws have had on traffic safety, see Peter W. Huber, and Robert E. Litan, eds., *The Liability Maze: The Impact of Liability Law on Safety and Innovation*, (Washington: The Brookings Institution, 1991).

23. The original formulation of this argument is in G. Calabresi, *The Costs of Accidents: A Legal and Economic Analysis*, (New Haven: Yale University Press, 1970).

24. A defense of the willingness to pay for safety as a measure of the benefits of safety devices is found in M.W. Jones-Lee, "The Value of Transport Safety," *Oxford Review of Economic Policy*, Vol. 6, No. 2 (Summer 1990), pp. 39–60.

25. Timothy L. McDaniels, "Reference Points, Loss Aversion, and Contingent Values for Auto Safety," *Journal of Risk and Uncertainty*, Vol. 5, No. 2 (May 1992), pp. 187–200.

26. See, for example, John D. Graham, ed., *Preventing Automobile Injury: New Findings from Evaluation Research* (Dover, Mass.: Auburn House, 1988).

27. Sam Peltzman, "The Effects of Automobile Safety Regulation," *Journal of Political Economy*, Vol. 83 (August–December 1975), pp. 677–725.

28. Robertson, Leon S., "A Critical Analysis of Peltzman's "The Effects of Automobile Safety Regulation," *Journal of Economic Issues* Vol. 11 (September 1977a) pp. 587–600.

29. For example, Keeler, in trying to explain his finding that the 55 mile per hour speed limit had no effect on fatality rates on rural expressways, assumes that drivers must have adjusted other aspects of driving behavior to accommodate the safer environment. Theodore E. Keeler, "Highway Safety, Economic Behavior, and Driving Environment," *American Economic Review*, Vol. 84, No. 3 (June 1994), pp. 684–693. See also Thomas L. Traynor, "The Effects of Varying Safety Conditions on the External Costs of Driving," *Eastern Economic Journal*, Vol. 20, No. 1 (Winter 1994), pp. 45–60.

30. Reviews of this research can be found in Glenn C. Blomquist, *The Regulation of Motor Vehicle and Traffic Safety* (Boston: Kluwer Academic Publishers, 1988) and Robert W. Crandall, Howard K. Gruenspecht, Theodore E. Keeler, and Lester B. Lave, *Regulating the Automobile* (Washington, D.C.: The Brookings Institution, 1986).

31. The best-known work on transportation deregulation and safety is in Leon N. Moses, and Ian Savage, eds., *Transportation Safety in an Age of Deregulation* (New York: Oxford University Press). For the effect of deregulation on road safety see also Donald L. Alexander, "Motor Carrier Deregulation and Highway Safety: An Empirical Analysis," *Southern Economic Journal*, Vol. 59, No. 1 (July 1992), pp. 28–38; Thomas L. Traynor, and Patrick S. McCarthy, "Trucking Deregulation and Highway Safety: The Effect of the 1980 Motor Carrier Act," *Journal of Regulatory Economics*, Vol. 3, No. 4 (December 1991), pp. 339–48; Alexander Kraas, "The Impact of the U.S. Motor Carrier Act of 1980 on Road Safety in California: An Econometric Policy Evaluation," *Logistics and Transportation Review*, Vol. 29, No. 2 (June 1993), pp. 179–192. Airline safety is considered in Clinton V. Oster, Jr., John S. Strong, and C. Kurt Zorn, *Why Airplanes Crash: Aviation Safety in a Changing World* (New York: Oxford University Press, 1992).

See also Nancy L. Rose, "Fear of Flying: Economic Analysis of Airline Safety," *Journal of Economic Perspectives*, Vol. 6, No. 2 (Spring 1992), pp. 75–94; Nancy L. Rose, "Profitability and Product Quality: Economic Determinants of Airline Safety Performance," *Journal of Political Economy*, Vol. 98, No. 5, Part 1, (October 1990), pp. 944–64; Richard A. Phillips, and Wayne K. Talley, "Airline Safety Investments and Operating Conditions: Determinants of Aircraft Damage Severity," *Southern Economic Journal*, Vol. 59, No. 2, (October 1992), pp. 157–64. Adib Kanafani and Theodore E. Keeler, "Airline Deregulation and Safety: Some Econometric Evidence from Time Series," *Logistics and Transportation Review*, Vol. 26 No. 3 (September 1990), pp. 203–209.

32. The goal of maintaining consumer goodwill is presumed to be an important incentive to invest in safety. This argument is analyzed by Severin Borenstein, and Martin B. Zimmerman, "Market Incentives for Safe Commercial Airline Operation," *American Economic Review*, Vol. 78. No. 5, (December 1988), pp. 913–935. See also Edward R. Bruning, and Ann T. Kuzma, "Airline Accidents and Stock Return Performance," *Logistics and Transportation Review*, Vol. 25, No. 2, (June 1989), pp. 157–168.; Andrew J. Chalk, "Market Forces and Commercial Aircraft Safety," *Journal of Industrial Economics*, Vol. 36, No. 1 (September 1987), pp. 61–81. Devra L. Golbe, "Safety and Profits in the Airline Industry," *Journal of Industrial Economics*, Vol. 34, No. 3 (March 1986), pp. 305–318.

33. Wayne K. Talley, and Philip A. Bossert, Jr., "Determinants of Aircraft Accidents and Policy Implications for Air Safety," *International Journal of Transport Economics*, Vol. 17, No. 2 (June 1990), pp. 115–130.

34. Drivers' hours policy is discussed in Thomas M. Corsi, and Philip Fanara, "Driver Management Policies and Motor Carrier Safety," *Logistics and Transportation Review*, Vol. 24, No. 2 (June 1988), pp. 153–163. See also R. Beilock, "Are Truckers Forced to Speed?" *Logistics and Transportation Review*, Vol. 21, pp. 277–291.

35. See for example T. Randolph Beard, "Financial Aspects of Motor Carrier Safety Inspection Performance," *Review of Industrial Organization,* Vol. 7, No. 1 (1992), pp. 51–64.

36. D. Mark Kennet, "Did Deregulation Affect Aircraft Engine Maintenance? An Empirical Policy Analysis," *Rand Journal of Economics*, Vol. 24, No. 4 (Winter 1993), pp. 542–558.

37. Kenneth D. Boyer, "The Safety Effects of Mode Shifting Following Deregulation," in L. Moses, and I. Savage, eds., *Transportation Safety in an Age of Deregulation* (Oxford: Oxford University Press, 1989).

NAME AND SUBJECT INDEX